Alan Roger

Spain & Portugal
2004

Quality Camping and Caravanning Sites

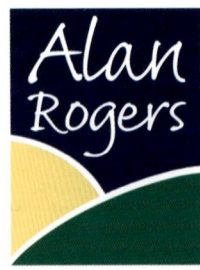

Compiled by: Alan Rogers Guides Ltd

Cover design: Paul Effenberg, Vine Cottage

Maps created by Customised Mapping (01769 560101) contain background data provided by GisDATA Ltd

Maps are © Alan Rogers Guides and GisDATA Ltd 2003

© Alan Rogers Guides Ltd 2003

Published by: Alan Rogers Guides Ltd, Burton Bradstock, Bridport, Dorset DT6 4QA

British Library Cataloguing-in-Publication Data:
A catalogue record for this book is available from the British Library.

ISBN: 0 901586 97 8

Printed in Great Britain by The Friary Press

While every effort is taken to ensure the accuracy of the information given in this book, no liability can be accepted by the authors or publishers for any loss, damage or injury caused by errors in, or omissions from, the information given.

All rights reserved. No part of this publication may be reproduced, stored in a retrieval system or transmitted, in any form or by any means, electronic, mechanical, photocopying, recording or otherwise, without prior permission in writing from the publishers.

Contents

- 4 Introduction
- 6 How to use this Guide
- 8 Alan Rogers TRAVEL SERVICE

21	SPAIN – Catalunya	127	Cantabria
69	Comunidad Valenciana	134	Pais Vasco-Euskadi
82	Murcia	137	La Rioja
86	Andalucia	139	Navarra
103	Extremadura	142	Aragón
106	Castilla La Mancha	150	PORTUGAL – Algarve
109	Madrid	156	Alentejo
112	Castilla y León	159	Lisbon & Vale do Tejo
120	Galicia	165	Beiras & Centre
123	Asturias	169	Porto & North

- 173 Driving in Europe
- 176 Driving in Spain & Portugal
- 177 Driving – Routes to Spain
- 188 Insurance
- 191 Open All Year
- 192 Dogs
- 193 Fishing, Horse Riding
- 194 Maps
- 200 Reader's Report form
- 201 Town and Village Index
- 202 Campsite Index by Number
- 204 Campsite Index by Region

WELCOME TO THE 2004 EDITION

the Alan Rogers approach

IT IS 36 YEARS SINCE ALAN ROGERS PUBLISHED THE FIRST CAMPSITE GUIDE THAT BORE HIS NAME. SINCE THEN THE RANGE OF TITLES HAS EXPANDED, WITH NEW GUIDES TO SPAIN & PORTUGAL AND ITALY BEING PUBLISHED FOR 2004. WHAT'S MORE THE ALAN ROGERS GUIDES ARE FAST BECOMING A FORCE TO BE RECKONED WITH IN THE NETHERLANDS TOO: IN 2004 ALL SIX TITLES WILL BE AVAILABLE FOR THE FIRST TIME, STOCKED BY WELL OVER 90% OF ALL DUTCH BOOKSHOPS.

There are many thousands of campsites in Spain and Portugal of varying quality: this guide contains impartially written reports on no less than 214 of the very finest, each being individually inspected and selected. Plus it incorporates a new section on our popular Travel Service (page 8), as well as all the usual maps and indexes, designed to help you find the choice of campsite that's right for you. We hope you enjoy some happy and safe travels – and some pleasurable 'armchair touring' in the meantime!

INDEPENDENT AND HONEST

Whilst the content and scope of the guides have expanded considerably since the early editions, our selection of campsites still employs exactly the same philosophy and criteria as defined by Alan Rogers 36 years ago.

'warts and all'

Firstly, and most importantly, our selection is based entirely on our own rigorous and independent inspection and selection process. Campsites cannot buy their way into our guides – indeed the extensive Site Report which is written by us, not by the site owner, is provided free of charge so we are free to say what we think and to provide an honest, 'warts and all' description. This is written in plain English and without the use of confusing icons or symbols.

" …the campsites included in this book have been chosen entirely on merit, and no payment of any sort is made by them for their inclusion."
Alan Rogers, 1968

A question of quality

The criteria which we use when inspecting and selecting sites are numerous, but the most important by far is the question of good quality. People want different things from their choice of campsite so we try to include a range of campsite 'styles' to cater for a wide variety of preferences: from those seeking a small peaceful campsite in the heart of the countryside, to visitors looking for an 'all singing, all dancing' site in a popular seaside resort. Those with more specific needs, such as sports facilities, cultural or historical attractions, are also catered for.

The size of the site, whether it's part of a campsite chain or privately owned, makes no difference in terms of it being required to meet our exacting standards regarding its quality and it being 'fit for purpose'. In other words, irrespective of the size of the site, or the number of facilities offered, the essentials (the welcome, the pitches, the sanitary facilities, the cleanliness and the general maintenance) must all be of a high standard.

Expert opinions

We rely on our dedicated team of Site Assessors, all of whom are experienced campers, caravanners or motorcaravanners, to visit and recommend sites. Each year they travel some 100,000 miles around Europe inspecting new sites and re-inspecting old ones. Our thanks are due to them for their enthusiastic efforts, their diligence and integrity and their commitment to the philosophy of the Alan Rogers Guides.

We also appreciate the feedback we receive from many of our readers, and we always make a point of following up complaints, suggestions or recommendations for possible new sites. Of course we get a few grumbles too – but it really is a few, and those we do receive usually arrive at the end of the high season and relate mainly to overcrowding or to poor maintenance during the peak school holiday period.

Please bear in mind that although we are interested to hear about any complaints we have no contractual relationship with the sites featured in our guides and are therefore not in a position to intervene in any dispute between a reader and a campsite. If you have a complaint about a campsite featured in our guides the first step should be to take the matter up with the site owner or manager.

Widely regarded as the 'Bible' by site owners and readers alike, there is no better guide when it comes to forming an independent view of a campsite's quality. When you need to be confident in your choice of campsite, you need the Alan Rogers Guide.

☑ Sites only included on merit
☑ Sites cannot pay to be included
☑ Independently inspected, rigorously assessed
☑ Impartial reviews
☑ 36 years of expertise

USING THE ALAN ROGERS GUIDES

Written in plain English, our guides are exceptionally easy to use, but a few words of explanation regarding the layout and content may be helpful. In Spain we have used the 15 official administrative regions, whilst in Portugal we use the five regions defined by the Portuguese Tourist Board. We provide a full page introduction to each region highlighting its main areas of interest and places to visit with details of the local cuisine.

Indexes
Our three indexes allow you to find sites by site number and name, by region and site name or by the town or village where the site is situated.

Campsite Maps
The maps will help you to identify the approximate position of each campsite within its region.

The Site Reports – *Example of an entry*

Number **Campsite Name**
Postal Address

A description of the site in which we try to give an idea its general features – its size, its situation, its strengths and its weaknesses. This column should provide a picture of the site itself with reference to the facilities that are provided and if they impact on its appearance or character. We include details on pitch numbers, electricity (with amperage), hardstandings, etc. in this section as pitch design, planning and terracing affects the site's overall appearance. Similarly we continue to include reference to pitches used for caravan holiday homes, chalets, and the like. Importantly at the end of this column we indicate if there are any restrictions, e.g. no tents, dogs.

Facilities
Lists more specific information on the sie's facilities, as well as certain off site activities.

At a glance
Welcome & Ambience	✓✓✓✓	Location	✓✓✓✓
Quality of Pitches	✓✓✓✓	Range of Facilities	✓✓✓✓

Directions
Separated from the main text in order that they may be read and assimilated more easily by a navigator en-route. Bear in mind that road improvement schemes can result in some road numbers being altered. Websites like **www.mappy.com** and others give detailed route plans.

Charges 2004

Reservations including contact details

Open

Facilities

Toilet blocks: We assume that toilet blocks will be equipped with at least some British style WCs, washbasins with hot and cold water and hot showers with dividers or curtains, and will have all necessary shelves, hooks, plugs and mirrors. We also assume that there will be an identified chemical toilet disposal point, and that the campsite will provide water and waste water points and bin areas. If not the case, we comment. We continue to mention certain features that some readers find important: washbasins in cubicles, facilities for babies, facilities for those with disabilities and motorcaravan service points. Readers with disabilities are advised to contact the site of their choice to ensure that facilities are appropriate to their needs.

Shop: Basic or fully supplied, and opening dates.

Bars, restaurants, takeaway facilities and entertainment: We try hard to supply opening and closing dates (if other than the campsite opening dates) and to identify if there are discos or other noisy entertainment.

Children's play areas: Fenced and with safety surface (e.g. sand, bark or pea-gravel).

Swimming pools: If particularly special, we cover in detail in the first column but reference is always included in the second column. Opening dates, charges and levels of supervision are provided where we have been notified.

Leisure facilities: For example, playing fields, bicycle hire, organised activities and entertainment.

Dogs: If dogs are not accepted or restrictions apply, we state it here. Check the quick reference list on page 192.

Off site: This briefly covers leisure facilities, tourist attractions, restaurants etc nearby. Geographical tourist information is more likely to be in the first column.

At A Glance: All Alan Rogers sites have been inspected and selected – they must meet stringent quality criteria. A campsite may have all the boxes ticked when it comes to listing facilities but if it's not inherently a 'good site' then it will not be in the guide.

These 'at a glance' ratings are a unique indication of certain key criteria that may be important when making your decision. Quite deliberately they are subjective and, modesty aside, are based on our inspectors' own expert opinions at the time of their inspection.

Charges: These are the latest provided by the parks. In those few cases where 2003 or 2004 prices are not given, we try to give a general guide.

Telephone numbers: All numbers assume that you are phoning from within Spain or Portugal. To phone Spain from outside that country, prefix the number shown with the International Code '00 34' and then the number indicated. To phone Portugal pefix the number shown with the International Code '00 351'.

Opening dates: Are those advised to us during the early autumn of the previous year – parks can, and sometimes do, alter these dates before the start of the following season, often for good reasons. If you intend to visit shortly after a published opening date, or shortly before the closing date, it is wise to check that it will actually be open at the time required. Similarly some sites operate a restricted service during the low season, only opening some of their facilities (e.g. swimming pools) during the main season; where we know about this, and have the relevant dates, we indicate it – again if you are at all doubtful it is wise to check.

Reservations: Necessary for high season (roughly mid-July to mid-August) in popular holiday areas (ie beach areas). You can reserve via our own Alan Rogers Travel Service or through tour operators. Or be wholly independent and contact the campsite(s) of your choice direct, using the phone, fax or e-mail numbers shown in the site reports, but please bear in mind that many sites are closed all winter.

Points to bear in mind

Some site owners are very laid back when it comes to opening and closing dates. They may not be fully ready by their opening date – grass and hedges may not all be cut or perhaps only limited sanitary facilities open. At the end of the season they also tend to close down some facilities and generally wind down prior to the closing date. Bear this in mind if you are travelling early or late in the season – it is worth phoning ahead.

The Camping Cheque low season touring system goes some way to addressing this in that participating campsites are advised to have all facilities open and running by the opening date and to remain fully operational until the closing date.

Whether you're an 'old hand' in terms of camping and caravanning or are contemplating your first trip, a regular reader of our Guides or a new 'convert', we wish you well in your travels and hope we have been able to help in some way. We are, of course, also out and about ourselves, visiting sites, talking to owners and readers, and generally checking on standards and new developments.

The Alan Rogers Team

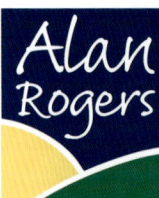

VALUE, VALUE, VALUE

service
and value

The Alan Rogers Travel Service was started three years ago in response to unrelenting requests from readers. We had so many requests asking us to take away the hassle of booking pitches on overseas campsites that we gave in. The Alan Rogers Travel Service was set up to provide a low cost booking service for readers: the next logical step to producing the guide books, allowing readers to browse through the guides, make a choice of campsite, then simply ask us to arrange everything.

Of course, with our contacts and relationships we can offer the pick of Europe's finest campsites. And, because we organise so many holidays, we can negotiate unbeatable ferry deals too. In fact the rates we get are so low that the ferry companies do not normally allow us to sell ferry crossings alone.

the **travel service**
TO BOOK THIS SITE
0870 405 4055
Expert Advice & Special Offers

Unbeatable Ferry Deals

WE ARE ALWAYS NEGOTIATING NEW OFFERS ON CHANNEL CROSSINGS. MAKE SURE YOU ASK US ABOUT OUR FAMOUS DEALS!

- ☑ **CARAVANS GO FREE**
- ☑ **TRAILERS GO FREE**
- ☑ **MOTORHOMES PRICED AS CARS**

At the Alan Rogers Travel Service we're always keen to find the best deals and keenest prices. There's always great savings on offer, and we're constantly negotiating new ferry rates and money-saving offers, so just call us on

0870 405 4055
and ask about the latest deals.

or visit
www.alanrogersdirect.com

THE AIMS OF THE TRAVEL SERVICE ARE SIMPLE.

- To provide convenience - when booking a campsite yourself can be anything but convenient.
- To provide peace of mind - when you need it most.
- To provide a friendly, knowledgeable, efficient service - when this can be hard to find.
- To provide a low cost means of organising your holiday – when prices can be so complicated.

HOW IT WORKS

1 Choose your campsite(s)
2 Choose your dates
3 Choose your ferry crossing

Then just call us for an instant quote

0870 405 4055

or visit

www.alanrogersdirect.com

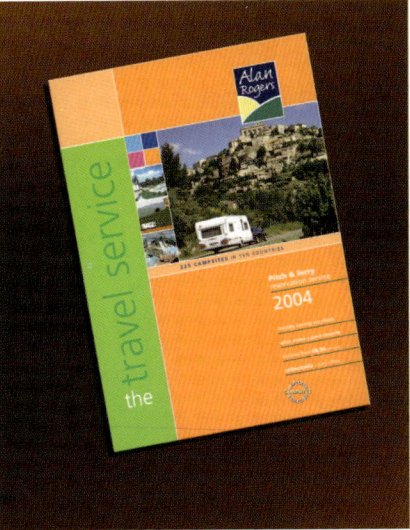

For full details see our FREE 2004 brochure

0870 405 4055

Ask about our incredible Ferry Deals:

☑ **Caravans GO FREE**

☑ **Motorhomes Priced as Cars**

Let us book your pitch and ferry for you

don't miss out
book early

Because so many of our best campsites are booked well in advance by those in the know, we do advise early action. We make it as simple as possible, and it's risk-free. A £100 deposit is all it takes to confirm those important campsite dates and secure the vital ferry crossing. The balance is not due until 10 weeks before departure, leaving you plenty of time to relax knowing that next year's holiday is 'in the bag'. Each year we unfortunately have to disappoint a number of would-be travellers who have left it just too late for the high summer dates (and ferry crossings) – please don't allow yourself to be one of them.

extra nights
FREE

Booking with The Alan Rogers Travel Service always means great value and real peace of mind. Now we've negotiated new special offers for 2004 – all designed to save you more money.

These are generally extra nights **FREE** of charge, subject to certain conditions and availability. Examples might be 7 nights for 6 or 12 nights for 10. Qualifying dates are usually in the off-peak period.

Ask for details or see our 2004 brochure (above).

PRICING YOUR HOLIDAY

WE ACT AS AGENTS FOR ALL THE CAMPSITES AND FERRY OPERATORS FEATURED IN THE TRAVEL SERVICE. AS SUCH, WE CAN BOOK ALL YOUR TRAVEL ARRANGEMENTS WITH THE MINIMUM OF FUSS AND AT THE BEST POSSIBLE PRICES. THE BASE PRICES BELOW INCLUDE 12 NIGHTS PITCH FEES AND RETURN FERRY CROSSING.

First night on site	Base Price 2 adults + car 12 nights	extra adult	child (0-13)	extra/fewer nights
Before 18 May	£294	£25	FREE	£12
18 May – 18 June	£314	£25	FREE	£12
19 June - 2 July	£345	£25	FREE	£12
3 July – 13 August	£415	£25	FREE	£12
14 August – 23 August	£375	£25	FREE	£12
From 24 August	£314	£25	FREE	£12

The base price of your holiday includes 12 nights pitch fees and a mid-week return ferry crossing from Dover to Calais with P&O Ferries for a car and five passengers (outward sailing times must be between 14:01 and 06:59. Inward sailing times must be between 20:01 and 14:59). Additional supplements are payable for caravans, trailers and motorhomes at all times and for cars at weekends and times outside those given above. There will also usually be a campsite supplement payable (see opposite). Call us on **0870 405 4055** for details and a quote.

If your holiday is longer or shorter than 12 nights, simply add or subtract £12 per night. Holidays must be for a minimum of 3 nights, with ferry (many sites have a minimum stay requirement). For holidays longer than 21 nights please call for a quotation. You may stay on as many sites as you wish, subject to individual site requirements, with a one-off £10 multi-site fee.

LOW £100 DEPOSIT
A special low deposit of just £100 secures your holiday
(full payment is required at the time of booking for travel within 10 weeks)

12 nights pitch fees + ferry for car and passengers	from **£294** DOVER - CALAIS
12 nights pitch fees + ferry for motorhome and passengers	from **£310** PORTSMOUTH - LE HAVRE/ CHERBOURG
12 nights pitch fees + ferry for car and caravan and passengers	from **£294** DOVER - CALAIS

* **Special Offers**: Look for our famous money-saving deals: Caravans Go Free, Motorhomes Priced as Car. Ask us for details.

Motorhomes Priced as Cars  **Caravans and Trailers GO FREE**

Site Supplements

All sites operate their own independent pricing structure, and in order to reflect the differences in cost from one site to another, we will add a nightly 'site supplement' to the Base Prices indicated above. Although some sites in our brochure have very low supplements (eg 80060 Val de Trie: 2 adults and car/ caravan/motorhome carries no supplement all season), others may carry much higher supplements. These reflect their location and amenities (eg 83020 Esterel Caravaning: 2 adults and car/caravan/motorhome = £28 supplement per night in high season).

Additional supplements can often apply for electricity, water and drainage or special pitches.

The simplest next step is to just call us for an immediate price quotation for your chosen site and all the available options, as well as any other important information, such as any minimum stay requirements.

CALL US NOW 0870 405 4055 FOR AN INSTANT QUOTE
OR VISIT www.alanrogersdirect.com

Leave The Hassle To Us

- All site fees paid in advance – you won't need to take extra currency with you.
- Your pitch is reserved for you – travel with peace of mind.
- No endless overseas phone calls or correspondence with foreign site owners.
- No need to pay foreign currency deposits and booking fees.
- Take advantage of our expert advice and experience of camping in Europe.

Already Booked Your Ferry?

We're confident that our ferry inclusive booking service offers unbeatable value. However, if you have already booked your ferry then we can still make a pitch-only reservation for you. Your booking must be for a minimum of 10 nights, and since our prices are based on our ferry inclusive service, you need to be aware that a non-ferry booking will always result in somewhat higher prices than if you were to book direct with the site.

You still benefit from:

- Hassle-free booking with no booking fees and foreign currency deposits.
- Comprehensive Travel Pack.
- Peace of mind: site fees paid in advance, with your pitch reserved for you.

FULL DETAILS IN OUR 64 PAGE 2004 COLOUR BROCHURE CALL
0870 405 4055

NEW FOR 2004

book on-line
and save money

NEW for 2004 www.alanrogersdirect.com is a brand new website designed to give you everything you need to know when it comes to booking your Alan Rogers inspected and selected campsite, and your low cost ferry.

Our glossy brochure gives you all the info you need but it is only printed once a year. And our friendly, expert reservations team is always happy to help on **0870 405 4055** – but they do go home sometimes!

Visit www.alanrogersdirect.com and you'll find constantly updated information, latest ferry deals, special offers from campsites and much more. And you can visit it at any time of day or night!

alanrogersdirect.com
book on-line and save

Campsite Information
- ✓ Details of all Travel Service campsites - **instantly**
- ✓ Find latest special offers on campsites - **instantly**
- ✓ Check campsite availability - **instantly**

Ferry Information
- ✓ Check ferry availability - **instantly**
- ✓ Find latest ferry deals - **instantly**
- ✓ Book your ferry online - **instantly**
- ✓ Save money - **instantly**

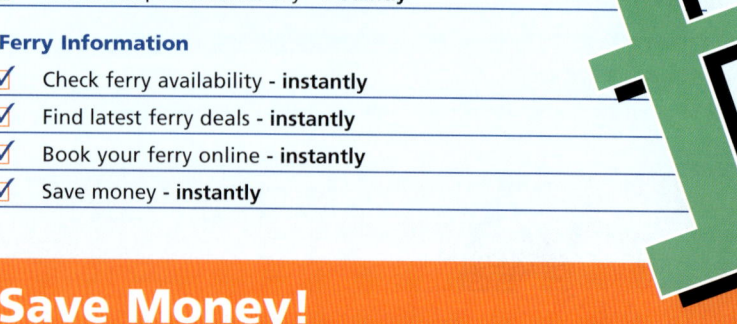

Save Money!
BOOK YOUR CAMPSITE AND FERRY - INSTANTLY

NEW Perfect Match
Find the campsite that's right for you

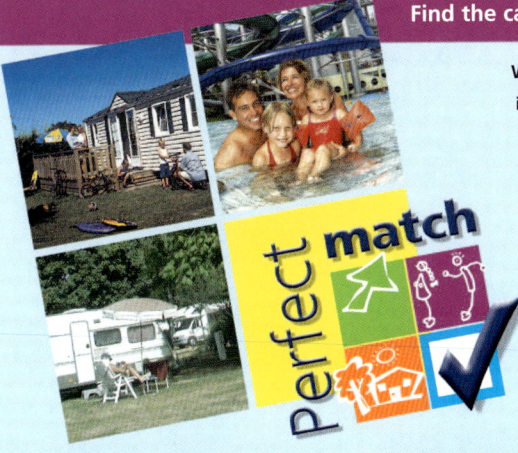

With so many sites to choose from it can be difficult to find a short-list. With the unique Alan Rogers Perfect Match system you can quickly find a campsite that meets your requirements. This powerful and searchable database of top campsites, all Alan Rogers inspected and selected, means you can quickly find an ideal site, book it on-line and relax in the knowledge that your holiday is safely reserved.

Ferry Deals On-line

FOR 2004 WE HAVE ARRANGED SOME EXCEPTIONAL OFFERS ON KEY CROSS-CHANNEL ROUTES. THESE ARE CERTAIN TO MAKE YOU WANT TO THINK ABOUT YOUR HOLIDAY NOW AND NOT RISK MISSING OUT.

Caravans Go FREE
Trailers Go FREE
Motorhomes Priced as Cars

Dover – Calais
Portsmouth – Cherbourg
Portsmouth – Le Havre

Portsmouth – Caen
Poole – Cherbourg

Conditions apply – ask for details or see page 26.

Don't delay – this offer is strictly subject to availability and will be first come, first served.

the travel service
TO BOOK THIS SITE
0870 405 4055
Expert Advice & Special Offers

IN ESTABLISHING OUR PROGRAMME, WE HAVE ENSURED A SELECTION OF SITES IN EVERY CORNER OF FRANCE AND, AS WELL AS OFFERING SITES IN WELL KNOWN AREAS AND WELL ESTABLISHED RESORTS, WE HAVE ALSO SOUGHT TO INCLUDE SOME SMALLER SITES IN LITTLE KNOWN AREAS, BUT WHICH ARE WELL WORTH A VISIT. THIS IS A SELECTION OF THE SITES WE CAN BOOK FOR YOU, WITH FERRY, IN 2004.

(C) Chalet (P) Pitch

Spain

ES8200 (P)
Cala Llevadó
Tossa de Mar
Beautifully situated cliff-side site with excellent facilities.

ES8390 (P)
Vilanova Park
Vilanova i la Geltru
Hillside site with views to sea, good facilities and large pool complex.

ES8035 (P)
L'Amfora
Sant Pere Pescador
Spacious, medium sized site with direct access to the beach.

ES8100 (P)
Inter-Pals
Platja de Pais
Well maintained, interesting site in pinewood, close to beaches.

ES8802 (P)
Cabopino
Marbella
A pretty site set beside a golf course and just 600m from the beach.

ES9000 (P)
Playa Joyel
Noja
High quality, comprehensively equipped busy site with pool, by superb beach.

ES8961 (C)(P)
El Helguero
Ruiloba
Well designed site with pool, close to good beaches.

MANY MORE SITES AVAILABLE AT

alanrogersdirect.com
book on-line and save

Crossing the Channel

One of the great advantages of booking with the Alan Rogers Travel Service is the tremendous value we offer. A package of 12 nights on site and return ferry costs from just £294 – check current public ferry fares and you'll see what incredible value this represents. As agents for all the cross-Channel operators we can book all your travel arrangements with the minimum of fuss and at the best possible rates.

Just call us for an instant quote
0870 405 4055
or visit
www.alanrogersdirect.com
Book on-line AND SAVE

Short Sea Routes

Hop across the Channel in the shortest possible time and you can be on your way. We offer all main routes at great prices (when you book a pitch + ferry 'package' through us). And why not take advantage of our Ferry Deals? Caravans and trailers can go **FREE** on Dover – Calais with P&O Ferries.

Caravans can even go **FREE** with **Eurotunnel** - ask for detals.

SEAFRANCE
DOVER-CALAIS FERRIES

Dover - Calais

Dover – Calais
Newhaven - Dieppe

EURO TUNNEL
Folkestone – Calais

Stena Line
Harwich – Hook of Holland

Special offers

Caravans Go **FREE**
Trailers Go **FREE**

Dover - Calais
Qualifying Dates

Travel can be all year long between 1 January 2004 – 31 Oct 2004 (excluding 16/7 to 31/8 outward and 24/7 to 5/9 inward).
Midweek crossings only (excludes Friday, Saturday outward, Saturday, Sunday inward).

Low prices available on other sailings - ask for details.

Don't delay – this offer is strictly subject to availability and will be first come, first served.

Just call us for an instant quote
0870 405 4055
or visit www.alanrogersdirect.com
BOOK ON-LINE AND SAVE

Longer Routes

Sometimes it pays to take a longer crossing: a more leisurely journey perhaps. Or a chance to enjoy dinner on board ship, followed by a night in a comfortable cabin, awaking refreshed and ready for the onward drive. Either way there are still savings to be had with our super Ferry Deals.

Portsmouth – St Malo/ Caen/Cherbourg
Plymouth – Roscoff/Santander
Poole – Cherbourg

Portsmouth – Le Havre/ Cherbourg/Bilbao
Hull - Rotterdam/Zeebrugge

Poole – St Malo

Special offers

Caravans Go FREE
Trailers Go FREE
Motorhomes Priced as Cars

Portsmouth – Cherbourg
Portsmouth – Le Havre

Portsmouth – Caen
Portsmouth – Cherbourg
Poole – Cherbourg

Qualifying Dates

Travel can be all summer long between 1 May 2004 - 31 October 2004. Midweek crossings only (excludes Friday, Saturday outward, Saturday, Sunday inward).

Low prices available on other sailings - ask for details.

1st time abroad?

PREPARATIONS FOR THAT FIRST TRIP CAN DE DAUNTING. BUT DON'T WORRY - WE'RE WITH YOU ALL THE WAY.

Don't delay – this offer is strictly subject to availability and will be first come, first served.

Just call us for an instant quote
0870 405 4055
or visit **www.alanrogersdirect.com**
BOOK ON-LINE AND SAVE

Save over 50% on your holiday

Camping Cheque

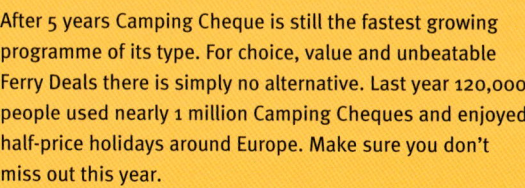

- **400 sites – all just £9.95 per night**
- **Maximum flexibility - go as you please**
- **Fantastic Ferry Deals**

After 5 years Camping Cheque is still the fastest growing programme of its type. For choice, value and unbeatable Ferry Deals there is simply no alternative. Last year 120,000 people used nearly 1 million Camping Cheques and enjoyed half-price holidays around Europe. Make sure you don't miss out this year.

Huge off peak savings

400 quality campsites in 18 European countries, including the UK, all at just £9.95 per night for pitch + 2 adults, including electricity. That's a saving of up to 55% off normal site tariffs. And with special free night deals (14 nights for 11 Cheques, 60 nights for 30 Cheques etc) the price can reduce to under a fiver a night!

ferry savings

Ask about our famous special offers

- ✓ **Caravans/trailers Go FREE**
- ✓ **Motorhomes Priced As Cars**

Conditions apply – ask for details

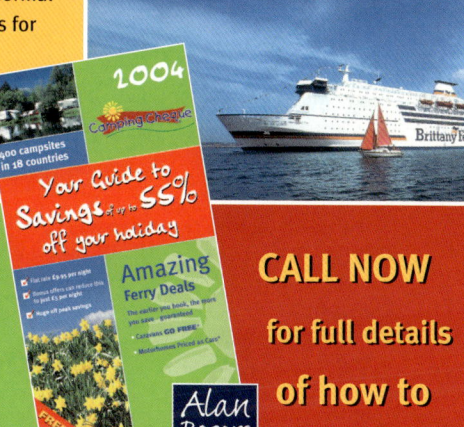

For full information visit the all-new website
www.campingcheque.co.uk
Buy Cheques, check ferry availability, book everything on-line AND SAVE!

CALL NOW for full details of how to save 50%

0870 405 4057

Portugal

Portugal is a relatively small country occupying the southwest corner of the Iberian peninsula, bordered by Spain in the north and east, with the Atlantic coast in the south and west. In spite of its size, the country offers a tremendous variety in both its way of life and traditions.

Most visitors looking for a beach type holiday head for the busy Algarve, with its long stretches of sheltered sandy beaches, and warm, clear Atlantic waters, great for bathing and watersports. With its monuments and fertile rolling hills, central Portugal adjoins the beautiful Tagus river that winds its way through the capital city of Lisbon, on its way to the Altantic Ocean. Lisbon city itself has deep rooted cultural traditions, coming alive at night with buzzing cafes, restaurants and discos. Moving south east of Lisbon the land becomes rather impoverished, consisting of stretches of vast undulating plains, dominated by cork plantations. Most people head for the walled town of Evora, an area steeped in two thousand years of history. The Portuguese consider the Minho area in the north to be the most beautiful part of their country, with its wooded mountain and wild coastline, a rural and conservative region with picturesque towns.

Population: 10 million

Capital: Lisbon

Climate: The country enjoys a maritime climate with hot summers and mild winters with comparatively low rainfall in the south, heavy rain in the north

Language: Portuguese, but English is widely spoken in cities, towns and larger resorts. French can be useful

Currency: The Euro (€)

Telephone: The country code is 00 351

Banks: Mon-Fri 08.30-11.45 and 13.00-14.45. Some large city banks operate a currency exchange 18.30-23.00

Shops: Mon-Fri 0900-1300 and 1500-1900. Sat 0900-1300.

Public Holidays: New Year; Carnival (Shrove Tues); Good Fri; Liberty Day 25 Apr; Labour Day; Corpus Christi; National Day 10 June; Saints Days; Assumption 15 Aug; Republic Day 5 Oct; All Saints 1 Nov; Immaculate Conception 8 Dec; Christmas 24-26 Dec

Tourist Office:
ICEP Portuguese Trade & Tourism Office,
Second Floor, 22/25a Sackville Street, London W1S 3LY

Tel: 09063 640 610   E-mail: iceplondt@aol.com
Fax: 020 7494 1868   Internet: www.portugalinsite.com

Spain

One of the largest countries in Europe, with glorious beaches, a fantastic sunshine record, vibrant towns and laid back sleepy villages, plus a diversity of landscape, culture and artistic traditions, Spain has all the ingredients for a great holiday.

Spain has a huge choice of beach resorts to choose from. With charming villages and attractive towns, the Costa Brava boasts spectacular scenery with towering cliffs and sheltered coves. There are plenty of lively resorts, including Lloret, Tossa and Calella, plus several quieter ones. Further along the east coast, the Costa del Azahar stretches from Vinaros to Almanzora, with the great port of Valencia in the middle. Orange groves abound. The central section of the coastline, the Costa Blanca, has 170 miles or so of silvery-white beaches. Benidorm is the most popular resort. The Costa del Sol lies in the south, home to more beaches and brilliant sunshine, whilst in the north the Costa Verde is largely unspoiled, with clean water, sandy beaches and rocky coves against a backdrop of mountains.

Beaches and sunshine aside, Spain also has plenty of great cities and towns to explore, including Barcelona, Valencia, Seville, Madrid, Toledo and Bilbao, all offering an array of sights, galleries and museums.

Population: 39.5 million

Capital: Madrid

Climate: Spain has a very varied climate. The north is temperate with most of the rainfall; dry and very hot in the centre; subtropical along the Mediterranean

Language: Castilian Spanish is spoken by most people with Catalan (northeast), Basque (north) and Galician (northwest) used in their respective areas

Currency: The Euro (€).

Banks: Mon-Fri 09.00-14.00. Sat 09.00-13.00

Telephone The country code is 00 34

Shops: Mon-Sat 09.00-13.00/14.00 and 15.00/16.00-19.30/20.00. Many close later

Public Holidays: New Year; Epiphany; Saint's Day 19 Mar; Maundy Thurs; Good Fri; Easter Mon; Labour Day; Saint's Day 25 July; Assumption 15 Aug; National Day 12 Oct; All Saints Day 1 Nov; Constitution Day 6 Dec; Immaculate Conception 8 Dec; Christmas Day

Tourist office:
Spanish National Tourist Office
22/23 Manchester Square, London W1U 3PX

Tel: 020 7486 8077   E-mail: info.londres@tourspain.es
Fax: 020 7486 8034   Internet: http://www.tourspain.es

The Regions of Spain

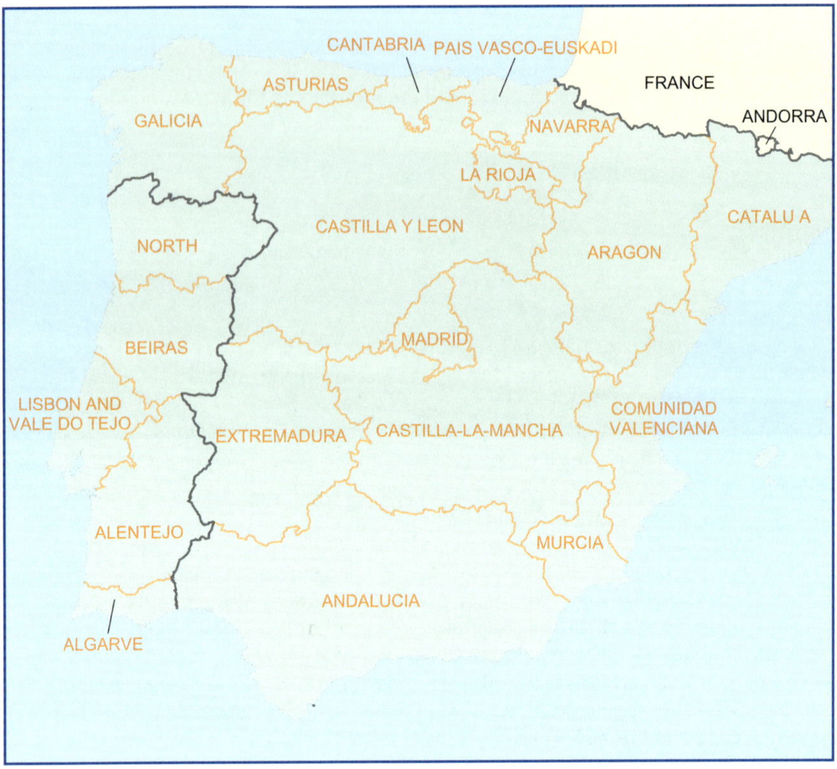

Cataluña-Catalunya

Flanked by the Pyrenees mountains and bathed by the Mediterranean Sea, Catalunya occupies the north eastern part of the peninsula. It has a strong identity, with a unique culture and language all of its own.

Catalunya is comprised of four provinces: Barcelona, Tarragona, Lleida and Girona

The regional capital is Barcelona

Barcelona is the historical capital of Catalunya and Spain's second leading city in both size and importance, after Madrid. The beautiful city has an impressive architectural heritage that includes the Gothic Quarter, with its cathedral, the old City Hall Building, the Episcopal Palace and the splendid Palace of the Generalitat. The city also boasts the work of the incomparable modernist architect Antonio Gaudí. In the centre of the fertile plain of the river Segre sits Lleida, capital of the province of the same name. Prominent atop a hill in the historic quarter of the city is the old cathedral or Seu Vella, symbol of the capital. The Costa Brava is the coastal zone that begins about 40 km. north of Barcelona and includes the entire shoreline of the province of Girona. It is an area of great natural beauty, formed by a succession of steep cliffs and small coves with finely grained sand. Some of its towns have been massively exploited for tourism but others, such as Tossa de Mar, still maintain their original size and fishing-village charm. The principal tourist centres on the coast include Roses, Sant Pere Pescador, L´Escala, L´Estartit, Palamos, Palafrugell, Platja d´Aro, S´Agaro, Sant Feliu de Guixols, Lloret de Mar and Blanes. There are daily boat services which operate along the coast for most of the year.

Cuisine of the region

Mediterranean influence with lots of tomatoes, garlic, fresh herbs, olive oil, onions, fish. Wild mushrooms in the autumn. Locally produced wines from Penedés, Conca de Barberá, Pla de Bages and Alella

Calçots: green onions grilled on a barbecue

Cod esqueixada: cod soaked in cold water then mixed with tomatoes, olives and onion

Escalivada: vegetable stew with roasted aubergine and peppers

Fuet, llonganisa, butifarra: local sausages

Suquet: seafood casserole

Recao de binefar: rice cooked with white beans, potatoes and chorizo

Places of interest

Empuries: Greco-Roman city

Figueres: birthplace of Salvador Dali, museum displaying his finest work

Girona: one of the oldest and most beautiful Catalan cities, 14th century cathedral

La Costa Dorada: stretches south from the Costa Brava to Tarragona, with beautiful, open, well maintained beaches

Parque Natural de Aigüamolls de L'Empordà: park made up of three reserves, with wildlife and over 320 bird species

Sitges: attractive beach town, museum of Cau-Ferrat featuring paintings by El Greco

Tarragona: Roman remains of Tarraco, the original Roman city

tip

FOR FREE TRAVEL ON PUBLIC TRANSPORT PLUS REDUCED ENTRY FEES INTO MANY MUSEUMS, SHOPS AND RESTAURANTS BUY A 1-3 DAY BARCELONA CARD FROM TOURIST OFFICES.

Cataluña-Catalunya

ES8005 Camping Cadaques
Ctra. de Port Lligat 17, 17488 Cadaques

Picturesque Cadaques is only accessible by a long winding road over the hills behind Roses and has an air of isolation. The attractive promenade is lined with restaurants and you can sit and watch the fishermen land their catches. Camping Cadaques is basic and mainly used by transit campers for short stays to visit the Dali attraction. Although it is not recommended for holidays, it is included to give an easier overnight visit to this difficult location. There are 200 pitches of 60-70 sq.m, some with a slight slope, and a separate area for tents. The large swimming pool is adjacent to the bar and restaurant with a terrace giving stunning views of the mountains, the Port of Lligat and the nature reserve. There are very few activities other than the pool and the site does look a little tired out of high season.

Facilities
Restaurant/bar. Good, well stocked supermarket producing its own bread. Swimming pool (high season). Laundry service and ironing. Dogs are not accepted. Off site: Fishing and bicycle hire 2 km. Riding 5 km. Golf 12 km.

At a glance
| Welcome & Ambience | ✓✓✓✓ | Location | ✓✓✓✓✓ |
| Quality of Pitches | ✓✓✓ | Range of Facilities | ✓✓✓ |

Directions
Leave autopista A7 (Figueres - Girona) at exit 4 and take C260 to Roses and on to Cadaqués. It is a long, winding road and the return journey is along the same route.

Latest charges
Per adult	€ 4.30
child	€ 3.20 - € 2.46
tent or caravan incl. electricity	€ 8.50
motorcaravan incl. electricity	€ 11.10
Plus 7% VAT.	

Reservations
Not generally necessary. Tel: 972 258 126.

Open
Easter - 15 September.

ES8020 Camping Internacional de Amberes
Playa de la Rubine, 17487 Empúria-Brava

Situated in the 'Venice of Spain', Empuria Brava is interlaced with inland waterways and canals. Internacional Amberes is large friendly site 50 metres from the wide, sandy beach, which is bordered on the east and west by the waterway canals (no access into them from the beach, only by car on the main road). The site can arrange temporary moorings for boats at Empuria Brava on request. The sea breeze here appears regularly during the afternoon so watersports are very good and hire facilities are available. Amberes is a surprisingly pretty and hospitable site where people seem to make friends easily and get to know other campers and the staff. The site has 798 touring pitches, most enjoying some shade from strategically placed trees. All have electricity and water connections. The restaurant and bar are close to the site entrance and the cuisine is so popular that locals use it too. Unusually the swimming pool is on an elevated terrace, raised out of view of most onlookers with sunbathing areas and a small children's pool adjoining. A shallow river runs through the site. A 'secret garden' style minigolf course is special to this site.

Facilities
Toilet facilities are in five fully equipped and recently renovated blocks. Washing machines. Motorcaravan services. Supermarket. Restaurant/bar. Disco bar and restaurant. Takeaway. Pizzeria. Watersports - windsurfing school. Boat moorings. Organised sports activities, children's programmes and entertainment. Swimming pool. Playgrounds. Football. Table tennis. Tennis. Volleyball. Apartments. Off site: Bicycle hire, riding and fishing 500 m. Golf 12 km.

At a glance
| Welcome & Ambience | ✓✓✓✓ | Location | ✓✓✓✓✓ |
| Quality of Pitches | ✓✓✓✓ | Range of Facilities | ✓✓✓✓ |

Directions
Empuria Brava is reached by the C260 Figueres - Roses road. Site is signed from main roundabout leading into Empuria Brava but it is easier to continue to second roundabout, turn towards Empuri Brava and follow road for some distance. Watch for site entrance (hidden by trees) on left on one of the many bends.

Charges 2004
Per person over 3 yrs	€ 3.00
pitch incl. electricity (55 sq.m)	€ 7.60 - € 19.50
pitch 70 sq.m.	€ 9.80 - € 22.70
pitch 100 sq.m.	€ 12.70 - € 27.20

Less 20% for pensioners for stays of 15 days or over in low seasons.

Reservations
Contact site for booking form. Tel: 972 450 507.
Email: info@inter-amberes.com

Open
1 April - 15 October.

ES8012 Camping Mas Nou

Ctra. Figueres-Roses, km 38, 17486 Castelló d'Empúries

Some two kilometres from the sea on the Costa Brava, this is a surprisingly tranquil site. Split into two parts, one contains pitches and sanitary blocks and the other houses the impressive leisure complex. There are 450 neat, level and marked pitches on grass and sand, a minimum of 70 sq.m. but most 80-100 sq.m, and 300 with electrical connections. The leisure complex is 80 metres from the main site across a very quiet road and features a huge L-shaped swimming pool with a paddling area. A more formal restaurant with ajoining bar, pleasant terrace crêperie and rotisseria under palms. Another barbeque/rotisseria in another part of the site offers takeaway meals (in season). The site owns the large souvenir shop on the entrance road. Lots of time and money goes into the cleanliess of this site and it is good very for families.

Facilities
Three excellent, fully equipped sanitary blocks include baby baths, good facilities for disabled visitors. These are amongst the best we have seen. Dishwashing and laundry sinks. Washing machines. facilities. Supermarket and other shops close by. Bar/restaurant. Takeaway. Swimming pool with life guard (from 1/6). Tennis. Minigolf. Basketball. Volleyball. Football. Mini club in dedicated building (July/Aug). Table tennis. Playground. Electronic games. Off site: Riding 1.5 km. Fishing and bicycle hire 2 km. Beach 2.5 km. National Park. Aquatic Park. Romanica tour of famous local churches.

At a glance
Welcome & Ambience	✓✓✓✓	Location	✓✓✓✓
Quality of Pitches	✓✓✓✓✓	Range of Facilities	✓✓✓✓✓

Directions
From A7 use exit 3. Mas Nou is 2 km. east of Castelló d'Empúries, on the Roses road, some 10 km. from Figueres.

Charges 2003
Per person	€ 3.70 - € 5.85
child (4-11 yrs)	€ 3.10 - € 4.15
caravan or tent	€ 3.70 - € 5.85
car or motorcycle	€ 3.70 - € 5.85
motorcaravan	€ 7.40 - € 11.70
electricity (6/10A)	€ 2.70 - € 3.10
dog	free - € 1.50

All plus 7% VAT. Camping Cheques accepted.

Reservations
Write to site. Tel: 972 454 175.
Email: info@campingmasnou.com

Open
12 April - 28 September.

Cataluña-Catalunya

Great on-line holiday deals alanrogersdirect.com

ES8030 Camping Nautic Almata

Ctra. St Pere Pescador, km 11.6, 17486 Castelló d'Empúries

Situated in the Bay of Roses, south of Empuria Brava and beside the Parc Natural dels Aiguamolls de l'Empordà, this is a site of particular interest for nature lovers (especially bird watchers). Beautifully laid out, it is arranged around the river and waterways, so will suit those who like to camp close to water and enjoy watersports and boating. It is worth visiting because of its unusual aspects and the feeling of being on the canals, as well as being a high quality beach-side site. It is a large site with 1,109 well kept, large, numbered pitches, all with electricity and on flat, sandy ground. There are some pitches right on the beach. The name no doubt derives from the fact that boats can be tied up at the small marina within the site and a slipway also gives access to a river and thence to the sea. Throughout the season there is a varied entertainment programme for children and adults. The facilities on this site are impressive. Some tour operators use the site.

Facilities

Sanitary blocks all of a high standard, attractively decorated. include some en-suite showers with basins, taps to draw hot water for dishwashing, laundry sinks and baby baths. Good facilities for disabled visitors and ramps where necessary. Washing machines. Gas supplies. Excellent supermarket. Restaurant and bar (recently refurbished), rotisserie and pizzeria near pool. Two separate bars by beach where discos held in main season. Water-ski and windsurfing schools. 300 sq. m. swimming pool. Tennis, squash, volleyball, fronton all free. Minigolf. Games room with pool and table tennis. Extensive riding tuition with own stables and stud. Children's play park (near river). Car, motorcycle and bicycle hire. Hairdresser. Torches are useful near beach. Off site: National Park and wetlands around site. Canal trips 18 km. Aquatic Park 20 km. Adventure sports 40 km. Excursions to Barcelona, Monserrat, Andorra and Dahli's museum.

Directions

Site is signed at 26 km. marker on C252 between Castello d'Empuries and Vildemat, then 7 km. to site. Alternatively, on San Pescador - Castello d'Empuries road head north and site is signed on right.

Charges 2003

Per pitch	€ 16.50 - € 33.00
person (over 3 yrs)	€ 1.45 - € 2.90
dog	€ 3.60 - € 4.60
boat or jet ski	€ 5.85 - € 7.90

All plus 7% VAT. No credit cards.

Reservations

Write to site. Tel: 972 454 477.
Email: info@almata.com

Open

15 May - 19 September, including all facilities.

At a glance

Welcome & Ambience	✓✓✓✓	Location	✓✓✓✓✓
Quality of Pitches	✓✓✓✓✓	Range of Facilities	✓✓✓✓✓

ES8010 Camping Castell Mar

Platja de la Rubina, 17486 Castelló d'Empúries

This friendly site is 350 metres from one of the very pleasant Gulf of Roses beaches, and within the large Aiguamolls de l'Empordà nature reserve. It is also convenient for (but quite separate from) the latest tourist development and facilities at Empuria Brava. With some 300 pitches, it is smaller than many sites in this part of Spain and is particularly suitable for families. There is a heated outdoor pool, a restaurant and bar and an large open-air auditorium where a varied entertainment programme is provided. A roof-top, terraced area is used for special occasions and enjoys pleasant views of the surrounding area. The pitches, most with electricity, are of average size for the Costa Brava and are on level ground with some artificial shade, mainly for tents, and natural shade from the trees and hedges. There are opportunities for most watersports nearby and reception can arrange excursions by canoe through the nature reserve. Security is very good – if you want to leave before 8 am. you must make prior arrangements. There are several tour operators (100 pitches) and a further 50 pitches have mobile homes to rent.

Facilities

The large, well maintained, modern toilet block is of a high standard. It provides some washbasins in cabins, facilities for disabled visitors and dishwashing with hot water. Washing machines. Bar, restaurant/pizzeria and takeaway (all season). Supermarket. Large screen satellite TV/video. Play area. Table tennis. Swimming pools (all season). Many organised activities and entertainment over a long season. Riding and children's donkey rides with cart. Exchange facilities. ATM. Torches required in some areas. Off site: Riding 1 km. Bicycle hire 3 km. Golf 10 km.

Directions

From A7 motorway exit 3 (Figueres N/Roses) take N11 south and exit on C260 Figueres - Roses road; site is signed on the right at km. 40.5, just after the second turn for Empuriabrava ; follow road for approx. 1.5 km.

Charges 2003

Per person	€ 3.00
child (3-10 yrs)	€ 2.00
pitch incl. electricity	€ 7.00 - € 28.00

VAT included. No credit cards.

Reservations

Necessary for July/Aug. and made with deposit (€ 12,02) for a min. of 8 days between 9/7-15/8. Tel: 972 450 822. Email: cmar@campingparks.com

Open

15 May - 26 September.

See advertisement on page 31

At a glance

Welcome & Ambience	✓✓✓	Location	✓✓✓✓
Quality of Pitches	✓✓✓	Range of Facilities	✓✓✓✓

Cataluña-Catalunya

ES8015 Camping Caravaning La Laguna

Apdo. de Correos 55, 17486 Castelló d'Empúries

La Laguna is a relaxed, spacious site on an isthmus within a Catalan national maritime park. It has direct access to the sandy beach and estuary of the river Muga. The new owners are continuing to spend much time and effort on improvements, including the large lagoon from which it takes its name. The approach is by a long (four km), and more or less private road. This is quite an unusual site for this area, being laid out very informally among mature pine trees. The 750 pitches (of which just 10 are occupied by mobile homes) are clearly marked on grass and sand, all with electricity (long leads may be useful). An attractive bar restaurant overlooks the lagoon and there is a swimming pool (July/Aug) and a disco across the road from reception. A riding school operates on site (May-Sept). The beach frontage is large and has a sailing school. It is said to be possible to cross over to Empuria Brava when the tide is out. The river Muga running along one side of the site is hidden by a high bank with a path along the top and there are many pleasant walks in this area. With the on-going improvements this is becoming a pleasant site for family holidays.

Facilities

Five toilets blocks, placed to avoid long walks, are simple in design. Three have been completely rebuilt (the others will follow); they all provide free hot water. Plenty of dishwashing sinks. Well equipped laundry room. Bar, restaurant and takeaway (all 15/3-20/10). Supermarket. Swimming pool (15/5-30/9). Tennis (free in low seasons). ATM. Minigolf. Sailing school (July/Aug). Fishing. Mini club. Bicycle hire. Riding. Dinner dance Thursday. 24 hour photo service. Animation programme and competitions. Off site: Bicycle hire 3 km. Golf 15 km.

At a glance

Welcome & Ambience	✓✓✓	Location	✓✓✓✓
Quality of Pitches	✓✓✓	Range of Facilities	✓✓✓✓

Directions

Site is signed from Castello d'Empuries bypass (C260 Figures - Roses) and is on the junction with the road for Sant Pere Pescador (signs for Camping). Follow approach road for approx. 4 km.

Charges 2003

Per person	€ 3.80 - € 6.55
child (3-10 yrs)	€ 3.10 - € 5.05
tent or caravan	€ 3.80 - € 6.55
motorcaravan	€ 7.20 - € 11.75
car	€ 3.80 - € 6.55
motorcycle	€ 3.10 - € 5.05
electricity (5A)	€ 3.10

Discounts for longer stays and pensioners. No credit cards.

Reservations

Contact site. Tel: 972 45 05 53. Email: info@campinglaguna.com

Open

1 March - 22 October.

ES8033 Camping Las Palmeras

Ctra. de la Platja, 17470 Sant Pere Pescador

A very polished site, the pleasant experience begins as you enter the palm bedecked site and are greeted at the air conditioned reception building. The 230 pitches are flat, very clean and well maintained, with shade and electricity. A few pitches are complete with water and drainage. Some smart mobile homes are placed unobtrusively around the site. A very pleasant pool complex has a lifeguard and the brightly coloured play areas are clean and safe. There is a huge array of activities, including some very exotic ones, which are booked at the site resulting in visits to various locations to indulge in what are known as 'active holidays' (extra charges). A full animation programme allows parents a break during the day and there is organised fun in the evenings in high season. Juan Alcantara, the owner is a kind gentleman who is very keen for you to enjoy your time at his family site. You will enjoy your stay here – there is a very happy atmosphere. The very pleasant beach is a 200 metres walk through a gate at the rear of the site.

Facilities

Two excellent toilet blocks are very clean, including first class facilities for disabled campers plus two well equipped baby rooms (key at reception). Facilites may become a little busy at peak periods and the family cabins are sought after. Washing machines. Motorcaravan services. Supermarket. Restaurant/bar (children's menu). Swimming pools (heated). Play areas. Table tennis. Tennis. Gym. Boule. Electronic games. Barbecue. Bicycle hire. Mini-club. Animation. Active holiday programme (ask at reception). Torches useful. Off site: Beach 200 m. Fishing. Boat launching 1 km. Riding 3 km. Golf 20 km.

At a glance

Welcome & Ambience	✓✓✓✓✓	Location	✓✓✓✓
Quality of Pitches	✓✓✓✓	Range of Facilities	✓✓✓✓

Directions

From A7/E15 Perpignoan - Girona road take Figueres exit and N11/C31 towards L'Escala. Turn for town of San Pescador and site is well signed around the town.

Charges 2003

Per adult	€ 2.00 - € 3.00
child (under 10 yrs)	€ 1.50 - € 2.00
pitch	€ 11.80 - € 26.10
electricity (5A)	€ 2.70
animal	€ 2.00 - € 3.50

Reservations

Made for min. 1 week with deposit (€ 100). Tel: 972 520 506. Email: info@campinglaspalmeras.com

Open

1 April - 31 October.

ES8035 Camping L'Amfora
Avenida Josep Tarradellas 2, 17470 Sant Pere Pescador

This is a large, friendly family site with a Greek theme, which is manifested mainly in the restaurant and pool areas. The site is clean and well kept and the owner is keen to operate in an environmentally friendly way. There are 850 pitches (730 for touring), all with electrical connections and most with a water tap, on level grass with small trees and shrubs. Of these, 64 pitches are large (180 sq.m.), made for two units per pitch and each with an individual sanitary facility (toilet, shower and washbasin). Some 200 more recently developed pitches have limited shade as yet. An inviting terraced bar and self-service restaurant overlook three large swimming pools (one for children) and a new one with two waterslides. Ambitious evening entertainment (pub, disco, shows) and children's animation are organised in season and a choice of watersports activities is available on the beach.

Facilities
In addition to the individual units, the two main sanitary blocks (one heated) offer free hot water, washbasins in cabins, hairdryers and baby rooms. There is extra provision near the pool area. Access is good for disabled visitors. Laundry facilities. Supermarket. Terraced bar, self service and waiter service restaurants, takeaway and pizza service. Restaurant and bar on the beach with limited menu (high season). Disco-bar for the young. Table tennis. Tennis courts. Bicycle hire. Minigolf. Football. Volleyball. Playground. Entertainment and organised activities for children. Evening shows. Windsurfing school. Sailing. Fishing. Doctor daily in season. Exchange facilities. Internet point. Car wash. Torches required in beach areas. Off site: Boat launching 1 km. Riding 6 km. Golf 15 km.

At a glance
| Welcome & Ambience | ✓✓✓✓ | Location | ✓✓✓✓✓ |
| Quality of Pitches | ✓✓✓✓ | Range of Facilities | ✓✓✓✓✓ |

Directions
From A7 motorway take exit 3 (Figueres/Roses) on N-11 towards Girona/Barcelona. Exit on C260 for Figueres/Roses towards Roses and, at roundabout near Castello d'Empuries turn right to Sant Pere Pescador. Site is signed through town.

Charges 2003
Per person	€ 2.90 - € 3.70
child (2-9 yrs)	free - € 3.00
pitch (100 sq.m.)	€ 11.50 - € 28.00
pitch with individual sanitary arrangements	€ 16.00 - € 38.00
large pitch (180 sq.m.) with sanitary	€ 18.50 - € 90.00
dog	€ 1.40 - € 3.40

Electricity (10A) included. Plus 7% VAT. Discounts for pensioners for longer stays. No credit cards. Camping Cheques accepted.

Reservations
Made with deposit (€ 61) and fee (€ 15.03); write to site. Tel: 972 520 540. Email: info@campingamfora.com

Open
3 April - 30 September.

travel service
TO BOOK THIS SITE
0870 405 4055
Expert Advice & Special Offers

Cataluña-Catalunya

ES8050 Camping Aquarius
Playa s/n, 17470 Sant Pere Pescador

A smart and efficient family site, Aquarius has direct access to a quiet sandy beach that slopes gently and provides good bathing (the sea is hsallow for quite a long way out). The site is ideal for those who really like sun and sea, with a quiet situation. One third of the site has good shade with a park-like atmosphere with the great variety of plants here being carefully labelled (Mr Rupp the owner is an enthusiast). An extension with less shade provided an opportunity to enlarge the pitches and they are now all at least 70-100 sq.m. There are 447 numbered pitches, all with electrical connections. Only five pitches are not used for tourers. The owner has an architectural background and a wealth of knowledge on the whole Catalan area and culture. He has written a booklet of suggested tours (from reception). The whole family is justifiably proud of their most attractive site and they continually make improvements. A small stage close to the restaurant is used for live entertainment in season. The spotless beach bar complex with shaded terraces and minigolf has marvellous views over the Bay of Roses. The 'Surf Center' with rentals, school and shop is ideal for enthusiasts and beginners alike.

Facilities
Attractively tiled, fully equipped, large toilet blocks provide some cabins for each sex. Excellent facilities for disabled people, plus baths for children and hot water for sinks. A superb new block has under-floor heating and features family cabins with showers and basins. Laundry facilities. Gas supplies. Car wash. Motorcaravan services. Full size refrigerators. Supermarket with butcher. Pleasant restaurant and bar with terrace. Takeaway. Children's play centre (with qualified attendant), playground and games hall. TV room with giant screen. 'Surf Center'. Table tennis. Volleyball. Minigolf. Bicycle hire. Football field. Boules. Barbecue and dance once weekly when numbers justify. Security boxes. Exchange facilities. ATM. Electronic games. Dogs are accepted in one section. (Note: no pool). Off site: Fishing and boat launching 3 km. Riding 6 km. Golf 15 km.

At a glance
| Welcome & Ambience | ✓✓✓✓ | Location | ✓✓✓✓✓ |
| Quality of Pitches | ✓✓✓ | Range of Facilities | ✓✓✓✓ |

Directions
From A7 motorway take exit 3 (Figueres/Roses) and take N11 south to join C260 towards Roses. At roundabout near Castello d'Empuries take road to and through San Pere Pescador. Site signed to left shortly after bridge south of town.

Charges 2003
Per adult	€ 2.75 - € 3.30
child (2-12 yrs)	free - € 2.40
pitch acc. to season and facilities	€ 6.80 - € 30.25
electricity (6A)	€ 2.50

All plus 7% VAT. Discounts for pensioners on longer stays. No credit cards.

Reservations
Made for any length with £50 deposit and £15 fee. (you are strongly advised to book early for any pitch near the beach). Tel: 972 520 003.
Email: camping@aquarius.es

Open
All year except 11 Jan - 14 March, with all facilities.

ES8040 Camping Las Dunas
Ctra. S M d'Empuries - Sant Pere, 17470 Sant Pere Pescador

Las Dunas is an extremely large, impressive and well organised site with many on site activities and an ambitious programme of improvements. It has direct access to a superb sandy beach that stretches along the site for nearly one kilometre with a windsurfing school and beach bar. There is also a much used swimming pool with large double children's pools. The 1,500 individual hedged pitches of around 100 sq.m. are laid out on flat ground in long, regular parallel rows. Electrical connections are provided on all pitches and shade is available in some parts of the site. Much effort has gone into planting palms and new trees here and the results are very attractive. Pitches are usually available, even in the main season. The large restaurant and bar have spacious terraces overlooking the swimming pools and you can also enjoy a more secluded cavern styled pub. A disco club is close by in a soundproof building (although people returning from this during the night can be a problem for pitches in the central area of the site). With free quality entertainment of all types in season and positive security arrangements, this is a great site for families with teenagers. Everything is provided on site so you won't need to leave.

Facilities
Five excellent large toilet blocks (with resident cleaners) have British style toilets, controllable hot showers and washbasins in cabins. One block has underfloor heating. Excellent facilities for children, babies and disabled people. Laundry facilities. Motorcaravan services. Extensive supermarket with bakery, good butcher and other shops. Large bar with terrace. Large restaurant. Takeaway. Ice-cream parlour. Beach bar in main season. Disco club. Swimming pool (30 x 14 m) with children's pool. Playgrounds. Tennis. Minigolf. Football and rugby pitches. Basketball. Boule. Volleyball. Sailing/windsurfing school and other watersports. Organised programme of events: sports, children's games, shows, music and entertainment, partly in English (15/6-31/8). Exchange facilities. ATM. Safety deposit. Dogs taken in only one section. Torches required in some areas.

At a glance
| Welcome & Ambience | ✓✓✓✓ | Location | ✓✓✓✓✓ |
| Quality of Pitches | ✓✓✓✓ | Range of Facilities | ✓✓✓✓✓ |

Directions
From A7 autostrada take exit 5 towards L'Escala (G1623) and turn north 2 km. before reaching L'Escala at sign to Sant Marti d'Ampurias. Site is well signed.

Charges 2003
Per adult	€ 3.00
child (2-10 yrs)	€ 2.50
standard pitch incl. electricity	€ 13.00 - € 35.50
water and drainage	€ 1.00 - € 3.00

All plus 7% VAT.

Reservations
Made for numbered pitches with deposit and fee. Address for information: Apdo. de Correus 23, 17130 La Escala (Girona). Tel: 972 521 717.
Email: info@campinglasdunas.com

Open
9 May - 25 September.

ES8060 Camping La Ballena Alegre 2
17470 San Pere Pescador

La Ballena Alegre 2, sister site to the Ballena Alegre south of Barcelona, is partly situated in a lightly wooded setting, and partly open, with some 1,800 m. of frontage facing directly onto an excellent beach of soft golden sand which is cleaned daily. They claim that none of the 1,629 pitches is more than 100 m. from the beach. The site has recently won Spanish tourist board awards and is keen on ecological fitness. The grass pitches are individually numbered and of decent size (over 200 are 100 sq.m.). Electrical connections are available in all parts and there are 70 fully serviced pitches. There are restaurant and bar areas beside the pleasant terraced pool complex (four pools including a children's pool). For those who wish to drink and snack late there is a pub open until 3 am. The soundproof disco has a covered approach and is firmly managed – a discount card doubles for easy identification of customers. A little train ferries people along the length of the site. Plenty of entertainment and activities are offered, including a well managed watersports centre, with sub-aqua, windsurfing and kite surfing, where equipment can be hired and lessons taken. You can also use a comprehensive open air fitness centre near the beach. A full animation programme is provided all season. An overflow area across the road provides additional parking and sports activities. The security barrier recognises your number-plate and opens automatically. A great site for families.

Facilities
All seven toilet blocks have been refurbished to a very high standard and are well maintained. These feature large pivoting doors for showers, wash cabins, etc, special low facilities for children, baby baths and facilities for disabled campers. Launderette. Motorcaravan services. Gas supplies. Supermarket. Chemist shop. Bar and self-service restaurant. Full restaurant (evenings all season). Takeaway. 'Croissanterie'. Pizzeria and beach bar in high season. Swimming pool complex (all season). Three tennis courts. Table tennis. Watersports centre. Fitness centre. Bicycle hire. Playgrounds. Sound proofed disco. Dancing twice weekly and organised activities, sports, entertainment, etc. all season but it is generally a quiet site. Safe deposit. Cash point. Resident doctor and site ambulance. Car wash. Dogs allowed in one zone (dog showers). Internet point. Torches useful in beach areas. Off site: Go-karting nearby with bus service. Fishing 300 m. Riding 2 km.

At a glance
| Welcome & Ambience | ✓✓✓✓ | Location | ✓✓✓✓✓ |
| Quality of Pitches | ✓✓✓✓ | Range of Facilities | ✓✓✓✓✓ |

Directions
From A7 Figueres - Girona autopista take exit 5 to L'Escala GI 623 for 18.5 km. At roundabout take sign to Sant Marti d'Empúries and follow camp signs. Access has now been entirely asphalted.

Charges 2003
Per person	€ 3.30
child (3-9 yrs)	€ 2.50
pitch incl. electricity (5A)	€ 14.90 - € 33.00
serviced pitch plus	€ 6.00 - € 11.00
drainage plus	€ 1.25 - € 2.10
dog	€ 2.10 - € 3.90

All plus 7% VAT. Discount of 10% on pitch charge for pensioners all season. No credit cards.

Reservations
Made with deposit (€ 200), min. 10 days 10/7-10/8; contact site for details. Winter address: Ave. Roma 12, 08015 Barcelona. Tel: 902 510 520.
Email: infb2@ballena-alegre.com

Open
15 May - 27 September.

Cataluña-Catalunya

ES8080 Camping El Delfin Verde
Ctra. de Torroella de Montgri, 17257 Torroella de Montgrí

A large, popular and high quality site in a quiet location, El Delfin Verde has its own long beach stretching along its frontage which campers have to themselves. A feature of the site is an attractive large pool in the shape of a dolphin with a total area of 1,800 sq.m. This has two island areas, one containing a huge fountain which can be lit at night. In the main season an elevated area with a large bar, full restaurant and a separate takeaway give wonderful views over the huge pool. There is a further restaurant with slightly cheaper, good value food in the main complex with an open air arena. This is a large site with nearly 6,000 visitors at peak times, well managed with friendly staff. Level grass pitches nearer the beach are marked and many are separated by small fences and newly planted hedging. All have electrical connections and access to water points and a stream runs through the centre of the site. There is shade in some of the older parts and a particularly pleasant area of pine trees in the centre provides marked but not separated pitches (sandy and not so level). El Delfin Verde is a large and cheerful holiday site with many good facilities, sports and a free family entertainment programme in season. Used by British tour operators (60 pitches).

Facilities
Six excellent large toilet blocks and a seventh smaller block, all with resident cleaners, have fully controllable showers using desalinated water and of good, comfortable size, and some washbasins in cabins. Laundry facilities. Motorcaravan services. Supermarket and other shops. Swimming pools (with lifeguard). Two restaurants, grills and pizzerias. Three bars - the main one closes 11 pm, pool bar open until 1 am; small bar by beach open in season. 'La Vela' barbecue and party area. Large sports area, football, volleyball, 8 tennis courts. 2 km. exercise track. Dancing and floor shows weekly in season. Disco. Excursions organised. General room with TV. Video room. Games room. Bicycle hire. Minigolf. Playground. Trampolines. Badminton. Fishing. Hairdresser. Car repairs, servicing and washing. Gas supplies. Dogs are not accepted in high season (12/7-15/8). Off site: Golf (20% discount) and riding 4 km.

At a glance
Welcome & Ambience	✓✓✓	Location	✓✓✓✓
Quality of Pitches	✓✓✓	Range of Facilities	✓✓✓✓✓

Directions
Site is at end of very long approach road leading off the C31 Torroella de Montgri - Palafrugell road (east of Girona). Watch out for white dolphin and flags by road side.

Charges 2003
Per person	€ 3.00
child (2-9 yrs)	€ 2.50
pitch incl. electricity	€ 19.00 - € 35.50
dog (excl 15/7-15/8)	€ 2.50

All plus 7% VAT. Special offers on long stays in low season.

Reservations
Only a guarantee to admit - no specific pitch allocated. Write (all year) with deposit (€ 91) to Apdo.43, 17257 Torroella de Montgri. Tel: 972 758 454. Email: info@eldelfinverde.com

Open
3 April - 17 October, incl. all amenities.

ES8070 Camping L'Escala
Cami Ample, 17130 L'Escala

Under the same ownership as Las Dunas (no. ES8040), but a complete contrast in terms of size, this is a small, traditional site with limited facilities. It takes just five minutes to walk to either the very pleasant beach or to the centre of this modestly sized, lively, yet historic holiday resort. Here you will find most of the usual seaside attractions. The site has a canopy of fir trees giving excellent shade. There are 140 pitches of which 90 are for touring units, so reservation is essential. All pitches have electricity, water and drainage. In season there is a bar and restaurant offering very good food with a pleasant enclosed terrace with a retractable candy-striped canopy. There is some road noise despite the very high wall between the site and the busy road alongside.

Facilities
The central toilet block is basic but clean, with British style toilets, washbasins (two in cabins for ladies), free hot water and 25 free showers. Dishwashing and laundry sinks with hot water. Shop, bar and restaurant (all high season). Basic play area. Off site: Fishing 100 m. Bicycle hire 500 m. Riding 3 km. Golf 15 km.

At a glance
Welcome & Ambience	✓✓✓	Location	✓✓✓
Quality of Pitches	✓✓✓	Range of Facilities	✓✓✓

Directions
Site lies on the north side of the town and the beach. Follow road for beach, then fork immediately left into Cami Ample to site on the right in 200 m. (watch for site name on wall and gate in high wall).

Charges 2003
Per adult	€ 2.10
child (2-10 yrs)	€ 1.80
pitch incl. electricity	€ 11.45 - € 16.00
dog	€ 2.10 - € 2.70

All plus 7% VAT.

Reservations
Essential in high season. Tel: 972 770 084. Email: info@campinglescala.com

Open
Easter - 25 September.

ES8007 Camping Castell Montgri

Ctra. Toroella - L'Estartit, km 4.7, 17258 L'Estartit

This is a large bustling site with all the modern paraphernalia of holiday-making. With over 50% of the site dedicated to catering for tour operators, it may come as a surprise that we should choose to feature it in a guide for independent campers and caravanners. However, the site does include three designated areas for independent campers and these provide 590 terraced and flat, pitches, some shaded but all with electricity. On arrival you are invited to find your own place. There is a busy bar/restaurant and terrace overlooking an attractive swimming pool with a pair of water slides (one large with attendant) close to these areas. The remainder of the site offers a very wide range of amenities and attractions, including one further, large pool with restaurant/bar and terrace areas higher on the site, and a new pool, bar and live music area at the very top with fantastic views. There are also two mini-pools for toddlers around the site along with various play areas, disco, sports facilities and a live entertainment programme. This site could be of interest to families with teenagers, offering the possibility for parents to rest whilst the youngsters enjoy their own type of holiday within the confines of the site.

Facilities
Toilet facilities are quite adequate, if not that luxurious, each area of the site having its own block, with dishwashing (H&C) and laundry facilities. Cleaning is continual (06.00-22.00 hrs) but with the numbers on site, litter may be a problem at times. Bars and restaurants. Pizzeria. Takeaway. Swimming pools. Supermarket and souvenirs. Football field. Tennis. Table tennis. Billiards. Volleyball. Minigolf. Playground. Large screen TV and videos. Disco. Entertainment programme and excursions. Exchange and safe deposit facilities. Car wash. Gas supplies. Free site bus to L'Estartit Torches required in some areas. Off site: Fishing 300 m. Riding 500 m. Bicycle hire 1 km. Golf 10 km. Seaside entertainment in Estartit.

At a glance
Welcome & Ambience	✓✓✓	Location	✓✓✓
Quality of Pitches	✓✓✓	Range of Facilities	✓✓✓✓✓

Directions
Site is on the main Torroella de Montgri - L'Estartit road GI 641 just north of the town on the left, just after town sign.

Charges 2003
Per person	€ 3.00
child (3-10 yrs)	€ 2.00
pitch incl. car and electricity	€ 8.00 - € 30.00

Prices include VAT. Minimum 7 day stay 6/7-18/8. Good discounts in low season. No credit cards.

Reservations
Made with non-returnable deposit (€ 12.02), to guarantee admission only. Tel: 972 751 630.
Email: cmontgri@campingparks.com

Open
8 May - 3 October.

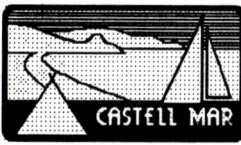

GRUP CASTELL. CAMPING PARKS
internet: www.campingparks.com

VIDEO / CD-ROM FREE !!!

* Write to us and we'll send you FREE a VIDEO or CD-Rom of Camping CASTELL MONTGRI, Camping CASTELL MAR and COSTA BRAVA.

* Rent of MOBILE HOMES and CHALETS.

* Animation programme in low season.

ES8075 Camping Estartit

Calle Villa Primavera 12, 17258 L'Estartit

This friendly, Belgian run site has limited facilities, but is only 300 m. from Estartit town. A short walk down the hill brings you into the heart of the town which is extremely popular and very commercialised, although you can find authentic tapas bars and street entertainment. The site itself is surprisingly quiet, considering its proximity to the town. Set amongst tall pine trees (which provide complete shade), in a narrow valley, it has 173 terraced pitches (132 for touring units), all with electrical connections. These are best suited for campers with tents as there are some very steep drops between the terraces. However, there are two sand/gravel areas for a small number of motorcaravans and caravans (booking essential in high season). The local beaches are extremely good but if the town is too frenetic the site has a very small swimming pool plus a sunbathing area with loungers. An attractive shaded area has a terrace beside the bar. Access around the site could be difficult for people with disabilities.

Facilities

The modern, fully tiled sanitary block is kept very clean and provides hot and cold showers (small fee for hot water), small laundry with washing machines and a separate baby area. Gas supplies. Bar/restaurant (1/6-15/9). Shop (1/6-15/9). Swimming pool (all season). Limited, small play area. Children's activities and adult social events (barbecue, bingo, etc). Excursions can be booked. Site is guarded day and night. Torches are necessary in the more remote parts of the site. Dogs are not accepted in high season (20/6-20/8). Off site: Fishing, bicycle hire and riding within 1 km. Golf 7 km.

At a glance

Welcome & Ambience	✓✓✓✓	Location	✓✓✓
Quality of Pitches	✓✓✓	Range of Facilities	✓✓✓

Directions

L'Estartit is approached on the E1641 which leaves the C31 road at Torroella de Montgri. Site is signed from Estartit town centre; follow the one-way system.

Charges 2003

Per person	€ 4.25
child (2-10 yrs)	€ 2.75
caravan or family tent	€ 4.70
car	€ 4.00
motorcaravan	€ 7.80
motorcycle	€ 2.80
electricity (2/6A)	€ 2.20 - € 2.80

Plus 7% VAT. Less 10-30% outside high season (10/6-31/8). No credit cards.

Reservations

Contact site. Tel: 972 751 909.

Open

Easter/1 April - 1 October.

ES8074 Camping Paradis

Avenida de Montgó 260, 17130 L'Escala

If you prefer a quieter site out of the very busy resort of L'Escala then this site is an excellent option. This large, friendly, family run site has a dynamic owner Marti, who is a most pleasant man with excellent English and very keen to help. The site is divided by the beach access road and has its own private access to the very safe and unspoilt beach. The site has 646 pitches, all with electricity, some on sloping ground although the pitches themselves tend to be flat. Established pine trees provide shade for most places with more coverage on the western side of the site. Non-stop maintenance ensures that all facilities at this site are of a high standard. There are three swimming pools, the largest with an idyllic and most unusual setting on the top of a cliff overlooking the Bay of Roses. The site operates its own well equipped sub-aqua diving school and campers can experience a free diving experience in the pool or more adventurous coastal diving where appropriate. A CCTV security system monitors the pools and general security from a purpose built centre.

Facilities

Modern, fully equipped sanitary blocks are kept very clean. Washing machines and dryers. Shop (1/4-30/9). Extensive modern complex of restaurants, bars and takeaways (1/4-30/9). Takeaway(1/4-15/9). Swimming pools (1/5-20/10). Pool bar. Play areas. Fishing. Basketball, volleyball and badminton. Kayak hire. Sub aqua school. Organised activities for children in high season. ATM machine. Private access to beach. Off site: Cala Montgo beach 100 m. with a charming bay of soft sand offering watersports, restaurants and a disco in season. Road train service to town centre from outside site. Riding 2 km. Golf 10 km.

At a glance

Welcome & Ambience	✓✓✓✓✓	Location	✓✓✓✓✓
Quality of Pitches	✓✓✓✓✓	Range of Facilities	✓✓✓✓✓

Directions

Leave autopista A7 at exit 5 heading for Viladimat, then L'Escala. Site is well signed from town centre.

Charges 2003

Per adult	€ 2.60 - € 4.40
child (3-9 yrs)	€ 1.85 - € 3.10
pitch	€ 10.00 - € 20.75
electricity (10A)	€ 3.15

Plus 7% VAT. No credit cards

Reservations

Advisable in high season. Tel: 972 770 200.
Email: info@campingparadis.com

Open

17 March - 20 October.

ES8072 Camping Les Medes

Paratge Camp De L'Arbre, 17258 L'Estartit

Les Medes is different from some of the 'all singing, all dancing' sites so popular along this coast and the friendly family of Pla-Coll are rightly proud of their award wining site. Set back from busy L'Estartit itself, it is only 800 metres to the nearest beach and a little train runs from near the site (June-Sept) to the town. With just 172 pitches, the site is small enough for the owners to know their visitors and, being campers themselves, they have been careful in planning their top class facilities. The level, grassy pitches range in size from 60-80 sq.m. depending on your unit. All have electricity and the larger ones (around half) also have water and drainage. They are clearly marked in rows, but with no separation other than by deciduous trees which provide summer shade. A cheery children's pool with fountains is behind the unusually shaped pool ringed by palms. This is part of an attractively landscaped feature with a false island, producing a relaxing atmosphere in front of the old Catalan farmhouse buildings. The open air dance floor has music twice weekly (in season). A classy indoor pool (heated) with sauna and solarium and good access for disabled campers is a great option out of high season.

Facilities
Two modern, spacious sanitary blocks, can be heated and are extremely well maintained, providing washbasins in private cabins, top class facilities for disabled people and baby baths. Washing machines and dryer. Dishwashing and laundry sinks. Motorcaravan services. Bar with TV and snacks (all year). Restaurant (1/4-31/10). Shop (all year, but only basics in winter). Outdoor swimming pool and paddling pool (15/6-15/9) with drinks stall. Indoor pool with sauna, solarium (15/9-15/6). Masseur. Children's play area. Indoor children's area. TV room. Internet terminals. Excursions organised in July/Aug. Diving activities arranged. Giant chess. Table tennis. Volleyball. Boules. Information folder on arrival. Bicycle hire. Diving organised from site. Tours arranged. Dogs accepted in parts of two low season periods – check with the site. Environmentally friendly. Torches are useful. Off site: Riding 400 m. Fishing 800 m. Nearest beach 800 m. Medes Natural Reserve 1.5 km. Estartit 2 km. Golf 8 km.

Directions
Site is signed from the main Torroella de Montgri - L'Estartit road GE641. Turn right after Camping Castel Montgri, at Joc's hamburger/pizzeria and follow signs.

Charges 2003

Per person	€ 3.00 - € 5.00
child (0-10 yrs)	€ 1.85 - € 3.60
pitch	€ 6.60 - € 11.20
electricity	€ 3.20
dog	€ 1.80

All plus 7% VAT. Discounts outside high season and special offers for low season longer stays. No credit cards.

Reservations
Advised for July/Aug. Write to site with € 31 deposit. Tel: 972 751 805.
Email: campingslesmedes@cambrescat.es

Open
All year except November.

At a glance
Welcome & Ambience	✓✓✓✓	Location	✓✓✓✓
Quality of Pitches	✓✓✓✓	Range of Facilities	✓✓✓✓

Cataluña-Catalunya

Only 2 km from L'Estartit, one of the most beautiful and ecological-minded villages of the Costa Brava, only 800m from the Beach. On our family site you will enjoy a fabulous holiday in the midst of nature. We have high quality installations: modern sanitary instal. With baby-baths, install. for the handicapped and free hot water, swimming pool (also indoors heated) bar, restaurant and supermarket... Leisure activities for the whole family: children's playground, watersports, bicycles for rent and a large programme of activities for all ages. And to relax a dive in our swimming pool with solarium and sauna.

telf.+34 972 751 805 – fax.+34 972 750 413 – www.campinglesmedes.com – campingslesmedes@cambrescat.es
paratge Camp de l'Arbre, apartado de correos, 140 - 17258 l'ESTARTIT, Girona   COSTA BRAVA

Great on-line holiday deals *alanrogersdirect*.com

ES8090 Camping Cypsela

Ctra. de Pals - Platja de Pals, 17256 Platja de Pals

This impressive, de-luxe site with lush vegetation and trees has many striking features, one of which is the sumptuous complex of sport facilities and amenities near the entrance. This provides a fine large swimming pool, a good children's pool and playgrounds, two excellent squash courts, a tennis court, fitness room, and other entertainment rooms. These include a children's playroom with mini-club and organised entertainment (including video screen), an amusements room with pool tables, football tables, video games, and a luxurious air-conditioned lounge. The 'Les Moreres' is a pleasant al fresco restaurant offering a varied menu plus good wines (it can become very busy). Another indoor restaurant offers a similar excellent service. You have the choice of a smart bar or the air conditioned cocktail bar. The main part of the camping area is pinewood, with 661 clearly marked touring pitches of varying categories on sandy gravel, all with electricity and some with full facilities. The 202 'Elite' pitches of 120 sq.m. are impressive. If you wish to travel to the beach there is a regular free bus service from the site. Cypsela is a busy, well administered site, only two kilometres from the sea, which we can thoroughly recommend, especially for families. It is very efficiently run, with good quality fixtures and fittings, all kept clean and maintained to a high standard, all your needs will be catered for here. The gates are closed at night. Several tour operators use the site (299 pitches).

Facilities
Four stylish sanitary 'houses' are of excellent quality with comprehensive cleaning schedules. Using solar heating, three have washbasins in cabins and three have amazing children's rooms with a battery of baby baths and larger ones for older children. Facilites for disabled people are superb. Serviced launderette. Ironing. Supermarket and other shops. Restaurant, cafeteria and takeaway. Bar. Hairdresser. Swimming pools. Tennis. Squash. Table tennis. Football field. Minigolf. Fitness room. Air conditioned social/TV room. Barbecue and party area. Children's club. Animation programme for children and adults in season. Organised sports and games activities. Games room. Business centre and internet centre. Doctor always on site. Car wash. Gas supplies. ATM. Dogs are not accepted. Off site: Bicycle hire 150 m. Golf 1 km. Fishing 2 km.

Directions
Cypsela is on the EN6502 road to Platja de Pals, leaving the C31 (Figueres - Palamos) road at roundavout near Pals.

Charges 2003
Per person	€ 4.24 - € 5.27
child (2-10 yrs)	€ 3.35 - € 4.22
pitch acc. to season and services	€ 18.92 - € 45.11

Reservations
Contact site. Tel: 972 667 696.
Email: info@cypsela.com

Open
15 May - 26 September.

At a glance
Welcome & Ambience	✓✓✓✓	Location	✓✓✓
Quality of Pitches	✓✓✓	Range of Facilities	✓✓✓✓

ES8101 Camping Playa Brava

Avda. del Grau, 1, 17256 Platja de Pals

This is a pleasant site with an open feel which has access to a large sandy beach (200 metres) and a freshwater lagoon. On both you can enjoy watersports and you may launch your own boat. The ground is level and very grassy with shade provided for the 500 pitches by a mixture of conifer and broad-leaf trees. Electricity is provided and about a third of the pitches (75-85 sq.m) have water and drainage. The air of spaciousness continues around the large pool and paddling pool (with lifeguard). There are no fences but huge grass sunbathing areas, the whole being overlooked by the restaurant and bar terrace. The restaurant is very pleasant and offers a most reasonable menu of the day including wine. An energetic entertainment programme runs during July and August. This is a green and pleasant family site.

Facilities
Five modern, fully equipped toilet blocks include facilities for disabled visitors. Dishwashing facilities under cover. Washing machines and dryers. Bar/restaurant. Takeaway. Supermarket. Swimming pool. Tennis. Volleyball. Minigolf. Play area on grass. Fishing. Watersports on river and beach, including sheltered lagoon for windsurfing learners. Gas supplies. Torches required in some areas. Dogs are not accepted. Off site: Two 18 hole golf courses 1 km. Bicycle hire 3 km. Riding 5 km.

Directions
Platja de Pals is reached via EN6502 road which leaves the C31 Figueres - Palamos road near Pals just north of Palafrugell. Site is well signed approaching village, then follow road for 3 km. (keeping golf course on your right) to site and beach.

Charges 2003
Per person	€ 1.40 - € 2.00
child	free - € 1.50
senior	free -€ 2.00
75 sq.m. pitch incl. electricity	€ 20.00 - € 30.00
85 sq.m.	€ 23.00 -€ 35.00

All plus 7% VAT. Discount for longer stays in low season. No credit cards.

Reservations
Write to site. Tel: 972 636 894.
Email: info@playabrava.com

Open
15 May - 11 September.

At a glance
Welcome & Ambience	✓✓✓	Location	✓✓✓✓
Quality of Pitches	✓✓✓	Range of Facilities	✓✓✓

ES8102 Camping Mas Patoxas

Ctra. Palafrugell-Pals, km 339, 17256 Pals

This is a mature and well laid out site for those who prefer to be apart from, but within easy travelling distance of the beaches (5 km) and town (1 km). It has a very easy access and is set on a slight slope with wide avenues on level terraces providing 400 grassy pitches of a minimum 72 sq.m. All have electricity and water, many have drainage as well. There are some very pleasant views and shade from a variety of mature trees. An air-conditioned restaurant/bar provides both waiter service meals and takeaway food to order (weekends only mid Sept-April) and entertainment takes place on a stage below the terraces during the high season. Both bar and restaurant terraces give views over the pools and distant hills. The restaurant menu is varied and very reasonable. We were impressed with the children's mini-club activity when we visited. There is a large, supervised irregularly shaped swimming pool with triple flume, a separate children's pool and a generous sunbathing area of the poolside and surrounding grass. Used by tour operators (40).

Facilities

Three modern sanitary blocks provide controllable hot showers, some washbasins with hot water, baby bath and three children's cabins with washbasin and shower. No specific facilities for disabled people, although access throughout the site looks to be relatively easy. Dishwashing facilities under cover (H&C). Laundry facilities. Restaurant/bar (1/4-30/9). Pizzeria. Takeaway. Well stocked shop (1/4-30/9). Swimming pool (15/6-30/9). Tennis. Table tennis. Volleyball. Football field. Entertainment in high season. Fridges for rent. Gas supplies. Torches useful in some areas. Off site: Bus service from site gate. Bicycle hire and riding 2 km. Fishing and golf 4 km.

At a glance

Welcome & Ambience	✓✓✓✓	Location	✓✓✓✓
Quality of Pitches	✓✓✓✓	Range of Facilities	✓✓✓✓

Directions

Site is east of Girona and approx. 1.5 km. south of Pals at km. 339 on the C31 Figueres-Palamos road, just north of Palafrugell.

Charges 2003

Per person	€ 3.60 - € 5.00
child (1-10 yrs)	€ 2.50 - € 3.00
caravan pitch	€ 14.00 - € 21.00
tent pitch with car	€ 11.00 - € 18.00
dog	€ 2.10

Plus VAT @ 7%. Special low season offers.

Reservations

Write to site. Tel: 972 636 928.
Email: info@campingmaspatoxas.com

Open

16 January - 15 December..

ES8103 Camping El Maset
Playa de Sa Riera, 17255 Begur

A delightful little gem of a site in lovely surroundings, El Maset has 115 pitches, of which just 20 are for caravans or motorcaravans, the remainder suitable only for tents. The owner of some 40 years, Sr Juan Perez is delightful, as is his secretary Josaphine, and longer stay customers may be presented with a memento of their visit. The site entrance is steep and access to the caravan pitches can be quite tricky. However, a new road has been cut out of the hillside and the owner's son will tow your caravan to your pitch. All these pitches have electricity, water and drainage with some shade. Access to the tent pitches, which are more shaded on attractive rock-walled terraces on the hillside seems quite straightforward, with parking for cars not too far away – the pitches are fairly small. All steep terraced pitches are safely fenced for children. For a small site the amenities are quite extensive, including an unusual elliptical shaped swimming pool. A bar and very homely restaurant offering excellent food, with a terrace giving very pleasant views over the pool and towards the other side of the valley. This small site provides the standard of service normally associated with the very best of the larger sites. It is situated in the tiny resort of Sa Riera with access to the beach (300 m), in a beautiful protected bay. There is a naturist beach (via a longer uphill path).

Facilities
Sanitary facilities are superb with marble tops, hair and hand dryers and soap. In three small blocks and very clean, they include baby facilities. Top quality washing up area (H&C), industrial washing machines and dryers. Unit for disabled campers. Bar/restaurant, takeaway (all season). Shop (from May). Swimming pool (all season). Solarium. Play area on astroturf. Area for football and basketball. Excellent games room. Dogs are not accepted. Off site: Fishing 300 m. Golf and bicycle hire 1 km. Riding 8 km.

At a glance
Welcome & Ambience	✓✓✓✓	Location	✓✓✓✓
Quality of Pitches	✓✓✓	Range of Facilities	✓✓✓

Directions
From the C31 Figueres - Palamos road south of Pals, north of Palafrugell, take GI653 to Begur. Site is 2 km. north of the town; follow signs for Playa de Sa Riera and site (steep entrance).

Charges 2003
Per person	€ 4.00 - € 5.50
child (1-10 yrs)	€ 3.00 - € 4.10
caravan	€ 5.10 - € 7.10
tent	€ 4.40 - € 6.50
motorcaravan	€ 5.60 - € 7.60
electricity	€ 3.00 - € 4.00

Plus 7% VAT. Discount in low season for 7 day stay.

Reservations
Write to site. Tel: 972 623 023.
Email: elmaset@jazzfree.com

Open
Easter - 24 September.

ES8104 Camping Begur
Ctra. d'Esclanya, km 2, 17255 Begur

The new owners here have made a massive investment in making the site a pleasant place to spend some time. It is a large site which has some good supporting facilities including a pleasant swimming pool and paddling pool at its centre. The bar and snack bar are part of this new pool complex and it has been well designed with terraces and sunbathing area. The touring areas are protected from the sun by mature trees and the 382 pitches are informally arranged on sloping sandy ground (chocks useful). Of these, 120 electrical connection, water and drainage. A few mobile homes and apartments are scattered around the slopes. Many improvements are being made and by 2004 most of the work will be complete. Many environmental activities are planned including visits to the revolutionary water cleansing plant deep in the woods. There are many sporting facilities including a well equipped weight training room (free). A huge supermarket is just outside the gate, used by locals and we are told a full restaurant will open here by 2004. The bays of the Costa Brava are just 1.5 km. away.

Facilities
Sanitary facilities in two modern blocks include hot water throughout and excellent facilites for disabled campers. Motorcaravan services. Bar and snacks. Restaurant planned. Supermarket just outside gate. Swimming pools (1/6-15/9). Table tennis. Boules. Weight training room. Play area. Volleyball. Football. Some animation in high season. Off site: Village and beaches 1.5 km. Fishing 3 km. Golf 10 km. Riding 15 km.

At a glance
Welcome & Ambience	✓✓✓✓	Location	✓✓✓✓
Quality of Pitches	✓✓✓✓	Range of Facilities	✓✓✓✓✓

Directions
From Girona take road east to La Bisbal and Palafrugell then Begur. Turn south towards Fornells the site is well signed 3 km. south of Begur.

Charges 2003
Per adult	€ 1.80 - € 3.20
child (3-1 yrs)	€ 1.20 - € 1.60
pitch	€ 5.70 - € 13.20
with electricity	€ 8.50 - € 20.80
animal	€ 2.80 - € 3.20

Reservations
Possible with € 100 deposit. Tel: 972 624 566.
Email: info@campingbegur.com

Open
25 April - 28 September.

ES8150 Camping Internacional de Palamos

Apto. Correus 100, 17230 Palamos

First impressions of this site are that it is unusual with a long perimeter wall covered with bright grafitti style murals. The site's strong point is the large swimming pool, plus children's pool, with attractive palms. It has a grass sunbathing area and its own modest white-washed bar/terrace in season. It might have space when others are full and has over 450 moderate sized, level, terraced pitches on a gentle slope. All pitches have a sink and variable shade, with electrical connections available in most parts. Access roads are gravel and may suffer in the case of heavy rain. Used by a tour operator (20 pitches). This is an improving site which is clean, welcoming and useful for exploring the local area from a peaceful base although it is pricey in high season.

Facilities
Three refurbished toilet blocks are fully equipped and include facilities for disabled people. Laundry room with washing machines, irons, etc. Small shop. Bar. Snack bar serving simple food and takeaway (from 1/6). Swimming pool (36 x 16 m.) with paddling pool. Torches necessary. Off site: Town 1 km. with hourly bus service. Nearest beach 400 m. Fishing 500 m. Bicycle hire and riding 1.5 km.

At a glance
Welcome & Ambience	✓✓✓✓	Location	✓✓✓✓✓
Quality of Pitches	✓✓✓✓✓	Range of Facilities	✓✓✓✓

Directions
Cars can approach site from central Palamós, but town streets are too narrow for caravans which should turn off C255 road just outside Palamós. Turn right just before Kings and from there follow Camping Internacional Palamos signs. Do not be confused by another site close by called Camping Palamos.

Latest charges
Per person	€ 2.70 - € 2.98
child (under 10 yrs)	€ 1.98 - € 2.18
pitch for car and tent/caravan	€ 15.15 - € 31.37
tent pitch (motorcycle but no car)	€ 5.65 - € 12.51
electricity (6A)	€ 4.21

All plus 7% VAT. No credit cards.

Reservations
Write to site with € 31 deposit. Tel: 972 314 736.

Open
1 April - 30 September.

ES8125N Camping Relax-Nat

Mont-Ras, 17230 Palamos

Enclosed by a perimeter wall, this extremely well maintained, small naturist site affords complete privacy. Set in pleasant countryside, eight hectares provide 310 pitches (all with 2A electricity) amongst a large variety of trees, spaced in such a manner as to provide sun and shade. Entering the site through the electronic security gate, you will find English spoken at reception. From this point you overlook the terraces fronting the bar, shop and pools. Although the site does not have a restaurant, there are many in the area offering good Spanish cuisine. A small picturesque bay, typical of those to be found along the Costa Brava and only five kilometres away, is for use by naturists. Naturism is increasingly popular in Spain and reservation is advised.

Facilities
The main toilet block, completely refurbished to a high standard, provided partitioned hot showers (free), facilities for babies and a unit for disabled visitors. Shop. Bar. Snack bar. Swimming pools, one 30 x 12 m. from mid-May, a smaller, heated one open all season with sun loungers, and a children's pool. Table tennis, boule, volleyball, basketball, football. Tennis (charged). Water activities. Minigolf. Two play areas. High season entertainment. Off site: Bicycle hire 2 km. Fishing and riding 5 km. Golf 20 km.

At a glance
Welcome & Ambience	✓✓✓	Location	✓✓✓
Quality of Pitches	✓✓✓✓	Range of Facilities	✓✓✓✓

Directions
Travelling along road C31 Palafrugell - Palamos (formerly C255), site is to east near km. 330 (opposite Mercamat store). If approaching from Palafrugell, use loop in front of store to turn across road.

Charges 2003
Per person	€ 4.95
child (under 10 yrs)	€ 3.90
pitch	€ 10.00 - € 17.60
electricity	€ 2.00
dog	€ 2.80

Plus VAT.

Reservations
Contact P.B. 19, 17230 Palamos (Girona) for details. Tel: 972 300818. Email: info@campingrelaxnat.com

Open
31 March - 30 September.

Cataluña-Catalunya

ES8120 Kim's Camping
Font d'en Xeco 1, 17211 Llafranc

This attractive, terraced site is arranged on the wooded slopes of a narrow valley leading to the sea and there are many trees including huge eucalyptus. A steep lower area rises to a very pleasant plateau where all the amenities are located. There are 350 grassy and partly shaded pitches, all with electric hook-ups, many of the larger pitches are on the plateau from which great views can be enjoyed. Whilst those on the terraces are connected by winding drives, narrow in places. The site has an excellent swimming pool (with lifeguard) and children's pool, a bar, and a pleasant restaurant with 'al fresco' eating. There are high standards of cleanliness and efficiency. The site is under one kilometre from the resort of Llafranc. This is a pleasant place for holidays where you can enjoy the bustling atmosphere of the village and beach, while staying in a quieter environment. The site provides an entertainment programme in high season and it is possible to organize a visit to the local sub aqua schools for all levels of diving. There is an outstanding view along the coastline and of the Pyrenees from Cap Sebastian close by. English is spoken by the very friendly management and staff.

Facilities
Sanitary provision is adequate and includes a small brand new block and toilet facilities for disabled visitors. Laundry facilities. Motorcaravan services. Car wash. Gas supplies. Well stocked shop. Bar. Bakery and croissanterie. Cafe/restaurant (15/6-20/9). TV room. Swimming pools. Tickets sold for the Girona bullfights. Excursions arranged - bus calls at site. Play areas and kid's club. Torches required. Off site: Fishing, Glass bottomed boat in Lafranc. Bicycle hire 500 m. Riding 4 km. Golf 9 km.

Directions
Llafranc is southeast of Palafrugell. Turn off the Palafrugell - Tamariu road at turn (GIV 6542) signed 'Llafranc, Club de Tennis'. Site is on right 1 km. further on.

Charges 2003
Per person	€ 2.25 - € 4.50
child (3-10 yrs)	€ 1.65 - € 2.55
pitch incl. electricity	€ 12.00 - € 22.55

Plus 7% VAT. Discounts for long stays and for senior citizens.

Reservations
Made with deposit (€ 90). Tel: 972 301 156. Email: info@campingkims.com

Open
Easter - 30 September.

At a glance
Welcome & Ambience	✓✓✓✓	Location	✓✓✓✓
Quality of Pitches	✓✓✓	Range of Facilities	✓✓✓✓

ES8140 Camping Treumal
Ctra. 253, km 47.5, 17250 Calonge

This very attractive terraced site has been developed on a hillside around the attractive gardens of a large, spectacular estate house which is close to the beach. The house is the focus of the site's excellent facilities, including a superb restaurant with terraces overlooking two tranquil beaches protected in pretty coves. The beaches are connected by a tunnel carved through solid rock through which you may safely walk. A multi-coloured, flower bedecked, and landscaped hillside leads down to the sea from the house with pretty paths and fishponds. There is a constant supply of fresh plants and flowers, and in summer the house area is a blaze of colour and very appealing. The site which reaches back to the road has 582 pitches on well shaded terraces. Of these 447 are accessible to tourers and there are some 50 pitches on flat ground alongside the sea – the views are stunning. Mobile homes and chalets occupy 135 pitches. There is a small round swimming pool in the lower areas of the gardens. Cars may not park by tents or caravans in high season, but must be left on car parks or roads. Electrical connections are available in all parts (5A for tents, 10A for caravans).

Facilities
Three well maintained sanitary blocks have free hot water in the washbasins (with some private cabins) and controllable showers, and a tap to draw from for the sinks. Washing machines. Motorcaravan services. Gas supplies. Supermarket and bar (1/5-30/9). Takeaway (1/6-15/9). Restaurant (15/6-15/9). Table tennis. Fishing. Play area and sports area. Games room. Off site: Bicycle hire 2 km. Riding and golf 5 km.

Directions
Site is on C253 (at km 47.5) Playa de Aro - Palomós coast road, 3 km south of Palomós. Avoid the town centre by using C31 (Girona - Palomós) road, leaving at km 320, dropping down to Sant Antóni de Calonge and turning right onto C253.

Charges 2003
Per person	€ 3.54 - € 6.10
child (4-10 yrs)	€ 2.03 - € 3.50
caravan, car and electricity	€ 13.05 - € 22.50
motorcaravan and electricity	€ 12.47 - € 21.50
tent, car and electricity	€ 12.47 - € 21.50

Plus 7% VAT. Discounts in low seasons. No credit cards.

Reservations
Made to guarantee admission (needed more for caravans than for tents) with deposit. Contact site at Aptdo Correos 348, 17250 Playa de Aro. Tel: 972 651 095. Email: info@campingtreumal.com

Open
1 April - 30 September.

At a glance
Welcome & Ambience	✓✓✓✓	Location	✓✓✓✓✓
Quality of Pitches	✓✓✓	Range of Facilities	✓✓✓

ES8130 Camping Internacional de Calonge
Ctra. S Feliu/Guixols - Palamos km 7.4, 17251 Calonge

This spacious, well laid out site has access to the fine beach by a footbridge over the coast road or you can take the little road train as the site is on very sloping ground. Calonge is a family site with two good sized pools on different levels, a paddling pool plus large sunbathing areas. These are overlooked by the restaurant terrace which has great views over the mountains. The site's 800 pitches are on terraces: all have electricity with 167 available for winter use. A large proportion are suitable for touring units (the remainder for tents) being set on attractively landscaped terraces. Access to some pitches may be a little difficult. There is good shade from the tall pine trees and some views of the sea through the foliage, although the views from the upper levels are taken by the tour operator and mobile home pitches. A nature area within the site is used for walks or picnics. A separate area within the site is set aside for visitors with dogs (including a dog shower).

Facilities
Generous sanitary provision in new or renovated blocks include some washbasins in cabins. One block is heated for winter use. Laundry facilities. Motorcaravan services. Gas supplies. Shop (Easter-30/10, supermarket 500 m). Bar/restaurant (Easter- 30/10). Patio bar (pizza and takeaway). Swimming pools with lifeguard (1/4-30/10). Playground. Electronic games. Rather noisy disco two nights a week (but not late). Bicycle hire. Table tennis. Tennis. Volleyball. Hairdresser. ATM. Internet. Security boxes. Torches necessary in some areas. Good security.
Off site: Fishing 300 m. Golf 3 km. Riding 10 km.

At a glance
Welcome & Ambience	✓✓✓✓✓	Location	✓✓✓✓✓
Quality of Pitches	✓✓✓✓✓	Range of Facilities	✓✓✓✓✓

Directions
Site is on the inland side of the coast road between Palamos and Platja d'Aro; take the C31 south to the 661 at Calonge. Follow signs to the C253 towards Platja d'Aro and on to site which is well signed.

Charges 2003
Per adult	€ 3.30 - € 5.80
child (2-10 yrs)	€ 1.70 - € 3.30
pitch for caravan or tent with car incl. electricity	€ 11.75 - € 21.10
motorcaravan incl. electricity	€ 10.10 - € 16.80

All plus 7% VAT. Discounts for longer stays Oct - end May. No credit cards.

Reservations
Write with deposit (€ 37). UK contact: Mr J Worthington (0161) 799 9562. Tel: 972 651 233. Email: intercalonge@intercalonge.com

Open
All year.

ES8160 Camping Cala Gogo
Ctra. S Feliu-Palamos, km 46.5, 17251 Calonge

Cala Gogo is a large traditional campsite with a pleasant situation on a wooded hillside with mature trees giving shade to most pitches. A small cove has a coarse sand beach and there is access to a further two small beaches along the sand. There are also two pools on the site (one heated in low season). The campsite facilities are contained in terraced buildings which have a supermarket, shops, small restaurant and a bar all with an adjoining terrace enjoying views over the pools down to the sea. A second floodlit bar pleasant restaurant and a takeaway are on the beach and open in high season. The 619 shaded touring pitches varying in size are in terraced rows, some with artificial shade, all have electricity and 250 have water and drainage. There may be road noise in eastern parts of the site. Some pitches are now right by the beach, the remainder are up to 800 metres uphill, but the tractor train, (all season) takes people from the centre of site to beach. The management is looking to make the site attractive to families. It is an active, bustling place, with over 2,500 campers when full. A huge aqua-park close by offers amazing waterslides and wave simulation. Used by tour operators (60 pitches), with 170 mobile homes and chalets to rent.

Facilities
Seven toilet blocks are of a high standard and are continuously cleaned. Some washbasins are in private cabins. Laundry. Motorcaravan services. Gas supplies. Super-market. General shop. Restaurants and bars. Swimming pools (25 x 12 m.) and paddling pool (lifeguards). Playground. Crèche and babysitting service for smaller children (extra charge). Sports centre with tennis, volleyball, basketball, etc, plus a mini-club. Programme of animation including sports, TV and video programmes daily, tournaments, entertainment. Bicycle hire. Limited table tennis. Kayaks (free). Fishing. Bureau de change. Medical service; nurse daily, doctor alternate days. Good 24 hr security service including video surveillance. Sponsored bus to local disco. Dogs are not accepted from mid June - end August. Off site: Bicycle hire and golf 4 km. Riding 10 km. Huge Aqua Park nearby with bus from site.

At a glance
Welcome & Ambience	✓✓✓✓	Location	✓✓✓✓
Quality of Pitches	✓✓✓✓	Range of Facilities	✓✓✓✓

Directions
Site is on inland side of coast road between Palomos and Platja d'Aro on the C253 at km 46.5 (4 km. south of Palomos). Avoid town centre by using C31 (Girona - Palomos) road, leaving at km 320, dropping down to Sant Antoni de Calonge, and turning right onto C253.

Charges 2003
Per person	€ 3.25 - € 5.50
child (3-12 yrs)	€ 1.50 - € 2.50
caravan or trailer tent incl. electricity (5A)	€ 12.00 - € 23.45
motorcaravan incl. electricity	€ 10.50 - € 20.10
tent pitch incl. electricity	€ 10.00 - € 19.10

Low season discounts. All plus 7% VAT. No credit cards.

Reservations
Made for min. 1 week with deposit (€ 150). Tel: 972 651 564. Email: calagogo@calagogo.es

Open
Easter or 12 April - 29 September.

Cataluña-Catalunya

ES8100 Camping Inter-Pals

Avda. Mediterrania, 17256 Platja de Pals

Sister site to no. ES8170 and set on sloping ground, with tall pine trees providing shade and about 500 m. from the beach, this site has 625 terraced pitches (including 280 for touring units and 250 for tents), on terraces and levelled plots, mostly with shade. Some of the terraced pitches have views of the sea through the trees. The main entrance and its drive resembles a pretty village street as the bungalows are set on both sides of the street lined with traditional lamp-posts. Continuing the village theme is a row of shops where you will find most camper's needs. The site is close to Platja de Pals which is a long sandy unspoilt stretch of beach, a discreet area of which is now an official naturist beach. The formal restaurant with good value menu and choice of takeaway overlooks the pools. The pretty town of Pals is close by along with a good golf course. The site will assist with touring plans of the area.

Facilities
Three well maintained toilet blocks include individual washbasins, dishwashing and laundry sinks and facilities for disabled campers. Washing machines and dryers. Gas supplies. Fridge/TV rental. Medical centre. Excursions. ATM. Diving and watersport arranged. Shops. Restaurant/bar with Pizzeria/croissenterie with dancing and entertainment area. Cafe/bar by entrance. Swimming pool. Basketball, volleyball and badminton courts. Tennis. Children's playground and organised activities and entertainment in high season. Electronic games. Pool tables. Some breeds of dog are excluded - check with site. Torch useful. Off site: Fishing 200 m. Bicycle hire 500 m. Golf 1 km. Riding 10 km.

At a glance
Welcome & Ambience ✓✓✓✓✓ Location ✓✓✓✓
Quality of Pitches ✓✓✓✓✓ Range of Facilities ✓✓✓✓

Directions
Site is on the road leading off the Torroella de Montgri-Bagur road north of Pals and going to Playa de Pals (Pals beach).

Charges 2003
Per person	€ 3.40 - € 4.80
child (3-10 yrs)	€ 2.25 - € 2.80
pitch	€ 15.20 - € 26.00
small tent and car	€ 13.00 - € 18.00
dog	€ 2.50

Plus 7% VAT. Discounts for long stays in low season. No credit cards. Camping Cheques accepted.

Reservations
Made in the sense of guarantee to admit only, without deposit. Tel: 972 636 179.
Email: interpals@interpals.com

Open
1 April - 30 September.

ES8170 Camping Valldaro

Apdo. Correus 57, Avda. Castell d'Aro, 63, 17250 Platja d' Aro

Valldaro is 600 metres back from the sea at Platja de Aro, a small, bright resort with a long, wide beach and plenty of amusements. It is particularly pleasant out of peak weeks and is popular with the British. Like a number of other large Spanish sites, Valldaro has been extended and many pitches have been made larger, bringing them up to 80 or 100 sq.m. There are now 1,200 pitches with 660 available for tourers. The site is flat, with pitches in rows divided up by access roads. You will probably find space here even at the height of the season. The newer section has its own vehicle entrance (the nearest point to the beach) and can be reached via a footbridge; it is brought into use at peak times. It has some shade and its own toilet block, as well as a medium-sized swimming pool of irregular shape with grassy sunbathing area and adjacent bar/snack bar and take-away. The original pool (36 x 18 m.) is next to the good Spanish-style restaurant which also offers takeaway fare. There are 400 permanent Spanish pitches and 150 mobile homes and chalets to rent, but these are in separate areas and do not impinge on the touring pitches.

Facilities
Sanitary facilities are of a good standard and are well maintained. Children's size toilets. Washbasins (no cabins) and adjustable showers (temperature perhaps a bit variable). Two supermarkets and general shops. Restaurant. Large bar. Swimming pools. Tennis. Table tennis, minigolf and tennis with snack bar. Playgrounds. Sports ground with football and basketball. Organised entertainment in season. Hairdresser. Air conditioned telephone/internet parlour. Gas supplies. Keen interest in environmental issues with many recycling bins. Off site: Fishing, bicycle hire and golf 1 km. Riding 4 km.

At a glance
Welcome & Ambience ✓✓✓✓✓ Location ✓✓✓✓
Quality of Pitches ✓✓✓✓ Range of Facilities ✓✓✓✓

Directions
Site is off the C31 Girona-Palamós road; follow signs for Platja de Aro.and site is signed off roundabout

Charges 2003
Per person	€ 3.15 - € 4.75
child (2-10 yrs)	€ 2.10 - € 2.75
pitch incl. electricity	€ 14.00 - € 23.75
dog	€ 2.10

All plus 7% VAT. Discounts in low seasons. Camping Cheques accepted.

Reservations
Made only in the sense of guaranteeing admission without deposit. Tel: 972 817 515.
Email: valldaro@valldaro.com

Open
26 March - 3 October.

ES8232 Camping Bella Terra

Platja de S'Abanell, 17300 Blanes

Camping Bella Terra is a very Spanish site, set in a shady pine grove facing a white sandy beach on the Mediterranean coast. There are 870 pitches with 590 for touring units, the rest taken by bungalows to rent (80) and by Spanish 'residents' (200). All pitches have 5/6A electricity and 24 are fully serviced. The site is in two sections, each with its own reception, on either side of a road which leads only to another campsite. The older part, with direct access to the beach, always fills up first and has the small supermarket with its own bakery, and the bar in front of which the children's activities and the evening entertainments take place. Main reception is on the right of the road as you approach, as are the restaurant with its own bar and the swimming pool, both of which (though already good) are due to be completely refurbished for 2004. This site has a real Spanish feel.

Facilities

The older sanitary blocks are quite adequate and fully equipped with provision for disabled visitors and laundry. The block on the newer side is much more modern and spacious, and an unusual feature is the suite of half-size showers, toilets and washbasins for young campers on both male and female sides. Shop, restaurant, bar and takeaway and outdoor swimming pool (all May - Sept). Playground. Fishing. Off site: Bicycle hire 500 m. Golf and riding 5 km.

At a glance

| Welcome & Ambience | ✓✓✓✓ | Location | ✓✓✓✓ |
| Quality of Pitches | ✓✓✓ | Range of Facilities | ✓✓✓✓ |

Directions

Site is south of Blanes. Follow signs from the town centre and site is just after Camping Blanes.

Charges 2003

Per person	€ 4.00 - € 4.30
child (3-10 yrs)	€ 3.30 - € 3.50
pitch	€ 12.30 - € 22.80
dog	€ 2.50 - € 4.00

Reservations

Contact site. Tel: 972 348017.
Email: cbellaterra@cbellaterra.com

Open

5 April - 30 September.

ES8225 Camping La Masia

C/Colon, 44, 17300 Blanes

A large resort site, Le Masia has 757 pitches with 300 for touring units. These pitches are flat, shaded by trees and in rows with some tour operater mobile homes inserted here and there. Two pools are in separate areas of the site, one having the restaurant terrace which also serves as the area for watching the entertainment programme. A large, central building houses the main bar and restaurant which offers a varied menu, including a menu of the day and full English breakfast. The jewel in the crown of the site is below this complex where you can enjoy spas, massage, plunge pools, exercise pools and pamper yourself in luxury in a Roman Bath type setting (extra charge). The tops of the buildings are for sunbathing or watching fireworks in the town. There is something for everyone in Le Masia and the resort town is just outside the gate, as is the fine beach.

Facilities

Five mature toilet blocks provide clean facilities with facilities for disabled campers and a well equipped baby room (key at reception). Motorcaravan services. Car wash. Washing machines and dryers. Supermarket. Bakery. Restaurants. Snack bars. Swimming pools. Spa centre. Play areas. Football. Boules. Basketball. Table tennis. Electronic games. Bicycle hire. Barbecue area. Entertainment programme. Internet. ATM. Exchange service. Security boxes. Torches useful. Off site: Resort town and beach outside the gate with usual attractions. Fishing. Boat launching 200 m. Bicycle hire 1 km. Riding 3 km. Golf 5 km.

At a glance

| Welcome & Ambience | ✓✓✓✓ | Location | ✓✓✓✓ |
| Quality of Pitches | ✓✓✓✓ | Range of Facilities | ✓✓✓✓✓ |

Directions

From A7, A19 or N11 take an exit to the coast for Blanes. Once at Blanes take Malgrat de Mar road and follow signs in town centre towards the beach. Site is very well signed in the town.

Charges 2003

Per adult	€ 3.90 - € 5.10
child (2-10 yrs)	€ 3.30 - € 4.40
pitch	€ 6.20 - € 19.95

Camping Cheques accepted.

Reservations

Contact site. Tel: 972 331013.
Email: info@campinglamasia.com

Open

1 May - 30 September.

Cataluña-Catalunya

ES8230 Beach Camp El Pinar
Avenida Villa de Madrid, 17300 Blanes

This is a pleasant, family orientated site adjoining a good beach. The name sums up the direction in which the owners are developing the site, with an emphasis on a more participatory approach to camping with an increase in the amount of activities and facilities offered – mostly directed towards sports. It is situated at the southern edge of Blanes beach, with direct access, and is about two kilometres from the town. The 587 touring pitches (250 on the new side), all with electricity and a minimum of 60 sq.m. are in two sections separated by the road, with both sides having direct access to the beach. The older side is mostly shaded by pine or broad leaf trees, the newer part has young trees that do not yet offer a great deal of shade. The newer side has its own modern sanitary block, plus a large swimming pool with a generous sunbathing area, and a children's pool (only used in July and August). This site will particularly appeal to families seeking easy access to a long beach (shelves quite steeply) and the attractions of a major resort.

Facilities
The sanitary blocks are tiled, have controllable hot showers, baby baths and open plan washbasins (all with hot water). The facilities on the original site have recently been refurbished. Dishwashing under cover. Laundry services. Motorcaravan services. Gas supplies. Bar/restaurant and takeaway. Small supermarket. Secure children's play area on grass. Swimming pool (small deposit for pass). Volleyball. Table tennis. Activities for adults and children organised in season (2/5-16/9) including dancing, bicycle excursions, aquagym. Excursions. Watersports near. No jetskis accepted. Regular bus service into the centre of Blanes.
Off site: Bicycle hire 1.5 km. Boat launching 2 km. Riding 8 km. Golf 15 km.

At a glance
Welcome & Ambience	✓✓✓	Location	✓✓✓✓✓
Quality of Pitches	✓✓✓	Range of Facilities	✓✓✓

Directions
Site is the last travelling south from Blanes town centre. Follow camping signs in Blanes until you see the El Pinar sign.

Charges 2003
Per person	€ 4.00 - € 4.80
child	€ 3.20 - € 4.20
pitch incl. electricity	€ 12.00 - € 15.00

Plus 7% VAT. Discounts for pensioners and low season longer stays.

Reservations
Write or phone site (no deposit). Tel: 972 331 083.
Email: camping@elpinarbeach.com

Open
31 March - 30 September.

ES8200 Camping Cala Llevadó
Ctra. de Tossa a Lloret, km. 3, 17320 Tossa de Mar

A beautifully situated cliff-side site, Cala Llevadó has fine views of the sea and coast below. It is shaped something like half a bowl with steep slopes. There are terraced, flat areas for caravans and tents on the upper levels of the two slopes, with a great many individual pitches for tents scattered around the site. Some of these pitches (without electricity) have fantastic settings and views. There is usually car parking close to these pitches, although in some places cars may be required to park separately. Electrical connections cover all caravan sectors and one tent area. High up in the site with a superb aspect, is the attractive restaurant/bar with a large terrace overlooking a play area and the pleasant swimming pool. One beach is for all manner of watersports within a buoyed area and there is a sub-aqua diving school. Some other pleasant little coves can also be reached by climbing down on foot (with care). The steepness of the site would make access difficult for disabled people or those with limited mobility. Cala Llevadó is luxurious and has much character and the atmosphere is informal and very friendly. Only 204 of the 575 touring pitches are accessible for caravans, so reservation in season is essential. There are also some tour operator pitches. The site is peacefully situated but only five minutes away from the busy resort of Tossa.

Facilities
Four very well equipped toilet blocks are well spaced around the site, built in an attractive style and immaculately maintained, with some washbasins in cabins, well equipped showers, and baby baths. Washing machines and dryer. Laundry service. Motorcaravan services. Gas supplies. Fridge hire. Large, well stocked supermarket. New restaurant/bar with terrace (5/5-28/9). Swimming pool (20 x 10 m.) and semi-circular children's pool. Three play areas. Entertainment for children (4-12 yrs). Sailing, water ski and windsurfing school. Fishing. Scuba diving. Excursions. Torches are definitely needed in some areas. Off site: Bicycle hire 3 km. The site is alongside a larger complex where all manner of sophisticated sports and adventure activities are available. Campers can also use the other pools here.

At a glance
Welcome & Ambience	✓✓✓✓✓	Location	✓✓✓✓✓
Quality of Pitches	✓✓✓	Range of Facilities	✓✓✓✓✓

Directions
Cala Llevadó is signed off the G1682 Lloret - Tossa road at km 18.9, about 3 km. from Tossa.

Charges 2003
Per person	€ 4.55 - € 7.00
child (3-14 yrs)	€ 2.80 - € 3.85
car	€ 4.55 - € 7.00
motorcycle	€ 4.55 - € 7.00
tent	€ 4.55 - € 7.00
caravan	€ 5.20 - € 7.50
motorcaravan	€ 7.70 - € 11.00
electricity	€ 3.55 - € 3.70
dog	€ 3.50

Plus 7% VAT.

Reservations
Accepted with deposit and fee. Tel: 972 340 314.
Email: info@calallevado.com

Open
1 May - 30 September, including all amenities.

ES8180 Camping Sant Pol

C. Doctor Fleming No.1, 17220 Sant Feliu de Guíxols

Sant Pol is a small, family owned site and Anna Genover speaks excellent English, with a good understanding of campers needs. On the Costa Brava, this hillside site is on the edge of Sant Feliu, only 350 metres from the beach (there may be some road noise on one side of the site). An attractive pool, bar and restaurant are the central focus of the site with shaded terraces and pitches of differing sizes curving down the slope. Higher terraces have the chalets and bungalows. There are only a few pitches for large units, but pleasant small terraces take tents and smaller units. The on site restaurant features regional dishes based on the best local produce available. San Feliu is an attractive seaside village with lots of cafés, restaurants and a crescent shaped white sandy beach. A great site for short stays, not for exploring the area.

Facilities
The clean and modern sanitary block has British style WCs and hot water. WC for disabled campers, but no shower (terrain would be difficult for wheelchairs). Washing machines and dryer. Motorcaravan services. Small supermarket for basics. Restaurant/bar. Swimming pools. Play area. Animation for children in high season. Minigolf. Library. Internet point. Electronic games. Excursions. Torches needed in some areas. Off site: Large supermarket 300 m. Beach 350 m. Regular bus service into town.

At a glance
Welcome & Ambience	✓✓✓	Location	✓✓✓✓
Quality of Pitches	✓✓✓	Range of Facilities	✓✓✓✓

Directions
San Feliu is southeast of Girona and is reached via the C65/C31 (Girona - Palomos) road. Leave this at km 312 signed S'Agaró. At roundabout take first exit signed to Sant Feliu and site, which is on left in a short distance.

Charges 2003
Per adult	€ 3.40 - € 7.10
child (5-10 yrs)	€ 2.15 - € 4.60
pitch	€ 7.40 - € 15.40
pitch incl. electricity and water	€ 11.60 - € 22.30
electricity	€ 2.85 - € 3.90

Discounts for stays in excess of 21 days. Low season special offers for senior citizens.

Reservations
Contact site. Tel: 972 327 269.
Email: info@campingsantpol.com

Open
15 March - 30 November.

ES9122 Camping Montagut

Ctra. Montagut-Sadernes, km 2, 17855 Montagut

This is a delightful, small family site where everything is kept in pristine condition. Jordi and Nuria, a brother and sister team, work hard to make you welcome and maintain the superb appearance of the site. Flowers and shrubs abound, with 90 pitches on attractively landscaped and carefully constructed terraces or on flat areas overlooking the pool. A tranquil atmosphere pervades the site and drinks on the pleasant restaurant terrace are recommended, along with sampling the authentic menu as you enjoy the views over the Alta Garrotxa. There is much to see in the local area between the Pyrenees and the Mediterranean. Walking and outdoor pusuits abound and the team will assist with bookings. This is a super site for relaxing and enjoying the wonderful scenery.

Facilities
The modern sanitary block has free hot showers, washing and laundry facilities plus a modern section for babies and disabled campers; everything was spotless when seen. Motorcaravan services. Restaurant and bar (1/3-31/10; weekends only in low season). Supermarket. Medium sized swimming pool with large sunbathing area and children's pool (1/5-30/9). Playground. Soccer. Petanque. Volleyball. Barbecue area. Torches are useful in some areas.

At a glance
Welcome & Ambience	✓✓✓✓	Location	✓✓✓✓✓
Quality of Pitches	✓✓✓✓	Range of Facilities	✓✓✓✓

Directions
Going west from Figueres on N260 Olot road, approx. 10 km. past Besalu at km. 75, turn right towards Montagut. At end of village turn left towards Sadernes and site entrance is 2 km.

Charges 2003
Per person	€ 3.95 - € 4.60
child (under 10 yrs)	€ 3.30 - € 3.95
caravan or tent	€ 4.30 - € 4.95
small tent	€ 3.45 - € 3.95
motorcaravan	€ 7.10 - € 7.43
car	€ 3.65 - € 4.30
electricity	€ 3.20

Plus 7% VAT. No credit cards.

Reservations
Contact site. Tel: 972 287 202.
Email: info@campingmontagut.com

Open
1 March - 31 October.

Cataluña-Catalunya

ES9144 Camping Stel
Ctra. N-152 Ramal-Llivia s/n, 17520 Puigcerdá

Sister site to nos. ES8420 and ES9143, this is an extremely efficient if pricey site. Part of a large, attractive building at the spacious entrance houses a modern reception (English is spoken). From here you will quickly be on your way to one of the flat, terraced pitches. Many of the pitches have shade and all are marked, clean and organized in rows with a water tap for each row. There is some road noise so, in order to avoid this and have views of the Cerdanya valley and the eastern Pyrenées, take one of the pitches on the upper terraces. The terrace closest to the facility block is occupied by new bungalows (2002). The rectangular pool with easy access is overlooked by the restaurant terrace, where you can enjoy a menu with local food, or the very reasonable menu of the day. You are very close to the French border here and thus you can enjoy sampling the two different cultures with ease.

Facilities
Sanitary facilities in the main building are of very high standard with all the little luxuries and are kept very clean. A small, smart block serves the upper terraces. Both blocks can be heated. Separate modern unit with facilities for disabled campers. Washing machines and dryer in main block. Shop, Bar/restaurant (all season). Swimming pool (July-Sept). Boules. Table football. Snooker. Novel adventure style play frame for children (supervision needed). Adventure club organizes all manner of watersports, and outdoor activities such as biking, tours, climbing, hang gliding, indoor archery and many others. Animation in high season only. Drinks machines. Animals accepted in separate area. Off site: Boat rental 2 km. Riding 5 km. Fishing and golf 7 km.

At a glance
Welcome & Ambience	✓✓✓✓	Location	✓✓✓✓
Quality of Pitches	✓✓✓✓	Range of Facilities	✓✓✓✓✓

Directions
From Perpignan take N116 to Prades and Andorra. At Puigcerdà take N152 to France (not the road with the security post) and the site is well signed.

Charges 2003
Per adult	€ 4.60
child (3-10 yrs)	€ 4.00
pitch	€ 16.00
electricity	€ 3.10

All plus 7% VAT. No credit cards.
Camping Cheques accepted.

Reservations
Advisable in July and August. Tel: 972 882 361.
Email: puigcerda@stel.es

Open
30 May - 28 September.

ES9143 Camping Pirineus
Ctra. Guils de Cerdanya, km 2, 17528 Guils de Cerdanya

This is a sister site to nos. ES8420 and ES9144, with a well organized entrance and one gets an immediate impression of space, green trees and grass – there is always someone watering and clearing up to maintain the high standards here. From the restaurant terrace you have fine views of the mountains in the background and the pool in the foreground. There is an open fire inside for cooler evenings and a huge mural of the mountains in case you cannot see the real thing out of the window. The pitches are neat, marked, of average size and organized in rows. Generally flat with some on a gentle incline, a proportion have water at their own sink on the pitch. There are many trees offering shade but watch overhanging branches if you have a high unit. There is much to see in the area.

Facilities
Two fully equipped, sanitary blocks of top quality and decorated with boxes of bright flowers, are kept spotlessly clean and can be heated when necessary. Smart washing machines and dryers. Motorcaravan service point. Shop (open all season). Bar/restaurant.(all season) TV room and well-equipped games room. Snooker. Heated swimming pool and circular paddling pool. Boules. Table football. Tennis. Table tennis. Basketball and five-a-side courts. Outdoor sports. Children's play area and clubhouse where youngsters can paint and play under supervision. Excursions. Entertainment (high season). Drinks machines. Dogs are not accepted. Off site: River fishing. Bicycle hire 2 km. Riding 4 km. Golf 6 km. French border and Andorra close by for duty free shopping.

At a glance
Welcome & Ambience	✓✓✓✓	Location	✓✓✓✓
Quality of Pitches	✓✓✓✓✓	Range of Facilities	✓✓✓✓✓

Directions
From Perpignan take N116 to Prades and Andorra. Exit at Piugcerda and take the road to Guils de Cerdanya for 2 km. Site is well signed from the town.

Charges 2003
Per pitch	€ 16.00
pitch with water	€ 19.70
adult	€ 4.60
child (3-10 yrs)	€ 4.00
electricity (3A)	€ 3.10

All plus 7% VAT. No credit cards.

Reservations
Advisable in July and August. Tel: 972 881 062.
Email: guils@stel.es

Open
22 June - 11 September.

www.alanrogers.com for latest campsite news

ES8063 Camping El Llac

Ctra. Circumval.lació de l'Estany, 17820 Banyoles

This is a cool, unassuming site which is is open most of the year and is close to an attractive lake. The 240 touring pitches are under many mature trees giving good shade and they are generally flat, with some very large pitches for big motorhomes (no full drainage). The bungalows, mobile homes and permanent units do not encroach on the touring pitches and the site is very restful. The pools are atop a large bar/restaurant and there are terraces for sunbathing. The supermarket is also in this central unit and pretty patios are at one end for relaxing with a cool drink. A novel barbecue unit is provided close to the pool and children can enjoy the wide variety of animals in the 'estany' (animal enclosure). This is a clean, peaceful site for exploring the area or as a transit stop.

Facilities
Four sanitary blocks provide clean facilities plus separate units for disabled campers (key at reception). Motorcaravan services. Supermarket. Restaurant/bar. Swimming pools. Play area. Table tennis. Tennis courts. Basketball. Gas. Medical centre. Barbecue. Torches useful.

At a glance
Welcome & Ambience	✓✓✓✓	Location	✓✓✓✓
Quality of Pitches	✓✓✓✓	Range of Facilities	✓✓✓

Directions
From A7 at Girona take C66 to Banyoles and then west to Olot. Look for campsite signs and directions to the lake. At lake look carefully for signs as only one of the many one-way streets lead to the site entrance.

Charges 2003
Per person	€ 3.15 - € 3.70
child (4-10 yrs)	€ 2.00 - € 2.8
pitch	€ 2.00 - € 7.00
electricity	€ 3.50
animal	€ 2.00

Reservations
Contact site. Tel: 972 570 305.
Email: c.llac@retemail.es

Open
15 January - 15 December.

ES8135 Eurocamping

Ctra. Palamós a Platja d'Aro, km. 49,2, 17251 Sant Antoni de Calonge

This very large campsite on the Costa Brava near Girona is attractively landscaped, with lawns, flowers and pretty features around the site, and 720 grass and gravel pitches. The size of the pitches varies, with some of good size and others that would struggle with larger units. Older areas of the campsite are shaded by tall trees creating a cooler zone, while the new areas have good size trees but are not yet under the same shade canopy. There are two pool complexes, one near the entrance with an unusual feature where one large pool cascades into another at a slightly lower level. Nearby are a paddling pool, outoor chess and a large grassy area. Central to the site, the larger lagoon style pool with its huge entertainment area also has a garden like atmospere. This can also be enjoyed at night when the pool is closed as there is a large restaurant with views over the pool and animation area. A small road train, popular with children, takes campers to the nearby beach. This family oriented site is very popular with visitors from Holland and Germany so it is a good idea to book ahead for busy periods.

Facilities
Four refurbished, clean toilet blocks vary in size and are well positioned. Almost all WCs are British style in comfortably sized cabins with shower and basin. Facilities for disabled visitors are very good as are baby rooms and many family rooms. Washing machines. Gas supplies. Supermarket just outside gate. Pleasant bars and good restaurant. Swimming pools. Playgrounds. TV in bar. Football field. 5 a-side. Volleyball. Basketball. Netball. Weight training room. Bicycle hire. Full animation programme including children's entertainment. Internet. ATM. Excursions. Beach train (July/Aug). Animal owners in two areas. Torches useful. Off site: Nearest beach 300 m. Fishing 300 m. Golf 6 km. Riding 15 km.

Directions
From N11 (Girona - Barcelona) take Palafrugall road and continue to St Antoni de Calogni where site is well signed (huge arched entrance on the main road of the town).

Charges 2003
Per pitch	€ 14.60 - € 23.05
water connection	€ 2.05
adult	€ 2.05 - € 4.90
child (3-9 yrs)	€ 1.80 - € 3.35

Reservations
Made with deposit (€ 70). Tel: 972 650 879.
Email: info@euro-camping.com

Open
1 April - 26 September.

At a glance
Welcome & Ambience	✓✓✓✓	Location	✓✓✓✓
Quality of Pitches	✓✓✓✓	Range of Facilities	✓✓✓✓✓

ES8210 Camping Tucan
Ctra. de Lloret - Blanes, 17310 Lloret de Mar

Situated on the busy, densely populated Costa Brava near Lloret de Mar, Camping Tucan is well placed to access all the attractions of the area. Views over the mountains are mixed with views of the development in the town. The 200 good size pitches all have electricity and are laid out in a herring-bone pattern with areas dedicated to singles, families with young children and couples who enjoy the quiet. Pitches are on terraces, flat surfaced with gravel and some are shaded. Activities on the site centre around the pleasant pool, bar, restaurant and terrace all of which are close to reception which allows staff to keep a watch on things. Tucan is a lively site with a wide variety of activities including an animation program for children and some entertainment at night. There is a separate, largely independent facility for young people at the rear of the site.

Facilities
The single toilet block. includes washbasins with hot water and facilities for disabled visitors, although access is difficult. All very clean when seen, we suspect the showers would be busy at peak periods. Washing machine. Gas supplies. Shop. Busy bar and good restaurant. Takeaway. Swimming pools. Playground. TV in bar. Volleyball. Basketball. Bicycle hire. Animation in season. Mini-club. Off site: Town 500 m. Nearest beach 600 m. Riding 1 km. Golf 4 km.

At a glance
| Welcome & Ambience | ✓✓✓ | Location | ✓✓✓ |
| Quality of Pitches | ✓✓✓✓ | Range of Facilities | ✓✓✓✓ |

Directions
From A7/E4, A19 or N11 Girona - Barcelona roads take an exit for Lloret de Mar. Site is 1 km. west of the town, well signed and is high on the hill off the main road. The entrance can get congested in busy periods.

Charges 2003
Per adult	€ 4.00 - € 5.70
child (1-9 yrs)	€ 3.10 - € 4.10
pitch	€ 4.00 - € 9.80
electricity	€ 3.20
animal	€ 1.50

Reservations
Contact site. Tel: 972 369 965. Email: info@campingtucan.com

Open
1 April - 30 September.

ES9123 Camping El Solsones
Ctra. Sant Llorenc, km 2, 25280 Solsona

Situated on a hillside, two kilometres from Solsona, this all year site has pleasant views of the hills on three sides and lots of mature trees giving a pleasant green shady appearance. With a lovely Spanish feel, it would be a pleasant spot for a short stay during any season. There are many weekend units here and although only 72 of the 269 pitches are for touring units (22 for caravans or motor-caravans and 50 for tents), we were told that finding a pitch was unlikely to be a problem. They are in separate sectuions of the site and are slightly sloping, with very little shade and electricity. The restaurant has attractive stained glass screens and a menu featuring Catalan style food and it is complemented by a large bar and casual eating area. A feature of the bar area is the central open fire-place. A large play area is provided, however parents are advised to supervise little ones as some of the equipment is of the older metal frame style which is not as child friendly as newer plastic play equipment. For winter visitors, the 'Ski Port del Conte' is 18 km. away. and there are facilities for riding, golf and walking in the vicinity. A friendly welcome is provided by the owner's daughter who speaks English, or sometimes by the owner himself who has no English, but good French.

Facilities
Modern sanitary facilities are in two buildings, with free hot water to the showers, washbasins, laundry and dishwashing sinks. Motorcaravan services. Large supermarket with fresh food. Restaurant and bar (24/6-15/9 and winter weekends). Simple meals and snacks are served indoors and outside on the terrace overlooking the pool. Swimming pool with lifeguard (24/6-16/9). Excellent sports complex and minigolf. Bicycle hire. Play area (see above). Petanque. Fronton. Aviary. Off site: Golf, riding and skiing nearby.

At a glance
| Welcome & Ambience | ✓✓✓✓ | Location | ✓✓✓ |
| Quality of Pitches | ✓✓✓ | Range of Facilities | ✓✓✓✓ |

Directions
Sologna is 45 km. northwest of Manresa, along the C55 and is on the C26 Lleida/Andorra - Barga road. Site is 2 km. out of town on the LV4241 signed to Sant Llorenc de Morunys and Ski Port del Comte.

Charges 2003
Per person	€ 4.60
child (2-10 yrs)	€ 4.30
caravan or tent	€ 4.60
motorcaravan	€ 8.25
electricity (4A)	€ 2.45
car	€ 4.60
motorcycle	€ 4.30
Plus 7% VAT.	

Reservations
Contact site for high season (in French).
Tel: 973 482 861. Email: info@campingsolsones.com

Open
All year.

Cataluña-Catalunya

ES9121 Camping de la Vall d'Ager
Ctra. Afores, s/n, 25691 Ager

Ager is not on a through-route to anywhere – hence the very peaceful situation – so if you are coming here it is likely to be for a specific reason. One of the main reasons could be that it is a hang-glider's paradise. The Montsec mountain range (1,677 m.) towers over the site in the Catalan pre-Pyrenees. Site activities revolve around flying; one of the launch points is just outside the perimeter. Climbing, walking, mountain biking, canoeing and other water sports are all available in the vicinity. There are 132 during pitches on slightly sloping ground, marked out by trees and with some shade. Electricity is available to all. There is a pleasant large bar with snack area and a restaurant which offers local fare at good prices. The pool is very pleasant and most welcome as it is hot and a little dusty hereabouts in high summer.

Facilities
A central sanitary building provides good facilities, including large showers (with divider and lots of room to change). Separate rooms for disabled visitors, facilities for dish-washing (hot water) and laundry (cold), plus a washing machine and dryer downstairs. Bar, snack bar and restaurant (all year). Shop (July/Aug). Bicycle hire. Delta-wing store. Swimming pools (high season). Boule. Barbecue. Play area. Torches are required. Off site: Village 300-400 m. Summer parties in the village. Riding 500 m. Fishing 7 km.

At a glance
Welcome & Ambience	✓✓✓✓	Location	✓✓✓✓
Quality of Pitches	✓✓✓✓	Range of Facilities	✓✓✓✓

Directions
Site is on northern edge of Ager village, at km. 201 on the C12 from Balaguer (which is 28 km. NNE of Lleida) to Tremp. From 2004 this will be the easiest access as major road works will have been completed. Alternatively, use the excellent C13 Lleida/Tremp road and turn west near km 67 onto the C12 (formerly L904) which has not been modernised and has old, narrow sections requiring attention.

Charges 2003
Per person	€ 4.20
child (under 10 yrs)	€ 3.80
tent or caravan	€ 4.20
motorcaravan	€ 8.10
electricity (10A)	€ 5.30
car	€ 4.20
motorcycle	€ 3.90

Reservations
Unlikely to be needed. Tel: 973 455 200. Email: iniciatives@valldager.com

Open
All year.

ES9142 Camping Solana del Segre
Ctra. N260, km 198, 25720 Bellver de Cerdanya

The Sierra del Cadi offers some spectacular scenery and the Reserva Cerdanya is very popular with Spanish skiers. This site is situated in an open, sunny lower valley beside the River Segré where the far bank is a National Park (unfenced so children will need supervision). The immediate area is ideal for walkers and offers many opportunities for outdoor sports enthusiasts. The site is in two sections, the lower one nearer the river being for tourists, mainly flat and grassy with 200 pitches of 100 sq.m. or more, shaded by trees with electricity. The upper area is taken by permanent units and the site can be busy at weekends. An indoor pool and gymnasium were planned. The climb to the disabled facilities on the upper level is steep and may be difficult for infirm campers. The plain restaurant offers a 'menu del dia' and the bar is co-located. Both have terraces where barbecue food may be bought in high season. A fair-sized swimming pool is overlooked from the terrace.

Facilities
Modern sanitary facilities are in three sections, one in a central building on the lower level, and two new, glass reinforced plastic 'portacabin' style units (unisex toilets/showers), one at each side of the lower level. Facilities for disabled campers are on the upper level and thus wheelchair users will experience problems. Hot water to most sinks. Modern area with dishwasher (€ 1) and deep sinks. Laundry with modern machines. Motorcaravan services. Shop, bar and restaurant (1/6-15/9). Swimming pool and paddling pool (1/5-9). Two play areas. Games room. River fishing. Dance area. Volleyball and petanque. Barbecue areas. Internet. Torches are required. Off site: Village has a range of shops bars and restaurants. Riding 1 km. Golf and bicycle hire 10 km. Ski-ing. Walking. Superb walking area.

Directions
Site is at the 198 km. marker on the N260 from Puigcerda to La Seu, well signed just beyond Bellver.

Charges 2003
Per unit incl. electricity (15A)	€ 16.25
adult	€ 4.50
child	€ 4.21
dog	€ 2.40
Plus 7% VAT.	

Reservations
Write to site. Tel: 973 510 310. Email: sds@solanadelsegre.com

Open
1 June - 15 September.

At a glance
Welcome & Ambience	✓✓✓✓	Location	✓✓✓✓
Quality of Pitches	✓✓✓	Range of Facilities	✓✓✓✓

Cataluña-Catalunya

ES8240 Camping Botànic Bona Vista Kim
Ctra. N-II, km.665, 08370 Calella de la Costa

While Calella itself may conjure up visions of mass tourism, this site is set on a steep hillside some three kilometres out of the town. Apart from perhaps some noise from the nearby coast road and railway, it is a quite delightful setting with an abundance of flowers, shrubs and roses (planted by the owner Kim, who has won several top Catalonian prizes for his roses). Of the 160 pitches, all with electricity, 130 are for tourers, they are 60-80 sq.m. or more and are situated on flat terraces on the slopes, with some shade. On arrival, park at the restaurant and choose a pitch – Kim is most helpful with siting your van. The access road is steep, with many of the pitches enjoying lovely views. The bar/restaurant is close to reception at the bottom of the site and is unusual in the attractive choice of Spanish décor and in having a circular, central open-hearth fire/cooker. There are two roof top terraces, the first with service from the restaurant and bar and above that (over 16 years), the computer controlled sauna, jacuzzi with pool sized filter, a well equipped gymnasium and a sunbathing area, all enjoying views over the sea. There are quite good beaches just across the road and railway, accessible via a tunnel and crossing (including a naturist beach). The site has recently won environmental awards.

Facilities
The standard of design in the three sanitary blocks is quite outstanding for a small site (indeed for any site). Some washbasins in cabins in the newest block. Baby room. Dishwashing under cover. Washing machines. Motorcaravan services. Bar/restaurant, takeaway and shop (1/4-1/10). Large children's playground. Recreation park. Satellite TV. Internet point. Games room. Barbecue and picnic area. No cycling allowed on site. Off site: Fishing 100 m. Bicycle hire 1 km. Riding and golf 3 km. Watersports near.

At a glance
Welcome & Ambience	✓✓✓✓	Location	✓✓✓✓
Quality of Pitches	✓✓✓✓	Range of Facilities	✓✓✓✓

Directions
From N11 coast road site is signed travelling south of Calella (at km. 665), and is on right hand side of road - care is needed as road is busy and sign is almost on top of turning (entrance shared with Camping Roca Grossa). Entrance is very steep. From Barcelona, after passing through Sant Pol de Mar, go into outside lane shortly after 'Camping 800 m.' sign and keep signalling left. Site entrance is just before the two lanes merge. (From C32 toll motorway, leave at exit 22 for Calella to join N11 south, then as above).

Charges 2003
Per person	€ 4.15
child (3-10 yrs)	€ 3.65
tent or caravan incl. electricity	€ 7.75
motorcaravan incl. electricity	€ 11.95
All plus 7% VAT. No credit cards.	

Reservations
Write to site. Tel: 93 769 24 88.
Email: info@botanic-bonavista.net

Open
All year.

ES8242 Camping Roca Grossa
Ctra. N-II, Km.665, 08370 Calella de la Costa

Translating from the Catalan as 'big rock', Roca Grossa celebrates its 50th year of business in 2004. The owners, the Bachs family, are very friendly and there is a very happy atmosphere in the campsite. Very steep slopes predominate at this site and there is a 100 m. climb from reception to the pool set at the top of the site. A road train runs all day to ferry you to the amenities, but the site is unsuitable for disabled campers and the infirm. The bonus is some great views over the sea from most of the terraced, but flat and reasonably sized pitches. Landrovers are used to site your unit. The permanent section of pitches is separated from the touring pitches and everything is kept very smart and clean. Clean and crisp, the pleasant pool enjoys fabulous views and the small restaurant/bar there is open all day. The sports facilities are also at this lofty point and if you wish to shop or use the main bar and restaurant, catch the train to the lower area near reception. The beach is just 50 m. across the road and the town is a short walk.

Facilities
An amazing array of clean sanitary blocks means there is not far to walk from any area of the site. Large and small, all blocks are well kept with hot water throughout. Washing machines. Gas supplies. Shop. Pleasant bar and restaurant. Swimming pools (May-Sept). Playground. TV in bar. Road train. Football field. 5 a-side. Volley ball. Two tennis couts. Animation programme including children's entertainment. Excursions. ATM. Torches useful. Off site: Beach, fishing and boat launching 50 m. Town 100 m. Riding 1 km. Golf 2 km. Watersports nearby.

At a glance
Welcome & Ambience	✓✓✓✓	Location	✓✓✓✓
Quality of Pitches	✓✓✓✓	Range of Facilities	✓✓✓✓✓

Directions
From A7 (Girona - Barcelona) take exit 9 or 10 for Malgrat del Mar on the N11. Turn south towards Calella and site is at 665 km. marker sharing an entrance with another campsite. Caravans are placed on pitches with site Landrover.

Charges 2003
Per adult	€ 4.11 - € 4.40
child (under 10 yrs)	€ 3.64 - € 3.89
pitch	€ 4.11 - € 8.80
electricity	€ 3.97 - € 4.25

Reservations
Made without deposit. Tel: 937 691 297.
Email: rocagrossa@rocagrossa.com

Open
1 April - 30 September.

ES9140 Camping Repos del Pedraforca

Ctra. B400, km 13.5, 08699 Saldés

Looking up through the trees in this steeply terraced campsite in the area of the Cadi-Moixero Natural Parc, you see the majestic Pedraforca mountain. A favourite for Catalan climbers and walkers, its amazing rugged peak in the shape of a massive stone fork gives it its name. The long scenic drive through the mountains to reach the site is breathtakingly beautiful. The natural beauty of the area, pretty villages, wild flowers, wonderful walks, and interesting local attractions including sea salt mountain and historic coal mines are what attract people to this area. The campsite owner, Alicia Font, is a charming hostess who speaks English. She has created excellent summer and winter facilities including an indoor heated pool, sauna, jacuzzi and gym complex, a large outdoor pool, rooftop relaxation area, upstairs social room, excellent restaurant and a popular bar. Access to the site is via a steep, curving road which could challenge some units. Pitches vary in size and accessibility, although there are excellent pitches for larger units.

Facilities
There are two clean, modern sanitary blocks. We found a low ratio of showers and toilet facilities, but all other sites in this area are the same. At peak periods there may be queues. British style WCs. Press button hot water and flowing cold water in the showers is a difficult system to manage, only one shower in each block has a privacy screen. Facilities for disabled campers. Washing machines and dryer. Restaurant/bar. Small supermarket for basic items. Heated indoor pool, gym and spa. Outdoor pool. Play areas. Animation for children and adults in high season. Games and social rooms. Rooftop relaxation area. Table tennis. Electronic games. Itinerary suggestions for excursions in the area. Torches required. Off site: Motorcaravan service point close but not within site. Restaurants.

Directions
Site is approx 90 minutes from Barcelona. Access to the site is gained from the C-16 Burga road. 2 km. south of Guardiola de Bergeda turn west to Saldes and site is well signed. It is 13.5 km. from the C-16.

Charges 2003
Per person	€ 4.45
pitch	€ 11.30
electricity (3-5A)	€ 3.20 - € 4.00

Discounts for stays of more than 3 nights and other offers for long stays (excluding high season).
Camping Cheques accepted.

Reservations
Contact site for details. Tel: 938 258 044.
Email: pedra@campingpedraforca.com

Open
All year.

At a glance
Welcome & Ambience	✓✓✓✓	Location	✓✓✓✓
Quality of Pitches	✓✓✓	Range of Facilities	✓✓✓✓

ES8310 Camping La Ballena Alegre

Autovia Castelldefels, km 12.5, 08840 Viladecans

La Ballena Alegre is a large site with good facilites, popular with the Spanish and other Europeans. About 16 kilometres from the centre of Barcelona, it has all the facilities for an extended holiday plus a superb sandy beach more than a kilometre long and 100 metres wide. Some may prefer the extremely pleasant lagoon style pool complex with slides and jacuzzi. It is a shaded, well laid out site, mostly covered by pine trees and divided into 1,450 pitches of about 70 sq.m. with 1,250 for touring units. Space is not usually a problem, certainly outside July/August. There is an attractive bar and a white linen restaurant with a terrace overlooking the pool. Entertainment is staged here in high season. A self service restaurant is close by serving great food, with some real Spanish dishes included at attractive prices if you have a large family. A further bar near the entrance is open late. The site has a lively atmosphere in high season, but with no noise after midnight. The airport is not far away and there is some aircraft noise, plus some road noise on one side of the site. However, the site is full of fun and ideal for families seeking a holiday with a Spanish flavour. Used by tour operators (75 pitches).

Facilities
The toilet blocks are good, varying in size and type. Two are new (these have some private cabins). Units for disabled visitors. Cleaning is good – a cleaner is on duty at each block during the day. Dog showers. Washing machines. Motorcaravan services. Large supermarket and other shops. Restaurant (24/6-30/8). Bar, snack bar and self service restaurant plus additional late bar near entrance. Swimming pool complex with slides and jacuzzi (25/5-25/9). Organised sports activities: aerobics, squash, roller skating, bicycle track, swimming, etc. Open area where folk dances, shows etc. are staged twice weekly (24/6-30/8). Soundproofed disco. Sports area with football. Playground. Tennis. Fishing. Garage (petrol and servicing) by entrance. Hairdressers. Bureau de change. Good treatment room with nurse; doctor calls daily. Gas supplies. Off site: Golf 2 km. Riding 3 km. Bicycle hire 6 km. Regular bus service to Barcelona.

Directions
From Barcelona on N11 either turn off on C245 road to Gava and Castelldefels or take motorway A2 spur towards Castelldefels - El Prat de Llobregat and continue to Castelldefels. Entrance leads directly off C246 dual-carriageway 'Autovia Castelldefels' on coast side of the road by a service station.

Charges 2003
Per person	€ 3.00 - € 4.50
child (under 10 yrs)	€ 2.00 - € 2.50
pitch incl. car and electricity	€ 13.00 - € 27.00
motorcycle with tent	€ 9.00 - € 16.00
dog	€ 2.00 - € 4.50

All plus 7% VAT.

Reservations
Only made in the sense of guaranteeing admission. Tel: 902 500 526. Email: ballena1@ballena-alegre.es

Open
1 April - 30 September.

At a glance
Welcome & Ambience	✓✓✓	Location	✓✓✓✓
Quality of Pitches	✓✓✓✓	Range of Facilities	✓✓✓✓✓

ES8392 Camping El Garrofer
Ctra. C246 km 39, 08870 Sitges

This is a large, pine covered site, alongside fields of vines, 800 m. from the beach and close to the pleasant town of Sitges. It has over 500 pitches of which 415 are for tourers and including 15 fully serviced pitches for large motorhomes. Everything is kept clean and the pitches are tidy and shaded, all with electricity. Dino is the young, dynamic, English speaking manager who has a vast programme of improvements which will make this a most attractive site. The permanent pitches are grouped in a completely separate area and the amenity buildings are along the site perimeter next to the road which absorbs most of the road noise. A varied menu is offered in the cosy restaurant with a small terrace. Everything is cooked to perfection (the restaurant has a local reputation and is used by non campers – the menu of the day is great value. A traditional bar is alongside and from here you can see the pretty mosaic clad play area. An ambitious animation programme is conducted for children in summer. Late evening Salsa classes were offered for adults when we visited. A small swimming pool with sunbathing areas is welcome on the hot summer days or you can walk to the very pleasant beach. Open most of the year, the site offers all manner of adventure activities (extra charge) which may be organized through reception and there are many things to see here.

Facilities
Three sanitary blocks with ample facilities are mature but clean – one is of a good standard, and another is to be replaced in 2002. Good facilities for disabled campers. Laundry. Bar/restaurant. Shop (reception in low season). Swimming pool. Golf packages. Practice golf. Tennis. Older play area with dated equipment, modern plastic module for toddlers. Boules. Car wash. Bus link from outside site to Barcelona airport and city.

At a glance
Welcome & Ambience	✓✓✓✓	Location	✓✓✓✓
Quality of Pitches	✓✓✓✓	Range of Facilities	✓✓✓✓

Directions
Sitges is roughly 30 km. southwest of Barcelona and the site is accessed from the C-246 km. 39, 2 km. from town towards Vilanova i la Geltrú.

Charges 2003
Per person	€ 2.41 - € 4.07
child (1-9 yrs)	€ 1.90 - € 3.26
pitch	€ 9.90 - € 13.65
motorcycle	€ 2.23 - € 3.74
electricity (6A)	€ 2.94
dog	€ 1.87

Plus 7% VAT.

Reservations
Contact site. Tel: 938 941 780.
Email: garroferpark@terra.es

Open
17 January - 17 December.

ES8390 Camping Vilanova Park

Ctra. de l'Arboc, km 2.5, 08800 Vilanova i la Geltru

This large, modern, hillside site has been equipped with costly installations of good quality and is open all year. The most remarkable feature is the excellent pool complex with one very large pool where there are water jets and a coloured floodlit fountain. Together with a smaller children's pool, this covers an area of some 1,000 sq.m. and enjoys wonderful views over the sea. In the same area is the shopping centre and the large bar and restaurant, set around a thoughtfully executed extension and refurbishment of old Catalan farm buildings where dancing and entertainment takes place. There is an ambitious animation programme for young and old throughout the high season, and at weekends for the remainder of the year. An unusual attraction is a Wildlife Park inhabited by deer and birdlife. Very pleasant, it has picnic areas and footpaths. At present there are 865 pitches with a very significant proportion occupied by a variety of well separated and screened static units. There are 150 pitches for touring units, located in separate areas of the site; 120 have their own water supply. Marked and of 70-100 sq.m, all have electricity and some larger pitches (100 sq.m.) also have water and drainage. The terrain, hard surfaced and mostly on very gently sloping ground, has many trees that provides shade. Used by tour operators (57 pitches).

Facilities
All the sanitary blocks, including a new one, are of excellent quality, can be heated and have washbasins (over half in cabins) with free hot water, and others of standard type with cold water. Sinks for dishwashing and clothes. Serviced laundry. Motorcaravan services. Supermarket (Easter - 30 Sept). Souvenir shop. Full restaurant and larger bar where simpler meals served (both all year). Swimming pools (Easter - 15 Oct). Games room. Tennis. Bicycle hire. Tennis. ATM and exchange facilities. Off site: Fishing 4 km. Vilanova town and beach are 4 km (local bus service). Golf 5 km. Barcelona is easily accessible – buses every hour in the main season or electric train from Vilanova i la Geltrú.

Directions
From Barcelona - Tarragona autopista take exit 29, towards Vilanova. There is no exit at no. 29 from Tarragona direction; take exit 30 into Vilafranca and turn right. The Vilanova bypass means one need not go into town. From N340 from L'Arboc turn directly on winding road for 11 km. for Vilanova i la Geltrú.

Charges 2003
Per person	€ 3.99 - € 6.32
child (4-12 yrs)	€ 2.49 - € 3.99
pitch incl. electricity (6A)	€ 11.91 - € 16.58

All plus 7% VAT. Excellent deals for retired people on longer stays. Camping Cheques accepted.

Reservations
Made in sense of guaranteeing to admit, with deposit. Tel: 93 893 34 02. Email: info@vilanovapark.es

Open
All year.

At a glance
Welcome & Ambience	✓✓✓✓	Location	✓✓✓✓
Quality of Pitches	✓✓✓✓	Range of Facilities	✓✓✓✓✓

An elegant site with country-club atmosphere!

50km South of Barcelona in the wine and champagne centre of Catalonia with more than 600 palm trees. Quiet situation. Very modern sanit. install. w. hot water everywhere. Swimming pool of 1,000 sq.m. and children's pool with big colour fountain (lighted in the evenings). Excellent restaurant "Chaine de Rotisseurs" in old catalan mansion. Superm. shops, English press, children's progr. activities. Large pitches w. electr. conn. Private, large ecological park of 50,000 sq.m. for beautiful walks and picnics.
Access: Motorway A-7, coming fr. Barcelona: exit 29; coming fr. Tarragona: exits 30 & 31; follow indic. Vilanova i la Geltru/Sitges.

Open throughout the year. We speak English.

CAMPING VILANOVA PARK
Apartado (postbus 64)
Tel. (34) 93 893 34 02 • Fax (34) 93 893 55 28
E-08800 Vilanova i la Geltrú (Barcelona)

ES8235 Camping Bon Repos

Malgrat de Mar, 08398 Santa Susana

If you enjoy the hustle and bustle of the Costa Brava in summer, then Bon Repos is ideal. It is a long, narrow coastal site with many pitches along the length of the attractive fine sand beach with direct access and no fence. The 500 pitches are of reasonable size, flat with a sand surface and lots of shade, and with 10A electricity. The beach is a strong point of the site having rocky outcrops and close by is the bar/restaurant with huge terrace. The pool is overlooked from here through perspex screens and the terrace was buzzing when we visited. Afternoon entertainment was in full swing with the hosts of Dutch campers enjoying the music and 'happy hour'. The railway runs close along one side of the site, which is good for train spotters but does create a noise problem. The play area is basic and there were some breakages, so children would need supervising. There is a separate paddling pool beside the main pool. This is a good site for a short visit or transits but the beach pitches are great and will need booking in high season.

Facilities

The two sanitary blocks are dated but clean. The number of showers is low and we suspect they are extremely busy at peak periods. Cold water at washbasins. Units for disabled campers. Well equipped baby room (key at reception). Washing machines and dryers. Motorcaravan services. Supermarket. Restaurant. Chicken bar. Giant TV in bar. Swimming pools (with lifeguard). Play area with some broken toys. Internet. Barbecue area. Tennis courts. Table tennis. Electronic games. Bicycle hire. Animation and happy hour. ATM. Security boxes. Torches useful. Off site: Resort town very close by. Boat launching 200 m. Bicycle hire 1 km. Riding 3 km. Golf 5 km.

At a glance

Welcome & Ambience	✓✓✓✓	Location	✓✓✓✓
Quality of Pitches	✓✓✓✓	Range of Facilities	✓✓✓

Directions

From A7 exit 9 (A19 exit 22) take road to Malgrat de Mar. Then turn south on coast road for Santa Susanna. Follow obvious campings signs - leading to site via a high tunnel under the railway on a minor beach road.

Charges 2003

Per adult	€ 4.15
child	€ 3.50
pitch incl. electricity	€ 22.00

Reservations

Contact site. Tel: 937 678 475.
Email: info@campingbonrepos.com

Open

All year.

ES8312 Camping Tres Estrellas

C-31, km 186,2, 08850 Gavá

The name translates as the 'three stars' and this beach site lives up to its name. The 407 pitches are mostly flat with electricity, informally placed under trees, with no permanent units. Many pitches are along the beach front, those closer to the beach having little shade, but they are very pleasant with great views – beach access is through a security fence. Amenities, including a large pool, are in a separate area of the site, nearer to but shielded from the road, keeping noise away from the pitches. Although busy, the site has a pleasant open feel. The bar and restaurant are close to the beach enjoying cool breezes in the evening. The bar is lively at times with everyone having great fun and it is located where there is little or no noise impact on the pitches, ideal in a site popular with all age groups. English is spoken and the staff are efficient and friendly. A modest entertainment programme is provided in high season. Tour operators use the site but have a separate area. This is a great site for visiting Barcelona as the bus stops outside the gate.

Facilities

Four traditional style toilet blocks provide clean facilities including neat facilities for disabled campers and a well equipped nursery room (key at reception). Washing machines and dryers. Motorcaravan services. Car wash. Supermarket. Restaurant. Bar. Snack bar. Swimming pool. Play areas. Football. Boules. Basketball. Internet. Animation. Table tennis. Electronic games. Bicycle hire. Entertainment programme. ATM. Security boxes. Torches useful. Off site: Bus outside gate into town. Fishing. Boat launching 200 m. Bicycle hire 1 km. Riding 3 km. Golf 7 km.

At a glance

Welcome & Ambience	✓✓✓✓	Location	✓✓✓✓
Quality of Pitches	✓✓✓✓	Range of Facilities	✓✓✓✓

Directions

On C31 south of Barcelona go towards Castelldefels and the site is at the 186 km. marker directly off the main road.

Charges 2003

Per adult	€ 4.31 - € 5.80
child (3-10 yrs)	€ 3.38 - € 3.84
pitch	€ 5.46 - € 13.19
electricity (5A)	€ 4.04
animal	€ 2.65 - € 3.32

Camping Cheques accepted.

Reservations

Contact site. Tel: 936 330637.
Email: fina@camping3estrellas.com

Open

15 March - 15 October.

ES8502 Camping-Caravaning Montblanc Park

Ctra. Prenefeta, km 1,8, 43400 Montblanc

Montblanc Park is a fabulous new site with 273 pitches, all of which have great views. Innovatively planned over 14 hectares, this is the camping site of the future. Visitors have first class facilities, a very high quality restaurant serves typically Spanish dishes, and a terrace area is available for those who would choose a less formal atmosphere. Both the restaurant and terrace enjoy views over the surrounding countryside and the exceptionally large lagoon style pool which has its own separate shallow toddlers' area. The pitches are on terraces so that all take advantage of the views of the Prades mountains, and gentle cooling afternoon breezes. They vary in size, are sloping (chocks useful) and have little shade as yet. An enthusiastic planting programmme, recently completed, will remedy this in the future. Wooden chalet style bungalows are located on the upper levels of the site. An animation team keep children amused during the day in July and August so parents can have a break. Sport is organised and there is live entertainment on Saturday night. This is a very professional operation, ideal for a relaxing holiday or exploring the many attractions of the local area.

Facilities
Two brand new sanitary blocks have all features a camper could wish for and include superb facilities for disabled campers and a well equipped baby room. Washing machines and dryers. Supermarket. Restaurant. Snack bar. Swimming pool and paddling pool. Play areas. Football. Boules. Basketball. Table tennis. Electronic games. Bicycle hire. Limited animation programme. Mini-club. Tents for hire. Off site: Riding 4 km. Beach 35 km. Golf 35 km.

At a glance
Welcome & Ambience	✓✓✓✓✓	Location	✓✓✓✓
Quality of Pitches	✓✓✓✓✓	Range of Facilities	✓✓✓✓✓

Directions
Site is off the A2 between Ileida and Tarragona. At C14 road intersection take road to Montblanc, then road to Prenefeta. Site is 1.8 km. out of Montblanc, very well signed in the town and on the road out.

Charges 2003
Per person	€ 3.00 - € 4.00
child (2-10 yrs)	€ 2.00 - € 3.00
pitch incl. electricity	€ 14.00 -€ 21.00
water	€ 2.00

Reservations
Contact site. Tel: 977 862544.
Email: info@montblancpark.com

Open
All year.

ES8506 Camping Serra de Prades

Sant Antoni, s/n, 43439 Vilanova de Prades

On the edge of the village of Vilanova, nestling in granite foothills with superb views from its elevation of 950 m, this is a welcoming and peaceful site. The 215 pitches are on terraces formed with natural stone and with good access. The upper tent pitches have wonderful views although you have a trek to the sanitary facility on the lower level. Hedges and trees separate pitches providing a pleasant green environment and some shade, and 90% of the pitches have electricity (176 with 6A, 13 with 10A). The site has won awards for its approach to ecology and solar power is used to heat water for the showers and the the pool, and recycling bins are used. The elegant new swimming pool (supervised) has a terrace for sunbathing. The bar/restaurant offers a limited range of meals including some regional dishes. The strength of this site is the range of adventure and outdoor activities on offer. These are most professionally organized and climbing is a favourite followed by abseiling, paint ball, cycling, archery and a host of others. There is an impressive horse riding area within the site and guided treks are offered. The helpful staff will organize any activity and if it is not on offer here they have contracts with outside agencies for further extensive activities. On site, less arduous activities are also organised for children and adults in season.

Facilities
The modern, well maintained sanitary block has British style WCs, hot water throughout and heating. Laundry facilities. Motorcaravan service point. Shop. Bar/restaurant. Swimming pool and children's pool (open and heated 1/4-15/10). Satellite TV. Archery. Basketball. Volleyball. Quad hire. Paint ball. 4 x 4 hire. Tennis. Riding with guided treks. Sports area. Entertainment organised in season. Safety deposit. Exchange facilities. Gas supplies. Torches required in some areas.

At a glance
Welcome & Ambience	✓✓✓✓	Location	✓✓✓✓
Quality of Pitches	✓✓✓✓	Range of Facilities	✓✓✓✓

Directions
From Tarragona on autopista A2 take exit 9 (Montblanc) and continue towards Lleida on N240. At km. 48 just west of Vimbodi, turn left towards Vallclara and Vilanova de Prades. Site is on roundabout at entrance to village. From Lleida leave A2 at exit 8 towards Tarragona on N240, the as above from km. 48 just before Vimbodi.

Charges 2003
Per person	€ 4.80
child (under 10 yrs)	€ 4.10
tent or caravan	€ 4.80
car	€ 4.80
motorcaravan	€ 9.50
electricity	€ 4.10

Plus 7% VAT. Camping Cheques accepted.

Reservations
Write to site. Tel: 977 869 050.
Email: info@serradeprades.com

Open
All year.

ES8395 Camping Arc de Bara

CN 340, km 1182, 43883 Roda de Bara

In comparison to the gigantic sites along this coastline, this smaller site has only 300 pitches of which most are taken up with static holiday caravans. The site is 60 m. from the superb beach, which is accessed by a rear gate in the site perimeter. The 30 pitches for tourers are generally shaded, are of average size (60-70 sq.m.) and are somewhat set apart from the very extensive permanent pitches but there is a distinct feeling of compression. The unusual feature of this site, perpetrated by one of the owners, is the modernistic design theme used on many of the camp building exteriors and interiors. This theme is continued at the attractive large heated swimming pool and children's pool elevated above the site's ground level and forming a curved arrowhead shape. Within the curve is a round observation area but this was unfinished when seen. The shop, bar and restaurant located close to the entrance are open every day between July and Sept. and at weekends only all other times of the year, as is the impressive bar/snack area near the beach access.

Facilities

Three very clean toilet blocks are of various designs (one a most unusual elevated circular building) and a fourth without showers. These offer free hot water to washbasins (some in cabins) and showers. Units for disabled visitors. Limited facilities for babies. Dishwashing and laundry (cold water only). A separate facility for disabled campers was under construction when we visited. Washing machines and dryers. Swimming pools. Bars. Restaurant. Snack bars. Supermarket. Small play area. Some animation in season. Torches required in some areas.

At a glance

Welcome & Ambience	✓✓✓	Location	✓✓✓✓
Quality of Pitches	✓✓✓	Range of Facilities	✓✓✓✓

Directions

From A7 autopista take exit 31 towards Tarragona. Site is on CN340 Barcelona - Tarragona road at 1182 km. marker just 50 meters from the Roman Arc. Use the approach turn for of camping Stel.

Charges 2003

Per person	€ 2.65 - € 4.25
child (3-9 yrs)	€ 1.60 - € 2.60
tent or caravan	€ 2.65 - € 4.25
car	€ 2.65 - € 4.25
motorcaravan	€ 4.25 - € 7.20
electricity	€ 2.60

Minimum charge € 20,44 per day for pitch and persons (1/7-31/8). All plus 7% VAT.

Reservations

Contact site. Tel: 977 800 902.
Email: camping@campingarcdebara.com

Open

All year.

ES8420 Camping Stel

Ctra. N340, km 1182, 43883 Roda de Bará

Camping Stel is part of a group also consisting of sites ES9143 and ES9144. The group's high standards are maintained here in Playa Bara, between the pre-Littoral mountains and the sea. The rectangular site is between the N340 road and the excellent beach, with the railway running close to the bottom of the site. Beach access is gained through a gate and under the railway – there is rail noise on the lower pitches. The main facilities are grouped around the pools which are very pleasant with a large flume to an extension of the main pool (heated all season), an octagonal paddling pool and pleasant grass area carefully set out with palms. The central complex containing all the services is impressive with a large bar, terrace and snack area overlooking the pools. A small restaurant is behind the bar. The pitches are generally in rows with hedges around the rows but at the lower end of the site the layout is less formal. Many pitches have individual sinks. There is a separate area where noise from radios or TVs is not allowed ensuring peace and quiet.

Facilities

There are four clean, fully equipped, sanitary blocks. One has been totally refurbished (2002) and offers new crisp facilities for children, excellent facilities for disabled campers and four high standard private cabins. Baby baths in the ladies' sections of blocks. One block in the chalet area is available to campers. Laundry. Motorcaravan service area. Supermarket and tourist shop. Bar/restaurant and snack bar. Swimming pools.(4 April - 28 Sep) Outdoor sports area. Gym. Animation for children and some adult entertainment in high season. Electronic games. Internet bar. Hairdresser. ATM. Overnight area for late arrivals. Dogs are not accepted. Torch useful. Off site: Fishing from beach. Golf, riding and bicycle hire 4 km. Travel to the many attractions in the area is simple by the nearby autopista, rail or bus services.

Directions

Site is at 1182 km. marker on the N340 near Arc de Bara, between Tarragona and Vilanova.

Charges 2003

Per adult	€ 6.00
child (3-10 yrs)	€ 4.60
pitch incl. electricity	€ 17.50 - € 19.60
with water and drainage	€ 21.00 - € 23.50

All plus 7% VAT. Camping Cheques accepted.

Reservations

Advisable in July/August. Tel: 977 802 002.
Email: stel@stel.es

Open

9 April - 28 September.

At a glance

Welcome & Ambience	✓✓✓✓	Location	✓✓✓✓✓
Quality of Pitches	✓✓✓✓✓	Range of Facilities	✓✓✓✓✓

ES8410 Camping Playa Bara

Ctra. N340, km. 1183, 43883 Roda de Bará

This is a most impressive site near the beach, which is family owned and has been carefully developed over the years. On entry you find yourself in a beautifully sculptured, tree-lined drive. Considering its size, with over 850 pitches, it is still a very green and relaxing site with an immense range of activities. It is well situated with a 50 m. walk to a long sandy beach via a tunnel under the railway (some noise) to a new promenade with palms and a quality beach bar and restaurant. Palms, shrubs and flowering plants give a pleasing tropical appearance to all aspects of the site. The owners have excelled themselves in the design of the impressive terraced Roman-style pool complex, which is the central feature of the site. An extremely well equipped gym with a dedicated instructor and a massage service. A separate attractive amphitheatre seats 2,000 and is used to stage ambitious entertainment in season. Pitches vary in size, the older ones terraced and well shaded with pine trees, the newer ones more open, with a variety of trees and bushes forming separators between them. All have electricity and a sink with water. Arrive early to find space in peak weeks. Used by some British tour operators.

Facilities
Excellent, fully equipped toilet blocks. Private cabins for both sexes in some blocks, children's and superb facilities for disabled visitors. Private sanitary facilities can be hired. Note: shower water is desalinated and thus rather salty but spring water is available from special taps. Washing machines and dryers. Undergound car parking. Motorcaravan service points. Supermarket. Butcher. Bakery. Fruit sold. Tabac. Souvenir shop. Full restaurant and larger bar where simpler meals and takeaway served, bars also in 3 other places, and pleasant bar/restaurant on beach. Picnic areas. Swimming pools. Jacuzzi/hydro-massage. Fronton and tennis courts (both floodlit). Roller skating. Football. Junior club. Sports area for children. Doctor (24 hr high season) on site. Windsurfing school. Volleyball. Basketball. Gymnasium. Massage parlour. Petanque. Minigolf. Fishing. Amphitheatre with stage and dance floor. Animation in several languages. Large games room with pool, football, table tennis, electronic machines; room for video's and satellite TV, with screen and seating. Cocktail bar/disco room (11- 4 am, weekends only outside high season). ATM. Deposit boxes. Hairdresser. Internet points. On site travel agent. Off site: Bicycle hire 2 km. Riding 3 km. Golf 4 km.

Directions
From A7 autoroute take exit 31 to Site entrance is at the 1183 km. marker on the main N340 just opposite the Arco de Bara Roman monument from which it takes its name.

Charges 2003

Per person	€ 2.97 - € 8.50
child (1-9 yrs)	€ 2.08 - € 5.95
large tent or caravan	€ 8.50
small tent	€ 5.95
car	€ 8.50
motorcycle	€ 5.95
motorcaravan	€ 14.50
electricity (5A)	€ 3.00

All plus 7% VAT. Low season reductions for pensioners and all sports charges reduced by 90%.

Reservations
Contact site for details. Tel: 977 802 701.
Email: info@barapark.es

Open
26 March - 26 September, with all amenities.

At a glance
Welcome & Ambience	✓✓✓✓	Location	✓✓✓✓
Quality of Pitches	✓✓✓✓	Range of Facilities	✓✓✓✓

ES8402 Camping Vendrell Platja

Avda. del Sanatori, s/n, 43820 Calafell

In the bustling Calafell area, this site is set back from the beach across a minor road. Popular with tourists for many years, the area has apartment buildings, bars and restaurants. An avenue of palms greets you on arrival here, and the pool with more tall palms and grassy areas, has two slides that delight children and adults alike. Around one side of the pool red umbrellas provide shade where cool drinks and snacks can be enjoyed. A large thatched area used in the evenings for entertainment, provides extra shade away from the pool. The very Spanish restaurant serves paella, pizza and family style meals. The site is bustling with activity and is crowded during high season. The small pitches (60 sq.m.) are partially shaded by trees yet to reach their full potential. Access to all the pitches is through one narrow central road which is busy with foot and vehicle traffic. As the pitches are very tightly packed this is not the site for campers who enjoy their privacy.

Facilities
Two well located toilet blocks provide clean facilities with a new unit for disabled campers and well equipped baby rooms. The numbers of showers and toilets are low - we think they would be stressed at peak periods. Washing machines. Motorcaravan services. Supermarket. Restaurant. Snack bar. Swimming pools and pool bar. Play areas. Football. Boules. Basketball. Table tennis. Electronic games. Bicycle hire. Very modest animation programme. ATM. Security boxes. Torches useful. Off site: Resort town and beach outside the gate with usual attractions. Fishing. Bicycle hire 200 m. Riding 2 km. Golf 3 km.

Directions
From A7 or A16 take exits for El Vendrel, east to Sant Salvador, then north on coast road towards Platja Calafell. Site is well signed west of the town centre.

Charges 2003

Per adult	€ 1.50 - € 5.50
child (3-11 yrs)	€ 1.15 - € 4.15
pitch	€ 5.50 - € 11.00
electricity	€ 3.30
dog	€ 1.00

Reservations
Contact site no deposit required. Tel: 977 694 009.
Email: vendrell@camping-vendrellplatja.com

Open
1 April - 30 September.

Cataluña-Catalunya

55

Great on-line holiday deals alanrogersdirect.com

ES8480 Camping & Bungalow Park Sanguli

Prolongacion Calle 'E' s/n, Apdo de Correos 123, 43840 Salou

Owned, developed and managed by a local Spanish family, Sanguli is a superb site boasting excellent pools and ambitious entertainment. Sister site to ES8481, it lies little more than 100 metres from the good sandy beach, across the coast road and a small railway level crossing (some train noise at times). Although large, Sanguli manages to maintain a quality family atmosphere due to the efforts of the very keen and efficient staff. There are four good sized, attractive pools (with children's pools), one near the entrance with a grassy sunbathing area partly shaded and a second deep one with water chutes that forms part of the excellent sports complex (with fitness centre, tennis and squash courts, a 'fronton', minigolf and football practice area). The third pool is the central part of the amphitheatre area at the top of the site which includes an impressive Roman style building with huge portals, containing a bar and restaurant with terraces. The amphitheatre seats 2,000 campers and treats them to very professional free nightly entertainment (1/5-30/9). All the pools have adjacent amenity areas and bars. The site is striving to achieve the 'Garden of Eden' that is the owners' dream. There are 1,214 pitches of varying size (75-90 sq.m) and all have electricity. A wonderful selection of trees, palms and shrubs provides natural shade. A real effort is made to cater for the young including teenagers with a 'Hop Club' (entertainment tailored for 13-17 year olds), along with a Computer Club which includes use of the internet. This is a large, professional site providing something for all the family, but still capable of providing peace and quiet for those looking for it. Used by British tour operators (132 pitches).

Facilities
The quality sanitary facilities are constantly improved and are always exceptional, including many individual cabins with en-suite facilities. All are kept very clean. Launderette with service. Motorcaravan services. Bars and restaurant with takeaway. Swimming pools. Jacuzzi. Fitness centre. Sport complex with tennis, squash, football practice ground, Sports area and fitness room (charged). Playground. Mini club, teenagers club and computer club. New minigolf. First-aid room. Gas supplies. Off site: Fishing and bicycle hire 100 m. Riding 3 km. Golf 6 km. Resort entertainment.

At a glance
Welcome & Ambience	✓✓✓✓	Location	✓✓✓✓
Quality of Pitches	✓✓✓✓✓	Range of Facilities	✓✓✓✓✓

Directions
On west side of Salou about 1 km. from centre, site is well signed from the coast road to Cambrils and from the other town approaches.

Charges 2003
Per adult	€ 5.00
child (4-12 yrs)	€ 3.00
pitch (70-75 sq.m)	€ 12.00 - € 29.00

Electricity i(7/10A) ncluded. All plus 7% VAT. Less 25-45% outside high season for longer stays. Special long stay offers for senior citizens.

Reservations
Advised for July/Aug. and made up to 1 March with sizeable booking fee; contact site. Tel: 977 381 641. Email: mail@sanguli.es

Open
19 March - 1 November.

Widely regarded as the 'Bible' by site owners and readers alike, there is no better guide when it comes to forming an independent view of a campsite's quality. When you need to be confident in your choice of campsite, you need the Alan Rogers Guide.

- ✓ Sites only included on merit
- ✓ Sites cannot pay to be included
- ✓ Independently inspected, rigorously assessed
- ✓ Impartial reviews
- ✓ 36 years of expertise

ES8481 Camping Cambrils Park

Apartado de Correos 123, 43850 Salou

A drive lined with palm trees and flowers leads from the large, very smart round reception building at this impressive modern site. Sister site to no. ES8480, it is set 500 m. back from the excellent beach in a generally quiet setting with outstanding facilities. The 684 slightly sloping, grassy pitches of around 90 sq.m. are numbered and separated by trees. All have electricity, 55 have water and waste water connections, some having more shade than others. The marvellous central lagoon pool complex with water slides is the main focus of the site with a raised wooden 'poop-deck' sunbathing area with palm surrounds that doubles as a stage for entertainment at night. There is a huge bar/terrace area for watching the magnificent floodlit spectacles, along with an excellent restaurant and an adjacent take-away. By day there is a small bar at a lower level in the pool where you can enjoy a cool drink from submerged stools, plus a dryer version on the far side of the bar or just relax on the spacious thick grassed sunbathing areas. There are a number of tour operator pitches and attractive thatched chalets. A fabulous jungle theme children's pool is nearer the entrance. This is a superb family site for your camping holiday and you will not need to leave what is really a holiday resort.

Facilities
Four excellent sanitary buildings provide some washbasins in cabins, superb units for disabled visitors, dishwashing, laundry and immaculate, decorated baby sections. Huge serviced laundry. Motorcaravan services. Car wash. Restaurant. Takeaway. Huge supermarket, souvenir shop and 'panaderia' (fresh-baked bread and croissants). Swimming pools. Minigolf. Tennis Football. Multi-games court. Basketball. Volleyball. Petanque. Animation and entertainment all season. Mini-club. Doctor on site daily all season. ATM. Gas supplies. Dogs are not accepted. Off site: Fishing and bicycle hire 400 m. Riding 3 km. Port Aventura theme park 4 km. Golf 7 km.

Directions
Site is about 1.5 km west of Salou. The entrance is signed about 700 m. west of Camping Sanguli (8480), on the coast road from Salou to Cambrils. Watch for camping signs to Sanguli but note that they are not the normal tent type signs – just the name.

Charges 2003
Per person	€ 4.50
child (4-12 yrs)	free - € 3.00
pitch incl. electricity (10A)	€ 12.00 - € 33.00
with water and waste water	€ 14.00 - € 35.00

All plus 7% VAT. Special offers, and low season discounts for pensioners. Camping Cheques accepted.

Reservations
Contact site. Tel: 977 351 031.
Email: mail@cambrilspark.es

Open
2 April - 12 October.

At a glance
Welcome & Ambience	✓✓✓	Location	✓✓✓✓
Quality of Pitches	✓✓✓	Range of Facilities	✓✓✓✓✓

ES8483 Camping Tamarit Park

N340 km 1172, Tamarit, 43008 Tarragona

This is an attractive, modern site, beautifully situated at the foot of Tamarit castle at one end of a superb one kilometre long beach of fine sand (with direct access). It is only nine km. from Tarragona and 16 km. from Port Aventura. The 710 pitches, 50 of which are virtually on the beach, are marked out on hard sand and grass and some are attractively separated by a variety of Mediterranean shrubs, pines and palm trees. All have electricity (6A) and are 70, 90 or 100 sq.m. in area. Long electricity leads and metal awning pegs may be required in places but wide internal roads give good access for even the largest of units (American motorhomes are accepted). Catering includes a beach-side waiter service restaurant with superb views and the terrace has tables just a few metres from the sea. A vast, attractively designed, lagoon-type swimming pool with bar and sun terrace has recently been added. The site is approached by a long access road, rather narrow but with passing places, reached across a new bridge (6 m.) over the railway line (there is train noise on the site). Tamarit Park is a site with good facilities, albeit on the expensive side. Security is provided but the very low wall which is the site beach boundary must be viewed with caution. This would be a good choice for windsurfing enthusiasts and an active family holiday by the sea.

Facilities
Sanitary blocks (one heated) are modern and tiled, providing good facilities. An unfortunate recent economy feature in the showers is the introduction of push-button controlled hot water with tap controlled cold, leading to a confusing mixture of temperatures. Private bathrooms to rent. Dishwashing with hot water. Laundry facilities incl. washing machines. Motorcaravan services. Gas supplies. Shop, bar/restaurant and takeaway service (all until 15/10). Swimming pool (15/5-15/10). Tennis. Volleyball. Petanque. Minigolf. Table tennis. Children's playground. Animation programme in season. Fishing. Exchange facilities and ATM. Barbecues not permtted on pitches. Off site: Riding 1 km. Bicycle hire 2 km. Golf 8 km.

Directions
From A7 take exit 32 towards Tarragona. At crossroads 'Urb. La Mora' go on towards Atafulla and after just 200 m. turn right to Tamarit. Site entrance is on left after 1 km.

Charges 2003
Per person	€ 4.25
child (1-12 yrs)	€ 3.25
pitch acc. to size and season	€ 15.00 - € 40.00

All plus 7% VAT. Discounts for students, pensioners, large families and longer stays in low season.

Reservations
Contact site. Tel: 977 650 128.
Email: tamaritpark@tamarit.com

Open
1 March - 1 November.

At a glance
Welcome & Ambience	✓✓✓	Location	✓✓✓✓
Quality of Pitches	✓✓✓	Range of Facilities	✓✓✓✓

ES8479 Camping Playa Cambrils – Don Camilo
Ctra. Cambrils - Salou Km 1.5, 43850 Cambrils

Almost completely canopied by trees which provide welcome shade on hot days, this site is 300 metres from the beach across a busy road. It is a mature site which has had some recent renovations (2003). The small (60 sq.m.) pitches are on flat ground, divided by hedges, there are many permanent units and half the site is given up to chalet style accomodation. Large units are placed in an area where the trees are higher. The pool complex includes a functional glassed restaurant and bar with a distinct Spanish flavour reflected in the menu and tapas available all day. The pool is long and narrow with separate children's pool and a large paved area for soaking up the sun. There is entertainment for children and the facilities for the animation team are good. A big building at one end of the site consists of the supermarket, an attended electronic games room and a large play room. As the site is popular with Spanish families, it would be good for pracising your language skills.

Facilities
One modern sanitary building, and one large plus one small refurbished block offer reasonable facilities with British style WCs and free showers in separate buildings. Washing machines, dishwashing (some hot some cold) and laundry sinks (cold only) are at the end of the block under cover. Facilities for disabled campers near the pool. Supermarket (Apr -Sep). Bar and separate restaurant (April-Sept). Playground. Animation in high season. Mini-club. Huge electronic games room. Torches useful. Off site: Bicycle hire 500 m. Fishing and golf 1 km. Riding 1.5 km.

Directions
Leave A7 at exit 37 and head for Cambrils, then the beach. Turn left along beach road. Site is 1 km. east of Cambrils Playa, well signed from Cambrils marina.

Charges 2003
Per pitch	€ 7.00 - € 21.00
adult	€ 2.50 - € 3.90
child (1-10 yrs)	free - € 2.90

Reservations
Write to site. Tel: 977 361 490.
Email: camping@playacambrils.com

Open
15 March - 12 October.

At a glance
Welcome & Ambience	✓✓✓✓	Location	✓✓✓✓
Quality of Pitches	✓✓✓	Range of Facilities	✓✓✓

CAMPING & BUNGALOW PARK
PLAYA CAMBRILS
(DON CAMILO)

E-43850 CAMBRILS (Tarragona)
(Postcode) Ap. Correos 315.
Tel. (34) 977 36 14 90
Fax (34) 977 36 49 88
www.playacambrils.com
camping@playacambrils.com

Access: Autopista A-7, exit 37, driving then towards Cambrils Puerto and Salou along the coast.

Well-shaded family campsite fronting the sea and the beach boulevard along the beach, in privileged surroundings for walking, leisure and sports activities, etc. All pitches with electr. supply. Fully equipped bungalows (also with TV). Modern and complete sanitary installations with free hot water. Bar-Restaurant, superrmarket. Animation activities in July and August. Large adult swimming pool and children's pool. Tennis court, (windsurf, catamaran, kayak,...)
Only 5 km from theme park Port Aventura (direct bus).

Costa Daurada

ES8470 Camping La Siesta
Ctra. Norte 37, 43840 Salou

La Siesta is only 250 m. from a pleasant sandy beach, divided into 470 individual pitches which are large enough and have electricity, with smaller ones for tents. Many pitches are provided with artificial shade, although there is considerable shade from the trees and shrubs. In high season, the siting of units is carried out by the management, who are friendly and helpful. Young campers are located separately to the rear of the site. There is a large, free swimming pool which is elevated above pitch level. The restaurant, which overlooks the pool, has a comprehensive menu, competing well with the town restaurants. There is also a bar with TV and a large terrace, where the entertainment takes place in high season. A suprisingly large supermarket caters for most needs in season.

Facilities
Three bright and clean sanitary blocks provide very reasonable facilities. Motorcaravan services. Supermarket. Various vending machines. Self-service restaurant and bar with cooked dishes to take away. Dancing some evenings till 11 pm. Swimming pool (300 sq.m; open all season). Children's playground. Medical service daily in season. ATM point. Torches may be required. Off site: Huge numbers of shops, restaurants and bars near. Port Adventura close. Bicycle hire 200 m. Fishing 500 m. Riding and golf 6 km.

Directions
Leave A7 at exit 35 for Salou. Site is signed off the Tarragona/Salou road.

Charges 2003
Per person	€ 3.70 - € 6.50
child (4-9 yrs)	€ 3.00 - € 3.70
pitch incl.electricity (10A)	€ 6.20 - € 15.90

All plus 7% VAT. No credit cards.

Reservations
Advised 1 July - 20 Aug. Deposit required.
Tel: 977 380 852. Email: siesta@tinet.fut.es

Open
14 March - 3 November.

At a glance
Welcome & Ambience	✓✓✓	Location	✓✓✓✓
Quality of Pitches	✓✓✓✓	Range of Facilities	✓✓✓✓

ES8482 Camping La Pineda de Salou

Ctra. Costa Tarragona - Salou km 5, 43481 La Pineda

La Pineda is just outside Salou towards Tarragona and this site is just 300 m. from the Aquapark and 2.5 km. from Port Aventura, to which there is an hourly bus service from outside the site entrance. There is some noise from this road. There is a medium sized swimming pool and children's pool, open from mid June, behind large hedges close to the entrance. A large terrace has sun loungers, and various entertainment aimed at young people is provided in season. The 366 flat pitches are mostly shaded and of about 70 sq.m. All have electricity connections. The simple restaurant/bar is shaded and has a large cactus garden to the rear. This is a plain, friendly and convenient site, with reasonable rates, probably best used for visiting the local area, rather than for extended stays. Note: this site is reasonably close to a large industrial centre.

Facilities

Sanitary facilities are mature but clean with baby bath, dishwashing and laundry sinks. Two washing machines in each block. The second building is opened in high season only. Gas supplies. Shop (1/7-31/8). Restaurant and snacks (1/7-31/8). Swimming pools (1/7-31/8). Bar (all season). Five-a-side soccer pitch. Small TV room. Bicycle hire. Games room with videos and drink and snack machines. Playground (3-12 yrs). Entertainment (1/7-30/8). Torches may be required. Off site: Beach 400 m. Fishing 500 m. Golf 12 km.

Directions

From A7 just southwest of Tarragona take exit 35 and follow signs to La Pineda and Port Aventura then campsite signs appear.

Charges 2003

Per person	€ 3.50 - € 5.00
child (1-10 yrs)	€ 2.40 - € 3.70
car	€ 3.30 - € 5.60
tent or caravan	€ 5.00 - € 6.70
motorcaravan	€ 6.90 - € 10.50
electricity (5A)	€ 3.10
dog	€ 1.50 - € 2.50

All plus 7% VAT.

Reservations

Made for high season (min. 7 nights) contact site.
Tel: 977 37 30 80. Email: info@campingpineda.com

Open

All year except 1 Jan. - 22 March.

At a glance

Welcome & Ambience	✓✓✓	Location	✓✓✓✓
Quality of Pitches	✓✓✓	Range of Facilities	✓✓✓✓

Different, natural unforgettable holidays

THE CAMPING SITE AND BUNGALOWS PARK IS OPEN FROM MARCH TO DECEMBER.

▲ The Camping Site is located at the Pineda beach, next to **Universal's-Port Aventura**, only 2.5 Km. away from the parking lot at the entrance, 3 Km. away from the center of Salou and 6 Km. away from the city of **Tarragona** (with its Roman walls, Circus, Amphitheatre, Aqueduct, Forum, Cathedral, museums, local "fiestas", "Castellers", night life, gastronomy, fresh fish).

▲ Booking of camping sites and renting of wooden **bungalows that are fully equipped** (TV, telephone, bed linen and towels) for 2/4 and 4/6 people, by telephone, fax or through the Internet (on-line bookings with a reliable server).

▲ During the off-peak season, our prices are low and we offer special rates for groups and young people.

Information and bookings: CAMPING LA PINEDA DE SALOU
Carretera de la costa Tarragona a Salou, km 5   E-43481 LA PINEDA (Tarragona)-Costa Daurada
Tel. (00-34) 977 37 30 80   Fax (00-34) 977 37 30 81   info@campingpineda.com

ES8530 Playa Montroig Camping & Bungalow Park

Aptdo 3, N-340 Km 1136, 43300 Montroig

What a superb site! Playa Montroig is about 30 km. beyond Tarragona set in its own tropical gardens with direct access to a very long soft sand beach. Bathing, windsurfing, surfboarding two diving rafts, a diving school and many beach sports are available. The main part of the site lies between the sea, road and railway (as at other sites on this stretch of coast, there is some train noise) and there is a huge underpass. The site is divided into spacious, marked pitches with excellent shade provided by a variety of lush vegetation including very impressive palms set in wide avenues. There are 1,950 pitches, all with electricity and 330 with water and drainage connections. Some 48 pitches are directly alongside the beach – they are somewhat expensive and extremely popular. The site has many outstanding features. There is an excellent pool complex near the entrance with two pools (one heated for children). A quality restaurant serves traditional Catalunian fare (seats 150 people) and overlooks an entertainment area where you may watch genuine Flamenco dancing and buffet food is served (catering for 1,000). A large terrace bar dispenses drinks and there is a disco and smaller bar. If you prefer international food there is yet another eating option in a very smart restaurant (seats 500). Above this is the 'Pai-pai' Caribbean cocktail bar with a more intimate atmosphere. Activities for children's are very ambitious (multi-lingual carers). 'La Carpa', a spectacular open air theatre, is an ideal setting for daily keep fit sessions and the professional entertainment provided. For children aged 5-11 yrs there is the 'Tam-Tam Eco Park', a 20,000 sq.m. forest zone, complete with experts who hold talks about the area. You can even camp out for a night (supervised) to study wildlife (a weekly event). Adults are also allowed in separate barbecues and other evening fun. This is an excellent site and there is insufficient space here to describe all the available activities. We recommend it for families with children of all ages and there is much emphasis on providing activities outside the high season.

Facilities

Fifteen sanitary buildings, some small, but of very good quality with toilets and washbasins, others really excellent, air conditioned larger buildings housing large showers, washbasins (many in private cabins) and separate WCs. Facilities for disabled campers and for babies. A 24 hour cleaning service operates. Water points around site (water said to be very pure from the site's own wells). Several launderettes. Motorcaravan services. Good shopping centre with supermarket, greengrocer, butcher, fishmonger, tobacconist and souvenir shops. Restaurants and bars. The 'Eurocentre', with 250 person capacity and equipped for entertainment and activities, large screen videos, films, shows and meetings (air conditioned). Fitness suite. Eco-park (see above). TV lounges (3) incl. satellite. Beach bar. Children's playground. Free kindergarten with multi-lingual staff. Skate-boarding. Jogging track. Sports area for volley-ball, football and basketball. Tennis. Minigolf. Table tennis. Organised activities for children and adults including pottery and gardening classes. Windsurfing and water skiing courses. Surfboards and pedaloes for hire. Boat mooring. Ladies' and men's hairdressers. Bicycle hire. Bureau de change. Safety deposit boxes. Telephone service. Gas supplies. Dogs are not accepted. TVs are not allowed outside your vehicle. Off site: Riding and golf 3 km.

Directions

Site entrance is off main N340 nearly 30 km. southwest from Tarragona. From motorway take Cambrils exit and turn west on N340 at 1136 km marker.

Charges 2003

Per person	€ 3.00 - € 5.00
child (under 10)	€ 2.00 - € 4.00
standard pitch with electricity	€ 21.00 - € 48.00
Premium pitch	€ 24.00 - € 60.00

All plus 7% VAT. Discounts for longer stays and for pensioners.

Reservations

Are possible and made with refundable booking fee (4,000 ptas). Contact Dept. de Reservas, Apdo 3. at site address. Tel: 977 810 637.
Email: info@playamontroig.com

Open

1 March - 31 October.

At a glance

Welcome & Ambience	✓✓✓✓	Location	✓✓✓✓✓
Quality of Pitches	✓✓✓✓✓	Range of Facilities	✓✓✓✓✓

ES8486 Camping Torre de la Mora
CN 340, km. 1171, 43080 Tarragona

Located on a promontory in a pleasant corner of the Costa Daurada with a village like atmosphere, Torre de la Mora takes advantage of its wonderful location, offering some pitches with cracking views over the white sandy beaches and rocky promontories of the coastline. The hinterland is pine forest and there are areas where you can pitch a tent, access electricity points and feel close to nature. The 200 touring pitches vary in just about every way, some are on the lower flat area, including a few with beach frontage, others are on steep terraces around the promontory. Many of the higher pitches around the old coastal defence fort and building have amazing views. It is important to select a pitch related to your level of fitness as the higher pitches and some of the lower terraces require an energetic approach (children should be supervised). We spoke to some campers who enjoyed Torre de la Mora so much they had been happily returning to the site for years. Some areas of the site reflect its age however we are told a program is underway to renovate the sports area, across a small road, which has a pleasant large pool in a garden-like setting.

Facilities
Two large and three small sanitary blocks are mature but the facilities within are clean with a unit for disabled campers. Careful selection of pitch is required for disabled campers or infirm visitors. There is a mixture of washing facilities some of which have hot water, others not and most are dated. Washing machine. Motorcaravan services. Supermarket. Restaurant. Chicken bar (high season). Swimming pool and sports area (to be renovated in 2004). Play area. Table tennis. Electronic games. Animation programme 5 nights a week. Torches useful. Off site: Pretty beach town outside the gate. Fishing. Bicycle hire 1 km. Golf 2 km. Riding 3 km. Boat launching 8 km.

Directions
From A7 Barcelona - Tarragona autopista take exit 32, then N340 towards Tarragona. Turn off for Punta del la Mora and site is well signed approaching the village. The final approach is via some narrow streets so watch for one way signs and there is an unusual entry through a high wire fence alongside road.

Charges 2003
Per unit incl. 1 person	€ 11.00 - € 19.00
extra person	€ 4.00 - € 6.00
child (under 10 yrs)	€ 3.00 - € 4.15
electricity (6A)	€ 3.30
dog	€ 2.50

Reservations
Contact site. Tel: 977 650277.
Email: camtmora@tinet.fut.es

Open
1 March - 31 October.

At a glance
Welcome & Ambience	✓✓✓	Location	✓✓✓✓
Quality of Pitches	✓✓✓✓✓	Range of Facilities	✓✓✓✓

ES8520 Camping Marius
Ctra. N340, km 1137, 43892 Miami-Playa

Quiet, well tended and not too huge, this agreeable site has a family atmosphere and a personal touch. One perimeter is on a good sandy beach with direct access and no roads to cross – you can almost fall out of bed and onto the beach. There is also a large beach bar. The site is divided into 345 individual pitches of adequate size so it does not become too overcrowded. They are quite shady with 300 electrical connections and eight pitches with water and drainage. Dog owners go on one half of the site which is split down the centre by a wall and large storm drain gully (clean). The lively fishing port of Cambrils, where you can buy freshly caught fish, is about seven kilometres It is an excellent watersports venue in high season. The use of TV sets outside your unit and the riding of bicycles on site is not permitted. Some train noise may be expected.

Facilities
Two of the sanitary blocks are dated but clean and a third is of an excellent standard. Free hot water in the showers and half the washbasins, plus 21 private cabins. Facilities for babies and disabled campers. Laundry room. Motorcaravan services. Bar and restaurant (1/6-30/9). Supermarket (15/4-30/9). Souvenir shop. Gas supplies. Children's club and playground. Hairdresser. Fishing. Table tennis. Torches required at night. Off site: Windsurfing, water ski and pedaloes nearby. Riding 4 km. Golf 10 km.

Directions
The site entrance is 28 km. from Tarragona on the Valencia road (N340).

Charges 2003
Per person	€ 5.00 - € 7.00
child (1- 10 yrs)	€ 2.50 - € 3.50
pitch incl. electricity	€ 12.00 - € 16.00
dog	€ 2.50 - € 3.50

Plus 7% VAT. Less 10-20% for longer stays.

Reservations
Contact site. Tel: 977 810 684.
Email: schmid@teleline.es

Open
1 April - 15 October.

At a glance
Welcome & Ambience	✓✓✓	Location	✓✓✓✓
Quality of Pitches	✓✓✓	Range of Facilities	✓✓✓

ES8540 Yelloh! Village La Torre del Sol

Ctra. N340, km 1136, 43300 Mont-Roig Del Camp

A pleasant banana tree-lined approach road gives way to avenues of palms as you arrive at Torre del Sol, a member of the French Airotel chain and the 'Yelloh' group of sites. Sister site to Templo del Sol (8537N), Torre del Sol is a very large site occuping a good position with direct access to the clean, soft sand beach, complete with a beach bar. Strong features here are 800m of clean beach-front and entertainment is provided all season. There is a separate area where the 'Happy Camp' team will take youngsters to camp overnight in the Indian reservation plus they can amuse them two days a week with other activities. The cinema doubles as a theatre to stage shows all season. A complex of three pools, thoughtfully laid out with grass sunbathing areas and palms has a lifeguard. There is good shade on a high proportion of the 1,500 individual, numbered pitches. All have electricity and are mostly of about 70-80 sq.m. There is usually space for odd nights but for good places between 10 July and 16 August it is best to reserve (only taken for a stay of five nights or more). Part of the site is between the railway and the sea so there is train noise. We were impressed with the provision of entertainment – parents could take a break whilst children were in the safe hands of the animation team.

Facilities

Four very well maintained, fully equipped, toilet blocks include units for disabled people and babies, and three blocks comprising private cabins with washbasins and hot showers. Washing machines. Gas supplies. Large supermarket, bakery, and souvenir shops at entrance, open to public. Full restaurant with soft-toy playpen area. Takeaway. Bar with large terrace where entertainment held daily all season. Beach bar. Coffee bar and ice cream bar. Pizzeria. Open roof cinema with permanent seating for 520. Three TV lounges (satellite TV); separate room for films or videos. Well-soundproofed disco. Swimming pools (two heated). Solarium. Sauna. Tennis. Table tennis. Squash. Volleyball. Language school (Spanish). Minigolf. Multi purpose hardcourt. Sub aqua diving from site. Bicycle hire. Fishing. Windsurfing school; sailboards and pedaloes for hire. Playground and crèche. Fridge hire. Library. Hairdresser. Car repair and car wash. No animals permitted. No jet skis accepted. Off site: Beach fishing. Riding 3 km. Golf 4 km.

Directions

Entrance is off main N340 road by 1136 km. marker, about 30 km. from Tarragona towards Valencia. From motorway take Cambrils exit and turn west on N340.

Charges 2003

Per person	€ 3.00 - € 7.25
child (0-7 yrs)	free - € 6.00
child (7-10 yrs)	€ 2.00 - € 6.00
pitch	€ 12.00 - € 22.00

All plus 7% VAT. Discounts in low season for longer stays. Camping Cheques accepted.

Reservations

Made only for Jul/Aug. before 15 June, in sense of guaranteeing admission, with booking fee (€ 18.03). Tel: 977 810 486. Email: info@latorredelsol.com

Open

15 March - 22 October.

At a glance

Welcome & Ambience	✓✓✓✓✓	Location	✓✓✓✓✓
Quality of Pitches	✓✓✓✓✓	Range of Facilities	✓✓✓✓✓

ES8533 Camping Els Prats

Ctra. N340, km 1137, 43892 Miami-Playa

A medium size, beach resort site with 250 pitches, El Prats is situated in a very popular part of the Costa Daurada, not far from Tarragona and the Port Adventura theme park. The pitches are fairly close together, mostly flat and shaded, and a few have access to the pleasant narrow, white sand and shingle beach. Bungalows are in one corner of the site, with an apartment block in another. A feature is the tropical style beach bar on stilts which serves drinks, snacks and ice cream. Attractive tropical plants adorn the site including many banana trees. The small irregularly shaped pool has two cascades which delight children, and a grassy area for sunbathing. A small pool bar serves drinks and ice creams. This is a family run site with the owner, his three sons and daughter in law, all working hard to make your holiday trouble free and give a more personalised service than some of the larger sites in the area. The site is popular with young people some of whom stay in a separate area and learn to windsurf. There is some road and rail noise on the western side of the site.

Facilities

Two blocks, one for each sex, provide clean facilities. Separate unit for disabled campers. Children's bathroom. Washing machines. Motorcaravan services. Supermarket. Restaurant, takeaway and three bars. Swimming pool (3/4-17/10). Play area. Table tennis. Bar billiards. Bicycle hire (organised trips). Windsurfing, canoeing and diving (free try dive Sat am). Medical room. Animation programme and some evening entertainment for adults in high season. Dogs and other animals not accepted 1/7-31/8. Torches useful. Off site: Riding 3 km. Golf 5 km. Cambrils 7 km. Port Adventura 15 km.

Directions

Site is between Miami Playa and Cambrils on the N340. Take exit 37 from the A7 autopista towards Cambrils, then 7 km. southwest of Cambrils at 1137 km. marker, take exit for Torre del Mar. Go under bridge and immediately right; site is 100 m further on.

Charges 2003

Standard pitch incl electricity (5A)	€ 8.50 - € 15.50
per adult	€ 2.80 - € 5.30
child (under 10 yrs.)	€ 2.30 - € 3.60
dog (not accepted 27/6-30//8)	€ 1.90 - € 2.20

Camping Cheques accepted.

Reservations

Contact site. Tel: 977 810 027. Email: info@campingelsprat.com

Open

6 March - 1 November.

At a glance

Welcome & Ambience	✓✓✓✓	Location	✓✓✓✓
Quality of Pitches	✓✓✓✓	Range of Facilities	✓✓✓✓

Cataluña-Catalunya

ES8537N Camping Naturista El Templo del Sol

43890 Hospitalet de L'Infant

El Templo del Sol is a large, luxurious terraced naturist site with a distinctly Arabesque style and superb buildings in Moorish style. The owner has designed the magnificent main turreted building at the entrance with fountains and elaborate Moorish arches. The three large, tiered swimming pools are wonderful with water cascading from one to the other and are part of a supporting complex containing a huge luxurious jacuzzi with cracking views over the sea, a large bar with snacks, a games area, plus a sunbathing area on the roof. Also included is a 'Solar Park' where visitors may learn about how solar energy is used and applied. The main building contains an impressive reception area and has an elegant restaurant with a terrace and an elegant mosaic central, open area with a fountain and a luxury cinema. This grouping of services are said to be among the best in European naturist sites. The site has 435 pitches, mainly rather small (60/70 sq.m), but 85 fully serviced. Pitches are on terraces giving rewarding views over the sea and ready access to the sandy beach. There is some shade. Site lighting is provided from pleasing serpent shaped light assemblies. The site is under French management (the same as ES8540 Torre del Sol) and English is spoken. There is some daytime rail noise especially in the lower areas of the site where the larger pitches are located.

Facilities
The sanitary blocks are amongst the best you will find in Spain providing everything you could require and extensive services for disabled campers. Washing machines. Well stocked supermarket. Health shop. Souvenir shop. Bars. Restaurant and snack bar (1/4-10/10). Swimming pools (20/3-15/10). Jacuzzi. Cinema. Games area. Volley ball. Boule. Separate round children's pool and play area. Miniclub. Doctor available. Library. Safety deposit boxes. Professional entertainment includes genuine Flamenco dancing. Hairdresser. Bicycle hire. ATM. Animals are not accepted. No jet skis. Off site: Fishing 100 m. Golf 2 km. (night time only). Bicycle hire and boat launching 3 km. Riding 7 km. Theme parks.

Directions
From N340 south of Tarragona, exit at km. 1123 towards L'Hopitalet and follow signs.

Charges 2003
Per person	€ 3.00 - € 6.50
child (under 10 yrs)	€ 1.80 - € 5.00
pitch incl. car and electricity	€ 11.00 - € 21.00
tent	€ 2.50 - € 5.00

Plus 7% VAT. Discounts for longer stays.

Reservations
Min. stay July/Aug. 5 nights, otherwise 3 nights. Naturist licence required. Contact site for details. Tel: 977 823 434. Email: info@eltemplodelsol.com

Open
28 March - 13 October.

At a glance
Welcome & Ambience	✓✓✓✓✓	Location	✓✓✓✓✓
Quality of Pitches	✓✓✓✓✓	Range of Facilities	✓✓✓✓✓

ES8536 Camping Caravanning Ametlla Village Platja

Apdo. Correus 240, Paraje Santes Creus, 43860 L'Ametlla de Mar

This site within a protected area is new (2000), has been well thought out and is startling in the quality of service provided, the finish and the materials used in construction. The 373 pitches are on a terraced hillside above colourful coves with shingle beaches and two small associated lagoons (with a protected fish species). The site is environmentally correct: local planning regulations are extremely tight including the types of trees that may be planted. The many bungalows here have been tastefully incorporated. There are great views, particularly from the friendly restaurant (which has a very good chef). Animation is organised for children in high season and there is a well equipped fitness room (free). There are good quality pools (with lifeguard) and a sub-aqua diving school operates on the site in high season and beginners may try a dive. This is a most attractive small site in an idyllic situation near the picturesque fishing village of L'Ametlla de Mar and within the Ebro Delta nature reserve. It is about 20 minutes from Europe's second largest theme park, Port Aventura, but as there is no regular bus service your own transport is required (the owners arrange free buses to the local disco each Wednesday). No transit traffic is allowed within the site in high season. Used by tour operators (30 pitches). This is a very good site for families or for just relaxing. There is some train noise.

Facilities
Three really good toilet blocks provide free hot water throughout, British style WCs, washbasins and some private cabins with WC and washbasin, plus others with WC, basin and shower. The showers are very clean, roomy and have hot water. Motorcaravan services. Gas supplies. Supermarket (1/4-30/9; small shop incl. bread at other times). Good restaurant with snack menu and bar. TV room (1/4-15/10). Swimming pool. Sub aqua diving. Kayaking. Fishing. Children's club and play area. Fitness room. Bicycle hire. Football. Basketball. Volleyball. Entertainment July/Aug. Barbecue area. Bicycle hire. Fishing. English is spoken. Off site: Boat launching 3 km. Golf 15 km. Riding 20 km. Theme parks.

Directions
From A7/E15 (Barcelona - Valencia) take exit 39 for L'Ametlla de Mar. Follow numerous large white signs on reaching village; site is 2.5 km. south of the village.

Charges 2003
Per person	€ 2.06 - € 5.00
child (under 10 yrs)	€ 1.69 - € 4.10
tent or caravan incl. electricity	€ 5.18 - € 8.80
motorcaravan incl. electricity	€ 6.86 - €12.90

All plus 7% VAT. Less for longer stays, especially in low season.

Reservations
Contact site. Tel: 977 267 784. Email: info@campingametlla.com

Open
All year.

At a glance
Welcome & Ambience	✓✓✓✓	Location	✓✓✓✓
Quality of Pitches	✓✓✓✓	Range of Facilities	✓✓✓✓

ES8535 **Camping-Pension Cala d'Oques**
43890 Hospitalet del Infante

This peaceful, and delightful site has been developed with care and dedication by Elisa Roller over 30 years or so. Part of its appeal lies in its situation beside the sea with a wide beach of sand and pebbles, its amazing mountain backdrop and the views across the bay to the town and part by the atmosphere created by Elisa, and staff – friendly, relaxed and comfortable. The restaurant with its homely touches has a super menu and a reputation extending well outside the site (the excellent cook has been there for many years) and the family type entertainment is in total contrast to that provided at the larger, brasher sites of the Costa Daurada. There are 255 pitches, mostly level and laid out beside the beach, with more behind on wide, informal terracing. Odd pine and olive trees are an attractive feature and provide some shade. Electricity is available although long leads may needed in places. Gates provide access to the pleasant beach with useful cold showers to wash the sand away. Torches are needed at night. For those interested, there is a naturist beach of fine sand around the little headland just south of the site. This is a pretty place to stay and Elisa gives a pleasant personal service but do not expect 'Costa' type entertainment. The village itself is well worth exploring.

Facilities
The main toilet facilities are on the front part of the building housing the restaurant, reception and the family home on the first level. Clean and neat, there is hot water to showers (hot water by token but free to campers – a device to guard against unauthorized visitors from the beach). An additional small block with clean toilets and washbasins is at the far end of the site. Restaurant/bar and shop (1/4-30/9). Play area. Five-a-side soccer. Fishing. Internet point. Gas supplies. Torches required in some areas. Off site: Village facilities, incl. shop and restaurant 1.5 km. Bicycle hire and riding 2 km.

At a glance
| Welcome & Ambience | ✓✓✓✓ | Location | ✓✓✓ |
| Quality of Pitches | ✓✓✓✓ | Range of Facilities | ✓✓✓✓ |

Directions
Hospitalet del Infante is south of Tarragona, accessed from the A7 (exit 38) or from the N340. From the north take first exit to Hospitalet del Infante at the 1128 km. marker. Follow signs in the village, site is 2 km. south, by the sea.

Latest charges
Per person	€ 4.50 - € 6.25
tent or caravan	€ 4.50 - € 6.25
car or motorcycle	€ 4.50 - € 6.25
motorcaravan	€ 6.00 - € 12.20
dog	€ 2.25 - € 2.40
electricity	€ 2.95

Discounts for seniors and for longer stays. No credit cards.

Reservations
Contact site. Tel: 977 823 254.
Email: eroller@nil.fut.es

Open
All year.

CAMPSITE INSPECTIONS

Every campsite in this guide has been inspected and selected by one our seasonal campsite inspection teams.

Our teams are required to visit typically between 30 and 50 sites and submit detailed reports on each site visited.

We now have a number of vacancies for campsite Inspectors and would be interested to hear from candidates with a good knowledge of camping and caravanning. A fee is paid for each inspection, as well as travel expenses.

For applications for these posts and further information, please contact:
Rod Wheat
Alan Rogers Guides Ltd, 96 High Street, Tunbridge Wells TN1 1YF
Fax: 01892 51 00 55   Email: contact@alanrogers.com

the travel service

Save Time, Save Money

THE LOW COST PITCH AND FERRY RESERVATION SERVICE FOR READERS OF THE ALAN ROGERS GUIDES

INSPECTED CAMPSITE & SELECTED

We'll book your preferred campsite(s)

Choose from 150 of the finest inspected and selected sites across Europe (look for the Alan Rogers logo alongside the site descriptions in all Guides). We can even book site-owned mobile homes and chalets (ask for our other brochure).

Ask about our incredible Ferry Deals:

- ✓ **Caravans GO FREE**
- ✓ **Motorhomes Priced as Cars**

We'll organise your low cost Channel crossing - call us for a quote or visit www.alanrogersdirect.com

We'll provide comprehensive information

Leave it to the experts and enjoy peace of mind. Our own unique Travel Pack, complete with map and guide book will prove invaluable.

Don't leave it to chance, leave it to us

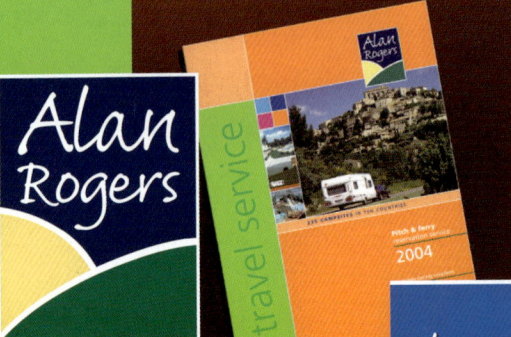

For your FREE colour brochure

0870 405 405

Alan Rogers

alanrogersdirect.com
book on-line and save

Comunidad Valenciana

This Mediterranean region is famous for its magnificent orange groves and beautiful long, sandy beaches. Centuries of Moorish presence have resulted in a profound Hispano-Moorish heritage.

Valenciana is made up of the provinces of Castellon, Valencia and Alicante

The capital of the region is Valencia

La Costa del Azahar (Orange-blossom Coast) stretches from Vinaros to Almanzora, with the great port of Valencia in the middle. Orange groves grow right down to the coast, particularly in the northern section. Good beaches can be found around Benicassim and Peñíscola. South of Valencia, the Costa Blanca derives its name from its 170 miles or so of silvery-white beaches – some of the best beaches are to be found on this coast, especially between Gandía and Benidorm. As a result it is one of the most popular tourist areas in Spain

The capital city of Valencia boasts a great nightlife and plays host to numerous festivals held throughout the year, including the unique fiesta of *Las Fallas de Saint Joseph*, when enormous papier-mache sculptures are set ablaze. Throughout it all are bullfights, music and fireworks. Alicante, the capital of the province of the same name, is dominated by the great Moorish castle of Santa Barbara, which offers marvellous views of the entire city. It also has several beaches in and around the town.

Cuisine of the region

Rice is the dominant ingredient, grown locally in paddy fields; the most famous dish is the *Paella Valenciana*. Soups and stews known locally as *ollas* are popular and seafood is readily available. Tiger nut milk is a soft drink exclusive to this region, usually accompanied by *fartons* (local pastries).

Arnadí: dessert with pumpkin and sweet potato

Arroz al horno: rice, baked with chickpeas

Arroz con costra: meat-based paella topped with baked egg crust

Arroz negro: rice cooked with squid

Bajoques farcides: stuffed peppers

Olla recapte: with potatoes and pork

Turrón: made of nuts and honey, either soft and flaky or hard like nougat

Places of interest

Castellón de la Plana: Santa Maria cathedral

El Puig: monastery, Museum of Print and Graphics (world's smallest book)

La Albufera: vast lagoon, home to 250 species of bird

Morella: medieval fortress town, dinosaur musuem

Oropesa: 16th century Tower of the King

Peñiscola: medieval castle

tip

JOIN IN THE FUN AT THE TOMATO-THROWING FESTIVAL OF BUÑOL (AUG). THE SPECTACULAR *LA TOMATINA* SEES SOME 30,000 PEOPLE HURL 120,000 TONNES OF TOMATOES AT EACH OTHER!

Comunidad Valenciana

ES8558 Camping Vinaros

Ctra. N340 km. 1054, 12500 Vinaros

Taking its name from the seaside town nearby, this uncomplicated site now has 179 numbered pitches of average size on flat ground. Mature trees provide shade and neat hedges separate the pitches, all of which have an individual sink. The site entrance is directly off the N340, with a spacious drive and lots of outside parking, but there is traffic noise. A pleasant small swimming pool has a sunbathing area and a paddling pool (May-Sept). The restaurant is nicely decorated, has a reasonable menu and serves snacks all year. Large blocks of natural stone have been used for decoration in the site and the theme is continued in the spotless sanitary block. Petanque is played and indoor games are available in the bar. This site is ideal as an all year stopover site and normally has several long stay British customers enjoying the peace and good discounts in low season. Nathalie, the chirpy manager speaks good English and has a keen sense of humour. This area reputedly enjoys 300 days of sunshine a year.

Facilities

Exceptionally clean, fully equipped, toilet block with clever use of marble and tiling creating a light crisp environment enhanced by potted shrubs. Some washbasins are in cabins. Washing machines and irons. Motorcaravan services. Camping essentials sold (tent pegs etc) and milk and bread can be ordered. Bar/restaurant (all year). Play area. Swimming pools (1/4-30/10). Petanque. Musical entertainment in season. Large aviary. Fax service. Ice for sale. Off site: Beach 800 m. Bus service outside gate. Rail station close by. Vinaros 500 m. with extensive choice of bars and restaurants. Golf 7 km.

Directions

Take exit 43 (Ulldecona) from the A7. Switch to the N340 and head towards Barcelona. Site is at 1054 km. marker directly off N340.

Latest charges

Per unit, all incl. € 12.40

All plus 7% VAT. Stay over 7 days in low season € 7.20 + 7% VAT.

Reservations

Contact site. Tel: 964 402424.

Open

All year.

At a glance

Welcome & Ambience	✓✓✓✓✓	Location	✓✓✓✓
Quality of Pitches	✓✓✓✓✓	Range of Facilities	✓✓✓✓✓

ES8560 Camping Playa Tropicana

Playa Tropicana, 12579 Alcossebre

Playa Tropicana is the living dream of the owners Vera and Charlie. It has been given a tropical theme with scores of 'Romanesque' white statues around the site including in the sanitary blocks. It has a delightful position away from the main hub of tourism, alongside a good sandy beach which shelves gently into the clean waters. There is a shingle beach for fishing nearby and a pretty promenade in front of the site, with statues. It is in a quiet position and it is a drive rather than a walk to the centre of the village resort. The site has 300 marked pitches separated by lines of flowering bushes under mature trees. Pitches vary in size (50-100 sq.m), most are shaded and there are electricity connections throughout (some need long leads). There are 50 places for motorcaravans with water and drainage and there is a scale of charges for the different pitches. The site has several large water features by the high quality restaurant. aviaries and small monkeys.

Facilities

Two sanitary blocks delightfully decorated, fully equipped and of excellent standard, include 16 washbasins in private cabins. Baby baths, some units with WC, basin and shower, and facilities for disabled people. Washing machine. Motor-caravan services. Gas supplies Large supermarket (all season). Superb restaurant, a little expensive (Easter-late Sept). Drinks served on terrace. Swimming pool (18 x 11 m.) and children's pool. Playground. Volleyball. Table tennis. Bicycle hire. Fishing. Torches necessary in some areas. No TVs allowed in July/Aug. Dogs are not accepted but cats are. Off site: Fishing and watersports on the beach. Riding and boat launching 3 km. Golf 25 km.

Directions

Alcoceber (or Alcossebre) is between Peniscola and Oropesa. Turn off N340 at 1018 km. marker towards Alcossebre on CV142. Just before entering town take right turn signed 'platjes Capicorb'. Follow road for approx. 2.5 km. turning right at beach. Site is on the right.

Charges 2003

Per person	€ 6.35
child (1-10 yrs)	€ 5.00
pitch	€ 25.00 - € 35.40

Electricity and VAT included. Discounts up to 45% out of season. Camping Cheques accepted.

Reservations

Made for min. 10 days with deposit (25%).
Tel: 964 412 463. Email: info@playatropicana.com

Open

15 March - 31 October.

At a glance

Welcome & Ambience	✓✓✓✓✓	Location	✓✓✓✓✓
Quality of Pitches	✓✓✓✓✓	Range of Facilities	✓✓✓✓✓

ES8570 Camping Torre La Sal 2

Cami L'Atall, 12595 Ribera de Cabanes

Torre La Sal 2 is a large site split in two by a fairly busy road, with a reception on each side. There are two pool complexes (one can be covered and heated) which are both on the west side, whilst the beach (shingle and sand) is on the east. Both sides have a restaurant (rather expensive) – the beach restaurant has two air conditioned wooden buildings and a terrace, but no views of the sea. Sports activities are on the western side, as is a children's park and large disco. The pools and the park are locked for certain periods during the day. The 240 flat pitches vary in size, some very large with their own sinks, and most have either shade from trees or very high artificial shading rigged on frames. All have electricity and are on sand, a few being close to the sea, but none with views. There is a plethora of bungalows, mobile homes, chalets and permanent pitches around the two areas. Many activities are organised in high season and the various amenities are scattered around the two locations.

Facilities

Toilet facilities are of a good standard in both sections, four to the west and two to the east, with facilities for disabled campers in both. Baby rooms. Hot water to some sinks. British style toilets. Washing machines. Motorcaravan services. Shop, bars and restaurants (all year). Swimming pools and paddling pools - one heated and covered. Large play area. Games room. Disco. Football. Tennis. Volleyball. Basketball. Petanque. Fronton. Car wash. Security boxes. Medical room. Torches are required. Off site: Village has a range of shops bars and restaurants. Riding 10 km. Golf 20 km.

Directions

From A7/E15 take exit 45 for Oropesa onto the N340. Move north to 1,000 km. marker and take road to the coast and town of Camil'atall. Site is well signed from here.

Charges 2003

Pitch incl. 2 persons and electricity	€ 12.30
extra person	€ 4.80
child (1-9 yrs)	€ 4.30
electricity (10A)	€ 4.30

Reservations

Write to site. Tel: 964 319 744.
Email: camping@torrelasal2.com

Open

All year.

At a glance

Welcome & Ambience	✓✓	Location	✓✓✓
Quality of Pitches	✓✓✓	Range of Facilities	✓✓✓✓

ES8580 Camping Bonterra

Avenida de Barcelona 47, 12560 Benicasim

If you are looking for a town site which is not too crowded and has good facilities this one may be for you, as there are few quality sites in the local area and this is open all year. It is a 300 metres walk to a good, shady beach, and parking is not too difficult. Good beach for scuba diving or snorkelling; hire facilities are available at Benicasim. The site has 375 pitches (70-90 sq.m), all with electricity, and a variety of bungalows on site. Bonterra has a clean and neat appearance with reddish soil, palms, grass and a number of trees which give good shade. There is a little road and rail noise. A well run, Mediterranean style site useful for visiting local attractions.

Facilities

Four attractive, well maintained sanitary blocks sensibly laid out, providing some private cabins, washbasins with hot water, others with cold. Showers have solar heating and include baby showers. Facilities for disabled campers. Laundry and motorcaravan services. Restaurant/bar. Shop (all year). Swimming pool, covered pool and children's pool. Playground (some concrete bases). Tennis. Multi-sport court. Table tennis. Disco. Bicycle hire. Off site: Town facilities. Fishing 500 m. Riding 3 km. Boat launching 5 km. Golf 10 km.

Directions

Site is east of Benicasim village, with entrance off the old main N340 road running a little back from the coast. Coming from the north, turn left at sign 'Benicasim por la costa'. On the A7 from the north use exit 45, from the south exit 46.

Charges 2003

Per adult	€ 2.03 - € 4.31
child (3-9 yrs)	€ 1.87 - € 3.95
pitch acc. to type and season	€ 7.50 - € 22.28
electricity	€ 3.13 - € 5.00

All plus 7% VAT. Less in low season and special long stay rates excl. July/Aug.

Reservations

Made if you write at least a month in advance.
Tel: 964 300 007. Email: info@campingbonterra.com

Open

All year.

At a glance

Welcome & Ambience	✓✓✓✓✓	Location	✓✓✓✓✓
Quality of Pitches	✓✓✓✓	Range of Facilities	✓✓✓✓

Comunidad Valenciana

Comunidad Valenciana

ES8612 Euro Camping
Playa de Oliva, 46780 Oliva

This English owned site is located beside the Playa de Oliva's golden sands. To reach it, you travel through the famous Valencia orange orchards. However be warned the final approach road to the site is very narrow and large units will find it necessary to drive through over-hanging foliage. The rectangular site has tarmac and gravel roads. The gravel pitches are on the small side but are well maintained and eucalyptus trees provide shade for many. The mature sanitary blocks are well maintained, although you will need to take a torch as the lighting is on a push-button timer and inevitably one is plunged into darkness which can be alarming (particularly in the disabled campers bathroom). The reception staff are helpful, speak excellent English and maintain a book swap library. A well stocked supermarket is on site and the restaurant complex looks over the sand dunes leading to the beach. Here you can enjoy food from the excellent menu including some delicious local delicacies and a good selection of regional wines. The bar and terrace area alongside the restaurant is a popular spot early in the evening to enjoy a drink with the sound of the waves in the background. Later in the evening entertainment is provided for adults while the children play happily on the adventure equipment nearby.

Facilities
Two mature sanitary blocks (and a third under construction) are well maintained. British style WCs, preset hot water in showers. Push-button lighting in sanitary blocks. Toilet facilities for disabled campers. Washing machines and dryer. Motorcaravan services. Well stocked supermarket. Restaurant/bar. Play area. Volleyball. Pentanque. Animation in high season. Refrigerator hire. Electronic games. Torches essential inside all sanitary blocks.

At a glance
Welcome & Ambience	✓✓✓✓	Location	✓✓✓
Quality of Pitches	✓✓✓✓	Range of Facilities	✓✓✓

Directions
From Alicante - Valencia autopista A7 take exit 61 onto N332 to Oliva. Exit at km. 213 or 210 and follow campsite signs.

Charges 2003
Per adult	€ 3.72
child (2-10 yrs)	€ 2.91
pitch	€ 10.39 - € 15.92
electricity	€ 2.56 - € 3.58
dog	€ 1.35

Camping Cheques accepted.

Reservations
Contact site. Tel: 962 854 098.
Email: eurocamping@interbook.net

Open
All year.

ES8625 Kiko Park Rural
46317 Villargordo del Cabriel

Approaching Kiko Park Rural, you will see a small hilltop village appearing within a landscape of mountains, vines and a jewel-like lake. Kiko was a small village and farm and the village now forms the campsite and its accomodation. Amenities are contained within architectually authentic buildings, some old and some new. Kiko Rural is run by four cousins from a family with 30 years of camping experience – a passionate and enthusiastic team with a vision of excellence. The 103 pitches (with 6A electricity) all have stunning views. Hundreds of trees planted in 2003 are yet to provide shade due to their size, although this will soon remedy itself. Generous hedge plantings have been made which already afford some privacy. There are swimming pools for adults and children, again with superb views. The restaurant serves delicious food. Kiko Rural is an ideal site for those folk, young and old, who enjoy adventurous activites, communing with nature, or relaxing with an occasional sightseeing excursion. A sister site to Kiko Park in Oliva Valencia (ES8615) Kiko Rural is like no other campsite. Old and new have combined to create an environment that is, within its catergory, outstanding.

Facilities
Three new sanitary blocks are very well equipped, including hot water throughout, preset showers and excellent facilities for disabled people. Gas supplies. Motorcaravan services. Excellent restaurant. Well stocked shop with reasonable prices. Pleasant bar with TV. Swimming pool and paddling pool. Very good playground. Bicycle hire. Many adventurous activities can be undertaken here, including white water rafting, gorging, orienteering, trekking, bungee and riding. Special programmes organised on application. Large families and groups catered for. Animation for children and adults in high season. Off site: All the arranged activities. Fishing, boating, canoeing and windsurfing on the lake. Boat launching. Village 3 km. with usual facilites. Tours to 'bodegas'. Tours to Valencia.

At a glance
Welcome & Ambience	✓✓✓✓✓	Location	✓✓✓✓✓
Quality of Pitches	✓✓✓✓	Range of Facilities	✓✓✓✓

Directions
From autopista A7/E15 on Valencia ring road (near the airport) take N111 to the west. Villagordo del Cabriel is about 18 km. towards Motilla. Take the village exit and follow the signs which lead through the village and over a hill - spot the village on a hill just 2 km. away. That village is the campsite!

Charges 2003
Per pitch	€ 5.00 - € 10.00
person	€ 3.60
child (up to 10 yrs)	€ 2.80

Camping Cheques accepted.

Reservations
Contact site. Email: kikoparkrural@kikopark.com

Open
All year.

ES8615 Kiko Park

Address 46780 Oliva

Kiko Park is a smart site nestled behind protective sand dunes, alongside a blue flag beach. There are sets of attractively tiled steps over the dunes or a long boardwalk near the beach bar (good for prams and wheelchairs) to take you to the fine white sandy beach and the sea. There is an award-winning restaurant with architecture that reminds one of a ship near the tropical style beach-bar, both overlooking the marina, beautiful beach and sea. The 200 large pitches all have electricity and the aim is to progressively upgrade all these to serviced 'super' pitches. There are plenty of flowers, hedging and trees adding shade, privacy and colour. This is an excellent site for watersport enthusiasts, as it is beside a marina for boat launching. A wide variety of entertainment is provided all year. The children's club area has a mini zoo, with lots of healthy looking animals (the 'burro' is popular, as are rabbits and the very strange Chinese duck that dances rather than walks). Spanish lessons are taught along with dance class and aerobics during the winter. The site is run by the second generation of a family involved in camping for 30 years and their experience shows. They are brilliantly supported by a friendly, efficient team who speak many languages. The narrow roads leading to the site can be a little challenging for very large units but it is worth the effort.

Facilities

Four modern sanitary blocks are very clean and fully tiled with free hot water, large showers, washbasins (a few in cabins), British style WCs and excellent facilities for disabled visitors (who will find a large part of this site flat and convenient). Laundry facilities. Motorcaravan services. Gas supplies. Restaurant. Bar with TV. Beach-side bar and restaurant (all year). Supermarket (all year, excl. Sundays). Playground. Watersports facilities. Diving school in high season (from mid-June). Mini club. Entertainment for children from mid-June. Petanque. Bicycle hire. Beach volleyball. Exchange facilities. Off site: The yacht club also offers its facilities of swimming pool, bar, restaurant and TV room to campers at Kiko. The footpath to the marina leads into the town – about a 10 minute walk. Indoor pool 1 km. Golf 5 km. Riding 7 km.

Directions

From A7 north of Benidorm take exit 61 to the town and then the beach; site is at the northwest end.

Charges 2003

Per person	€ 5.20
child (under 10 yrs)	€ 4.20
pitch acc. to services and season	€ 8.90 - € 24.80
dog	€ 2.10
electricity (16A)	€ 2.10

Reservations

Write to site. Tel: 962 850 905.
Email: kikopark@kikopark.com

Open

All year.

At a glance

Welcome & Ambience	✓✓✓✓✓	Location	✓✓✓✓✓
Quality of Pitches	✓✓✓✓	Range of Facilities	✓✓✓✓

Comunidad Valenciana

Comunidad Valenciana

ES8675 Camping Vall de Laguar
C/Sant Antonio 24, La Vall de Laguar, 03791 Campell

Near the pretty mountain-top village of Campell, this new campsite is perched high on the side of a mountain with breathtaking views of hilltop villages, the surrounding hills and distant sea. The pitches, pool, terrace and restaurant all share the views. Enrique and Consuello and their children Nico and Neus efficiently run this charming country site. Consuello cooks the most wonderful food and Nico is a font of information about the local area. A good time to be here is at the end of October when campers join in the festivities in the local village after the 'walk with history' when over a thousand people dine on paella. The 68 average size gravel pitches are on terraces and all have electricity and water. Trees and hedges have been planted but are yet to reach their potential. This is a great site to get away from the coastal hustle, bustle and high rise of the beaches. The restaurant has a pretty terrace and the pool is served by a small pool bar. There is a tight steep turn at the entrance although there is room to manoeuvre. This is a new site showing great promise for the future.

Facilities
Two new sanitary blocks have excellent clean facilities including some for disabled campers. Washing machines and dryers. Shop. Restaurant. Bar and pool bar. Swimming pool. Small entertainment programme in high season. Barbecue area with sinks. Torches useful. Off site: Attractive town close by. Donkey excursions 1 km. Beach and golf each 18 km.

At a glance
Welcome & Ambience	✓✓✓✓	Location	✓✓✓✓
Quality of Pitches	✓✓✓✓	Range of Facilities	✓✓✓

Directions
Site is about 20 km. west of Xabia/Javea. From A7/E15 take exit 62 and head to Beniarbeig on minor road. From there go to Sanet, Benidoleig and finally Vall de Laguar. Site is well signed from the town and sits above it. There are some winding and narrow sections on the way.

Charges 2003
Per unit	€ 8.42 - € 12.02
person	€ 3.61 - € 3.61
child (over 3 yrs)	€ 3.00
electricity	€ 2.00

Minimun charge Easter week and July-Aug € 19.23.

Reservations
Contact site. Email: info@campinglaguar.com

Open
All year.

ES8680 Camping Armanello
Av de la Communidad Valenciana, 03500 Benidorm

This small, uncomplicated site is in a slightly scruffy area one kilometre back from the eastern Benidorm beach (the one on the other side of the town is less crowded), Armanello is quietly situated just far enough away from the main coast road to avoid excessive noise. It is a plain and mature site, with small pitches (60 sq.m.) marked out in bays of ten or twelve in former citrus and olive groves. There is a small and much-used swimming pool. About 103 units are taken on flat ground with elecricity available throughout. The site is popular with long stay units in winter. The approach road from the main N332 is narrow and bumpy. The facilities here are rather basic and we see this as a site for transit stops and short stays, rather than as a holiday site, but the rates are very good.

Facilities
Two heated toilet blocks (arranged back to back) have washing and shower facilities with hot and cold water, British style toilets and some washbasins in cabins. Hot water for laundry and dishwashing. Facilities near reception include a washroom, shower and WC for disabled people. Washing machines and dryer. Gas supplies. Motorcaravan services. Well stocked shop (all year). Bar. Restaurant (high season). Swimming pool. Aviary. Off site: Fishing, bicycle hire or riding within 1.5 km. Golf 10 km.

At a glance
Welcome & Ambience	✓✓✓	Location	✓✓✓
Quality of Pitches	✓✓✓	Range of Facilities	✓✓✓

Directions
From new bypass (N332) take Levante Beach road into Benidorm; watch for site signs after 1 km. directly off this road. From autopista junction 65 take Benidorm exit and at second traffic lights turn left. Site approach road is 1 km. on right. As you leave the site turn right not left for the main road as the road becomes impossibly rough and narrow.

Latest charges
Per adult	€ 4.81
child	€ 4.21
pitch	€ 15.03
car	€ 4.81
tent	€ 4.81
electricity (16A)	€ 2.70

Plus 7% VAT. Reductions in low season, plus special winter prices.

Reservations
Contact site for details (it also has much winter trade when reservation is advisable). Tel: 965 853 190. Email: arenablanca@ctv.es

Open
All year.

ES8681 Camping Villasol

Avda. Bernat de Sarria, 03500 Benidorm

Benidorm is increasingly popular for winter stays and Villasol is a genuinely excellent, purpose built modern site. There is a small indoor pool, heated for winter use and a very attractive, large outdoor pool complex (summer only) featuring a lovely, sheltered free-form pool in a beautifully landscaped, grassy sunbathing area where palm trees and Mediterranean shrubs and flowers create a colourful and exotic atmosphere. The pool is overlooked by the bar/restaurant and restaurant terrace. Many of the 314 well separated pitches are on wide terraces which afford views of the mountains surrounding Benidorm. All pitches (80-85 sqm) have electricity and satellite TV connections, with 160 with full services for seasonal use. Shade is mainly artificial as yet. The town and Levante beach are within easy walking distance (1.3 km) leaving your car on site. If you are looking for first class amenities in Benidorm, in pleasant and fairly quiet surroundings, this site would make an excellent choice. Reservation is advised even in winter. We hear that part of the site may be lost to a road widening scheme, but the owner is developing a new site elsewhere. We are following its progress.

Facilities
Modern, well fitted sanitary blocks provide free, controllable hot water to showers and washbasins and British WCs. Good facilities for disabled campers. Laundry facilities. Good value restaurant. Bar. Shop. Swimming pools, outdoor and indoor. Playground. Evening entertainment programme. Dogs are not accepted. Off site: Fishing and bicycle hire 1.3 km. Golf 8 km.

Directions
From the autopista take Benidorm exit (no. 65) and turn left at the second set of traffic lights. After 1 km. at another set of lights turn right, then right again at next lights. Site is on right in 400 m. From northern end of N332 bypass follow signs for Benidorm Playa Levante. In 500 m. at traffic lights turn left, then right at next lights. Site is on right after 400 m.

At a glance
Welcome & Ambience	✓✓✓✓	Location	✓✓✓
Quality of Pitches	✓✓✓✓	Range of Facilities	✓✓✓✓

Latest charges
Per person	€ 4.17 - € 5.64
child (1-9 yrs)	€ 3.24 - € 4.17
pitch	€ 8.53 - € 15.26
electricity	€ 3.24

All plus 7% VAT. Good discounts for longer stays in winter.

Reservations
Only accepted for 3 month min. stay, starting 1 Oct. Write to site. Tel: 965 850 422.
Email: camping-villasol@dragonet.es

Open
All year.

ES8682 Camping Villamar

Carre Del Albir, 03503 Benidorm

A new all year site with all the amenities a camper could desire, Villamar is a superb site, operating to high standards and rules. The central Lake style pools and amenities complex with its extensive grassed areas, dotted with palms, is cleverly designed and very smart. Sit on the terraces looking over the tropical scenery as you enjoy an English breakfast or diner later in the day, and you will find it difficult to remember the teeming town of Benidorm is close by. The 650 pitches are occupied by a myriad of foreign guests and we are told the owners intend to create a small camping area planned for 2004. The pitches are very big, flat, with some shade from young trees. The entertainment programme and indeed the whole site is aimed at a mature population though there are few things for children to do. The sports area has many courts for boules and other sedate activities such as darts, centred in the restaurant area. The restaurant is attractively decorated and has lounges and terraces for relaxation along with internet terminals and electronic games. All round this is a great site. There are no tour operator pitches.

Facilities
The four new sanitary blocks include open style washbasins (some partitioned), free controllable hot showers, baby areas and units for disabled campers. Dishwashing and separate laundry sinks outside each block. Well stocked shop with reasonable prices. Restaurant. Snack bar. Motorcaravan services. Car wash. Two outdoor swimming pools (one heated for the winter guests), one indoor pool (lifeguards in high season). Small play area. TV room, games room and leisure area. Boules. ATM. Internet point. Adult animation programme in the reataurant area. Dogs are not accepted. Off site: Resort town and beach close with usual attractions. Golf, riding, bicycle hire and boat launching 2 Km. Excursions.

Directions
Site is North East of Benidorm at Platja de L'abril. From the A7, A19 or N11 take the exit for Benidorm (Platja de L'Abril). Once at the end of the exit road from the autoroute look for the very obvious camping signs.

Charges 2003
Per person	€ 4.50 - € 6.90
child ((1-3 yrs)	€ 3.50 - € 4.30
pitch	€ 9.20 - € 16.00
electricity	€ 3.50

Reservations
Contact site. Tel: 96 681 1255.
Email: camping@campingvillamar.com

Open
All year.

At a glance
Welcome & Ambience	✓✓✓✓✓	Location	✓✓✓✓
Quality of Pitches	✓✓✓✓✓	Range of Facilities	✓✓✓✓

Comunidad Valenciana

Comunidad Valenciana

ES8683 Camping Benisol

Avda. de la Comunidad Valenciana s/n, 03500 Benidorm

Camping Benisol is a well developed and peaceful site with lush, green vegetation and a mountain background. Mature hedges and trees afford privacy to each pitch and some artficial shade is provided where necessary. There is an excellent restaurant serving traditional spanish food at great prices, with a pretty, shaded terrace overlooking the pool with palms and a thatched pool bar. The 298 pitches of which around 115 are for touring units (60-80 sq.m), all have electrical hook-ups and 75 have drainage. All the connecting roads are now surfaced with tarmac and the large internationally themed minigolf area is very popular with children. Amenities include a good-sized, pleasant swimming pool which is open late (22.00 in summer), with tall palms, a tropical ambience, cascades and small water slides. The pool has a pleasant sunbathing area. Some day-time road noise should be expected.

Facilities

Modern sanitary facilities with free hot water in the showers, heated in winter and kept very clean, have free, solar heated hot water to the washbasins, showers and sinks for laundry and dishwashing. Laundry facilities and clothes lines. Car wash. Gas supplies. Restaurant with terrace and bar (all year, closed 1 day a week). Shop. Swimming pool (Easter - Nov). Sports ground. Small, old-style play area. Minigolf. Table tennis. Jogging track. Tennis. Golf driving range. Doctor's room. ATM. Car wash. Off site: Riding 1 km. Bicycle hire and fishing (sea) 3 km. Golf 14 km. Bus route.

Directions

Site is northeast of Benidorm. Exit N332 at 152 km. marker and take turn signed Playa Levant. Site is 100 m. on left off the main road, well signed.

Charges 2003

Per pitch	€ 11.45 - € 15.65
person	€ 4.20 - € 4.50
child (1-10 yrs)	€ 3.60 - € 3.90
electricity (4/6A)	€ 2.40

All plus 7% VAT. Less 15-60% in low seasons. No credit cards.

Reservations

Contact site. Tel: 965 851 673.

Open

All year.

At a glance

Welcome & Ambience	✓✓✓	Location	✓✓✓✓
Quality of Pitches	✓✓✓✓	Range of Facilities	✓✓✓✓

ES8685 Camping Caravaning El Raco

AddressAvda. Doctor Severo Ochoa, s/n, 03500 Benidorm

This purpose built site with excellent facilities and very competitive prices provides 780 pitches (180 for touring units). There is wide access from the Runcon de Loix road. The site is quietly situated 1.5 km. from the town, Levante beach and promenade. The road has both footpaths and a cycle track. There are wide tarmac roads and pitches of 80 sq.m. or more, separated by low, clipped cypress hedging, which provide some shade. Free satellite TV connections are provided to each pitch and there are 94 with all services with electricity available. The whole site is on a slight downward slope away from the entrance and affords excellent views of the rugged mountains in the hinterland, although this open aspect could be a disadvantage in windy weather. The restaurant, bar and elegant outdoor and indoor pools are all at the entrance, some distance from the touring pitches. There are large numbers of permanent pitches and many seasonal pitches are occupied by wintering campers (lots of British) and the site has a mature, cheerful atmosphere. This is a clean, tidy and good quality site.

Facilities

Three large toilet blocks are well equipped. Facilities for disabled people. Dishwashing sinks. Laundry facilities. Gas supplies. Motorcaravan services. Restaurant. Bar. Well stocked shop with reasonable prices. Busy bar with TV also open to public and good value restaurant. Outdoor swimming pool, no slides or diving board (1/4-31/10). Indoor heated pool (1/11-31/3). Playground. ATM. Off site: Beach 1 km. Bicycle hire 2 km. Golf 6 km. Theme parks.

Directions

From autopista take Benidorm exit (no. 65) and turn left at the second set of traffic lights. After 1 km. at another set of lights turn right, then straight on at next lights for 300 m. to site on right. From northern end of N332 bypass follow signs for Benidorm Playa Levante. In 500 m. at traffic lights turn left, then straight on at next lights for 300 m. to site on right.

Charges 2003

Per person	€ 4.30 - € 4.51
child (1-9 yrs)	€ 3.10 - € 3.31
tent	€ 4.66 - € 4.96
caravan	€ 5.41 - € 5.86
car	€ 4.06 - € 4.96
motorcaravan	€ 4.12 - € 9.02
motorcycle	€ 3.61 - € 3.91
electricity (10A)	€ 2.71 - € 2.86

Discounts for longer stays. VAT included. No credit cards.

Reservations

Not accepted. Tel: 96 586 8552.
Email: campingraco@inicia.es

Open

All year.

At a glance

Welcome & Ambience	✓✓✓✓	Location	✓✓✓✓
Quality of Pitches	✓✓✓✓	Range of Facilities	✓✓✓✓✓

www.alanrogers.com for latest campsite news

ES8686 Excalibur Medieval Camping

Camino Viejo del Albir s/n, 03580 Alfaz del Pi

This is a site you could either love or loathe. Unlike other campsites, it has a theme of medieval times. An American theme park approach has been attempted here and we saw lots of families enjoying themselves. However, we also saw that there was a constant struggle to keep up with the high maintenance a site with as many guests as this demands. There are 386 level pitches with bitumen access roads and gravel surfaces and some shade; 128 of these are for tourers. In addition, there are also 150 chalets to rent. The large pseudo-medieval dining room has a self-service menu, as has the breakfast room. Meals can be included in the daily rate here and many visitors take an inclusive package. At peak times amenities appear to be stressed. However, some campers may find the circus-like chaos, the medieval dinner and show with its knights in shining armour on horseback, the giant Excaliburlooming above the pool area with its large playground, sauna, gym and underground indoor pool, enough compensation. This is a site where close attention needs to be paid to children's welfare as the unfenced pools and giant play areas are side by side – there are slippery areas and steps without rails all in the same area.

Facilities
Four matching sanitary blocks are showing signs of heavy usage and the breakages within are extensive; this extends to the facilities for disabled campers. Washing machines. Motorcaravan services. Large multiple pool complex with jacuzzis. Sauna. Roman style indoor pool below main pool complex. Snack bar. Self service restaurants. Basic shop with souvenirs. Football. Boules. Basketball. Huge outdoor play areas. Inside play area with American style games (everything is free). Table tennis. Electronic games. Bicycle hire for children. ATM. Internet terminal. Security boxes. Torches useful. Off site: Resort town and beach near with usual attractions. Riding 100 m. Bicycle hire 1 km. Fishing 3 km. Golf 20 km. Excursions.

Directions
Site is northwest of Benidorm in Playa de L'Albir. From A7/E15 or N332 roads from the north leave at first exit for Benidorm. At end of the exit road there are numerous signs for Excalibur.

Charges 2004
Per person	€ 4.65 - € 6.10
child (1-9 yrs)	€ 3.60 - € 4.50
pitch	€ 9.50 - € 17.00
electricity	€ 3.13

Reservations
Contact site. Tel: 966 866 928.
Email: c-m@camping.medieval.com

Open
All year.

At a glance
Welcome & Ambience	✓✓✓	Location	✓✓✓
Quality of Pitches	✓✓✓✓	Range of Facilities	✓✓✓

ES8687 Camping Cap Blanch

Playa Cap Blanch, 03590 Altea

This well run site in a coastal location, is open all year and very popular for winter stays. It is alongside the beach road and has direct access to the pebble beach and is within a few hundred yards of all Albir's shops and restaurants. Campers can join in a host of activities organised by the site, from tennis and walking to painting and Spanish lessons. The site tends to be full in winter and is very popular with several nationalities, especially the Dutch. For winter stays, it would pay to get there before Christmas as January and February are the peak months. Although it is on the coast, the site is well sheltered and something of a sun-trap, the 250 pitches on flat, hard gravel are of a good size and well maintained with electricity.

Facilities
The refurbished sanitary block can be heated and provides good facilities including some washbasins in private cabins, baby facilities and a room (locked) with facilities for disabled visitors. Motorcaravan services. Gas supplies. Laundry. Bar and restaurant. Playground. Tennis. Boules. Fitness centre. Organised entertainment and courses. ATM.
Off site: Restaurants, shops and commercial centre close.

Directions
Site is on Albir - Altea coast road and can be reached from either end. From N332, north or south, watch for sign Playa del Albir and proceed through Albir until you reach the coast road. Site is on north side of Albir, well signed.

Charges 2003
Per person	€ 5.50
child (3-12 yrs)	€ 4.50
caravan	€ 6.50
tent	€ 5.50
car	€ 5.50
motorcaravan	€ 8.50
electricity (5A)	€ 4.50

VAT included. Less 10-35% for low season stays 7-30 days, special rates for long stays.

Reservations
Contact site. Tel: 965 845 946.
Email: capblanch@ctv.es

Open
All year.

At a glance
Welcome & Ambience	✓✓✓	Location	✓✓✓✓
Quality of Pitches	✓✓✓	Range of Facilities	✓✓✓✓

Comunidad Valenciana

Comunidad Valenciana

ES8689 Camping Playa del Torres

Partida Torres Norte 11, Apdo. Correus 243, 03570 Villajoyosa

Jacinto and Mercedes have a pretty beachside site with the lower part set under eucalyptus trees. Reception is placed in one of the site's tasteful wooden buildings close to the beach (excellent English is spoken). The 85 lower pitches, some large, are on flat ground with shade. Ten good pitches are right alongside the beach fence (book early). All have electricity, some are fully serviced and there are ample water fountains around the site along with efficient, modern lighting. The upper levels of the site have chalets and mobile homes. A modest sized pool with a sunbathing area is set in the centre part of the site between the building housing the bar, cafeteria and shop and the separate clean toilets block (a short walk from the beachside pitches). Boats can be launched from the sand and shingle beach, sub-aqua diving and other watersports can be organised. If you prefer small sites away from the 'high rise' and bustle of Benidorm which is of high quality, this could be for you.

Facilities

The sanitary building is of a high specification, as are the fittings within, including excellent showers. Laundry. Bar. Cafeteria. Shop. Swimming pool. Children's play area. Petanque. Fishing. Barbecues. Freezer. Fridge hire. Reception will assist with all tourist activities. Off site: Riding 100 m. Golf 18 km. Serious or recreational walking and climbing is possible about 20 minutes away from the site. Benidorm is very close.

At a glance

Welcome & Ambience	✓✓✓✓	Location	✓✓✓✓✓
Quality of Pitches	✓✓✓✓	Range of Facilities	✓✓✓

Directions

From Villajoyosa on N332, 1 km. after town, 300 m. past traffic lights, sign on right, follow road 800 m. to site. From Benidorm after 3 km. site on left, but left turn prohibited. Proceed 400 m. to traffic lights, circle onto other carriageway, then as above. From autoroute leave at Benidorm or Villajoyosa onto N332, then as above. Do not confuse with two older sites (Hercules and Sartorium) which are adjacent sites.

Charges 2003

Per person	€ 3.44 - € 3.82
child (4-13 yrs)	€ 2.57 - € 2.85
pitch	€ 3.22 - € 7.15
caravan	€ 3.57 - € 3.97
car	€ 3.44 - € 3.83
motorcaravan	€ 6.44 - € 7.15
electricity (16A; plus meter)	€ 3.31

Plus 7% VAT. Less 5-50% for low season stays of 7 days or more.

Reservations

Contact site. Tel: 966 810 031. Email: capto@ctv.es

Open

All year.

ES8741 Camping Florantilles

03193 San Miguel de Salinas

Florantilles is an unassuming site, some four kilometres. behind the coast, with some views over the top of the neighbouring citrus groves to a distant salt lake. It is open all year and in winter and spring the delicious scent of orange blossom fills the air. Mimosa trees provide shade for the 271 good-sized pitches (around 90 sq.m.) which are laid out on wide terraces; some very large pitches are available at extra cost. Electricity connections are provided for each pitch, together with water and a raised drain. There are many long stay customers including lots of British visitors. The entrance has a large parking area with car wash facilities, with the entrance to the camping area fitted with a barrier. Amenities include a good sized pool and a children's pool. There is a restaurant with a standard tourist menu. Some light entertainment may be organized in season. Many watersports are possible in the nearby noisy beach resort of Torrevieja and walking clubs are popular, plus bird watching, cycling and golf (discounts available). There is noise from the new motorway on the north side of the site. We see this as a transit site or for short visits to explore the area, rather than for family holidays.

Facilities

Two main toilet blocks provide controllable hot showers. Several smaller blocks dotted around the site have toilets and showers but no hot water. All of these facilities were showing signs of wear and tear. Laundry facilities. Bar (all year). Restaurant (summer only). Shop (limited hours in low seasons). Swimming pool (supervised in peak season, closed in winter). Tennis. Boules. Playground. Only 20 dogs are accepted on the site so a call is advised to ascertain acceptability. Torches required in some areas. Off site: Golf 4 km. Fishing, bicycle hire 5 km. Major resort entertainment in Torrevieja.

At a glance

Welcome & Ambience	✓✓✓	Location	✓✓✓✓
Quality of Pitches	✓✓✓✓	Range of Facilities	✓✓✓✓

Directions

Leave A7 Valencia - Alicante autopista at Crevillente exit 724 on to recently upgraded and renumbered A37 Alicante - Cartegena autopista. The exit for the camping is immediately after the first toll, exit 758 for Torrevieja (Sur). A the roundabout turn right (site is now signed), at 300 m. turn first right. Site is on left.

Latest charges

Per unit	€ 9.02
adult	€ 3.61
child (1-12 yrs)	€ 3.01
electricity	€ 2.70

All plus 7% VAT. Special low season discounts.

Reservations

Contact site. Tel: 965 720 458.

Open

All year.

ES8742 Camping Internacional La Marina
Ctra. N332 km. 76, 03194 La Marina

Efficiently run by a friendly Belgian family, La Marina has 370 pitches of seven different types and size of pitch ranging from about 50 sq.m. for tents to 100 sq.m. with electricity, TV, water and drainage. Artificial shade is provided and the pitches are extremely well maintained on level, well drained ground with a special area allocated for tents in a small orchard. The Lagoon swimming pool complex is absolutely fabulous and has something for everyone (with lifeguards). The quality restaurant and bustling terraces overlook the Lagoon making for a most relaxing meal. A fine fitness centre and covered, heated pool (14 x 7 m) is close by. A pedestrian gate is at the rear of the site to give access to the long sandy beach through the coastal pine forest that is a feature of the area. You can be assured of quality at La Marina and thus we recommend it very highly whatever type of holidaying camper you may be.

Comunidad Valenciana

Facilities
The elegant sanitary blocks offer the very best of modern facilities. Heated in winter, they include private cabins and facilities for disabled visitors. These facilities are amongst the best we have seen on the Mediterranean coast. Laundry facilities incl. irons. Modern motorcaravan services. Gas supplies. Supermarket. Bar/restaurant serving traditional Spanish dishes (all year). Swimming pools (1/4-15/10). Indoor pool. Fitness centre with massage. Sauna. Extensive activity and entertainment programme. Tennis. Table tennis. Huge playground. Hairdresser. Good security. Off site: Fishing 800 m. Boat launching 5 km. Golf 7 km. Bicycle hire 8 km. Riding 15 km. Hourly bus service from outside the gate to Alicante or Murcia. Theme parks.

At a glance
Welcome & Ambience	✓✓✓✓✓	Location	✓✓✓✓✓
Quality of Pitches	✓✓✓✓✓	Range of Facilities	✓✓✓✓✓

Directions
Site is 2 km. west of La Marina. Leave N332 Guardamara de Segura - Santa Pola road at the 75 km. marker if travelling north, or the 78 km. marker if travelling south. Site is well signed.

Charges 2003
Per person	€ 5.00 - € 6.00
child (under 10 yrs)	€ 3.50 - € 4.00
pitch acc. to type and season	€ 16.00 - € 31.00
electricity	€ 2.40
dog	€ 1.00 - € 2.00

Plus 7% VAT. Seven grades of pitch. Less in low season, plus good discounts for longer stays 16/9-14/6, excluding Easter.

Reservations
Made with deposit (€ 30,05), min. 5 days Easter and Aug. Tel: 965 419 200.
Email: info@camping-lamarina.com

Open
All year.

Comunidad Valenciana

ES8754 Camping Jávea
Ctra. Cabo de la Nao, km 1, 03730 Jávea

The 200 metre access road to this site is a little unkempt as it passes some factories, but all changes on the final approach with palms, orange and pine trees, the latter playing host to a colony of parakeets. English is spoken at reception. The boxed hedges and palms surrounding this area with a backdrop of hills dotted with villas presents an attractive setting. The site's three hectares provides space for 246 numbered pitches with 146 for touring units. Flat, level and rectangular in shape, the pitches vary in size (60-80 sq.m. and not advised for caravans or motorhomes with an overall length exceeding 7 metres). All have a granite chip surface and electricity. Being a typical Spanish site, the pitches are not separated so units may be close to each other. Some pitches have artificial shade, although for most the pruned eucalyptus and pepper trees will suffice. The area has a large number of British residents so a degree of English is spoken by many shopkeepers and many restaurants provide multi-language menus. Besides being popular for a summer holiday, Camping Javea is now open all year and could be of interest to those that wish to 'winter' in an excellent climate. Discounts can make an extended stay extremely viable.

Facilities
Two very clean, fully equipped, sanitary blocks include two children's toilets plus a baby bath, dishwashing and laundry sinks. Two washing machines. Small bar and restaurant where in high season you purchase bread and milk. Large swimming pool and children's pool with lifeguard and sun bathing lawns. Play area. Table tennis. Boules. Five-aside football. Basketball. Electronic barriers (deposit for swipe card). Off site: Sandy beach 3 km. Javea within easy walking distance with supermarkets and shops catering for all needs. Market Thursday.

At a glance
Welcome & Ambience	✓✓✓	Location	✓✓✓
Quality of Pitches	✓✓✓	Range of Facilities	✓✓✓

Directions
Exit N332 for Javea on A134, continue in direction of Port (road number changes to CV 734). On reaching roundabout and Lidl supermarket turn right signed Arenal Platges and Cabo de la Nao (also camping sign). Straight on at next roundabout to camping sign and slip road in 100 m. If you miss slip road go back from next roundabout.

Charges 2003
Per adult	€ 3.46 - € 3.85
child	€ 2.95 - € 3.95
pitch 60 sq.m.	€ 9.20 - € 10.22
pitch 70 sq.m.	€ 10.82 - € 12.02
pitch 80 sq.m.	€ 12.44 - € 13.82
electricity (8A)	€ 2.58

Reservations
Necessary for high season. Tel: 965 791 070. Email: info@campingjavea.com

Open
All year.

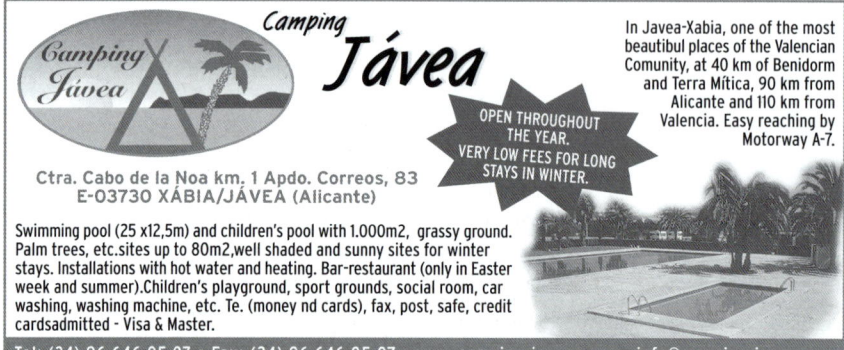

Camping Jávea

In Javea-Xabia, one of the most beautibul places of the Valencian Comunity, at 40 km of Benidorm and Terra Mítica, 90 km from Alicante and 110 km from Valencia. Easy reaching by Motorway A-7.

OPEN THROUGHOUT THE YEAR. VERY LOW FEES FOR LONG STAYS IN WINTER.

Ctra. Cabo de la Noa km. 1 Apdo. Correos, 83
E-03730 XÁBIA/JÁVEA (Alicante)

Swimming pool (25 x12,5m) and children's pool with 1.000m2, grassy ground. Palm trees, etc.sites up to 80m2,well shaded and sunny sites for winter stays. Installations with hot water and heating. Bar-restaurant (only in Easter week and summer).Children's playground, sport grounds, social room, car washing, washing machine, etc. Te. (money nd cards), fax, post, safe, credit cardsadmitted - Visa & Master.

Tel: (34) 96 646 05 05 • Fax: (34) 96 646 05 07 • www.camping-javea.com • info@camping-javea.com

ES8743 Complejo Ecoturistico Marjal
Ctra. N-332, km 73.4, 03140 Guardamar del Segura

MarJal is located beside the estuary of the Segura river, alongside the pine and eucalyptus forests of the Dunas de Guardamar natural park. It is a new site with a huge lagoon-style pool and a superb sports complex. There are 246 pitches on this award winning site, all with water, electricity, drainage and satellite TV points, the ground covered with crushed marble making the pitches clean and pleasant. There is little shade as yet and the site has an open feel with lots of room for manoeuvring. The large leased restaurant overlooks the pools and the river that leads to the sea in the near distance. This situation is shared with the taperia (high season) and bar with large terraces fringed by trees, palms and pomegranates. The impressive pool/lagoon complex (1,100 sq.m) has a water cascade, an island bar plus bridge, one part sectioned as a children's pool and a jacuzzi. The extensive sports area is also impressive with qualified instructors who will customise your fitness programme whilst consulting the doctor. No effort has been spared here, the quality heated indoor pool, light-exercise room, sauna, solarium, beauty salon, fully equipped gym and changing rooms, including facilities for disabled visitors, are of the highest quality. Aerobics and physiotherapy are also on offer. All activities are discounted for campers. A programme of entertainment is provided for adults and children in season by a professional animation team. The fine sandy beach can be reached through the forest (800 m).

Facilities
Three excellent heated sanitary blocks have free hot water, elegant separators between sinks, spacious showers and some cabins. Each block has high quality facilities for babies and disabled campers, modern laundry rooms with washing machines, dryers, ironing boards and dishwashing rooms (complete with drainers and paper drying rolls). Car wash. Well stocked supermarket. Restaurants. Bar. Large outdoor pool complex (1/6-31/10). Heated indoor pool (low season). Fitness suite and gymnasium. Sauna. Beauty salon. Solarium. Aerobics and aquarobics for the more mature camper. Play room for children. Minigolf. Floodlit tennis and soccer pitch. Volleyball. Bicycle hire. Games room. TV room. ATM. Off site: Riding and golf 4 km.

At a glance
Welcome & Ambience	✓✓✓	Location	✓✓✓✓
Quality of Pitches	✓✓✓✓	Range of Facilities	✓✓✓✓✓

Directions
On N332 40 km. south of Alicante, site is on the sea side between 73 and 74 km. markers.

Charges 2003
Per person	€ 4.00 - € 6.00
child	€ 2.50 - € 4.00
pitch	€ 16.00 - € 28.00
dog	€ 2.00 - € 3.00
electricity (per kw)	€ 0.21

All plus 7% VAT.

Reservations
Contact site. Tel: 966 725 022.
Email: marjal@futurnet.es

Open
All year.

ES8755 Camping Caravanning Moraira
Camino Paellero 50, 03724 Moraira-Teulada

This small hillside site with some views over the town and marina is quietly situated in an urban area amongst old pine trees and just 400 m. from a sheltered bay. Terracing provides shaded pitches of varying size (access to some of the upper pitches may be difficult for larger units). A few pitches have water and waste water facilities and a few have sea and marina views. There are electricity connections (6/10A). A large, painted water tower stands at the top of the site. An attractive irregular shaped swimming pool with paved sunbathing terrace is below the small bar/restaurant with terrace. The pool, which is heated in winter, has observation windows where you can watch the swimmers. The pool is used for sub-aqua instruction and the site runs a professional diving school for all levels (the diving here is good and the water warm even in winter). A sandy beach is 1.5 km.

Facilities
The high quality toilet block, with polished granite floors and marble fittings, is built to a unique and ultra-modern design with extra large free hot showers. Washing machine and dryer in separate room. Motorcaravan services. Bar/restaurant and shop (main season). Small swimming pool. Tennis. Sub-aqua with site boat and instruction. Electronic games. Comprehensive security system. Torches may be required. Off site: Shops, bars and restaurants within walking distance.

At a glance
Welcome & Ambience	✓✓✓	Location	✓✓✓✓
Quality of Pitches	✓✓✓	Range of Facilities	✓✓✓

Directions
Site is best approached from Teulada. From A7 take exit 63 onto N332. In 3.5 km. turn right signed Teulada and Moraira. In Teulada fork right to Moraira. At junction at town entrance turn right signed Calpe and in 1 km. turn right into road to site on bend immediately after Res. Don Julio. Do not take the first right as the signs seem to indicate otherwise you will go round a loop.

Latest charges
Per person	€ 3.60
child (4-9 yrs)	€ 2.70
pitch incl. car and unit	€ 9.91
electricity	€ 3.00

All plus 7% VAT. Less 15-60% in low seasons.

Reservations
Write to site for details. Tel: 965 745 249.

Open
All year.

Murcia

In the province of Murcia you'll find sandy beaches, dunes and unspoilt coves along the coast; inland hills and valleys plus the regional parks of Sierra de Carche, Sierra de la Pila, Sierra de Espuña, and Carrascoy and El Valle.

The capital of the region is Murcia

Murcia, the capital of the region, was founded in the ninth century by the Moors on the banks of the Río Segura. The square of Cardinal Belluga houses two of the town's architectural gems, the Episcopal Palace and the Cathedral, and there are a range of museums and exhibitions to visit. With narrow medieval streets, the characterful town of Cartagena has lots of bars and restaurants plus two nautical museums: the National Museum of Maritime Archaeology and the Naval Museum. Also on a nautical theme, the International Nautical Week is celebrated here in June. Along the coast there are numerous beaches offering a wide range of water sports: sailing, windsurfing, canoeing, water skiing and diving. And the area between the coastal towns of Águilas and Mazarrón is a breeding ground for tortoises and eagles.

Inland are the historic towns of Lorca and Caravaca de le Cruz. The former is known as the 'baroque city' with its examples of baroque architecture, seen in the parish churches, convents, and houses; the latter too is home to beautiful churches, including El Santuario de Vera Cruz.

Cuisine of the region

Vegetables are important and found in nearly every dish. Fish is also popular, cooked in a salt crust or *a la espalda* (lightly fried and baked), and usually accompanied by rice. Fig bread is a speciality of the region.

Bizcochos borrachos: sponge soaked in wine and syrup

Cabello de Ángel: pumpkin strands in syrup

Caldero: made of rice, fish and the hot ñora pepper

Caldo con pelotas: stew made of turkey with meatballs

Chuletas de cordero al ajo cabañil: suckling lamb chops served with a dressing of garlic and vinegar

Tocino de cielo: dessert made with egg yolks and syrup *Yemas de Caravaca*: cake made with egg yolks

Places of interest

Águilas: seaside town with good beaches

Moratalla: pretty village, castle offering stunning views of the surrounding countryside and forests

Puerto de Mazarrón: Enchanted City of Bolnuevo - a small area of eroded rocks, nature reserve and lagoon at La Rambla de Moreras

San Pedro del Pinatar: seaside resort, La Pagan beach is renowned for its thearapeutic mud, which reputedly relieves rheumatism and is good for the skin

Santiago de la Ribera: upmarket resort with sailing club

 **tip**

MANY PLACES OF INLAND MURCIA ARE NOT EASILY ACCESSIBLE BY PUBLIC TRANSPORT; A CAR IS THE MOST CONVENIENT WAY TO VISIT THE AREA.

www.alanrogers.com for latest campsite news

Murcia

ES8748 Camping Los Madriles
Ctra. de la Azohia, km. 4.5, 30868 Isla Plana

An extraordinary site with super facilities, Los Madriles is run by a hard working team, with constant improvements being made. Twenty kilometres west of Cartegena, the approach to the site and the surrounding area is fairly unremarkable, but the site is not. It provides huge rectangular and lagoon stlye pools with water sprays and jacuzzis which are fed by thermal waters used by the ancient Romans. Unbelievably the pools are emptied every night after they close at 10 pm. and are refilled by morning with fresh water thus doing away for the need for chlorination. A fairly steep access road leads to the 311 flat, good to large size terraced pitches. Some have shade from large trees, with others in the newer area having less shade but panoramic views of the sea and behind to the mountains (ideal for winter visits). Private cabins are available. Simple snacks and prepackaged meals are served in the bar and attractive area near the pools. The campsite is immaculately clean and has excellent sports facilities. The guests we spoke to were really enjoying their stay. Local excursions can be made to the Campillo de Adrentro now a picnic spot, but once a military base.

Facilities
Five sanitary blocks provide excellent facilities, including facilities for disabled campers. Washing machines and dryers. Motorcaravan services. Car wash. Restaurant/snack bar. Bar. Shop. Swimming pools with jacuzzi. Five-a-side football. Boules. Basketball. Table tennis. Play areas. Electronic games. Bicycle hire. ATM. Dogs and other animals are not accepted. Torches useful. Off site: Town close by. Beach and boat launching 600 m. Fishing. Riding 6 km. Golf 20 km. Excursions.

At a glance
Welcome & Ambience	✓✓✓✓	Location	✓✓✓✓
Quality of Pitches	✓✓✓✓	Range of Facilities	✓✓✓✓✓

Directions
From A7/E15 take km. 627 exit to Mazarron (southeast of Murcia) and go east on coast road towards Cartegena. Site is well signed before entering town of La Azohia.

Charges 2003
Per person	€ 3.50
pitch	€ 10.48

Reservations
Contact site. Tel: 968 152 151.

Open
All year.

ES8745 Camping La Fuente
30709 Banos de Fortuna

Located in an area known for its thermal waters since Roman and Moorish times, La Fuente is a gem with just 62 pitches. The main attraction here is the huge pool complex where the water is constant at 22 degrees for 365 days of the year. Fed from thermal springs this is really good for old bones! Importantly there is a long gentle ramp into the pool, for the not so agile or where a bath chair could be lowered into the water. A daily charge applies to use of the pool and jacuzzis (€ 3.61 but well worth it). There is a very good restaurant and separate bar. The site is in two sections, one where pitches are in standard rows and the other where they are in circles around blocks. The flat pitches have electricity, some with shade, and the unusual thing is that all have their own very modern mini-sanitary block. The site's buildings are a cheery yellow colour and the pool has a large terraced area and pool bar. There is accommodation on site but it is separate from the camping area. Unusually winter is high season here.

Facilities
All pitches have their own high quality facilities including a unit for disabled campers. Washing machines and dryers. High quality restaurant shared with accomodation guests. Snack bar by pool. Supermarket. Bicycle hire. Communal barbecues. Off site: Spa town, massage therapies, hot pools. Golf and riding 20 km.

At a glance
Welcome & Ambience	✓✓✓✓	Location	✓✓✓✓✓
Quality of Pitches	✓✓✓✓✓	Range of Facilities	✓✓✓

Directions
From A7/E15 Alicante - Murcia road take C3223 to Fortuna then follow signs to Banos de Fortuna. The site with its bright yellow walls can be easily seen from the road and is very well signed in the town.

Charges 2003
Per person	€ 2.10
child	€ 1.20
pitch (with private sanitary facilities)	€ 7.81
dog	€ 0.90
electricity (10A; per kw/h on meter)	€ 0.19
Pitch prices discounted after five days.	

Reservations
Contact site. Tel: 968 685017.
Email: campingfuente@terra.es

Open
All year.

ES8752N Camping Naturista El Portus
El Portus, 30393 Cartagena

Set in a secluded, mountain fringed, south facing bay, El Portus is a fairly large naturist site with direct access to a sand and shingle beach and enjoying magnificent views. With its own micro-climate, this part of Spain enjoys almost all year round sunshine; mid-day temperatures which seldom drop below 20 degrees. There are some 400 pitches, half for tourers, ranging from 60-100 sq.m, all but a few having electricity, mostly on fairly level, if somewhat stony ground. El Portus has a reasonable amount of shade from the trees and every pitch has views. Permanent units are situated on the hillside above the site. A large, supervised swimming pool and paddling pool are sheltered and landscaped with grass areas for sunbathing. At other times there may be a smaller heated pool above the camping area. One of the bar/restaurants is open all year. This is relaxed site with welcoming, English speaking reception staff.

Facilities
Five toilet blocks of varying styles are fully equipped. Opened as required, they are clean and bright, some are unisex. Open plan dishwashing and laundry facilities. Showers all with hot water,. Facilities may be a little busy in peak season. Unit for disabled visitors, key from reception. Washing machines. Motorcaravan services. Three drinking water points clearly marked near the steps to restaurant. Non-drinking water points well spaced around site. Well stocked shop. Bar with TV and libary. Restaurant with 'menu del dia' high season, snack bar by beach acts as restaurant low season. Swimming pools. Play area. Tennis. Volleyball. Table tennis. Petanque. Yoga. Scuba-diving club (high season). Windsurfing. Spanish lessons. Small boat moorings. Disco and entertainment (high season).
Off site: Fishing from beach. Riding and golf 40 km.

At a glance
Welcome & Ambience	✓✓✓✓✓	Location	✓✓✓✓✓
Quality of Pitches	✓✓✓✓	Range of Facilities	✓✓✓✓✓

Directions
Site is on the coast, 10 km. west of Cartagena. Follow signs to Mazarron then take E22 to Canteras. Site is well signed for 4 km. to El Portus.

Charges 2003
Per person	€ 5.49
child (3-9 yrs)	€ 4.04
pitch	€ 12.31
pitch with electricity (6A)	€ 17.20
dog	€ 3.73

Plus 7% VAT. Special discounts for longer stays and in low season. Camping Cheques accepted.

Reservations
Made with € 181 deposit. Tel: 968 553 052.
Email: elportus@elportus.com

Open
All year.

www.alanrogers.com for latest campsite news

ES8753 Caravaning La Manga
Autovia Cartagena - La Manga exit 15, 30370 La Manga del Mar Menor

The site is a very large well equipped, 'holiday style' site with its own beach and pool. With a good number of typical Spanish long stay units, the length of the site is impressive (one kilometre) and a bicycle is very helpful for getting about. La Manga is a 22 km. long narrow strip of land, bordered by the Mediterranean on one side and by the Mar Menor on the other. There are sandy bathing beaches on both sides and considerable development in terms of hotels, restaurants and night clubs. You cannot drive all round this narrow strip of land as there is a gap in the centre, however, the very end of the southern part is great for 'getting away from it all'. The campsite is situated on the approach to 'the strip' and enjoys the benefit of its own semi-private beach alongside the Mar Menor, with a sailing, canoeing and windsurfing school and the site's excellent restaurant (traditional Spanish Tapas and food) and bar right beside the beach. The beach is dotted with impressive tall palm trees and the sea is very shallow and warm, so it is ideal for families with small children or choose between the outdoor or indoor pools. There are some 1,000 touring pitches of two sizes (84 or 110 sq m), regularly laid out in rows on slightly sloping gravel. They are smart, separated and shaded by high hedges, all have electricity and water connections. This site's excellent facilities are ideally suited for holidays in the winter when the weather is very pleasantly warm.

Facilities
Seven clean toilet blocks of standard design well spaced around the site. They include washbasins (with hot water in five blocks), and covered cold water sinks (three with hot water) for washing up and laundry. Laundry. Gas supplies. Large well stocked supermarket. Restaurant. Bar. Snack bar. Swimming pool complex, supervised, (April - Sept). Indoor pool, gymnasium, sauna and jacuzzi. Open air cinema (April - Sept). Tennis. Petanque. Minigolf. Basketball. Volleyball. Football area. Children's play area. Watersports school. Off site: Golf, bicycle hire and riding 5 km.

At a glance
Welcome & Ambience	✓✓✓✓✓	Location	✓✓✓✓✓
Quality of Pitches	✓✓✓✓✓	Range of Facilities	✓✓✓✓✓

Directions
Use exit 15 from MU312 dual-carriageway towards Cabo de Palos, signed Playa Honda (site signed also). Cross road-bridge and double back on yourself. Site entrance is clearly visible beside dual-carriageway with many flags flying.

Charges 2003
Per 84 sq.m. pitch incl. 2 persons	€ 14.50 - € 22.00
3 persons	€ 14.50 - € 24.25
4 persons	€ 14.50 - € 27.25
110 sq.m. pitch incl. 2 persons	€ 15.00 - € 26.00
3 persons	€ 15.00 - € 29.00
4 persons	€ 15.00 - € 32.00
dog	€ 1.00

Electricity (10A) included. All plus 7% VAT. Prices for up to 8 persons available; child under 6 yrs free. Less 10, 20 or 25% for stays of more than 7, 14 or 21 days in low season. Special prices for long winter stays.
Camping Cheques accepted.

Reservations
Contact site. Tel: 968 563 014.
Email: lamanga@caravaning.es

Open
All year.

Ctra. de El Algar a Cabo de Palos, km 12.
E-30370 **La Manga del Mar Menor**
Cartagena (Murcia)
Tel.: (34) 968 56 30 19
       (34) 968 56 30 14
Fax: (34) 968 56 34 26

www.caravaning.es • lamanga@caravaning.es

A paradise between two seas. Come for a lovely, warm winter to the borders of the Mar Menor, there where you can enjoy the sun 3000 hours per year. Not far from the historical towns Cartagena and Murcia. In winter in-door swimming pool, jacuzzi, sauna and gym and up till 50% reduction.

Andalucia

Famous for its sun, its beautiful traditions, its poets, original folklore, age-old history and magnificent heritage left behind by the Moors, Andalucía is one of the most attractive regions in Spain.

This comprises eight provinces: Almeria, Cadiz, Cordoba, Granada, Huelva, Malaga, Jaen and Seville

The regional capital is Seville

With the River Guadalquivir running through it, the charming city of Seville is one of the most visited places in the region. The old city, with its great monuments; the Giralda tower, Cathedral and the Alcázar, plus the narrow, winding streets of Santa Cruz, is particularly popular. Also on the Guadalquivir, Cordoba is located northeast of Seville. It too has a picturesque Jewish Quarter along with a rich Moorish heritage. Indeed, the Mezquita is one of the grandest mosques ever built by the Moors in Spain.

Located further east on the foothills of the Sierra Nevada Mountain Range, Granada is home to the impressive Alhambra, a group of distinct buildings including a Royal Palace, splendid gardens, and the fortress of Alcazaba. The Sierra Nevada, Spain's highest range, offers good skiing and trekking. Further south, you'll find the fine beaches and tourist areas of the Costa Tropical and the Costa del Sol, including the developed resort of Malaga. There are more beaches on the west coast plus one of the oldest settlements in Spain, the bustling port of Cádiz.

Cuisine of the region

Andalucía has more tapas bars than anywhere else in Spain. Sea food in abundance, fresh vegetables and fruit: oranges from Cordoba; persimmons, pomegranates, figs, strawberries from Alpujarra; avocados, mangos, guavas, papayas from the coast of Granada and Malaga. Locally produced wine and sherry.

Alboronia: vegetable stew

Alfajors: almond and nut pastry

Gazpacho ajoblanco: cold soup with garlic and almond

Gazpacho salmorejo: much thicker and made with tomatoes only

Pestiños: honey coated pastries

Tocinillo de cielo: pudding made with egg yolks and syrup

Places of interest

Almeria: preserved Moorish heritage with greatest purity. Located on a beautiful bay

Casa-Museo Pablo Ruiz Picasso: art museum including collection of originals by Pablo Picasso

Jaen: medieval fortress, Renaissance cathedral, 11th century Moorish baths, Santa Catalina castle

Jerez de la Frontera: birthplace of sherry and Spanish brandy, site of renowned equestrian school

Mijas: enchanting village, with narrow streets bordered by brilliantly white-washed houses

Parque Natural de las Sierras de Cazorla y Segura: largest park in Spain with mountains, river gorges, forests and wildlife

Ronda: beautiful town on the edge of an abrupt rocky precipice

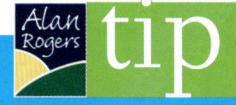

tip

JOIN IN THE FERIA DE ABRIL. HELD IN SEVILLE SHORTLY AFTER THE HOLY WEEK FESTIVITIES, IT IS A WEEK-LONG PARTY OF FOOD, DRINK AND FLAMENCO.

www.alanrogers.com for latest campsite news

ES8749 Camping Sopalmo

Sopalmo, 04638 Mojacar

This is a tiny, homely, site run by a cheerful man called Simon and his charming mother Isabel. They are full of fun and determined that you will enjoy your stay. The site is on two levels, the upper site (be prepared for a fairly steep gravel track to the gates) for 20 tourers and the lower section for 12 tents. All pitches are marked, level and on gravel with electricity. It is unspoilt and has much rustic charm with the family house providing the focal point of the site. The attractive trees and shrubs around the site include olives, figs, mimosa and cacti. Reception is a pretty little room in the front section of the quaint house and a few steps take you into a small but typically Spanish bar. There are informal 'al fresco' gatherings and late barbecues on the lovely terrace, especially at Christmas. We recommend the site for the more mature camper who wishes to get away from it all and be very much within a family atmosphere. Lots of British campers winter here. Ask to see the baby tortoises that Simon rescues and then releases back into the wild when mature.

Facilities

The small sanitary block is very clean and fully equipped. Facilities for disabled campers. Hot showers assisted by solar power. Basic laundry and dishwashing facilities in a pleasant roofed area near reception. Bar. Breakfast available in summer, and the baker calls at 10.30 daily. Torch useful. Off site: The beach is 2 km. (naturism permitted) and the nearest serious shops are 5 km. Riding and bicycle hire 10 km.

At a glance

Welcome & Ambience	✓✓✓✓✓	Location	✓✓✓✓
Quality of Pitches	✓✓✓✓✓	Range of Facilities	✓✓✓

Directions

Exit from main coast road (N340) at junction 520 (northeast of Almeria). Take the AL152 (formerly A150) to Mojacar Playa and continue south towards Carboneras. Site is 6 km south of Mojacar Playa, signed off the road

Latest charges

Per adult	€ 3.70
child	€ 2.90
pitch	€ 7.40
electricity	€ 2.00

Plus 7% VAT. Reductions for low season and longer stays. No credit cards.

Reservations

Contact site. Tel: 950 478413.

Open

All year.

ES8751 Camping Cuevas Mar

Cuevas del Almanzora, 04618 Palomares

The site opened in '95 is managed by Pedro, a friendly Frenchman and is gaining a reputation for its excellent service, comfortable facilities and immaculate appearance. Cuevas Mar is a welcome addition in a region very popular with British visitors who appreciate its year-round dry, sunny climate. Quietly situated just back from the coast road (a little road noise on the site) and 500 m. across the road from the beach, the site offers 200 large, smart pitches (80-100 sq.m), all with electricity connections and firm dry surfaces. The newer section for large motorhomes is closest to the road. The older pitches are screened by hedges and young trees which afford some shade and have easy access from wide roads (some artificial shade is provided). The most attractive sheltered, tiled, oval-shaped pool is surrounded by a grassy sunbathing area and has a thoughtfully provided long ramp to help the elderly or infirm to enter the water. Although there are few additional facilities here it is a most pleasant site and there are good restaurants within easy walking distance.

Facilities

The well designed neat central sanitary block is generous in size, adequate and fully equipped. Good laundry and dishwashing facilities under cover. Washing machines and dryer. Two drinking water points on site (in common with many other sites in this very dry area, drinking water is supplied from tanks refilled by tanker and the remainder of the water on site is non-potable). Shop. Bar with terrace by pool. Snacks may be offered in high season. Swimming pool (14 x 9 m; May - Sept). Jacuzzi. Off site: Restaurants 200 m. Mojaca 7 km. for seafood and lively bars. Fishing from beach 200 m. Bicycle hire 3 km. Golf 4 km.

At a glance

Welcome & Ambience	✓✓✓✓✓	Location	✓✓✓✓
Quality of Pitches	✓✓✓✓✓	Range of Facilities	✓✓✓

Directions

From N340 (Murcia - Almeria) leave at 537 km. for Cuevas del Amanzora, then follow the road to Vera and Palomares. Site is signed from Vera.

Latest charges

Per person	€ 4.20
child	€ 3.20
caravan or tent	€ 4.20
car	€ 4.20
motorcaravan	€ 8.42
motorcycle	€ 3.01
dog	€ 1.80
electricity (6A)	€ 3.01

Generous discounts for longer winter stays. No credit cards.

Reservations

Contact site. Tel: 950 467 382.
Email: cuevasmar@arrakis.es

Open

All year.

Andalucia

ES8760 Camping Mar Azul
Playa de San Miguel s/n, 04711 Almerimar

Right beside the sea, on flat ground and with direct access to a sandy beach, Mar Azul is in a dry and sunny area of Spain where there are few other campsites. The landscape to the north is dominated by the Sierra Nevada. This is the case for 120 kilometres along this part of the coast. The 890 individual, numbered pitches here are quite attractively laid out with many palm trees and at 90 sq.m. are larger than most in Spain. Artificial shade is provided on most pitches. Some serviced pitches for large units have been added recently. A circular, unheated swimming pool with children's pool, a terrace and sun-beds, is near the beach. Another pool, a toilet block and a sports area at the centre of the site are effectively abandoned and await redevelopment. Work is in progress in various areas of the site. This site lies out on its own, but the large development of Almerimar with golf course, large hotel, restaurant and shops is little over 1 km. along the beach. The town of El Ejido is 8 km. with excellent shellfish restaurants and if you stroll through the sand dunes you will be treated to the spectacle of flamingos and other protected species in the adjacent lagoons.

Facilities
Four, fully equipped, toilet blocks of good quality are heated when required. Washing machines. Motorcaravan services. Gas supplies. Fridge hire. Comprehensive shopping facilities and supermarket. Bar. Restaurant. Swimming pool. Tennis. Fronton. Squash. Table tennis. Fitness centre. Boules. Volleyball. Badminton. Basketball. Riding. Archery. Bicycle hire and circuit. Roller skating. Minigolf. Football practice area. Fishing. Windsurfing school and equipment for hire. Riding school. Children's club (April - June). English is spoken. Torch useful. Off site: Golf 1.5 km.

At a glance
Welcome & Ambience	✓✓✓✓	Location	✓✓✓✓
Quality of Pitches	✓✓✓✓✓	Range of Facilities	✓✓✓✓

Directions
Turn off main N340/E15 road at km. 409 for Almerimar. After 4 km. turn right at entrance to town and follow signs for site, which is west of the town.

Charges 2003
Per person	€ 3.80 - € 4.80
child (2-10 yrs)	€ 3.00 - € 4.00
tent or caravan	€ 3.80 - € 5.00
car	€ 3.80 - € 5.00
motorcaravan	€ 6.00 - € 7.00
dog	€ 0.80 - € 1.60
electricity	€ 2.70 - € 3.20

All plus 7% VAT. Reductions for longer stays (up to 60%). Camping Cheques accepted.

Reservations
Made for any length. Tel: 950 497 585. Email: info@campingmarazul.com

Open
All year.

ES8765 Camping La Garrofa
Ctra. Nacional 340 - km 435,4, 04002 Almeria

One of the earliest sites in Spain (dating back to 1957), La Garoffa is a simple site nestled into a cove with a beach that is virtually private. The shingle beach cannot be accessed other than by sea or through the campsite. It is rather dramatic with the tall mountain cliffs behind. Many of the rather small 102 flat and sloping sandy pitches here are shaded, some are virtually on the beach, most very close to the water. An old fortress looks down on the campsite – you can walk to it via a valley at the back of the site and across an old Roman bridge. These are all on land owned by the family who also own the campsite. La Garoffa was let for many years and is now back in the hands of the family who are working hard to return the site to its full potential. Sites in this area are generally poor and this is good by comparison. The impact of the high road bridges to the back of the site is minimal. There is a small restaurant that served delicious food in a rather relaxed way. It's all very relaxed here and that is part of its rather unique rustic, simple charm.

Facilities
A single sanitary block is mature but clean. No facilities for disabled campers. Restaurant/snack bar. Shop. Play area. Torches useful. Fishing. Off site: Town close by. Walks. Sub aqua diving. Bicycle hire 2 km. Golf 8 km. Excursions – tickets to attractions sold.

At a glance
Welcome & Ambience	✓✓✓✓	Location	✓✓✓✓
Quality of Pitches	✓✓✓	Range of Facilities	✓✓✓

Directions
Site is west of Almeria Take 438 exit from the N 340 and follow the camping signs. The site is below the minor road on the beach side and easy to find.

Charges 2003
Per person	€ 3.70
child	€ 3.25
motorcaravan	€ 6.30
caravan	€ 3.90
tent	€ 3.70
car	€ 3.25
electricity	€ 3.30

Reservations
Contact site. Tel: 950 235770.

Open
All year.

ES9270 Camping Suspiro del Moro

Ctra. Bailén - Motril, km. 145., Puerto Suspiro del Moro, 18630 Granada

Suspiro Del Moro is 11 km. south of Granada just off the Motril road or, alternatively, can be approached on the scenic mountain road from Almunecar. Based high in the Sierra Nevada mountain range, the area offers spectacular views from just outside the site, with trees and fences inhibiting the views inside. The site is small and rectangular with a cool and peaceful atmosphere and noise from the road is reduced by the high perimeter wall. Many locally made colourful pottery items are on sale in the rear of reception. Family run, it is well kept with gravel paths leading to the flat, grass pitches which all benefit from the shade of mature trees. The site is part of a business which includes a very attractive Olympic sized swimming pool and there is a direct access path from the site. Above this is a huge restaurant and bar both with terraces. The restaurant has a most extensive menu and waiter service and it is a real treat to eat there whilst enjoying the views over the Sierra Nevada. This is an ideal site to investigate the local area and has the great advantage of impressive additional facilities.

Facilities
Three small toilet blocks are situated around the camping area with British WCs and free hot showers. Laundry and washing up facilities are of a good standard. Small shop. Small restaurant/bar (high season). Functions are sometimes held here which can be noisy until late at night. Bar. TV lounge. Swimming pool with children's end (high season only). Small play area on gravel. Table tennis. Table football. Pool table.

At a glance
Welcome & Ambience	✓✓✓	Location	✓✓✓
Quality of Pitches	✓✓✓	Range of Facilities	✓✓✓

Directions
Leave the new Granada to Motril road at junction 144 if from the south or 139 from the north and follow the un-named campsite signs. There is only one site here.

Charges 2003
Per person	€ 3.61
child	€ 2.40
pitch	€ 7.81
electricity	€ 2.40

Less 20% in low season.

Reservations
Contact site. Tel: 958 555 411.
Email: suspirodelmoro@eresmas.com

Open
All year.

ES9280 Camping Sierra Nevada

Avenida Madrid 107, 18014 Granada

This is a good site either for a night stop or for a short stay while visiting Granada. For a city site it is surprisingly pleasant. Quite large, it has an open feeling and, to encourage you to stay a little longer, an irregular shape pool with a smaller child's pool open in high season. There is some traffic noise around the pool as it is on the road boundary. With **148** pitches for touring units, the site is in two connected parts with more mature trees and facilities to the northern end. Artificial shade is available throughout the site if required. Electrical connections are available. There is a small tour operator presence but it is not intrusive.

Facilities
Two very modern sanitary blocks, with excellent facilities, include cabins, very good facilities for disabled people and babies. Additional high standard sanitary facilities by the pool made available at peak times. Washing machines. Motorcaravan services. Gas supplies. Shop (15/3-15/10). Swimming pools with lifeguards and charge of € 1.5 (15/6-15/9). Bar/restaurant by pool. Tennis. Table tennis. Petanque. Large playground. Doctor lives on site. Off site: Fishing 10 km. Golf 12 km. Bus station 50 m from site.

At a glance
Welcome & Ambience	✓✓✓✓✓	Location	✓✓✓✓✓
Quality of Pitches	✓✓✓✓	Range of Facilities	✓✓✓✓

Directions
Site is just outside the city to north, on road to Jaén and Madrid. From autopista, take Granada North - Almanjayar exit 123 (close to central bus station). Follow road back towards Granada and site is shortly on the right, well signed.

Charges 2003
Per person	€ 4.62
child (3-10 yrs)	€ 3.91
pitch	€ 10.50
electricity (10A)	€ 3.16

VAT included.

Reservations
Made for camping or motel. Tel: 958 150 062.
Email: campingmotel@terra.es

Open
All year.

Andalucia

ES9275 Camping Los Avellanos de Sierra Nevada

Ctra. de la Fábrica s/n, 18152 Dilar

This is a fascinating tiny business with a philosophy of peace and tranquillity, a world apart from other sites in southern Spain. This has been achieved by Pilar and her brother Idvier. There is a fabulous old house and 20 beautifully terraced pitches (mainly for tents) with amazing views. You can pick fruit from the scores of fruit trees and collect the 'huevos corral' – free range eggs or pick your own vegetables from the plot (small charge). There is a shaded area with a spring set aside for reading and dreaming and as you walk to the sanitary block, birds fly out of holes in the bank. The vine-covered patio overlooks the small raised pool and commands wonderful views of the mountains. The narrow approach roads are interesting for larger units and a few motorcaravans may be accepted in an informal lower area where electricity can be supplied. A phone call is a good idea if you are driving a large unit- ask for Pilar as her English is very good. Expect a different experience here but we stress this is mainly for tents and better for summer visits.

Facilities

Toilet facilities are modern and clean. Pretty bar/restaurant serves typical local fare and sells basic supplies (very limited in low season). Kitchen for hire. Restaurant/bar. Swimming pool (high season only). Table tennis. Darts. Bicycle hire. Riding. Fishing in river Dilar. Details of walks from reception. Torches essential. Excellent rooms to let. Off site: Tours of Granada (20 minutes away), especially the Alhambra, organised. Site also useful for skiing in Sierra Nevada in season.

At a glance

Welcome & Ambience	✓✓✓✓	Location	✓✓✓✓✓
Quality of Pitches	✓✓✓✓	Range of Facilities	✓✓

Directions

From Granada going south take the A323, then the GR05 road to Otura. Go through the town following signs for Dilar where you will find signs for the site. Note: Do not stray from the route indicated by the signs through town, as the roads are extremely narrow.

Latest charges

Per person	€ 3.16
child	€ 2.70
tent	€ 3.61
car	€ 3.01
motorcycle	€ 2.70

Reservations

Contact site. Tel: 958 596016.
Email: Avellano@Teleline.es

Open

All year.

ES9285 Camping Las Lomas

Ctra. de Sierra Nevada, 18160 Güejar-Sierra

This site is high in the Güejar Sierra and looks down on the Patano de Canales reservoir. After a wonderful drive to Güéjar-Sierra, you are rewarded with a site having excellent facilities. It is set on a slope but the pitches have been levelled to a great degree and are quite private, with high separating hedges and with many mature trees giving good shade (some pitches have sinks and most have electricity). The large bar/restaurant complex has a patio with wonderful views over the lake and an impressive huge central fire that is lit in winter. The pools also share this view, and have a grassed area for sunbathing that runs down to the fence looking over the long drop to the lake below (safe fencing). A new feature is luxury rooms for hire, including one with a superb spa which is for hire by the hour. Any infirm visitors will need a car to get around as the inclines are extreme.

Facilities

Pretty blue tiled sanitary blocks (heated in winter) provide clean facilities. First class facilities for disabled campers and well equipped baby room (key at reception). Spa for hire. Motorcaravan services. Supermarket. Restaurant/bar. Swimming pool. Play area. Table tennis. Minigolf. Basketball. Many other activities available including parascending. Barbecue. Torches useful. Off site: Buses run from outside site to village and Granada (15 km).Tours of the Alhambra organised with guides supplied if required. Useful site for winter skiing.

At a glance

Welcome & Ambience	✓✓✓✓	Location	✓✓✓✓
Quality of Pitches	✓✓✓✓	Range of Facilities	✓✓✓✓

Directions

Using A323 (Jaén - Motril) take exit 135 at Granada to Sierra Nevada which brings you to the A395. At 4 km. marker take exit 5B for Sierra Nevada. Pass 7 km. marker and turn immediately right towards Cenes de la Vega and Güéjar-Sierra and right again after 200 m. onto GR420, then left to Güéjar-Sierra. Site is signed - drive uphill past the dam and enjoy the views to the site.

Latest charges

Per person	€ 3.01
child	€ 2.40
pitch	€ 7.81

VAT included. No credit cards.

Reservations

Contact site. Tel: 958 484 742.

Open

All year.

ES9290 Camping El Balcon de Pitres
18414 Pitres

A simple country site perched high in the mountains of the Alpujarras, El Balcon de Pitres has its own rustic charm. Some 15 years ago the mountain top was terraced and many thousands of trees were planted around the site; many of these provide shade. There are stunning views from some of the 175 level grassy pitches. On Saturday evenings in summer there is a wide variety of live entertainment around an exotic Morrocan tent, which serves as a bar and which is far enough away from the pitches not to disturb sleeping campers. Local visitors often add to the 'hot august night' ambience. The large restaurant serves excellent, typically Spanish meals. The pool is very popular in summer with locals as well as campers. The Lopez family, have built this site from barren mountain top to cool oasis in the mountains in just fifteen years. There are lots of opportunities in the area for mountaineering sports such as canyoning and parascending, plus trekking.

Facilities
Two toilet blocks provide adequate facilities but the steeply sloping site is unsuitable for disabled campers and thus there are no facilities for them. Restaurant/snack bar. Bar. Shop. Swimming pools (extra charge, € 2.40 adult € 1.50 child). Bicycle hire. Torches useful. Off site: Town close by. Fishing. Canyoning. Trekking. Parascending. Quad bikes. Village sports centre providing football.

At a glance
Welcome & Ambience	✓✓✓✓	Location	✓✓✓✓
Quality of Pitches	✓✓✓✓	Range of Facilities	✓✓✓

Directions
Site is about 30 km. northeast of Motril. From coastal N340 take N323 and E902 north to Lanjaron. On E348 proceed towards Orgiva and just before town turn left to Soportuja, Pampaneira and finally Pitres where site is signed. From Orgiva the roads are very winding so allow plenty of time.

Charges 2003
Per adult	€ 3.31
child	€ 2.50
electricity	€ 1.95

Reservations
Contact site. Tel: 958 766111.
Email: info@balcondepitres.com

Open
All year.

ES8711 Nerja Camping
Ctra. N340, km. 297, 29787 Maro

This site is set on the lower slopes of the Sierra Almijara, two kilometres from the excellent beaches. Nerja Camping is a small, slightly jaded site of 55 pitches (30 with electricity and no static units) with impressive views of the surrounding mountains and the Mediterranean. Being situated slightly above but alongside the main coast road, it is easy to find – the price you pay is some traffic noise but this seems hardly to detract from the relaxing ambience (however, the new autopista will pass close by in 2004 and this may change). The pitches are on the small side and set on slopes with some terracing along with some artificial shade. The roads, although sloping, should present few problems for siting units. The small hut-style restaurant doubles as a bar and has a small terace where you can order snacks. The owners help with all activities and also recommend restaurants in the area. We see this as a site for transit rather than for extended stays.

Facilities
The single sanitary block has adequate facilities but needed cleaning when we visited. There are some free hot showers, washbasins (1 only with hot water), undercover dish-washing sinks (cold water) and laundry facilities. Small swimming pool and paddling pool (March - Sept). Small restaurant/bar (March - Sept). Essentials from the bar. Off site: Bus service nearby. The Nerja limestone caves 1 km. Fishing 3 km. Bicycle hire and riding 5 km. Sub-aqua diving, parascending and watersports close by. Day trips to Granada or Gibraltar can be taken using tour operators.

At a glance
Welcome & Ambience	✓✓✓	Location	✓✓✓✓
Quality of Pitches	✓✓✓	Range of Facilities	✓✓✓

Directions
Site is signed from main N340 coast road about 5 km. east of Nerja after the 296 km. marker. If coming from Nerja, go 500 m. past site entrance (opposite the red and white radio masts) to cross the extremely busy main road.

Latest charges
Per person	€ 4.00
child (2-10 yrs)	€ 3.25
tent	€ 4.00 - € 5.30
caravan	€ 5.30
car	€ 4.00
motorcaravan	€ 6.00
motorcycle	€ 3.25
electricity (15A)	€ 3.00

Reservations
Write to site. Tel: 952 529 714.

Open
All year except October.

Andalucia

ES8782 Camping Caravaning Laguna Playa

Prolongacion Paseo Maritimo, 29740 Torre del Mar

Laguna Playa is a pleasant and peaceful site alongside one of the Costa del Sol beaches, run by a father and son team (the son speaks excellent English) who give a personal service. Trips are organised to the famous Alhambra Mosque in Granada on a weekly basis and the site is well placed for visits to Malaga and Nerja. The pitches are flat, of average size and with good artificial shade supplementing that provided by the many established trees on site. All pitches have electricity. The busy restaurant with a terrace offers good value for money and many locals use it. The site has a distinctly Spanish flavour in August. Animation is organised for children in high season and you could visit the new cinema near reception. Various competitions including petanque are organised in summer. Good off peak discounts are available.

Facilities

Two well equipped, modern, sanitary blocks, both recently refurbished, include baby baths and good facilities for disabled campers. Laundry facilities. Supermarket. Bar and busy restaurant also used by locals (all open all year). Swimming pools (open high season). Play area. Drinks machine. Children's entertainment. Off site: Beach promenade 200 m. Bicycle hire 500 m. Regular bus service 700 m. outside site. Riding 2 km. Golf 1.5 km.

At a glance

Welcome & Ambience	✓✓✓✓	Location	✓✓✓✓
Quality of Pitches	✓✓✓	Range of Facilities	✓✓✓✓

Directions

Site is on the sea front west of the town of Torre del Mar, off the main N340 Malaga - Nerja road. Follow signs and take care not to enter the first camp site you meet on the beach as this is inferior and will be demolished in new development in the near future.

Latest charges

Per adult	€ 3.67
child	€ 2.91
tent	€ 3.67
caravan	€ 4.06
car	€ 3.67
motorcaravan	€ 13.22
motorcycle	€ 2.94
electricity (metered in winter)	€ 2.10

Reservations

Write to site. Tel: 952 540 631.

Open

All year.

ES8790 Camping La Laguna

Ctra. La Rábita s/n, 29620 Fuente de Piedra

In a remote area of Andulucia, this tiny campsite of just 30 pitches looks over the salty lakes and marshes of the Laguna de Fuente. The average size pitches are on a sloping, terraced hillside, with views of the lake. They are mostly flat (chocks useful on some pitches) with a gravel surface and little shade. There is a separate grassy area for tents near the pool and bungalows. This is the area of the Parque National de Donana, ranked amongst Europe's greatest wetlands. This particular area is known for its 15,000 wonderful pink Greater Flamingos. Unusually for a site of this size there is a pool and an excellent bar, snack bar and huge restaurant which serves beautiful Spanish food. Try the excellent, inexpensive 'menu del dia'.

Facilities

One neat block has clean facilities including for disabled campers. Washing machines. Restaurant. Bar with TV. Snack bar. Shop. Swimming pool. Pool bar. Electronic games. Bicycle hire. Torches useful. Off site: Bicycle hire 1 km. Fishing 5 km. Riding 10 km. Golf 40 km. Excursions.

At a glance

Welcome & Ambience	✓✓✓✓	Location	✓✓✓✓
Quality of Pitches	✓✓✓✓	Range of Facilities	✓✓✓✓✓

Directions

Site is some 20 km. northwest of Antequera. From Antequera take A92 and take exit at 132 km. point and follow road to the town. Site is well signed from the town but the signs are small white on black and there are two campsites. This one is on the northeast corner of the lake.

Charges 2003

Per person	€ 3.75 - € 4.10
child (0-12 yrs)	€ 2.25 - € 2.40
pitch incl. car	€ 4.85 - € 6.45
electricity	€ 3.00

Reservations

Contact site. Tel: 952 73 52 94.
Email: info@camping-rural.com

Open

All year.

ES8783N Camping Naturista Almanat
Carril de la Torre Alta s/n, 29749 Almayate

With direct access to a one kilometre grey sand and shingle naturist beach, this established all year naturist site, set amongst agricultural land with mountain backdrop, is proving a firm favourite with many British seeking winter sun. English is spoken at the modern reception adjacent to the security barrier. The site also has a night guard. The entire two hectare site is flat with a fine shingle surface on dirt. A large number of trees planted when the site opened in 1998 have now matured, providing much needed shade in the summer months. The 160 touring pitches with electricity, vary in size and shape with the majority demanding physical manoeuvring of a touring caravan. Some pitches are long and narrow which could prevent the erection of an awning and you may feel quite close to your neighbour. The facilities on site are to a very high standard.

Facilities
The large, unisex toilet is fully equipped, regularly cleaned and all under cover. Good facilities for disabled campers near reception (approach surface may cause minor difficulty for wheel chair users). Between the campsite and beach, a sheltered grass area ideal for sunbathing and a bar/restaurant with terrace overlooking the sea provides good food at acceptable prices. Small shop for basic provisions. Large unheated swimming pool. Play area. TV in bar. Sauna and fully equipped gym. Basketball, paddle tennis. Cinema (56 seats) showing VHS tapes or DVD. Weather permitting, one is expected to be nude which is obligatory in the swimming pool area and bar during the day. Off site: Torre del Mar is 2 km. with many shops, restaurants, a street market on Thursdays and internet café. Regular bus service from end of approach road (1 km). Fishing, riding nearby.

At a glance
Welcome & Ambience	✓✓✓✓	Location	✓✓✓✓
Quality of Pitches	✓✓✓✓✓	Range of Facilities	✓✓✓✓✓

Directions
Approaching this site from the east (Torre del Mar) it is necessary to make a left turn to access the 600 m. single-track tarmac lane leading to the site entrance. It is currently illegal to make that left turn and you will be fined if caught by the authorities. We recommend that whether travelling from the east or west exit the N340 autovia at junction 265 signed Cajiz Iznate and Costa 340a. Take the Costa direction and on reaching the coast turn left onto 340a toward Torre del Mar. Site well signed in 4 km. on right shortly after passing 'Bull' hoarding.

Charges 2003
Per person	€ 3.90
child (2-10 yrs)	€ 3.10
tent	€ 3.90
caravan	€ 4.40
car	€ 3.90
motorcaravan	€ 8.30
electricity (16A)	€ 2.30
dog	€ 1.65

All plus 7% VAT. No credit cards.

Reservations
Contact site. Tel: 952 556 462.
Email: almanat@arrakis.es

Open
All year.

ES8800 Camping Marbella Playa
Ctra. N-340, km. 192,800, 29600 Marbella

This large site is 12 km. east of Marbella with public transport available to the town centre and local attractions. A sandy beach is about 150 m. away with direct access. There are 430 individual pitches of up to 70 sq.m. with natural shade (additional artificial shade is provided to some), and electricity available throughout. A large swimming pool complex with a restaurant/bar with large patio, palm trees, banana plants and lush grass for sunbathing provides a very attractive feature. The site is busy throughout the high season but the high staff/customer ratio and the friendly staff approach ensures a comfortable stay.

Facilities
Four sanitary blocks of mixed ages, are fully equipped and well maintained. Three modern units for disabled visitors. Laundry and dishwashing areas in good order. Large supermarket with butcher and fresh vegetable counter. Bar, restaurant and café. All amenities open all year. Supervised swimming pool (free - April/Sept). Playground (on gritty sand). Torches necessary in beach areas.

At a glance
Welcome & Ambience	✓✓✓✓	Location	✓✓✓✓✓
Quality of Pitches	✓✓✓✓	Range of Facilities	✓✓✓✓✓

Directions
Site is 12 km. east of Marbella with access close to the 193 km. point on the main N340 road.

Latest charges
Per person	€ 3.55
child (1-10 yrs)	€ 3.01
car	€ 3.55
caravan or tent	€ 6.01
motorcycle	€ 3.25
motorcaravan	€ 8.41
electricity (10/20A)	€ 2.46
minimum pitch fee	€ 9.02 - € 16.65

All plus 7% VAT. Reductions (up to 50%) for long stays and senior citizens outside 16/6-31/8.

Reservations
Write to site. Tel: 952 833 998.

Open
All year.

Andalucia

ES8802 Camping Cabopino
Ctra. N340, km 194.7, 29600 Marbella

This large mature site is alongside the main N340 coast road in the Costa del Sol, also known as the Costa del Golf, and fittingly there is a major golf course alongside the site. Just 600 metres from the beaches and dunes, a short walk over the road and down the hill brings you to a restaurant on the beach and an unofficial naturist area. You are seven kilometres from Marbella which is extremely popular with British visitors and very commercialised, although you can find authentic tapas bars in the old town. The site is set amongst tall pine trees which provide shade, and the pitches are large and sandy (with some huge areas for large units). The upper areas of the site are filled with permanent pitches and bungalows are scattered around the remainder. The 385 touring pitches all have electrical connections and there is a separate area on the west side for groups of younger guests. At the other side of the site you will find a fenced pool with a grass sunbathing area. Close to the entrance, the terrace to the restaurant enjoys shade and is very pleasant. The white linen restaurant offers great food, good service and a reasonable wine cellar, competing well with the town restaurants.

Facilities
Four mature but clean sanitary blocks provide hot water throughout. Washing machines. Bar/restaurant. Shop. Swimming pool (all season). Play area. Some children's activities and adult entertainment is planned for next year. Excursions can be booked. Torches necessary in the more remote parts of the site. Off site: Fishing, bicycle hire and riding within 1 km. Golf 7 km.

At a glance
Welcome & Ambience	✓✓✓	Location	✓✓✓
Quality of Pitches	✓✓✓✓	Range of Facilities	✓✓✓✓

Directions
Site is 7 km. from Marbella. Approaching Marbella from the east, leave the N340 at the 194 km. marker (signed Cabopino). Site is off the roundabout at the top of the slip road.

Charges 2003
Per person	€ 3.00 - € 5.00
child	€ 2.00 - € 4.00
pitch	€ 5.80 - € 11.90
dog	€ 2.25
electricity (10A)	€ 3.00

Plus 7% VAT. Discounts outside high season.
Camping Cheques accepted.

Reservations
Contact site. Tel: 952 834 373.
Email: info@campingcabopino.com

Open
All year.

ES8803 Camping La Buganvilla
Ctra. N340, km 188.8, 29600 Marbella

This site has a grand total of 1,000 pitches, of which 300 are for touring units. They are mostly on terraces so there are some views across to the mountains and hinterland of this coastal area. La Buganvilla is a large, uncomplicated site with mature trees providing shade to some pitches. The terrain is a little rugged in places and the buildings are older in style but all were clean when we visited. A pool near the bar and restaurant is ideal for cooling off after a day's sightseeing. The restaurant offers barbecue style meals. Next to the campsite a large area of common land provides pleasant walks. A footbridge crosses the N340 road and there is a gradual 400 m. downhill walk to the beach, where there are some bars and restaurants. The staff are friendly and some English is spoken but you will get a chance to practice your Spanish. There is a multi-language book swap, and internet point in the small reception area.

Facilities
Three painted sanitary blocks are clean and adequate with laundry facilities. Large bar/restaurant with terrace overlooking the pool area. Extremely well stocked mini supermarket. Play area. Basketball and tennis in high season. Dogs are not accepted in July/Aug. Off site: Bus service close to site entrance. Fishing and watersports 400 m. Resort type entertainment close. Bicycle and scooter hire 1 km. Golf 5 km.

At a glance
Welcome & Ambience	✓✓✓✓	Location	✓✓✓✓
Quality of Pitches	✓✓✓✓	Range of Facilities	✓✓✓

Directions
Site is between Marbella and Fuengirola off the N340. Access at 188.8km marker on the N340 can only be achieved when travelling in a westerly direction, i.e. from Fuengirola towards Marbella. If travelling in the opposite direction, continue past the site until reaching the 'cambio de sentido' signed Elviria. Take U-turn over the dual carriageway. Site is signed.

Charges 2003
Per adult	€ 3.50 - € 4.00
child (under 10 yrs)	€ 2.50 - € 3.50
caravan	€ 4.00 - € 6.00
car	€ 3.50 - € 4.50
motorcaravan	€ 5.00 - € 7.00
electricity	€ 2.60
dog (not July/Aug)	€ 2.00

All plus 7% VAT. Discounts in low season.

Reservations
Contact site. Tel: 952 831 973.
Email: info@campingbuganvilla.com

Open
All year.

www.alanrogers.com for latest campsite news

Andalucia

ES8809 Camping El Sur

Ctra. Ronda - Algeciras, km 1,5, Apartado de Correos 127, 29400 Ronda

The generous manoeuvring area and delightfully decorated entrance to this site are a promise of something different which is fulfilled in all respects. The very friendly family who run the site have worked hard for many years combining innovative thinking with excellent service. The 114 terraced pitches have electricity and water, and are partially shaded by olive and almond trees. Most have relaxing views of the surrounding mountains but at an elevation of 850 m. the upper pitches (the very top 45 pitches are for tents only) allow a clear view of the town of Ronda. The various leisure facilities are very clean, well maintained and the personal touches of the owners are obvious which make using them more enjoyable. This is one of the best small sites we have seen in Andalucia with prices that are extremely competitive.

Facilities

The immaculate sanitary block is fully equipped (toilet paper purchased from reception). Laundry facilities in little separate blocks. Gas supplies. Bar and very large, high quality restaurant serving excellent food at reasonable prices (closed 71 15/1). Kidney shaped pool most welcome in summer as the temperatures soar (1/6-30/9). Playground and adventure play area. Separate camping area for groups. Minigolf. Dogs on leads with site permission. Barbeques on pitch with site permission. Off road bicycle hire. Internet terminal. Off site: The famous town of Ronda with all its attractions. The coast is approximately one hours drive. National parks to the north.

At a glance

Welcome & Ambience	✓✓✓✓✓	Location	✓✓✓✓✓
Quality of Pitches	✓✓✓✓✓	Range of Facilities	✓✓✓✓✓

Directions

Site is well signed from the town centre (do not stray off the signed route as there are some very narrow roads) and it is off the Algeciras road, 1.5 km. south of Ronda.

Charges 2003

Per person	€ 4.04
child (under 10 yrs)	€ 3.67
tent	€ 3.47 - € 4.50
car or motorcycle	€ 3.47
caravan	€ 4.74 - € 6.93
motorcaravan	€ 7.87 - € 11.02
electricity (5-10A)	€ 3.36 - € 4.81

Plus 7% VAT. Less 40% in low season. No credit cards.

Reservations

Advised for July/Aug. Tel: 952 875 939.
Email: info@campingelsur.es

Open

All year.

ES8850 Camping Paloma

Ctra. Cadiz-Malaga, km 70, 11380 Tarifa

A spacious, neat and tidy, family orientated site popular with Spanish families and young people of all nations in high season. Paloma is well established with many tall palms placed around the site, just 700 m. from a fabulous beach with white sands and enormous dunes. The area is famous for its ideal kite and windsurfing conditions. The site has 353 pitches on mostly flat ground, although the westerly pitches are sloping. They are of average size with some places for extra large units, some are separated by hedges and most are shaded by mature trees; around 200 pitches have electrical connections. A large, smart restaurant serves excellent Spanish fare and the bar with large courtyard buzzes with activity, tapas and snacks are served here. There is a small swimming pool with a paved and grassed sunbathing area and an attractive thatched, stone bar.

Facilities

There are two sanitary blocks, one of a good size, although it is a long walk from the southern end of the site. The other block is smaller and open plan, serving the sloping areas of the site. The sanitary blocks have been refurbished to a high standard. WCs are British style with some Turkish, washbasins have cold water. Facilities for disabled visitors are in the smaller block with access from sloping ground, also a babies room. All very clean when seen. Washing machine. Gas supplies. Shop. Busy bar and good restaurant. Swimming pool with adjacent bar (high season only). Playground. TV in bar. Excursions (June-Sept). Off site: Nearest beach 700 m. Bicycle/scooter/quad hire 5 km. Riding 10 km. Tarifa 12 km. with lots of night life and bars. Golf 25 km.

At a glance

Welcome & Ambience	✓✓✓✓	Location	✓✓✓✓
Quality of Pitches	✓✓✓✓	Range of Facilities	✓✓✓✓

Directions

Site is signed off N340 Cadiz road at Punta Paloma, about 10 km. northwest of Tarifa, just west of km. 74 marker. Watch carefully for the site sign - no advance notice. Be sure to use the slip road to turn left if coming from Tarifa. Follow the signs down a sandy road for 300 m. and site is on the right.

Latest charges

Per person	€ 4.81
child	€ 3.91
car	€ 3.01
motorcycle	€ 2.70
tent	€ 3.31
caravan	€ 3.31
motorcaravan	€ 5.11
electricity	€ 2.70

Reservations

Made for one part of site, for any length and without deposit. Tel: 956 684 203.

Open

All year.

Andalucia

ES8812 Camping Chullera 2

Ctra. N340, km 141.5, 29692 Sabinillas-Manilva

This is an uncomplicated site with a friendly owner on the Costa del Sol with an attractive 'al-fresco' type restaurant and bar close to the beach. The bar is a simple affair, the food is very good and cheap. The eight kilometres of sandy beach is safe (shelving at low tide), clean, and a major attraction – there are several desirable pitches alongside the beach, with electricity. Most of the larger than average pitches have artificial or natural shade and are well cared for, some being on a gentle slope. There are a number of static pitches here (30%) and the weekends can be lively when the Spanish campers relax. If you wish for something a little quieter then go to the sister site Chullera 3, just one kilometre east, where there are 250 touring pitches with similar facilities but no statics (Chullera I is under the building development to the west of Chullera 2). Excellent food is served at the San Raphael restaurant belonging to Raphael, the site owner, just outside the main entrance. Here smart waiters serve traditional food and there is a very good cellar. A short walk east along the beach brings you to the pretty town of Casares where there are many superb seafood restaurants, some on the beach. We see this as a site for visiting the area rather than a family holiday site. There is some road noise in the northern part of the site.

Facilities
There are two mature sanitary blocks (cleaning may be variable). No facilities for disabled campers. Laundry facilities. Bar/café close to beach with TV. Well stocked supermarket by entrance. Basic play area. Torches advised in the beach areas. Bus service from outside site to Marbella and La Linea.

At a glance
Welcome & Ambience	✓✓✓	Location	✓✓✓
Quality of Pitches	✓✓✓	Range of Facilities	✓✓✓

Directions
Site is well signed off the main N340 at the 141.5 km. marker, 16 km. west of Estepona.

Latest charges
Per adult	€ 3.31
child (above 10 yrs)	€ 2.70 - € 3.31
caravan	€ 3.31
car	€ 3.31
motorcaravan	€ 6.61
motorcycle	€ 2.70
electricity (6A)	€ 2.55

All plus 7% VAT.

Reservations
Write to site. Tel: 952 890 196.

Open
All year.

ES8855 Camping Tarifa

Ctra. N340, km 78.87, 11380 Tarifa

The long, golden sandy beach is a good feature of this site, with private access, and is ideal for windsurfing and safe for swimming. The site has a pleasant, open feel and is reasonably sheltered from road noise. It has been thoughtfully landscaped and planted out with an amazing variety of shrubs and flowers and is remarkably clean. There is a smart, modern reception area with an attractive water feature close by. The 265 level pitches are of varying sizes and are surrounded by pine trees which provide ample shade. All have electricity and there are adequate water points. A pleasant restaurant/bar area provides fast food and drinks. The pool is rather small and crowded in summer but has pleasant views of the distant mountain range.

Facilities
Two modern, fully equipped sanitary blocks include facilities for campers with disabilities and baby room. All spotless when seen. Motorcaravan services. Gas supplies. Supermarket and excellent bar/restaurant - fast food only, all open all year with patio. Swimming pool complex with bar. Large children's play area with modern activities. Drinks machines. Good security. Off site: Fishing 100 m. Riding 300 m. Bicycle hire 5 km. Excursions.

At a glance
Welcome & Ambience	✓✓✓✓	Location	✓✓✓✓
Quality of Pitches	✓✓✓	Range of Facilities	✓✓✓

Directions
Site is on main N340 Cadiz road at the 78.87 km. marker, 7.5 km. northwest of Tarifa. There are large modern signs well ahead of the site with a deceleration lane if approaching from the Tarifa direction, large gaily coloured signs mark the approach to the site.

Latest charges
Per person	€ 4.81
child	€ 3.61
tent	€ 2.70
caravan	€ 3.01
car	€ 2.70
motorcycle	€ 2.40
motorcaravan	€ 4.81
electricity (5/10A)	€ 2.55

Reservations
Advised for July/Aug. Tel: 956 684 778.
Email: camping-tarifa@camping-tarifa.com

Open
All year.

Andalucia

ES8860 Camping Fuente del Gallo
Apto. 48, 11140 Conil de la Frontera

Fuente del Gallo extends a warm welcome to British visitors particularly as one half of the ownership is Irish. The attractive pool, restaurant and bar complex with its large, shaded terace, are particularly welcoming in the height of summer. The site is well maintained with 221 pitches allocated to touring units. Although the actual pitch areas are generally a good size, the majority are long and narrow. This could, in some cases, prevent the erection of an awning and your neighbour may feel close. In low season it is generally accepted to make additional use of an adjoining pitch. Each pitch has electricity and a number of trees create shade to some pitches. Good beaches are relatively near at 300 metres with access gained by steps through new houses with palm-lined roads. Helpful, friendly staff will assist in booking discounted trips to nearby attractions or even further afield to Africa.

Facilities
Two modernised and very clean sanitary blocks include excellent services for babies and disabled visitors and hot water at all facilities. Two new blocks provide additional areas for washing dishes and clothes (cold water only). Laundry room with two washing machines. Motorcaravan services. Gas supplies. Well-stocked shop. Attractive bar and restaurant (breakfast served). TV and games rooms. Swimming pool (all season, lifeguard in high season when there is a small charge) with large grass area for sunbathing and children's pool. Play area. Excursions. Torches useful. Safety deposit boxes. Off site: Watersports on beach. Fishing 300 m. Riding 1 km. Bicycle and motor scooter hire 2 km. Golf 5 km.

At a glance
Welcome & Ambience	✓✓✓✓	Location	✓✓✓✓
Quality of Pitches	✓✓✓✓	Range of Facilities	✓✓✓✓

Directions
From Cadiz-Algeciras road (N340) at km. 23.00, follow signs to Conil de la Frontera town centre, then shortly right to Fuente del Gallo and 'playas' following signs.

Charges 2003
Per person	€ 4.00
child (3-10 yrs)	€ 3.50
tent	€ 3.50
caravan	€ 3.80
car	€ 3.20
motorcycle	€ 2.80
motorcaravan	€ 6.70
electricity (10A)	€ 3.20

All plus 7% VAT. Less 11-30% for longer stays (except Jul/Aug).

Reservations
Contact site. Tel: 956 440 137.

Open
Easter - 3 September.

ES8865 Camping Playa Las Dunas de San Anton
P Maritimo de la Puntilla, 11500 El Puerto de Santa Maria

This site lies within the Parque Natural Bahia de Les Dunes and is next to the long and gently sloping golden sands of Puntilla beach. A ten minute walk takes you into the bustling heart of Puerto Santa Maria, a traditional Spanish resort. This is a pleasant and peaceful site (though very busy in August) with 400 separate marked pitches, 140 for tourers, with much natural shade and ample electrical connections. Motorcaravans park in an area called the Oasis which is very pretty. The tent and caravan pitches, under mature trees, are terraced and separated by low walls. This is a spacious site with a tranquil setting and it is popular with people who wish to 'winter over' in peace.

Facilities
Immaculate modern sanitary facilities with separate facilities for disabled campers and a baby room. Laundry facilities are excellent. Gas supplies. Bar/restaurant (all year). Supermarket (high season). Very large swimming pool (supervised) and toddlers pool (high season). Play areas. Night security all year. Off site: Fishing 500 m. Riding or golf 2 km. Municipal sports centre close by offers all manner of sporting activities and the beach provides additional free sports facilities such as volleyball. Local buses for town and cities visits and a ferry to Cadiz.

At a glance
Welcome & Ambience	✓✓✓✓	Location	✓✓✓✓
Quality of Pitches	✓✓✓✓✓	Range of Facilities	✓✓✓✓

Directions
Site is 5 km. north of Cadiz off N1V route. Take road to Puerto Santa Maria, site is very well signed throughout the town (small yellow signs high on posts).

Latest charges
Per person	€ 3.37 - € 3.73
child	€ 2.88 - € 3.19
tent	€ 3.64 - € 4.06
car	€ 2.88 - € 3.19
motorcycle	€ 2.31 - € 2.58
motorcaravan	€ 4.81 - € 5.35
electricity (5A)	€ 2.43 - € 2.67

Reservations
Advised for August; contact site. Tel: 956 872 210. Email: campinglasdunas@terra.es

Open
All year.

Andalucia

ES8889 Camping Los Alcornocales
11330 Jimena de la Frontera

Camping Los Alcornocales takes its name from the surrounding Los Alcornocales Natural Park which is one of Europe's largest Mediterranean forests. A small and charming new site, it is off the beaten track in unspoilt countryside. The site has been well planned and the owners have been environmentally strict in its construction and situation. The result is a most pleasant experience of nature if you tire of the beaches. There are magnificent views over the Natural Park and the river Hozgarganta. Within minutes you are in 170,000 hectares of park containing amazing landscapes and an abundance of wildlife. The 97 pitches (27 for tourers) have been thoughtfully hedged and grassed and all have electricity. Trees such as catalpa, maple and hibiscus ensure a tranquil feeling. The administration building has a natural thatch roof and contains a superb restaurant with an open fire. The theme is continued throughout with a pretty bar using the natural wood and stone of the area and cleverly decorated with cork from the magnificent oaks, which abound. This is a superb site for those who love nature.

Facilities
The sanitary block is very much in keeping with the surroundings. It offers free hot water and the modern facilities include very large showers with excellent facilities for disabled campers. The mirrors used are genuine ships' portholes and are a pleasant touch. Small shop sells essentials but we recommend you stock-up. Bar/restaurant (all year). Playground. Football pitch. Swimming pool. English is spoken. No transit traffic is allowed within the site in high season. All forms of outdoor activity planned for 2003 but check before arrival. Off site: Walking in National park. Fishing 1 km. Riding and bicycle hire 15 km. Golf 40 km.

At a glance
Welcome & Ambience	✓✓✓✓✓	Location	✓✓✓✓✓
Quality of Pitches	✓✓✓✓✓	Range of Facilities	✓✓✓✓✓

Directions
From N340 San Roque - Algeciras take exit 115. Follow C369 for approx. 30 km. then turn left on C3331 to Ubrique. Turn left after 80 km. marker signed Jimena de la Fronterra. Site is on the right. Don't be put off if the gate is shut on arrival someone will appear.

Charges 2003
Per person	€ 3.60
child (2-12 yrs)	€ 2.40
car	€ 3.00
tent or caravan	€ 3.60 - € 4.00
motorcaravan	€ 6.00
electricity (16A)	€ 3.00

All plus 7% VAT. No credit cards. Discounts for longer stays over 1 month.

Reservations
Contact site. Tel: 956 640060.
Email: camping@arrakis.es

Open
All year.

ES8871 Camping Giralda
Ctra. Provincial 4117, 21410 Isla Cristina

The fountains at the entrance and the circular 'thatched' reception building set the tone for this very large, well managed and pleasant site. The 520 pitches are quite spacious on sand, most benefitting from the attractive mature trees which abound on the site. The majority of pitches have electricity (142 are for tents). Access to the excellent beach is gained by a short stroll, crossing the minor road alongside the site and passing through attractive pine trees. There is a separate area within this huge site where organised groups come to enjoy the activities offered within a dedicated adventure area (low season only). A quiet site out of the main tourist area with good leisure and adventure facilities.

Facilities
Four large, modern, semi-circular 'thatched' sanitary blocks are very clean and fully equipped. Laundry. Shop, bar and snacks (all year). Restaurant (April - Sept). Swimming pools. Basketball. Archery. Volleyball. Petanque. Soccer. Mountain biking. Beach games. Table tennis. Watersports school. Play area. Organised activity area for groups low season. Excursions booked. Site contract security all year. Off site: Beach 200 m. Fishing 200 m. Bicycle hire 1 km. Golf 4 km. Riding 7 km.

At a glance
Welcome & Ambience	✓✓✓✓✓	Location	✓✓✓✓
Quality of Pitches	✓✓✓✓✓	Range of Facilities	✓✓✓✓

Directions
Leave E1/A49 motorway at exit 113 signed Lepe on N444. Turn right on N431, use Lepe bypass, then left to Le Antilla and on to Isla Cristina. Site is on right (signed) just as you reach Isla Christina (this route avoids Pozo del Camino and many speed bumps).

Charges 2003
Per person	€ 4.60
child (2-10 yrs)	€ 3.35
tent	€ 4.30
caravan	€ 5.00
car	€ 3.85
motorcycle	€ 3.00
motorcaravan	€ 8.75
electricity	€ 3.50
animal	€ 1.00

Plus 7% VAT. Winter discounts.

Reservations
Advised for July/Aug. Tel: 959 343 318.
Email: campinggiralda@infonegocio.com

Open
All year.

ES9081 Camping Villsom

Ctra. Sevilla - Cadiz, km. 554.8, 41700 Sevilla

This is a fine city site that was one of the first to operate in Spain and it is still owned by the same family. The administrative building consists of a peaceful and attractive, bar with patio and satellite TV (where breakfast is served) and there is a pleasant, dedicated reception area. Minigolf and table tennis are available. There are no static caravans here, and the site has a nice homely feel. It is excellent for visiting Seville with a frequent bus service to the centre (20 minutes, bus stop close by). Camping Villsom has around 180 pitches which are level and shaded. A huge variety of trees and palms are to be seen around the site and in summer the bright colours of the flowers are very pleasing. We are told that the oranges from the trees are sold to Britain for marmalade. The site has a most inviting, large, palm surrounded pool which is quite secluded. Temperatures can be hotter here than almost anywhere in Spain and the pool seems essential. It is essential to book if you intend to visit this site in peak weeks.

Facilities
An excellent new sanitary block supplements the recently modernised existing facilities. Laundry facilities. Small shop selling basic provisions. Bar with satellite TV (open July/Aug). Swimming pool (June-Sept). Large minigolf course. Table tennis. Drinks machine. Off site: Restaurant and supermarket close.

At a glance
Welcome & Ambience	✓✓✓✓	Location	✓✓✓✓
Quality of Pitches	✓✓✓	Range of Facilities	✓✓✓

Directions
This needs care as an error results in extensive driving along the main road to turn around. From Cadiz to Seville on NIV look for 'Carrefour' store and sign on left at the 554 km. marker and turn right signed Salida dos Hermanas - Isla Menor. Take the left to Isla Menor, and once you have passed under a concrete road bridge; the site is immediately on the right.

Latest charges
Per adult	€ 3.16
child	€ 2.76
tent	€ 3.28
caravan	€ 3.43
car	€ 3.28
motorcaravan	€ 4.09
motorcycle	€ 2.73
electricity	€ 2.04

All plus 7% VAT.

Reservations
Write to site. Tel: 954 720 828.

Open
All year.

ES9082 Camping Sevilla

Ctra. N-IV, km 534, 41007 Sevilla

This site just south of the perimeter of Seville airfield, by day with your ear defenders, you can practice your plane-spotting, but thankfully the usual mandatory respite exists at night, although you are fairly close to the main Seville - Madrid road. This is a flat, sandy site with 85 pitches of varying size for motorcaravans and caravans, plus 450 for tents. Electricity is available. Trees provide some pitches with shade, others have artificial shade. The kidney shaped pool and paddling pool area are very welcome in the summer heat. There is the constant change-over bustle of all nationalities coming and going to visit Seville; this site is ideal for a short stay to enjoy the city.

Facilities
Buildings housing the sanitary and supporting facilities are round in shape and a happy yellow colour. To reinforce the reality of the intense summer temperatures, half of the showers are cold water only. The remainder provide free hot (very) water, but only cold for all other washing functions. Blocks kept very clean. Supermarket, bar and restaurant (high season). Small bar/snack area (out of main season). Swimming pools (June - Sept); adult € 1,20, child € 0,50). Drinks machines. Electronic games. Two excellent motorhome service points. Off site: Bus service runs to city centre leaving from inside site (high season). 'Magic Island' theme park 3 km.

At a glance
Welcome & Ambience	✓✓✓✓	Location	✓✓✓
Quality of Pitches	✓✓✓✓	Range of Facilities	✓✓✓

Directions
From any route follow signs to the airport (very easy) and you will pick up signs for the campsite from any direction. Be sure to follow signs carefully If you miss the turn the quickest way to cross the autoroute is to go through the airport.

Latest charges
Per person	€ 3.00
child (3-11 yrs)	€ 2.40
car	€ 3.00
caravan	€ 3.00
tent	€ 2.50 - € 3.00
motorcaravan	€ 4.50
motorcycle	€ 2.00
electricity (6/10A)	€ 2.00

Plus 7% VAT. No credit cards.

Reservations
Advised in July and August. Tel: 954 514 379.
Email: campingsevilla@wanadoo.es

Open
All year.

ES9078 Camping Los Villares

Parque Periurbano, Avenida de l Fuen Santa 8, 14071 Cordoba

This is a site with a difference. Unusually it is part of one of Spain's natural parks and environmental rules must be strictly followed when you stay here. If you wish for a peaceful, simple site with no frills then this may be your cup of tea. There are bountiful pine, olives, gums and other trees providing shade and, as the site is within the Parque, the setting is absolutely natural. Thoughtfully some natural stone tables and benches are scattered around the site. The natty little bar and restaurant provide a simple menu and drinks. The 170 tent pitches are delightfully informal. Find your place with its considerable privacy or make your way to the fenced area for 30 caravans or motorcaravans – access is fine. The friendly warden will assist as necessary. All touring pitches have electricity but you will most certainly need torches as you find your way home through the densely wooded area beyond the site. This is great site with reasonable prices, which will suit those who do not need the artificial entertainment of bigger sites and just wish to relax at one with nature.

Facilities

The single toilet facility is centrally located, provides free hot water and is of good quality. Washing machines. Restaurant/bar. Shop. Five-a-side soccer. Off site: Natural Parque (protected), with walks and wildlife.

At a glance

| Welcome & Ambience | ✓✓✓ | Location | ✓✓✓ |
| Quality of Pitches | ✓✓✓✓ | Range of Facilities | ✓✓✓ |

Directions

The site is about 7 km. north of Cordoba. It is on the north side of the river which bisects the city and it is simpler to go to the centre to find the small access road to Parque and site. Follow the Parador (state run hotel) signs if you cannot see the signs for the Parque Periurbano which have small camping sign inside the fairly large green edged signs. Also follow signs for municipal camping which help. All these will bring you past the municipal camping – then look for a major right turn and follow clear signs out of city. Site is a stiff climb of several thousand feet out of city.

Latest charges

Per person	€ 2.55
child	€ 1.95
tent or caravan	€ 2.55 - € 3.91
car or motorcycle	€ 2.10
motorcaravan	€ 4.21
electricity	€ 2.40

No credit cards.

Reservations

Contact site. Tel: 957 330145.
Email: campingvillares@latinmail.com

Open

All year.

www.alanrogers.com for latest campsite news

ES9080 Camping Municipal El Brillante
Avenida del Brillante 50, 14012 Córdoba

For a municipal site this is impressive. Cordoba is one of the hottest places in Spain and the superb pool here is more than welcome. It is large and has pleasant terraced gardens where you can sunbathe as you admire the colourful flowers and shrubs. The 120 neat pitches are attractively spaced alongside the canal (securely fenced for safety) which runs through the centre of the site. The upper pitches are now covered by artificial and natural shade but the lower, newer area has little shade. Here the pitches are more spacious if you have a larger unit. The site becomes very crowded in high season. The entrance is narrow and may be congested so care must be exercised – there is a lay-by just outside and it is easier to walk in initially. The bar/restaurant is close to reception and there is a pleasant terrace bar/restaurant which overlooks the pool gardens in high season. Buses go from outside the site to town. If you really want to stay in the city, then this site is a good choice.

Facilities
The toilet blocks have been renovated and an impressive new block added with facilities for babies and disabled people. Motorcaravan services. Gas supplies. Bar and restaurant (1/4-30/9). Shop (all year). Swimming pool (15/6-15/9). Play area. Off site: Bus service to city centre from outside site. Large supermarket 300 m.

At a glance
Welcome & Ambience	✓✓✓	Location	✓✓✓✓
Quality of Pitches	✓✓✓	Range of Facilities	✓✓✓

Directions
Site is on the north side of the river. Entering Cordoba by NIV/E25 road from Madrid, drive into city centre. After passing the Mosque/Cathedral, turn right onto the main avenue, continue and take right fork where the road splits, and follow signs for campsite and/or district of El Brillante. Keep a sharp eye out for camp signs as they are partially hidden behind foliage.

Latest charges
Per unit incl. 2 adults	€ 15.93
tent and car incl. 2 adults	€ 14.72
tent without car	€ 10.97
extra adult	€ 3.45
child (1-10 yrs)	€ 2.58
electricity	€ 2.55

No credit cards.

Reservations
Not made. It is essential to arrive early in high season. Tel: 957 403 836.

Open
All year.

ES9085 Camping Carlos III
Ctra. Madrid - Cadiz, km 430, 14100 La Carlota

This is a good alternative site for Cordoba being 25 km. from the city. A very large, busy site especially at weekends, it has many supporting facilities including a good swimming pool for adults and separate children's pool. With the bar and catering services open all year, the site has a more open feel than the bustling municipal site in Cordoba itself. The touring areas are canopied by trees which offer considerable shade for the 300 separated pitches. On sandy, gently sloping ground, around two-thirds have electrical connections. Permanent units, mobile homes and bungalows are in a separate area, where there are also sporting facilities. There may be some slight road noise.

Facilities
Sanitary facilities in two modern blocks have British (40%) and Turkish style WCs, with hot showers in the block near reception. Motorcaravan services. Bar/restaurant, shop (all year). Swimming pools (1/6-15/9). Aviary. Table tennis. Boules. Minigolf, Play area. Volleyball. Football. Hairdressers. Off site: Bus service outside site. Riding 500 m. Village 2 km.

At a glance
Welcome & Ambience	✓✓✓	Location	✓✓✓
Quality of Pitches	✓✓✓	Range of Facilities	✓✓✓✓

Directions
From N-IV Cordoba-Seville motorway take La Carlota exit at km. 429 point; site is well signed.

Latest charges
Per person	€ 3.60
child (under 12 yrs)	€ 2.70
car	€ 3.30
motorcycle	€ 2.70
tent	€ 3.45
caravan	€ 3.60
motorcaravan	€ 4.95
electricity (5A)	€ 2.70

Plus 7% VAT. Discounts (10-20%) for longer stays in low season.

Reservations
Probably necessary in July/Aug. Tel: 957 300 697. Email: campingcarlos@navegalia.com

Open
All year.

ES9084 Camping La Campiña

Ctra. Altea Quintana-Pte Genil km 11,5, 14547 Santaella

What a charming site – literally amongst the olive trees and set high on a hill to catch cool summer breezes. Everything is immaculately kept and we rarely see sites of this size with such excellent amenities and standards. There is a large pool in a garden setting with cool green lawn and the restaurant with its traditional rustic charm, has a delightful menu of home made food. The 'menu del dia' was delicious and very good value. Fresh bread and croissants are cooked to order in the morning, or you can have an inexpensive breakfast on the terrace. The 35 pitches are level and most have shade, the surface is gravel and there are views over the olive fields to the surrounding hills. The area is famous for its natural beauty, wine and olives (excursions can be arranged to see olive oil made, and to a local 'bodega' for the wine making). The Martin-Rodriguez family are enthusiastic and work hard to make a visit here a delightful experience.

Facilities
Two small traditional sanitary blocks have clean services including facilities for disabled campers (key at reception). Washing machines. Restaurant. Snack bar. Shop. Swimming pool. Table tennis. Basketball. Torches useful. Off site: Bus from gate to Cordoba. Town 2 km. Riding 15 km. Golf 40 km.

At a glance
Welcome & Ambience	✓✓✓✓	Location	✓✓✓
Quality of Pitches	✓✓✓✓	Range of Facilities	✓✓✓

Directions
From A92 Sevilla- Malaga road take exit 106 for Herrera. Then right on N340 towards Puente-Genil. Go through Puente-Genil crossing the river and take the Cordoba road. Turn left for Aguilar and then very quickly left again for Santaella. Travel north for about 24 km. to find camp site signs north of Santanaella on the road to La Rambla. Do not go into the town of Santanaella. Site is tucked off the road on the right behind high hedging.

Charges 2003
Per adult	€ 3.50
child	€ 3.40
pitch	€ 16.50

Reservations
Contact site. Tel: 957 315 303.
Email: camping_campina@bch.navegalia.com

Open
21 January - 19 December.

ES9089 Camping Despenaperros

Ctra. Infanta Elena, 23213 Santa Elena

Despeñaperros is a very smart, new site in the heartland of La Mancha, run by a co-operative of five very friendly people who employ helpful staff. This site is an ideal break point for those travelling from Madrid towards the Costa del Sol, or those wishing to explore the local attractions. The site is located in a 30-year-old pine grove which is part of the Despeñaperros nature reserve. All 116 pitches are of a good size, have natural shade from the mature pine trees and unusually have their own electricity, water, TV connections and waste water drainage.

Facilities
Two central sanitary blocks are of a high standard. Washing machines. Motorcaravan services. Gas supplies. Shop. Excellent bar (all year) and charming restaurant (12/3-20/10). Swimming pools (15/6-15/9). Tennis. First aid room. Caravan storage. Night security.

At a glance
Welcome & Ambience	✓✓✓✓	Location	✓✓✓✓
Quality of Pitches	✓✓✓✓	Range of Facilities	✓✓✓

Directions
On N1V- E5 Autovia de Andalucia between Bailén and Madrid at km. 257, at the village of Santa Elena; site is well signed.

Latest charges
Per adult	€ 2.85
child	€ 2.34
tent	€ 3.01
car	€ 2.85
caravan	€ 3.01
motorcaravan	€ 5.05
motorcycle	€ 1.83
electricity (10A)	€ 2.70

All plus 7% VAT.

Reservations
Contact site. Tel: 953 664 192.

Open
All year.

Extremadura

This is one of the most beautiful, and perhaps least known, regions of inland Spain. Its beautiful cities, first Roman and Moorish, then medieval and aristocratic, gave birth to many of the conquistadors - conquerors of the New World.

Extremadura has two provinces: Badajoz and Cáceres

Extremadura is a large and sparsely populated region in the west of Spain, bordering central Portugal and consisting of two provinces, both of which bear the name of their main town. Cáceres, to the north, has a fascinating old quarter, ringed by old Moorish walls and superb watchtowers. Nearby Plasencia is home to a splendid Gothic cathedral, old medieval walls and beautiful Baroque and Renaissance palaces. And the attractive town of Trujillo, birthplace of Pizzoro, the conqueror of Peru, has palaces, churches and a bustling town square.

To the south is Badajoz, the second province and the largest in Spain. With its fortified main town and Alcazaba (citadel), the city of Badajoz is located on the *Vía de la Plata* (Silver Route), an old pilgrimage route to Santiago de Compostela used during the Middle Ages. Located on this route, Mérida is one of the best preserved archaeological sites in Spain. Indeed, the city boasts more Roman remains than any other city, including a Roman theatre and amphitheatre, a Roman Bridge spanning over 800 metres long, with 60 arches, Roman villas and a Museum of Roman Art.

Cuisine of the region

Local cuisine includes the Iberian cured ham and a variety of cheeses; *Torta del Casar, La Serena, Ibores, Gata* and *Cabra del Tietar*. Game abounds in this region (partridge, pigeon, turtledove, rabbit, hare, wild boar, deer) served with wild mushrooms, truffles or wild asparagus. Honey, thyme, heather, rosemary, lavender, lime and eucalyptus are used to prepare a great variety of desserts.

Alfeñiques: caramel dessert
Nuégados: egg yolk and orange buns
Perrunillas: small round cakes
Rosquillas: ring-shaped biscuits
Técula-mécula: cinnamon, almond and tea

Places of interest

Alcántara: six-arched Roman bridge, castle, mansions

Corio: quiet old town enclosed by 4th century Roman walls, cathedral

Cuacos de Yuste: town with 15th century Jeronimos Monastery

Guadalupe: old pilgrimage centre, church and monastery

Jerez de los Caballeros: birthplace of various conquistadores

Olivenza: town with strong Portuguese influence, castle, ethnographic museum, 17th century church

Pedroso de Acim: Convento del Palancar – said to be the smallest monastery in the world

tip

VISIT THE MONFRAGÜE NATURE RESERVE; A PROTECTED AREA WITH FORESTS, MEADOWS, RIVERS AND RESERVOIRS, WITH OVER 200 ANIMAL SPECIES INCLUDING THE SPANISH LYNX.

www.**alanrogers**.com for latest campsite news

Extremadura

ES9087 Camping Merida
Ctra. NV Madrid-Port, km 336.6, 06800 Mérida

Camping Mérida is situated alongside the main N-V to Madrid, the restaurant, café and pool complex separating the camping site area from the road where there is considerable noise. The site has 80 good sized pitches, most with some shade and on sloping ground, with ample electricity connections (long leads may be needed). No English is spoken, but try out your Spanish. Reception is open until midnight. Camping Mérida is ideally located to serve both as a base to tour the local area or as an overnight stop en route when travelling either north/south or east/west.

Facilities
Central sanitary facility include hot and cold showers, dishwashing sinks (H&C) and laundry sinks (cold only) under cover. Gas supplies. Small shop for essentials. Busy restaurant/cafeteria and bar. Medium sized swimming pool and children's pool with lifeguard (May-Sept). Bicycle hire. Playground. Caravan storage. Torches useful. Off site: Town 4 km.

At a glance
Welcome & Ambience	✓✓✓	Location	✓✓✓✓
Quality of Pitches	✓✓✓✓	Range of Facilities	✓✓✓

Directions
Site is alongside road NV (Madrid-Lisbon), 5 km. east of Mérida, at km. 336.6 point.

Latest charges
Per adult	€ 3.15
child	€ 2.70
tent or caravan	€ 3.15
car	€ 3.15
motorcaravan	€ 4.35
electricity	€ 2.70

All plus VAT.

Reservations
Write to site. Tel: 924 303 453. Email: proexcam@jet.es

Open
All year.

ES9027 Camping Parque Natural de Monfrague
Ctra. Plasencia-Trujillo km 10, 10680 Malpartida de Plasencia

Situated on the edge of the Monfrague National Park, this well managed site owned by the Barrado family, has fine views to the Sierra de Mirabel and delightful surrounding countryside. Created as a National Park in 1979, Monfrague is now recognised as one of the best locations in Europe for anyone with any degree of interest in birdwatching. Many of the 128 good-sized pitches are grassed on slightly sloping terraced ground. Scattered trees offer a degree of shade, there are numerous water points and electricity is rated at 10A. Used by locals, the air-conditioned restaurant provides good quality food at acceptable prices. An evening meal on the veranda as the sunsets will install fond memories of a rewarding holiday. On rare occasions a goods train travels along the nearby railway line.

Facilities
Large modern toilet blocks, fully equipped, are very clean. Facilities for disabled campers and baby baths. Laundry. Supermarket/shop. Restaurant, bar and coffee shop. TV room with recreational facilities and fire for cooler times. Swimming pools and children's pool (June - Sept). Play area. Tennis. Basketball. Bicycle hire. Riding. Animation for children in season. Barbecue areas. Off site: Large supermarket at Plasencia.

At a glance
Welcome & Ambience	✓✓✓✓	Location	✓✓✓✓✓
Quality of Pitches	✓✓✓✓✓	Range of Facilities	✓✓✓✓

Directions
Approaching on the N630 - From the north take the EX-208 (previously C524) Plasencia - Trujillo; site on left in approx. 6km. From the south turn right just south of Plasencia onto EX-108 (previously C511) in direction of Malpartida de Plasencia. Right at main junction onto EX-208 to site.

Charges 2003
Per adult	3.20
child	2.50
tent or caravan	3.20
car	2.50
motorcaravan	4.50
electricity	2.50

VAT included. Camping Cheques accepted.

Reservations
Write to site. Tel: 927 459 233.

Open
All year.

ES9028 Camping Las Villueracas

Ctra. Villanueva, 10140 Guadalupe

This rural site nestles in an attractive valley northwest of Guadalupe. The pools and restaurant are of a very high standard and the restaurant leads to a pretty patio with overhead vines and potted plants allowing elevated views of the pools. There is a separate patio across the village street which is pleasant for sitting out with drinks whilst the management provide a barbecue and more casual food. The 70 pitches are level and of a reasonable size; some are marked, although the logic of the numbering is difficult to follow in places and large units may experience difficulty in getting into the more central pitches. There is limited shade from young trees and a more shaded area in a 'spinney'. A river runs alongside the site and we are told that the ground can be muddy in very wet periods. The site is co-located with hostel accommodation.

Facilities

The single toilet block is in the older style but very clean, one area for women and one for men, providing British type WCs, washbasins and free hot showers (although hot water is from a 40 litre immersion heater which could be overwhelmed in busy periods). There are no facilities for disabled campers as yet. Restaurant. Bar. Swimming pools. Shop. Tennis. Small playground. Barbecue area. Safe deposit. Medical post. Car wash.

At a glance

Welcome & Ambience	✓✓✓	Location	✓✓✓
Quality of Pitches	✓✓✓	Range of Facilities	✓✓✓✓

Directions

From NV/E90 Madrid - Mérida exit at Navelmoral de la Mata. Follow south to Guadalupe on CC713 (approx. 83 km). Site is 2 km. from Guadalupe, near the Monastery.

Latest charges

Per adult	€ 2.40
child	€ 2.10
tent	€ 2.10 - € 2.40
car	€ 2.25
caravan	€ 2.40
motorcycle	€ 2.10
motorcaravan	€ 3.61
electricity	€ 2.10

No credit cards.

Reservations

Write to site. Tel: 927 367 139.

Open

All year.

Extremadura

Widely regarded as the 'Bible' by site owners and readers alike, there is no better guide when it comes to forming an independent view of a campsite's quality. When you need to be confident in your choice of campsite, you need the Alan Rogers Guide.

✓ Sites only included on merit

✓ Sites cannot pay to be included

✓ Independently inspected, rigorously assessed

✓ Impartial reviews

✓ 36 years of expertise

INSPECTED & SELECTED CAMPSITES

Great on-line holiday deals alanrogersdirect.com

Castilla-La Mancha

This region is located south of Madrid and occupies what was the southern part of the ancient kingdom of Castille, including the area known as La Mancha, universally famous as the setting for Miguel de Cervantes great novel *Don Quijote de la Mancha*.

Castilla-La Mancha has five provinces: Albacete, Ciudad Real, Cuenca, Guadalajara and Toledo

The capital of the region is Toledo

The terrain can be divided into two distinct parts: the plateau, an extensive flat land with very few mountains, and the mountainous areas, which encircle the plateau around the region's borders, including the foothills along the massifs of the Central mountain range, the Iberian mountain range and the Sierra Morena.

Toledo is crammed with monuments and nearly all the different stages of Spanish art are represented with Moorish-Mudejar-Jewish buildings; Gothic structures, such as the splendid cathedral; and Renaissance buildings. Toledo was also home to El Greco and many of his paintings are displayed in the Museum of El Greco. The region of Cuenca is surrounded by mountainous, craggy countryside, with the city itself home to extraordinary houses which hang over the cliff tops of the deep gorges. One of these has been converted into the Museum of Abstract Art. In the heartland of La Mancha, through the region of Ciudad Real, you can follow the Ruta de Don Quixote and see the famous windmills at Campo de Criptana.

Cuisine of the region

Local produce features heavily: aubergines, garlic, peppers, tomatoes, olive oil, meat, including both game and farm animals. Wine from La Mancha, Valdepeñas, Méntrida, Almansa, Dominio de Valdepusa and Finca de Elez

Alajú: an almond and nut pastry

Bizcochás de Alcázar: a tart soaked in milk with sugar, vanilla and cinnamon

Caldereta manchega: lamb stew

Morteruelo: paté made of pork and game birds

Pisto manchego: a type of ratatouille with tomatoes, red and green peppers, courgettes, served either hot or cold

Tiznao: filleted cod which is flame-grilled in an earthenware dish with pepper, tomatoes, onions and garlic.

Places of interest

Almagro: home of international theatre festival

Albacete: renowned for its knife-making industry, 16th century cathedral

Guadalajara: preserved Moorish walls, 10th century bridge, Santa Maria la Mayor, 15th century Duque del Infantado Palace

tip

VISIT LA CIUDAD ENCANTADA IN CUENCA, AN AREA OF LIMESTONE OUTCROPS, AND SEE HOW EROSION HAS SCULPTED THE ROCK TO CREATE ANIMAL-LIKE AND ABSTRACT FORMS.

www.alanrogers.com for latest campsite news

ES9088 Camping de Fuencaliente

km.105, N420 Cordoba-Tarragona, 13130 Fuencaliente

This quiet site nestles in an attractive valley between the Sierra Modrona and the Sierra Morena. It is ideal as a stopover if crossing Spain coast to coast. With very few other desirable sites in this region of Castilla-La Mancha, this one is open all year round and is very peaceful with good views through pined slopes. The site is spacious with some shade from young trees but most is provided by artificial means. The 91 well maintained pitches are generous at over 100 sq.m. and all have electricity (6A) and water. There are areas allocated for tents. The large swimming pool with a separate children's area is most welcome in summer, as this part of Spain gets very hot. The site has a good restaurant overlooking the pools, with very reasonable prices – the food was excellent when we visited. The local village of Fuencaliente is 5 km. south and provides the usual village facilities including some very good Spanish restaurants and bars.

Facilities
The large, modern toilet block has excellent facilities. Laundry sinks. Swimming pool (1/6-15/9; free). Restaurant/bar (all year). Supermarket. Children's playground. Barbecue facilities.

At a glance
Welcome & Ambience	✓✓✓	Location	✓✓✓
Quality of Pitches	✓✓✓	Range of Facilities	✓✓✓

Directions
Site is on N420 road at 105 km. marker approx. 5 km. north of Fuencaliente.

Latest charges
Per person	€ 3.61
child	€ 3.31
tent	€ 3.61
caravan	€ 5.71
car	€ 2.10
motorcycle	€ 1.80
motorcaravan	€ 9.32

Electricity included. Plus 7% VAT.

Reservations
Advised for July/Aug. Tel: 926 698 170.

Open
All year.

ES9094 Camping La Aguzadera

Ctra. N-IV, km. 197.5, 13300 Valdepeñas

This is a small, unassuming site which will be useful to travellers, especially if you wish to enjoy some excellent Spanish fare in the restaurant. There are few other campsites open all year in this area. With pleasant views of the mountains, the site is part of a huge sports complex where there is lots of activity, although the site is quite separate with lots of room to manoeuvre. The 66 pitches are of average size and are on sloping sand with a few trees providing a little shade. There is some road noise as the site is just off the N4. The sophisticated restaurant overlooks a pool with terraces and sunbathing areas but food is also available in the bar. It is primarily a transit site but useful if you are following the Valdepenas wine route.

Facilities
The central sanitary block is average, unheated, but clean. Washbasins have cold water only. Restaurant plus bar and attached eating area. Essentials from bar. Swimming pool and paddling pools (high season only), Play area. Tennis. Large sports complex alongside (charges apply). Dogs are not accepted. Torches required.

At a glance
Welcome & Ambience	✓✓✓	Location	✓✓✓
Quality of Pitches	✓✓✓	Range of Facilities	✓✓✓✓

Directions
Site is directly off N4 Madrid - Cadiz at 197 km. marker at Valdepenas exit. Look for the 'Angel of Peace' statue - the site is directly opposite and is well signed.

Latest charges
Per person	€ 3.55
child	€ 2.57
car	€ 3.71
caravan	€ 3.95
tent	€ 3.01
motorcaravan	€ 5.88
electricity	€ 3.01

Reservations
Contact site. Tel: 926 310 769.
Email: la-aguzadera@manchanet.es

Open
All year.

Castilla-La Mancha

ES9090 Camping El Greco
Ctra. CM-4000 km. 0,7, Puebla de Montalban, 45004 Toledo

Toledo was the home of the Grecian painter and the site that bears his name boasts a beautiful view of the ancient city from the restaurant, bar and superb pool. The friendly, family owners make you welcome and are proud of their site which is the only one in Toledo. There is an attractive, tree-lined approach and ivy clad pergolas run down each side of the swimming pool. A large shaded terrace offers shelter from the sun which can be very hot here. The 150 pitches are of 80 sq.m. with electrical connections and shade from strategically planted trees. Most have hedges that separate and give privacy, with others in herring bone layouts that make for interesting parking in some areas. Access to some pitches may be tricky for caravans (narrow and at an angle). The river Tagus streches alongside the site but fishing in it is a better bet than swimming (it was being re-fenced when we visited). This site makes a relaxing base to return to after a hard day visiting the local sights.

Facilities
Two sanitary blocks, both modernised include facilities for disabled campers and everything is modern and kept clean. Laundry. Motorcaravan services. Swimming pool (15/6-15/9; with charge). Restaurant/bar (1/4-30/9) with good menu and fair prices. Shop in reception. Volleyball. Playgrounds. Barbecues. Ice cube machine. Off site: Fishing in river. Golf 10 km. Riding 15 km. An hourly air-conditioned bus service runs from the gates to the city centre, touring the outside of the walls first. Warner Brothers movie theme park 40 mins. Madrid 1 hour drive.

At a glance
Welcome & Ambience	✓✓✓✓	Location	✓✓✓✓✓
Quality of Pitches	✓✓✓✓✓	Range of Facilities	✓✓✓✓✓

Directions
Site is on C4000 road on the edge of the town, signed towards Puebla de Montelban; site signs also in city centre. From Madrid on N401, turn off right towards Toledo city centre but turn right again at the gates to the old city. Site is signed from the next right turn.

Charges 2003
Per person	€ 4.40
child (3-10 yrs)	€ 3.70
caravan or tent	€ 4.24
car	€ 4.24
motorcycle	€ 3.50
motorcaravan	€ 8.49
electricity (6A)	€ 3.18

Plus 7% VAT.

Reservations
Not necessary and not made. Tel: 925 220 090. Email: elgreco@retemail.es

Open
All year.

Madrid

The region of Madrid lies right in the middle of the Spanish mainland bordering Castilla-La Mancha and Castilla and Leon. At the centre lies the city of Madrid, which since the 16th century has been the country's capital.

The region of Madrid is a one province autonomy, also called Madrid

The mountainous region of Madrid can be divided into two areas: the sierra, in the north and west of the region, which includes part of Somosierra and Guadarrama; and the central and southern parts, where the area is flatter and forms part of the plateau of La Mancha and La Alcarria.

Founded by the Moors in the 9th Century, Madrid is now a modern, vibrant city offering innumerable attractions to the visitor. Its architectural heritage is immense. Some of the oldest parts of Madrid lie around the Puerta del Sol; a good starting place for exploring the city. Full of outdoor resturants and bars, Plaza Mayor is considered to be one of the finest in Spain, and in summer bcomes an outdoor theatre and music stage. The city also has a large number of parks and gardens, among them el Retiro, the Botanical Gardens, the Parque del Oeste and the Casa de Campo; and numerous museums and art galleries. Outside the capital, the Sierra de Madrid is ideal for winter sports and the beautiful town of Aranjuez, home to the Royal Palace and glorious gardens, is a popular retreat from the city.

Cuisine of the region

Tapas is popular with typical dishes including seafood: steamed mussels, anchovies in vinegar and pickled bonito plus croquettes and mini-casseroles. Sea bream and cod is used a lot. Local produce includes beef from the Guadarrama Mountains, olives from Campo Real, aniseed from Chinchón and asparagus from Aranjuez. Madrid is also a good place to experience every regional style of Spanish cooking

Buñuelos: a type of fritter which is filled with custard, chocolate and cream

Cocido: meat, potato and chickpea stew

Con gabardina: prawns cooked in beer

Torrijas: bread pudding

Places of interest

Alcala de Henares: university town, birthplace of Cervantes, author of Don Quixote, Cervantes House Museum, Archiepiscopal Palace Cathedral

Chinchón: 15th century castle, beautiful medieval square, 19th century church with painting by Goya, home of Alchoholera de Chinchón – aniseed liquer!

Parque Natural de la Cumbre: moutain park, highest mountains in the Madrid region.

San Lorenzo de El Escorial: town in heart of Guadarrama Mountains, Monastery of El Escorial, Royal Pantheon

THE VERANOS DE LA VILLA (JULY-SEPT) AND FESTIVAL DE OTONO (SEPT-NOV) IN MADRID HAS THEATRE, CINEMA, FLAMENCO AND MUSIC CONCERTS. MANY EVENTS ARE FREE.

Madrid

ES9091 Camping Municipal Soto del Castillo

Soto del Rebollo s/n, 28300 Aranjuez

Aranjuez, supposedly Spain's version of Versailles, is worthy of a visit with its beautiful palaces, leafy squares, avenues and gardens. It is 47 km. south of Madrid and 46 km. from Toledo, and is therefore a useful and popular site, ideal for enjoying the local attractions or for an en-route stop. Two little tourist road trains run from the site to the palaces daily. This unusually well equipped municipal site is alongside to the River Tajo in a park-like situation with mature trees. The 225 touring pitches, all with electricity, are set on flat grass, unmarked amid tall trees. Siting is informal but pitches are of moderate size. Canoes may be hired from behind the supermarket and there is a lockable moat gate to allow access to the river. There is good security backed up with CCTV around the river perimeter.

Facilities

The largest of three modern and good quality sanitary blocks is heated in winter and well equipped with some washbasins in cabins. Two smaller blocks of more open design have been refurbished. Washing up facilities have only cold water. Laundry facilities. Gas supplies. Small shop (15/6-15/9). Bar/restaurant (all year) with attractive riverside patio (also open to the public). Takeaway. TV room. Swimming and paddling pools (15/6-15/9). Play area. Volleyball. Bicycle hire. Boat launching and Canoe hire. Drinks machines. Torch useful. Off site: Within walking distance of palace, gardens and museums. Riding 5 km. Golf 20 km.

At a glance

Welcome & Ambience ✓✓✓✓✓ Location ✓✓✓✓✓
Quality of Pitches ✓✓✓✓ Range of Facilities ✓✓✓✓✓

Directions

Using the A305 from Madrid to Arunjez look for the 8 km. marker on the outskirts of town. Then follow campsite signs - these lead you back onto the A305 (going north now) and the site is signed off right at 300 m. on the first left bend. Follow signs down the narrow road for 400 m. If coming from the south ensure that you have the A305 to Madrid - there are other roads signed to Madrid. If in doubt ask as it is very confusing if the A305 road is missed.

Latest charges

Per person	€ 3.00 - € 3.91
child (3-10 yrs)	€ 2.55 - € 3.15
caravan	€ 3.45 - € 4.36
tent	€ 2.70 - € 4.21
car	€ 2.55 - € 3.30
motorcaravan	€ 3.76 - € 4.81
electricity (10A)	€ 3.30

Plus 7% VAT. Discounts for groups or long stays.

Reservations

Write to site. Tel: 918 911 395.

Open

All year.

ES9092 Camping Lagos Coto Cisneros

Ctra. Pte Arganda - Chinchon, 28500 Arganda del Rey

This is a large, lively site with a very simple Spanish flavour, 20 km. from Madrid, which could be used for exploring the capital or as a stopping point if travelling to the south as it is about half-way through Spain. The 340 marked pitches are of reasonable size, all have electricity and most are shaded by mature trees. There is a large representation of permanent Spanish pitches but the touring pitches are generally separate and in pleasant surroundings. There are several lakes, two near the entrance and the other is surrounding more than half the site boundary. All are safely fenced but the friendly ducks have their own accesses and may well join you for a meal. The lakes are good for fishing and watersports are available (nothing involving engines). If you arrive late out of season persevere and the security guard will let you in. We see this mostly as a transit stop-over.

Facilities

Unsophisticated, unheated sanitary blocks but clean and neat with facilities for disabled campers. (Note one block has push button hot water with free flow cold water to the shower which is irritating). Staged area for animation in summer. Restaurant/bar (hours vary in winter and they may only open at weekends). Swimming pool and paddling pool (supervised in season). Play area. Watersports. Fishing. Football. Tennis. Bicycle hire. Petanque. Torch useful. Off site: Theme park 16 km. Madrid 20 km.

At a glance

Welcome & Ambience ✓✓✓ Location ✓✓✓✓
Quality of Pitches ✓✓✓ Range of Facilities ✓✓✓

Directions

From Madrid - Alabcete E901/NIII take the M832 Morata de T/Chinchon road at 20.5 km. from Madrid. Chincon. The site is 3 km further on and well signed.

Latest charges

Per person	€ 3.61
child	€ 3.01
caravan or tent	€ 3.61
car	€ 3.61
motorcaravan	€ 6.62
electricity (5A)	€ 3.31

No credit cards.

Reservations

Contact site. Tel: 918 719 695.

Open

All year.

Madrid

ES9200 Caravanning El Escorial

Apdo. Correos 8, Ctra. M600, km 3500, 28280 El Escorial

There is a shortage of good sites in the central regions of Spain, but this is one (albeit rather expensive). El Escorial is very large, there are 1,358 individual pitches with artificial shade (ensure you get a pitch without low tree acanopy if you have a 3m high motorcaravan. Of these, 750 are occupied by permanent units but are totally separate from the touring and tent areas – weekends can be lively in the bar. There are another 250 pseudo 'wild' spaces for tourists on open fields, with good shade from mature trees (long cables may be necessary for electricity). The general amenities on site are good and include three swimming pools (unheated), plus a children's pool in a central area with a bar and restaurant with terrace and plenty of grassy sitting out areas.

Facilities

Three large refurbished toilet blocks, plus two smart, small blocks for the 'wild' camping area, are all fully equipped with some washbasins in private cabins. Baby baths and facilities for disabled campers. The blocks can be heated in cool weather. Large supermarket (1/3-31/10) and souvenir shop. Restaurant/bar and snack bar (1/3-31/10). Disco-bar. Swimming pools. Three tennis courts. Two football pitches. Basketball. Fronton. Volleyball. Two well equipped playgrounds on sand. ATM. Off site: Riding and golf 7 km. Town 3 km.

At a glance

Welcome & Ambience	✓✓✓✓✓	Location	✓✓✓✓
Quality of Pitches	✓✓✓✓✓	Range of Facilities	✓✓✓✓✓

Directions

From the south go through the town of El Escorial, follow the M600 - Guadarrama road - the site is near the 8 km. marker, 3.5 km north of town on the right. If approaching from the north use the A6 autopista take exit 47 and the M600 towards El Escorial town. Site is on the left.

Charges 2003

Per person	€ 4.60
child (3-10 yrs)	€ 4.45
caravan or tent	€ 4.60
car	€ 4.60
motorcaravan	€ 7.90
electricity	€ 3.30
VAT included.	

Reservations

May be made in writing to guarantee admission.
Tel: 918 902 412. Email: info@campingelescorial.com

Open

All year.

ES9210 Camping Pico de la Miel

Ctra. NI Madrid - France, km. 58, 28751 La Cabrera

Pico de la Miel is a very large site 70 km. north of Madrid. It is well signed and easy to find, two or three kilometres southwest off the main N1 road, with an amazing mountain backdrop. Mainly a long-stay site for Madrid hence there are a huge number of very well established, fairly old statics. There is a small separate area with its own toilet block for touring units. The 60 pitches are on rather poor, sandy grass, some with artificial shade. Others, not so level, are under sparse pine trees and there are yet more pitches for tents (although the ground could be hard for pegs). Electricity connections are available. Tall hedges abound and trees make it resemble a giant maze, no internal signs are provided and the long walk to the pool can be a challenge. The noise level from the many Spanish customers is high and you will have a chance to practice your Spanish!

Facilities

Dated but clean tiled toilet block, with some washbasins in cabins and free hot water to laundry and washing up sinks. It can be heated and has an en-suite unit with ramp is provided for disabled visitors. Motorcaravan services. Gas supplies. Shop. Restaurant/ Bar (all year). Excellent swimming pool complex, supervised (15/6-15/9). Tennis. Playground. Off site: Bicycle hire and riding 200 m. Fishing 8 km.

At a glance

Welcome & Ambience	✓✓✓✓	Location	✓✓✓✓
Quality of Pitches	✓✓✓✓	Range of Facilities	✓✓✓✓✓

Directions

Site is well signed from the N1. Going south use exit 60, going north exit 59 or 60, and follow site signs.

Latest charges

Per person	€ 4.40
child (2-9 yrs)	€ 4.00
caravan or tent	€ 4.40
car	€ 4.40
motorcaravan	€ 7.00
electricity	€ 3.00
All plus 7% VAT. Less 10-25% for longer stays.	

Reservations

Contact site. Tel: 918 688 082.
Email: pico-miel@sierranorte.com

Open

All year.

Castilla y León

The large region of Castilla y León is located inland, bordering Portugal to the west. It has a rich legacy dating back to the Romans, with an extraordinary wealth of castles, cathedrals and mansions, historic cities and towns.

The region is made up of the following provinces:
Avila, Burgos, Leon, Palencia, Salamanca, Valladolid, Zamora, Segovia and Soria

Steeped in history and architectural sights, the major towns and cities of the provinces all have something to offer. In the south, the town of Ávila is set on a high plain, surrounded by 11th century walls; and the graceful city of Salamanca was once home to one of the most prestigious universities in the world. Its grand Plaza Mayor is the finest in Spain. In the east, Segovia is well known for its magnificent Roman aqueduct, with 163 arches and 29 metres at its highest point; the cathedral; and the fairy-tale Alcazár, complete with turrets and narrow towers. And the attractive city of Soria still retains a Romanesque legacy in its network of medieval streets. Burgos in the north, is the birthplace of El Cid and has a Gothic cathedral of exceptional quality, making it one of the finest in Spain. The lively university city of Leon boasts a Royal Pantheon, decorated by Romanesque wall paintings, and also an impressive Gothic cathedral. There too is a Gothic cathedral in Palencia plus an archaeology museum. South of Leon, the old walled quarters of Zamora have a retained medieval appearance, with a dozen Romanesque churches. And in the centre of the region, Valladolid is famous for its extravagant and solemn processions during the Holy Week celebrations.

Cuisine of the region

The region is best known for its roast pork and lamb which has earned it the nickname *España del Asado* (Spain of the Roast). Other local products include trout from Leon and Zamora, and a variey of pulses: white, red and black beans, Castilian and *Pedrosillano* chickpeas, and various types of lentils. Soups feature a lot in winter: trout soup, typical of Órbigo de Leon; garlic soup; Zamora soup, a garlic soup with ripe tomatoes and hot chilli peppers

Bizcochos de San Lorenzo: sponge cakes

Farinatos: sausages made from breadcrumbs, pork fat and spices

Hornazos: sausage and egg tarts

Judias del barco con chorizo: haricot beans with sausage

Yemas: a sweet made with egg yolks and sugar

Places of interest

Astorga: city of Roman origin, chocolate museum, cathedral

Ciudad Rodrigo: Renaissance mansions, cathedral, 12th century walls

Coca: impressive Mudejar castle, birthplace of the famous Roman emperor Theodosius the Great

Pantano de Burgomillodo: reservoir, great for bird-watchers

Parque Natural del Cañón del Río Lobos: park created around the canyon of the River Lobos with rock formations, cave and good walking tracks

Parque Natural del Lago de Sanabria y alrededores: mountainous area with deep valleys and glacier lagoons, variety of flora and fauna including 76 types of birds and 17 large mammals

THE PLAZA DEL COSA IN PEÑAFIEL MAKES ONE OF THE MOST SPECTACULAR BULLRINGS IN SPAIN WHEN BULLFIGHTS ARE HELD IN AUGUST.

ES9019 Camping La Pesquera
Ctra. de Caceres - Arrabal, 37500 Ciudad Rodrigo

This modest site has just 54 pitches and is located near the Rio Agueda looking up to the magnificent fortress ramparts of Ciudad Rodrigo. Entry to the site is through a municipal park with a large play area. Whilst the site is small it can take even the largest units, the centrally located facilities have all been refurbished to a high standard, the pitches are flat and grassy and the roads are well maintained gravel. The pitches are shaded by trees by day and there is site lighting at night although you may find torches useful due to the tree canopy. The reception and a small bar which serves snacks in summer is near the front of the site. There is a touch of old Spain directly alongside the site – an old farmhouse with its trailing grape vine and ancient well.

Facilities
Attractive new ochre/stone sanitary building with British WCs and free hot showers. Washing machine, dishwashing (H&C) and laundry (C) sinks. Facilities for disabled campers. Basics sold from bar in high season. Bar/snacks (April - Sept). Playground outside gates. Barbecue outside gate. Torches useful. Off site: Fort in town to explore. Riding 5 km. River fishing 1 km. Superb walking area.

At a glance
Welcome & Ambience	✓✓✓✓	Location	✓✓✓✓✓
Quality of Pitches	✓✓✓✓✓	Range of Facilities	✓✓✓

Directions
Site is southwest of Salamancar close to Ciudad Rodrigo. From the E80 N260, any direction, take the 526 to Coria. Site is alongside river directly off the road and well signed.

Charges 2003
Per adult	€ 2.80
child (up to 12 yrs)	€ 2.50
tent	€ 2.50 - € 2.80
caravan	€ 2.80
car	€ 2.80
motorcaravan	€ 5.00
electricity	€ 2.50
dog	€ 1.80

Reservations
Contact site. Tel: 923 481 348.

Open
25 April - 30 September.

ES9026 Camping El Burro Blanco
Camino de las Norias s/n, 37660 Miranda del Castañar

Set on a hill top, within the Sierra Peña de Francia is the romantic walled village of Miranda del Castañar with its charming, crumbling castle. The site has been developed by a Dutch team including husband and wife Jeff and Yvonne and their friend Paul. You are welcomed at the gate and are walked around the facilities. A copy of the site regulations is provided to all campers along with your own rubbish bin. The 48 shady pitches are 60 sq.m, with two at 130 sq m and are mostly level with some terracing and all with electricity. The pitches are beautifully set in 3.5 hectares of the most attractive woodland complete with rough tables and chairs made from local stone, unusual statues, a fountain fed by a well and a small stream which traces a route though the site. The owners keep an exhaustive list of all the birds and other wildlife spotted around the campsite, and in one area (wet in winter, but dry in summer) there are beautiful luminous green tree frogs and other aquatic reptiles.

Facilities
One central modern sanitary facility, fully equipped includes a baby-bath. Two washbasins have hot water and one hot tap serves both the dishwashing and laundry sinks. Out of season part of the unit is closed and therefore facilities are unisex. Launderette. Gas supplies. Reading room with many books and a small bar. Off site: Restaurants, bars and shops in village 600 m. Municipal swimming pool nearby, river swimming and fishing 1.5 km. If you wish to explore some of the unique villages in the area, avoid Alberca which has been spoiled by over-exploitation. Try instead Cepecla or Casas del Corde.

At a glance
Welcome & Ambience	✓✓✓✓	Location	✓✓✓✓
Quality of Pitches	✓✓✓✓	Range of Facilities	✓✓✓

Directions
Take C512 Salamanca - Coria road southwest for approx. 70 km. or C515 Bejar - Ciudad Rodrigo road turning south on C512. The road to Miranda del Castañar is approx. 7 km. northeast of the village of Cepeda.

Charges 2003
Per caravan	€ 4.00
child (0-5 yrs)	€ 3.00
pitch	€ 9.00
electricity	€ 1.20

Plus 7% VAT. No credit cards (ATM in village).

Reservations
Contact site. Tel: 923 161 100.
Email: elbb@infonegocio.com

Open
1 April - 1 October.

ES9025 Camping Regio

Ctra. de Madrid, km. 4, 37900 Santa Marta de Tormes

Salamanca is one of Europe's oldest university cities, and this beautiful old sandstone city has to be visited. This is also a useful staging post en-route to the south of Spain or central Portugal. The site is seven kilometres outside the city on the old road to Madrid. It is behind the Hôtel Regio and campers can take advantage of the hotel facilities which include a quality restaurant, a somewhat cheaper cafeteria (discounts for campers), an excellent swimming pool and children's pool (small charge). There is a pool bar and a shaded patio. The site itself has a small bar and restaurant. The pitches (with a large area for tents) are clearly marked on slightly sloping ground, with some shade in parts. There are plentiful electricity points in little red-roofed towers and many water points with unusual taps.

Facilities
Very large fully equipped sanitary block has very good facilities for disabled campers. Washing machines in a dedicated room - all very clean. Gas supplies. Excellent motorcaravan services. Restaurant, cafe and swimming pool at adjoining hotel. Bar. Supermarket (1/4-30/9). Play area. Tennis. Basketball. English is spoken. Off site: Bus to town terminates at hotel car-park. Town centre 7 km. Fishing 2 km. Bicycle hire 4 km. Golf 7 km.

At a glance
Welcome & Ambience	✓✓✓	Location	✓✓✓✓
Quality of Pitches	✓✓✓✓✓	Range of Facilities	✓✓✓✓✓

Directions
Take the main N501 route from Salamanca to Avila, then to St Marta de Tormes 7 km east of the city. Hôtel Regio is on the old road into St Marta on the left at the 90 km. marker. Combined yellow camping signs are through the city and on the roads to the east.

Latest charges
Per adult	€ 2.40 - € 2.90
child	€ 2.10 - € 2.55
tent	€ 2.40 - € 2.90
caravan	€ 2.40 - € 2.90
car	€ 2.40 - € 2.90
motorcycle	€ 2.10 - € 2.55
motorcaravan	€ 4.70 - € 7.20
electricity (10A)	€ 2.40 - € 2.90

Reservations
Write to site. Tel: 923 138 888.
Email: recepcion@campingregio.com

Open
All year.

ES9022 Camping El Folgoso
49361 Vigo de Sanabria

After a pleasant drive through the Sanabria National Park you reach this unspoilt site alongside a beautiful lake. It has green hills to the west and a lake to the east. It is a large site with the majority of the pitches given over to tents, as the terrain is rugged and strewn with enormous rocks, whilst being sheltered by fine dense oaks. The pitches are informal and tents are placed anywhere on terraces or the lower levels. Pitches for caravans and motorcaravans are in more formal lines at the far end of the site with electricity available. All buildings are primarily of wood and stone and designed to be in sympathy with the surroundings. The nearby lake shores are public areas but there are toilets along with picnic and barbecue facilities. There are magnificent walks all around the site and much to see in the area. The owners have another smaller site, also near the lake, if you prefer to really get away from it all.

Facilities
Three sanitary blocks, two refurbished and one new unit close to the restaurant, provide pre-set showers on payment (100 ptas coin slot), facilities for disabled campers and a variety of washing facilities but all with cold water. Bar with snacks (open all year). Self-service and full restaurants (April - Oct). Drinks machines. Torches essential.
Off site: Children's playground very close. Supermarket (April - Oct) just outside site. Gate at rear of site leads to lake 50 m. to fish, swim or enjoy the watersports.

At a glance
Welcome & Ambience	✓✓✓	Location	✓✓✓✓
Quality of Pitches	✓✓✓	Range of Facilities	✓✓✓

Directions
From the free N525 Orense/Ourense - Benavente autovia or the parallel A525, take any exit for Puebla de Sanabria and follow the signs for the Sanabria National Park. This will place you on the ZA 104 heading north. Pass through the villages of El Puente, Cubelo and Galende to 11 km. marker and site is signed to the right.

Latest charges
Per person	€ 3.46
child (under 10 yrs)	€ 2.55
car	€ 3.31
caravan	€ 4.36
tent	€ 3.76
motorcaravan	€ 5.26
electricity (5A)	€ 2.25

Reservations
Not necessary. Tel: 980 626774.

Open
All year.

ES9021 Camping Municipal Fuentes Blancas
Ctra. Cartuja - M'flore, km 3,5, 09000 Burgos

Fuentes Blancas is a comfortable municipal site within easy reach of the Santander ferries. There are around 350 marked pitches of 70 sq.m. on flat ground, 112 with electrical connections and there is good shade in parts. A small shop caters for most needs, the typically Spanish bar serves snacks and in the evening a restaurant is open. The site has a fair amount of transit trade and reservations are not possible for August, so arrive early. Burgos is an attractive city which is ideally placed for overnight stops en-route to the south of Spain.

Facilities
Clean, modern, fully equipped sanitary facilities in five blocks, but not all open outside July/Aug. Facilities for babies. Washing machine. Motorcaravan services. Small shop (all season). Bar/snack bar (all season). Swimming pool (15/5-15/9). Playground. Table tennis. Basketball. Football. English is spoken. Off site: Fishing 150 m. Bicycle hire 2 km. Bus service to city or a fairly shaded walk.

At a glance
Welcome & Ambience	✓✓✓✓✓	Location	✓✓✓✓✓
Quality of Pitches	✓✓✓✓	Range of Facilities	✓✓✓✓

Directions
From the north (Santander) follow signs for E5/N1 (E80/N620) Valladolid - Madrid on the main through road (dual-carriageway). Immediately after crossing river turn left at 'Fuente Blancas Parc' signs leading to yellow camp signs and follow river east in direction of Cartuja de Miraflores for 3 km. Site well signed on left.

Latest charges
Per pitch incl. electricity (6A)	€ 10.75
adult	€ 3.50
child (2-10 yrs)	€ 2.50

Plus 7% VAT.

Reservations
Not made. Tel: 947 486 016.

Open
1 April - 30 September.

Castilla y León

ES9023 Camping Camino de Santiago

Casco Urbano, 09110 Castrojeriz

This tranquil and uncomplicated site lies to the west of Burgos on the outskirts of Castrojeriz, an unspoilt original small Spanish rural town. In a superb location, almost in the shadow of the ruined castle high on the adjacent hillside, it will appeal to those who like peace and a true touring campsite without all the modern trimmings, and at a reasonable cost. Out of main season the bar/restaurant are closed but ask to be directed to the 'Taberna' restauraranT in town for a real treat of old Spanish cuisine in classical unspoilt surroundings. The 50 marked pitches are level, grassy and divided by hedges, with electricity, water and drainage available to all. Mature trees provide shade and there is a pretty orchard in one corner of the site. English is spoken here.

Facilities

Adequate sanitary facilities with showers (three hot per sex), British and Turkish style WCs, and washbasins with cold water only. Laundry and washing up sinks with hot tap. These facilities are in older style, but are well maintained and clean. Washing machine. Small shop with basic necessities (1/6-31/8). Bar. Cafeteria/coffee shop with two terraces (1/6-31/8). Games room with table football, pool table, table tennis. Tennis. Play area. Bicycle hire. Barbecue area. House with three pleasant rooms to let.

At a glance

| Welcome & Ambience | ✓✓✓✓ | Location | ✓✓✓✓✓ |
| Quality of Pitches | ✓✓✓✓ | Range of Facilities | ✓✓✓ |

Directions

From N120 (Osorno-Burgos) road, turn onto BU404 for Villasandino and Castrojeriz. Turn left at crossroads on southwest side of town and then left at campsite sign.

Charges 2003

Per person	€ 3.00
child	€ 2.00
tent	€ 2.50 - € 3.00
caravan	€ 4.00
car	€ 3.00
motorcycle	€ 3.00
electricity (5A)	€ 3.00

All plus 7% VAT.

Reservations

Write or fax site for details. Tel: 947 377 255.
Email: campingcastro@eresmas.com

Open

1 March - 30 November.

ES9044 Camping Monumento al Pastor

Ctra. Madrid - Irun km. 308, 09219 Ameyugo

This is a very small simple site which makes a very good transit stop and is very special if you wish to sample traditional Spanish fare cooked to perfection whilst enjoying spectacular views. There are 15 pitches terraced on grass with one area allocated for tents. In high season there is a small hardstanding for two additional vehicles. Electricity is available to all the grass pitches. There are also some 50 permanent pitches. In high season a small hut serves as reception, otherwise go to the bar. The site itself lays at the foot of Napoleon Hill. A large bar/restaurant provides magnificent views of the Obareues mountains and surrounding hills which are designated to become a natural Park in the near future. The owner's son speaks good English.

Facilities

Sanitary facilities are quaint, clean and adequate. Essentials sold in the bar. Fabulous stylish restaurant offering campers top Spanish cuisine or a special 'menu del dia', also very popular with locals. Children's playground. Basketball. Five-a-side soccer. Off site: Local bus/train service 3 km. Bilbao 70 km. Co-located restaurant with smart uniformed waiters, most impressive wine list and excellent food.

At a glance

| Welcome & Ambience | ✓✓✓✓✓ | Location | ✓✓✓✓✓ |
| Quality of Pitches | ✓✓✓✓ | Range of Facilities | ✓✓✓ |

Directions

Nearest large town is Miranda de Ebro. Site is very easy to find as it sits on the N1 between Gastiez Vitoria and Burgos. Madrid - Irun (A68/E80 Bilbao - Burgos) road at 308 km. marker. The monument makes it impossible to miss the site, but take care as the access is can be dangerous if crossing the main road. A safer option is off the N625 250 m. from the main road access.

Latest charges

Per adult	€ 2.84
child	€ 2.35
caravan	€ 3.05
tent	€ 2.40 - € 3.36
car	€ 2.84
motorcycle	€ 1.82
motorcaravan	€ 4.42
electricity (5A)	€ 2.25

Reservations

Contact site. Tel: 947 344355.

Open

All year.

ES9250 Camping Costajan

Ctra.- NI/E5, km. 162, 09400 Aranda de Duero

This site is well placed as an en-route stop for the ferries, being 80 km. south of Burgos. This is the capital of the Ribera del Duero wine region that produces many fine wines of Spain, competing with the great Rioja. The welcome here is warm and friendly with 225 pitches provided, all with electricity, and with around 100 available for all types of tourer. Large units may find access to the variably sized pitches a bit tricky among dense olive and pine trees and on the slightly undulating sandy ground but the trees provide good shade. In high season there is a good sized swimming pool to relax in. The river Duero runs close by and there is much of historical interest in the area. A café is here for snacks in season but there is a really good restaurant just 400 metres away any many more in the local area.

Facilities
Good, heated, modern sanitary facilities have hot and cold water, plus dishwashing and laundry sinks. Facilites for disabled people. Washing machine. Reception opens 08.00-14.00 and 18.00-22.00. Gas supplies. Shop with essentials (all year). Cafe with snacks and bar. Large swimming pool open to public (all 15/5-15/9). Tennis. Football. Minigolf. Torch useful. Off site: Riding 2 km. Fishing 3 km.

At a glance
Welcome & Ambience	✓✓✓✓	Location	✓✓✓
Quality of Pitches	✓✓✓✓	Range of Facilities	✓✓✓✓

Directions
From N1/E5 take exit to North signed Aranda de Duero at 164.5 km, follow N1 towards town and the campsite is at the 162 km mark.

Latest charges
Per person	€ 3.50 - € 3.65
child	€ 3.50
caravan	€ 3.50 - € 3.65
tent	€ 3.35 - € 3.65
car	€ 3.50 - € 3.65
motorcaravan	€ 5.50 - € 6.00
electricity	€ 3.50
dog	€ 1.60

Reservations
Said to be unnecessary. Tel: 974 502 070.
Email: costajan@circulopyme.com

Open
All year.

ES9253 Camping Picon del Conde

Ctra. NI, km. 263, 09292 Monasterio de Rodilla

This all year site is unusual, in that it has been amazingly decorated by the owner, Pedro Fasseler Sagredo who is extremely lively and friendly, as are his family. The experience begins as you drive under an art nouveau style entry arch and enter a pleasant site with a variety of unusual sculptures that include Don Quixote and his companion Sancho Panza. The theme is continued in the friendly restaurant and bar with use of decorative local rock on most surfaces. The 60 level, grass pitches, all with electricity, are of a reasonable size with separating hedges giving some privacy and trees offering shade. There is some traffic noise from the busy N1 alongside the site and the picnic site and terrace directly outside the restaurant are always busy in season, the adjacent motel being responsible for some of this. Compared to other sites in the area this is a good option for a stopover if heading for the ferry or for exploring the area. If you visit around Christmas you will see the amazing nativity scene the father constructs, with a profusion of working models with lights and decorations.

Facilities
The first floor, unheated sanitary block is modern, very clean and fully equipped. A central elevated Venus de Milo statue is accentuated by mirrors and natural lighting. Good facilities for disabled campers are beneath the main sanitary facilities. Motorcaravan service point. Restaurant and friendly bar. Swimming pools. Play area. Tennis and fronton. Off site: Burgos 15 minutes away.

At a glance
Welcome & Ambience	✓✓✓✓✓	Location	✓✓✓✓
Quality of Pitches	✓✓✓✓✓	Range of Facilities	✓✓✓✓

Directions
Nearest town Monasterio de Rodilla (Burgos) From autopista A1 take exit 3 at Briviesca on the N1. Then exit 2 at Rubena heading north on N623 towards Irun. Site is on the N1 at the 263 km. marker, well signed midway between Burgos and Briviesca.

Latest charges
Per adult	€ 2.90
child	€ 2.60
caravan	€ 3.20
tent	€ 2.90 - € 3.20
car	€ 3.20
motorcycle	€ 2.70
motorcaravan	€ 4.40
electricity (5A)	€ 3.10

Reservations
Contact site. Tel: 947 594 355.

Open
All year.

Castilla y León

ES9254 Camping Puerta de la Demanda
Ctra. de Pineda, km. 2, 09199 Villasur de Herreros

This recently built site is being improved and shows great promise. On flat ground, it is overlooked on three side by the hills and mountains of the Sierra de la Demanda which give the site its name. There is little shade over 50 well marked large pitches all of which have electricity and drainage. The modern buildings are of local stone and wood in sympathy with the quiet surroundings, yet providing an excellent set of facilities. Just 300 m. away is a dam which may provide non-powered watersports and a river is very close for swimming and fishing. The whole site is securely fenced. When inspected the support facilities were being put into place but the owners assure us that everything would soon be in place.. Burgos is close by with all its attractions.

Facilities
Attractive new ochre/stone sanitary building with British WCs and free hot showers. Washing machine, dishwashing (H&C) and laundry (C) sinks. Facilities for disabled campers. Basics sold from bar in high season. Bar and snacks (April - Sept). Torches useful. Off site: River fishing 1 km. Superb walking area.

At a glance
Welcome & Ambience	✓✓✓✓	Location	✓✓✓✓
Quality of Pitches	✓✓✓✓	Range of Facilities	✓✓✓✓

Directions
From the N120 Burgos - Lograno road, exit at Ibeas de Juarros (approx 7km east of Burgos) towards Villalbura, Arlanzon, Villasue de Herreros and site on road no. 8201.

Charges 2003
Per adult	€ 2.81
child (up to 12 yrs)	€ 2.30
tent	€ 2.62 - € 2.91
caravan	€ 2.91
car	€ 2.91
motorcaravan	€ 4.90
electricity (5A)	€ 2.30
dog	€ 1.80

Plus 7% VAT.

Reservations
Contact site. Tel: 983 796819.

Open
Easter - September.

ES9251 Camping Cañon del Rio Lobos
Ctra. Burgos de Osma - S. Leonardo de Yagü, 42317 Ucero

This is a smart and 'proper' site with vast amounts of flowers, set among attractive limestone cliffs of the Burgos canyons. The site is pricey but all facilities are immaculate and there are few others in the area. Reception is purpose built and control of the security barrier is from within – everything here is very organised. The campsite logo depicts a bird of prey and you will see many of these wheeling above the site. You can practise your Spanish here as little English is spoken, but there is tourist information in English. The very attractive swimming pool is within a secure walled area, which again has many flowers and shrubs and is private from the road that runs alongside the site (some road noise). Children will need supervision in the pool as there is no barrier between the shallow and deep areas. If you wish to take advantage of the stunning scenery and explore the area the site staff will assist with routes and maps.

Facilities
Spotless fully equipped toilet blocks. Bar/restaurant (high season) or a set 'menu del dia' in the bar. Basic shopping from bar. Swimming pool (extra charge). Two excellent tennis courts (extra charge). Play area. Bicycle hire. Fishing. Torch useful. Off site: Local bus service 1 km to town (Wed & Sat). Excellent walking routes.

At a glance
Welcome & Ambience	✓✓✓✓✓	Location	✓✓✓✓✓
Quality of Pitches	✓✓✓✓✓	Range of Facilities	✓✓✓✓✓

Directions
On N234 Burgos - Soria road take right fork in village of San Leornado de Yagüe. Turn right again after village signed El Burgos de Osma. Site is on this road and well signed south of Ucero.

Charges 2003
Per person	€ 11.60
pitch	€ 11.60
child	€ 3.45
electricity	€ 4.30

All plus 7% VAT.

Reservations
Contact site. Tel: 975 363565.

Open
March - November.

ES9240 Camping El Cantosal

Ctra. de Santiuste, km. 2, 40480 Coca

On the 'Ruta de Mudejar' (route of Mudejar castles and buildings), near the nature reserve 'Hoces del Duraton' is this tiny campsite of 50 pitches. The setting has a fairy tale air about it – the magnificent 15th century Castillo de Coca can be seen from most of the site. The history of the village is fascinating and the climb to the tallest tower of the castle is rewarded with views of the village, its ancient bull ring and the surrounding countryside. The grass and sand pitches are flat and shaded by tall trees in the daytime, and lit by pretty post lights at night. The bar serves snacks and excellent coffee and has a lovely open fire for cooler evenings. There is an arrangment for campers to use the local pool at a special rate, the campsite is set alongside a river where there are lots of wooden picnic tables under the trees and stone barbeques.

Facilities
The modern sanitary building with British style WCs and free showers is central. Washing machine, dishwashing (H&C) and laundry sinks under cover. Facilities for disabled campers. Shop (high season). Bar with snacks (all season). Large playground just outside the site. Off site: Village with shops bars and restaurants. Fishing 2 km. Golf 20 km. Village of Coca 2 km.

At a glance
Welcome & Ambience	✓✓✓✓✓	Location	✓✓✓✓✓
Quality of Pitches	✓✓✓✓✓	Range of Facilities	✓✓✓

Directions
From Valladoid south on the N601 to Olmedo then east on the vp1105 to Coca. At T-junction marked Coca 2 km, Santuiste 7 km, turn into campsite road through stone pillars situated on the left and signed Zona De Picnic El Cantasol.

Charges 2003
Per adult	€ 2.80
child (up to 12 yrs)	€ 2.50
tent	€ 2.60 - € 2.80
caravan	€ 2.80
car	€ 2.80
motorcaravan	€ 5.00
electricity	€ 2.55
dog	€ 1.80

Reservations
Write to site. Tel: 983 796819. Email: info@asecal.net

Open
Easter - September.

ES9029 Camping El Astral

Camino de Pollos 8, 47100 Tordesillas

The site is in a prime position alongside the wide River Duero (safely fenced). It is homely and run by a charming man, Eduardo Gutierrez, who has excellent English and is ably assisted by brother Gustavo and sister Lola. The site is generally flat with 154 pitches (on separated by hedges). They vary in size from 60 to 80 sq.m. with mature trees providing shade. We recommend a walk across the bridge to investigate the bustling town of Tordesillas which is steeped in Spanish history. Visits to local Bodegas (wineries) can be organised. This is a friendly site ideal for exploring the area as you move through Spain. There is an electricity pylon tucked in the corner of the site but this does not detract from the pleasant ambience here and the quality stay offered.

Facilities
One attractive sanitary block including two cabins with WC, bidet and washbasin. Quality facilities provided for disabled campers, including ramps throughout site. Baby room in ladies' area. Washing machines. Motorcaravan services. Supermarket. Bar. Very good restaurant fequented by locals. Swimming and paddling pools (15/6-15/9; lifeguard at all times). Playground. Tennis. Minigolf. English speaking staff. Local bus service. Animation daily in high season. Torches are useful.

Directions
Tordesillas is 28 km. southwest of Valladolid. From all directions, leave the main road towards Tordesillas and follow signs to campsite or 'Parador' (a hotel near the campsite).

Charges 2003
Per person	€ 3.10 - € 3.95
child (0-12 yrs)	€ 2.45 - € 3.25
caravan or tent	€ 3.10 - € 3.95
car	€ 2.65 - € 3.40
motorcycle	€ 2.65 - € 4.40
motorcaravan	€ 5.25 - € 6.25
electricity (5A)	€ 2.80

Plus 7% VAT. Discounts in low season and for longer stays. Camping Cheques accepted.

Reservations
Not necessary. Tel: 983 770 953. Email: info@campingelastral.com

Open
1 April - 30 September.

At a glance
Welcome & Ambience	✓✓✓✓✓	Location	✓✓✓✓✓
Quality of Pitches	✓✓✓✓✓	Range of Facilities	✓✓✓✓✓

the travel service
TO BOOK THIS SITE
0870 405 4055
Expert Advice & Special Offers

Castilla y León

Galicia

With a coastline of inlets and wide, rocky estuaries, sheltering traditional old fishing villages and fine beaches, Galicia is perhaps best known for Santiago de Compostela, the place where the famous pilgrim's route comes to an end.

This region is made up of four provinces: Ourense, Lugo, A Coruña and Pontevedra

The obvious highlight in the region has to be the beautiful medieval city of Santiago de Compostela, capital of Galicia and world famous centre of the old European pilgrimage. Now a World Heritage Site, the city boasts an impressive Romanesque cathedral with more churches, convents and monasteries dotted around. One of the best times to go to Santiago de Compostela is during the Festival of St James on 25 July, which has also been designated Galicia Day. Following the route into the city, are the towns of Portomarín and Samos. Near Samos, the Lóuzara valley and the Sierra do Oribio are ideal for those interested in hiking and wildlife. There are also places to go paragliding or potholing.
The Galician coastline is characterized by high cliffs and estuaries collectively known as the Rías Atlas and Rías Baixas with the Costa da Morte or Coast of Death separating them; so called because of the hundreds of shipwrecks that litter the cliffs and rocks. It was also once considered by the pilgrimages to be the 'end of the world'. Along the coast are medieval towns and villages including Noia, Muros, A Coruña and Finisterre. Corcubión, Camariñas and Corme-Laxe are other rias with fishing villages and home to some of the best barnacles in the region.

Cuisine of the region

Local cuisine features heavily in fiestas and throughout the region are numerous markets. Good quality seafood is found in abundance; *percebes* (barnacles) are a favourite. *Pulpo* (octopus) is also popular and special *pulperias* will cook it in the traditional way. Vegetable dishes include the Galician broth, made with green beans, cabbage, parsnip, potatoes and haricot beans. *Aguardiente gallego*, a regional liquer, is used to make the traditional mulled drink known as *queimada*, where fruit, sugar and coffee grains are added and then set alight.

Caldeirada: fish soup

Caldo gallego: thick stew of potato cabbage

Empanada: light-crusted pastries often filled with pork, beef, tuna or cod.

Lacon con grelos: ham boiled with turnip greens

Places of interest

A Coruña: medieval quarters, Romanesque churches, Roman lighthouse

Baiona: one of the region's best resorts

Camariñas: town on the 'end of the world', good barnacle hunting ground, lacemaking traditions

Lugo: town completely enclosed within preserved Roman walls, along which are 85 towers

Malpica: seaside harbour, jumping off point for nearby islands

Pontevedra: picturesque old town with lively atmosphere

Vigo: fishing port, beaches

Viveiro: beaches, old town surrounded by Renaissance walls

tip

WITH GOOD BEACHES, WALKING TRACKS, BARS AND RESTAURANTS, THE ATLANTIC ISLANDS NATIONAL PARK HAS FOUR GROUPS OF ISLANDS INCLUDING THE CÍES AND ONS ISLANDS.

www.alanrogers.com for latest campsite news

ES9024 Camping As Cancelas

Rue do 25 de Xulio 35, 15704 Santiago

The beautiful city of Santiago has been the destination for European Christian pilgrims for centuries and they now follow ancient routes to this unique city which is now a National Monument. The As Cancelas campsite is excellent for sharing the experiences of these pilgrims in the city and around the magnificent cathedral. It has 156 marked pitches (30-70 sq.m), arranged in terraces and divided by trees and shrubs. On a hillside overlooking the city, the views are very pleasant, but the site has a steep approach road and access to most of the pitches can be a challenge for large units. Electrical hook-ups are available, the site is lit at night and a security guard patrols. There are many legendary festivals and processions here, the main one being on July 25, especially in holy years (when the Saint's birthday falls on a Sunday).

Facilities

Two very modern, luxurious toilet blocks are fully equipped, with ramped access for disabled campers. The quality and cleanliness of the fittings and tiling is outstanding. Dishwashing and laundry facilities. Small mini market (open July/Aug.). Restaurant. Bar/ TV. (open all year). Well kept, unsupervised swimming pool and children's pool. Small playground. Off site: Regular bus service runs into the city from the bottom of the hill outside site. Huge covered commercial centre (open late and handy for off season use) five minutes level walk away.

At a glance

Welcome & Ambience	✓✓✓✓	Location	✓✓✓✓
Quality of Pitches	✓✓✓	Range of Facilities	✓✓✓✓

Directions

From the east on N634 Lugo road site is signed at junction with N550 road (on dual-carriageway filter right following signs for right for La Coruña N550 and also site). Turn at the sports stadium and site is 800 m. on left.

Charges 2003

Per adult	€ 3.46 - € 4.00
child (up to 12 yrs)	€ 2.40 - € 3.07
car	€ 3.46 - € 4.18
tent	€ 3.46 - € 4.18
caravan	€ 3.46 - € 4.30
motorcycle	€ 2.55 - € 3.28
motorcaravan	€ 6.91 - € 8.35
electricity (5A)	€ 2.76

All plus VAT.

Reservations

Write to site. Tel: 981 580 476.
Email: info@campingascancelas.com

Open

All year.

BUNGALOWS AND RURAL TOURISM ACCOMODATIONS

CAMPING "AS CANCELAS"

Situated north of the city, access by San Cayetano and Avenida del Camino Francés.

OPEN THROUGHOUT THE YEAR

In quiet surroundings, though not far from historical pilgrims town with its famous cathedral. Good bus connection to town and its historical monuments. Site has first class installations, incl. swimming and paddling pool, as well as first class ablution blocks.

Ruo de 25 de Xulio, 35   E-15704 SANTIAGO DE COMPOSTELA (La Coruña)
Tel.: (34) 981 58 02 66 - 58 04 76 • Fax. (34) 981 57 55 53

Galicia

ES8942 Camping Los Manzanos

Ctra. Sta Cruz - Meiras, km. 0,7, 15179 Santa Cruz

This large site is to the east of the historic port of La Coruña, not far from some ria (lagoon) beaches and with good communications to both central and north Galicia – it is only an hour and a half drive from Santiago de la Compostela, for example. The site has a steep sloping access and is divided by a stream into two main sections, linked by a wooden bridge. Some huge interesting stone sculptures create focal points and conversation pieces. The lower section is on a gentle slope. Pitches for larger units are marked and numbered, all with electricity and, in one section, there is a fairly large, unmarked field for tents. The site impressed us as being very clean, even when full, which it tends to be in high season. Señor Sanjurjo speaks good English and visitors are assured of a friendly welcome. Some aircraft noise should be expected (but only six aircraft per day – none at night).

Facilities

Two good toilet blocks provide modern facilities including free hot showers. Swimming pool – clean, with a lifeguard, free to campers, and open most of the day, evening and all season. Small shop with fresh produce daily. High quality restaurant/bar (Easter - Sept) serving good food and a range of wines at reasonable prices. Playground. Barbecue area. Telephone and post box. Medical post. Excellent bungalows for hire. Off site: Beach 800 m. Bicycle hire 2 km. Golf and riding 8 km.

At a glance

Welcome & Ambience	✓✓✓✓✓	Location	✓✓✓✓
Quality of Pitches	✓✓✓✓✓	Range of Facilities	✓✓✓✓

Directions

Nearest large city is La Coruna. From A9/E1 going south, take exit 7 for 'O Burgo'. The site is on the Santa Cruz - Meiras road, north of Oleiras and is well signed from there.

Charges 2003

Per adult	€ 4.40
child	€ 3.40
caravan or tent	€ 4.40 - € 4.80
car	€ 4.40
motorcycle	€ 3.60
motorcaravan	€ 8.80
electricity	€ 2.90

All plus 7% VAT.

Reservations

Write to site. Tel: 981 614 825.
Email: info@camping-losmanzanos.com

Open

Easter - 15 September.

Asturias

Like its neighbouring province, Cantabria, Asturias also has a beautiful coastline, abeit more rugged and wild, with the Picos range separating them. In the south the Cantabrian mountains form a natural border between Asturias and Castilla-León.

This is a one province region

The capital is Oviedo

Situated between the foothills of the Picos mountains and the coast is the seaside town of Llanes, in the east. It has several good beaches, beautiful coves and given its location, is a good base for exploring the Picos del Europa. Along the coast towards Gijón are more seaside resorts including Ribadesella, with its fishing harbour and fine beach. The cities of Gijón and, in particular, Avilés are renowned for their Carnival festivities, a national event which takes place in late February. This week-long party involves dancing, live music, fireworks and locals who dress up in elaborate fancy-dress costumes. South of here towards the centre of the province is the capital, Oviedo. The city boasts a pedestrian old quarter with numerous squares and narrow streets, a cathedral, palaces, a Fine Arts Museum, Archaeological Museum plus various remarkable churches that date from the 9th century. There are also plenty of *sidrerías* (cider houses).The west coast of Asturias is more rugged. One of the most attractive towns along here is Luarca, built around a cove surrounded by sheer cliffs. With a fishing harbour and an array of good restaurants and bars, the town's traditional character is reflected in its *chigres* – old Asturian taverns – where visitors can learn the art of drinking cider.

Cuisine of the region

Local specialities include *fabada,* a type of stew made with haricot beans called *fabes, potes* (soups) and of course cider, which can be drunk in *sidrerias*. The customary way to serve cider is to pour it from a great height, a practice know as *escanciar*, into a wide-mouthed glass only just covering the *culin* or bottom. Rice pudding is the traditional dessert and *frixuelos* (crepe), *huesos de santo* (made from marzipan) and *tocinillo de cielo* (syrup pudding) are eaten during festivals.

Brazo de gitano: a type of Swiss roll

Carne gobernada: beef in white wine with bacon, eggs, peppers and olives

Fabada asturiana: haricot beans, chorizo, cabbage, cured pork shoulder and potatoes

Pastel carbayón: almond pastry

Places of interest

Avilés: 14th and 15th century churches and palaces

Cuillero: small, charming fishing port

Gijón: 18th century palace, beaches, museums

Villahormes: seaside town with excellent swimming coves

Villaviciosa: atmospheric old town, 13th church, cider factory

 **tip**

VISIT THE CIDER FACTORY AT VILLAVICIOSA AND SEE HOW THE *LAGARES* WORK – THE PRESSES USED TO EXTRACT THE JUICE, BEFORE SAMPLING THE LOCAL TIPPLE.

Asturias

ES8940 Camping Los Cantiles

Ctra. N - 634, km. 502,7, 33700 Luarca

Luarca is a picturesque little place with a pretty inner harbour and two sandy beaches. Los Cantiles is two kilometres to the east on a cliff top that juts out into the sea, giving excellent views from some pitches and the sound of the waves to soothe you to sleep. The owners speak excellent English and Hubert, who is Dutch, and Cornelia, who is German, are charming and eager that you enjoy your stay here. The site is well maintained and is a pleasant place to stop along this under-developed coastline. The 230 pitches, 83 with electricity are mostly on level grass, divided by huge hedges of hydrangeas and bushes. Some pitches have gravel surfaces. There is a separate area for late arrivals in high season. You can take the car to the Laurca beaches and the small town is within walking distance downhill. This is a pleasant site as a base for exploring the area or as a transit site if moving to or from Portugal.

Facilities

Two modern, fully equipped sanitary blocks (one in low season) are kept very clean, as is the whole site. Mainly British style toilets. The block used in winter is heated. Large solar heating system for hot water. Facilities for disabled people and babies. Water is recycled for flushing purposes – the owners have a 'green' attitude. Laundry. Freezer service. Gas supplies. Small shop (all year). Bar with hot snacks (15/6-1/10). Day room for backpackers with tables, chairs and cooking facilities (less gas). Lounge/reading room. Bicycle hire. Torches are required. English is spoken. Off site: Indoor swimming pool, sauna and fitness centre 300 m. Fishing 70 m. Riding 6 km.

At a glance

| Welcome & Ambience | ✓✓✓✓✓ | Location | ✓✓✓✓✓ |
| Quality of Pitches | ✓✓✓✓✓ | Range of Facilities | ✓✓✓✓ |

Directions

Turn off main N632 at 154 km. marker onto N634. At the km 502.7 point east of Laurca, site is well signed through an estate.

Charges 2003

Per adult	€ 3.27 - € 3.50
child (4-10 yrs)	€ 2.85 - € 3.05
tent	€ 3.04 - € 3.60
caravan	€ 3.64 - € 3.90
motorcaravan	€ 6.54 - € 7.00
car	€ 3.27 - € 3.5
electricity	€ 1.82 - € 2.55

Plus 7% VAT. No credit cards.

Reservations

Advised for mid July - end Aug and made by post with deposit (€ 15). Tel: 985 640 938.
Email: cantiles@conectia.net

Open

All year.

ES8945 Camping Lagos de Somiedo

Valle de Lago, 33840 Somiedo

This is a most unusual gem of a small site in the moutainous Parque Natural de Somieda. Winding narrow roads with challenging rock overhangs, hairpin bends and breathtaking views (for eight km) finally bring you to the lake and campsite at an elevation of 1,200 m. This is a site for 4x4s, powerful small campervans, cars, backpackers of endurance – not advised for medium or large motorhomes, and caravans are not accepted. It is not an approach for the faint hearted! The friendly Lana family make you welcome at their unique site, which is tailored for those who wish to explore the natural and cultural values of the Park without the 'normal' campsite amenities. There is no electricity. A charming building, in keeping with the area, provides all the amenities and contains many items of natural interest. A small bar/restaurant set tight into the vertical rock face offers traditional Asturian food, but watch out for the local's stilted wooden clogs scattered in the entrance hall. There is a cool wind here most of the time and a torch is essential at night. Cars are parked away from the pitches here. Look out for the bears, wolves, capercailles and a unique wild goat which frequent these mountains.

Facilities

There are British style toilets and free hot water to clean hot showers, washbasins, laundry sinks and for dishwashing (outside, under cover). Facilities for babies and children. Washing machine. Combined reception, small restaurant, bar and reference section. Bread, milk and other essentials, plus local produce and crafts are sold in the site shop and bar. Horses for hire, trekking. Lectures on flora, fauna, history and culture. The river Valle runs through the site allowing trout fishing (licence required). Barbecue area. Small play area. Telephone. Gas supplies. Off site: The very small village is within 500 m.

At a glance

| Welcome & Ambience | ✓✓✓✓ | Location | ✓✓✓✓ |
| Quality of Pitches | ✓✓✓ | Range of Facilities | ✓✓✓ |

Directions

From N634 via Oviedo turn left at 442 km. marker on AS-15 signed Parque Natural de Somiedo. At 9 km. marker past village of Longoria, turn left on AS-227. At 38 km. marker, turn left into Pol de Somiedo, signed Centro Urbano. Follow signs for Valle de Lago and El Valle; 8 km. of hairpin bends from Pola, passing Urria on the left, brings you to the valley. Site is signed on the right.

Latest charges

Per adult	€ 3.46
child	€ 2.85
tent incl. 2 persons	€ 3.46
car	€ 2.85
motorcycle	€ 2.40
motorcaravan	€ 6.01

All plus 7% VAT.

Reservations

Not necessary. Tel: 985 763 776.

Open

Easter - 15 October.

ES8950 Camping Costa Verde

Playa de la Griega, 33320 Colunga

This busy site with a marked Spanish flavour, some 1.5 km. from the town of Colunga, has some very nice features and the owners aim to please. The most attractive feature, just outside the gate, is a spacious, supervised beach with a low tide lagoon which is ideal for younger children. There are 160 regularly laid out pitches which are very busy in high season. They are flat, but with little shade, and electricity is available throughout (long leads needed in places). A new sports and play area, with a dedicated barbecue and a picnic area is at the end of the site across a bridge. Whilst the river is mainly fenced off, children could possibly find their way to the river and thus should be supervised. This area is the real Jurassic Park with the footprints of dinosaurs having been discovered and preserved locally, along with some dinosaur fossil remains. Ask at reception for details and guides.

Facilities
The single toilet block is of a high standard with a mixture of British and Turkish style toilets (all British for ladies), large showers and free hot water throughout. Laundry. Well stocked shop. Bar/restaurant is traditional and friendly. Sports field. Barbeque. Playground. Torches needed. Little English spoken. Off site: Nearby towns of Ribadesella, Gijón and Oviedo. Excellent beaches. Fishing in river alongside site. Golf 18 km.

At a glance
Welcome & Ambience	✓✓✓✓✓	Location	✓✓✓✓✓
Quality of Pitches	✓✓✓✓	Range of Facilities	✓✓✓✓

Directions
From Santander take N634 to Ribadesella, and continue for 21 km. along the N632 coast road towards Gijón. Take right turn towards Lastres from the centre of Colunga.

Latest charges
Per adult	€ 3.70
child (over 5 yrs)	€ 3.15
tent	€ 3.25 - € 3.40
caravan	€ 4.20
car	€ 3.15
motorcycle	€ 2.85
motorcaravan	€ 6.00
electricity (6A)	€ 2.55

VAT included.

Reservations
Essential for peak weeks and made for exact dates with deposit. Send for booking form.
Tel: 985 856 373.

Open
Easter - early October.

ES8955 Camping Caravaning Arenal de Moris

Ctra. 632, 33344 Caravia Alta

This peaceful, rural site is close to three fine sandy beaches and is surrounded by mountains in the natural reservation area known as the Sueve. A hunting reserve, this is important for a breed of short Asturian horses, the 'Asturcone'. It is an ideal area for sea and mountain sports, horse riding, walking, birdwatching and cycling. Camping Arenal's 350 grass pitches are of 40-70 sq.m. and electricity connections (5A) are available. With little shade, some pitches are terraced with others on an open, slightly sloping field with views of the sea. The restaurant with a terrace serves local dishes and overlooks the pool to hills and woods. There was little noise when we visited but this must be considered a possibility. The excellent beach is a short walk.

Facilities
Three sanitary blocks provide comfortable, controllable showers (no dividers) and vanity style washbasins, laundry facilities and external dishwashing (cold water). Supermarket. Restaurant. Swimming pool. Tennis. Play area in lemon orchard. English is spoken. Off site: Fishing 200 m. Golf 10 km. Riding 15 km. Shops, bar and restaurants in local village.

At a glance
Welcome & Ambience	✓✓✓✓	Location	✓✓✓
Quality of Pitches	✓✓✓✓	Range of Facilities	✓✓✓

Directions
Site is signed from the N632 Ribadesella - Gijón road at km. 14 point.

Charges 2003
Per person	€ 3.95
child	€ 3.70
caravan	€ 5.15
tent	€ 3.70 - € 3.95
car	€ 3.95
motorcycle	€ 2.90
motorcaravan	€ 6.50
electricity	€ 2.40

Reservations
Contact site. Tel: 985 853 097.
Email: camoris@teleline.es

Open
1 June - 31 August.

Asturias

ES8960 Camping La Paz

Ctra. N-634 Irun - Coruna, km. 292, 33597 Vidiago-Llanes

On arrival here you may well be reminded of the fortress towns of old Spain. The reception building is opposite a solid rock face and many hundred feet below the site and the climb to the site is quite daunting but the staff will place your caravan for you, although motorcaravan drivers will have an exciting drive to the top. Once there it is all worth it as the views are absolutely outstanding. The site is arranged on numerous terraces with lower areas in a valley floor. The way down to the beach is very steep but the views, both to the Picos de Europa and to seaward are most impressive. There are 434 pitches with electricity of between 30-70 sq.m, but many are only suitable for tents with no electricity. Because of the steep access, units may be positioned on upper terraces by site staff using Range Rovers. An area back from the beach is more suitable for very large units. There is a cliff-top restaurant and bar with commanding views over the ocean and beach. It is best to book in high season since the site is deservedly popular and one of the best managed along this coast. With the extreme slopes, we think it would appeal most to visitors who are not infirm. Children will require supervision on the steep slopes.

Facilities

Four, first class sanitary blocks, with some interesting and unusual design features (such as being cut into solid rock), are modern, well equipped and spotlessly clean. They include hot showers with electronic controls and a baby bath. Full laundry and dishwashing facilities. Spring water is available from a number of taps throughout the site. Motorcaravan services. Mini-market. restaurant and bar. Lounge. Watersports. Table tennis. Games room. Fishing. Superb Beaches. Torches essential. English spoken.
Off site: Well placed for excursions to the eastern end of the Picos de Europa.

At a glance

Welcome & Ambience	✓✓✓✓✓	Location	✓✓✓✓✓
Quality of Pitches	✓✓✓✓✓	Range of Facilities	✓✓✓✓✓

Directions

From Santander take N634 towards Llanes. Site is signed from the main road at km.292, before you arrive in Vidiago.

Latest charges

Per adult	€ 3.58
child	€ 3.34
tent	€ 3.40
caravan	€ 4.78
car	€ 3.58
motorcycle	€ 2.98
motorcaravan	€ 5.98
electricity	€ 2.52

All plus VAT @ 7%.

Reservations

Advised for peak weeks. Tel: 985 411 012.
Email: delfin@campinglapaz.com

Open

1 June - 20 September.

ES8965 Camping Picos de Europa

33556 Avin-Onis

This site is newly developed and the dynamic owner, Jose is very pleasant and nothing is too much trouble. There is direct access off the AS114 in a valley situation beside a pleasant, fast flowing river. Local stone has been used for the L-shaped building at the main entrance which houses reception and a very good restaurant. The bar has an unusual circular window and small terrace overlooking the river. The 140 marked, smallish pitches have been developed in three corridor type avenues, on level grass backing on to hedging and with electricity to most. The tent area is over the bridge past the fairly small, round swimming and paddling pool. The site specialises in caving activities and is youthful.

Facilities

The main sanitary facilities are in the reception building. Additional toilet facilities, showers, baby bath, etc are in the tent area. Laundry and dishwashing facilities. Washing machine. Shop (Jul - Sep). Bar, restaurant serves a menu of the day at lunchtimes (all local fare). All year Swimming pool. Canoeing, riding and exceptional caving. Torches necessary. Excursions can be arranged in the mountains (on horseback if wished) and canoes can be hired. Off site: Site runs a most professional Speleology school with a hostel 3 km. away with 100 beds. Riding 12 km. Covadonga with its lakes and national park 13 km. Coast at Llanes 25 km. Golf 35 km.

At a glance

Welcome & Ambience	✓✓✓✓✓	Location	✓✓✓✓✓
Quality of Pitches	✓✓✓✓	Range of Facilities	✓✓✓✓✓

Directions

Site is 15 km. east of Cangas on AS114 road.

Latest charges

Per adult	€ 3.30
child (under 14 yrs)	€ 3.00
small tent	€ 3.30
large tent or caravan	€ 3.90
car	€ 3.00
motorcycle	€ 2.40
motorcaravan	€ 5.40
electricity	€ 2.40

All plus 7% VAT.

Reservations

Not needed outside July/Aug. Tel: 985 844 070.
Email: info@picos-europa.com

Open

All year.

Cantabria

The region of Cantabria in the north of Spain offers the best of both worlds. On the one hand there is the glorious coastline with beautiful beaches and pretty fishing villages; while inland there are a number of national parks including the moutainous, Picos de Europa.

Cantabria is a one province region

The capital is Santander

The capital, Santander, is an elegant city which extends over a wide bay with views of the Cantabrian Sea. Its historic quarter is situated against a backdrop of sea and mountains, although the town is best known for its beaches; the Playa de la Magdalena, which has a summer windsurfing school, and the popular El Sardinero beach. There is also a Maritime Museum and Museum of Prehistory and Archaeology plus a small zoo housed in the gardens of the old royal palace. A short distance from the city is the pretty medieval village of Santillana del Mar and the prehistoric Caves of Altamira. Despite being closed indefinitely for restoration work, the adjacent Altamira Museum houses a replica of these caves and their impressive prehistoric drawings. Also on the outskirts of the capital is the Cabárceno Nature Park with more protected areas scattered around the region, including those at Oyambre, Peña Cabarga and Saja-Besaya. The largest is the mountain range of Picos de Europa, a national park which shares it territory with Asturias and Castilla-León. With river gorges, valleys, woodlands and an abundance of wildlife, it is popular with walkers, trekkers and climbers.

Cuisine of the region

Seafood is used a lot, including fresh shellfish, sardines, *rabas* (fried squid), *bocartes rebozados* (breaded whitebait). Cheese is produced throughout the region; *queso de nata* (cream cheese), *picón* from Treviso Bejes, and smoked cheeses from Áliva or Pido. A typical dish of the region is the Cantabrian stew, which contains haricot beans, cabbage, rice and sausage. Desserts include the traditional cheesecakes of the Pas Valley and pastries. The local tipple is *orujo*, a strong liquor.

Maganos encebollados: squid with onion

Quesada: cheesecake

Sobaos pasiegos: sponge cakes

Sorropotún: type of fish stew

Places of interest

Castro Urdiales: beaches, Gothic church, Roman bridge, old quarter

Comillas: rural town, beaches, Gaudí-designed villa

Laredo: lively seaside resort, 13th church, 5 km. long sandy beach

Lierganes: 17th and 18th architecture, spa

Potes: on east side of Picos de Europa, mountain bike hire, paragliding available

San Vicente de la Barquera: picturesque fishing port

tip

THERE ARE MORE PREHISTORIC CAVES AT PUENTE VIESCO, ONE OF WHICH, CASTILLO, IS OPEN TO TOURS; IT'S BEST TO BOOK IN ADVANCE. IT ALSO HAS REMARKABLE PAINTINGS.

www.alanrogers.com for latest campsite news

Cantabria

ES8961 Camping El Helguero
Ctra. Santillana-Comillas, 39527 Ruiloba

This site, surrounded by tall trees and impressive towering rock formations, caters for around 240 units on slightly sloping ground. There are many marked pitches on different levels, all with access to electricity, but with only a little shade in parts. There are also attractive tent and small camper sections set close in to the rocks. The reasonably sized swimming pool and children's pool has an access lift for disabled campers. This is a good site for disabled visitors, in a peaceful location, and is excellent value out of main season. One can generally find space here even in high season, but arrive early. The site is used by tour operators and there are some site owned chalets. There is a large Spanish presence at weekends, especially in high season, so if you don't want to share the boisterous culture, choose one of the many pitches away from the restaurant area.

Facilities
Three well placed toilet blocks, although old, are clean and cared for, and include facilities for disabled visitors and children. Dishwashing, laundry sinks and washing machines. Motorcaravan services. Well-stocked supermarket (July/Aug. 9 am - 1 pm). bar snacks, separate more formal restaurant, Swimming pool with (limited opening with lifeguard on duty, caps compulsory – sold on site). Playground. Animation in high season. Games machines. Activities for children and entertainment for adults. Bicycle hire. ATM. Torches required. Off site: Restaurants in village. Fishing and riding 3 km. Santillana del Mar 12 km. Beaches near.

At a glance
Welcome & Ambience	✓✓✓	Location	✓✓✓
Quality of Pitches	✓✓✓✓	Range of Facilities	✓✓✓✓

Directions
From the C6316 road from Santillana del Mar to Comillas, turn left at Sierra. Site is signed as Camping Ruiloba (we don't know why) and is 200 m. on the left.

Latest charges
Per adult	€ 3.00 - € 3.60
child (4-10 yrs)	€ 2.50 - € 3.10
caravan or tent	€ 3.00 - € 3.60
car	€ 3.00 - € 3.60
motorcaravan	€ 6.00 - € 7.20
electricity (6A)	€ 2.15

Camping Cheques accepted.

Reservations
Write to site. Tel: 942 722 124.
Email: elhelguero@ctv.es

Open
1 April - 30 September.

the travel service
TO BOOK THIS SITE
0870 405 4055
Expert Advice & Special Offers

ES8962 Camping La Isla
Picos de Europa, 39570 Turieno-Potes

La Isla is beside the road from Potes to Fuente Dé, with excellent mountain views and good shade, which makes it a popular site for families with young children. Established for over 25 years, a warm welcome awaits you from the owners, who speak good English, and a most relaxed and peaceful atmosphere exists in the site. The 160 unmarked pitches are arranged around an oval gravel track (one-way system), under a variety of fruit and ornamental trees. Electricity is available to all pitches, though some may require long leads. A small bar and restaurant is cleverly placed at a lower level, by the small river which runs through the site. Everything here is in the traditional style and very pleasing. There are opportunities for riding and 4x4 safaris (site provides details) in the region, together with all the other mountain sports and active outdoor pursuits.

Facilities
Single, clean and smart sanitary block retains the style of the site. It includes washbasins, laundry and dishwashing sinks all with cold water. Washing machine. Gas supplies. Freezer service. Small shop. Restaurant/bar with local dishes. Takeaway. Small swimming pool, bathing caps compulsory (15/5-15/10). Playground. Barbecue and picnic area. Fishing. Bicycle hire. Riding. Drinks machine. Off site: Monastery at Toribio nearby. Interesting town of Potes, with Monday morning market 4 km.

At a glance
Welcome & Ambience	✓✓✓✓	Location	✓✓✓✓
Quality of Pitches	✓✓✓✓	Range of Facilities	✓✓✓✓

Directions
Site is on right hand side, 4 km. outside Potes, on N621 Potes to Espinama/Fuente Dé road.

Latest charges
Per adult	€ 2.91
child (0-10 yrs)	€ 2.37
tent	€ 2.73
caravan or trailer tent	€ 2.91
car	€ 2.73
motorcycle	€ 1.71
motorcaravan	€ 6.61
electricity (3A)	€ 1.98

All plus VAT. Low season reductions.

Reservations
Write to site. Tel: 942 730 896.
Email: campicoseuropa@terra.es

Open
1 April - 30 October.

www.alanrogers.com for latest campsite news

ES8963 Camping La Viorna

Ctra. Santa Toribio, 39570 Potes

The wonderful views down the valley from the open terraces of this site make it an attractive base from which to tour this region or to relax by the excellent swimming pool. It is popular with both familes and couples. There are beds of flowers and the trees are maturing, providing shade on many pitches. Access is good for all sizes of unit to the 110 pitches of around 70 sq.m, all of which have electricity. In high season, however, tents may be placed on less accessible, steeply sloping areas. The restaurant (fixed menu) has a terrace overlooking the pools. A pleasant feature is that all roofs are of the same design that is in sympathy with the town. This extends to a large picnic area behind the main block and even to small covered sitting out areas around the pool. All the buildings are in local stone with chunky wood fittings which look extremely attractive.

Facilities

Single, neat sanitary block of high standard, clean and modern. Washbasins with cold water. Facilities for disabled visitors double as unit for babies (key from reception). Laundry room has plenty of sinks, washing machine and ironing board. Dishwashing room with many sinks all cold water. Shop. Restaurant/bar with terrace. Heated swimming pool (23 x 13 m) and children's pool (bathing caps compulsory). Playground. Games room. Covered area with electronic games. Tourist information. Some English spoken. Many sporting activities can be arranged such as parascending, mountain biking, rafting and canoeing. Off site: Potes 2 km. (Monday market). Toribio Monastery close. Fuente Dé short spectacular drive.

At a glance

| Welcome & Ambience | ✓✓✓✓ | Location | ✓✓✓✓✓ |
| Quality of Pitches | ✓✓✓✓✓ | Range of Facilities | ✓✓✓✓✓ |

Directions

Take road N621 from Unquera to Potes. After town take left fork signed Toribio de Liebana and site is on right after 800 m.

Latest charges

Per person	€ 2.85
child	€ 2.40
caravan/tent	€ 2.85 - € 3.91
car	€ 2.85
motorcycle	€ 2.40
electricity (3/6A)	€ 2.10

All plus VAT.

Reservations

Write to site. Tel: 942 732 021.

Open

Easter/1 April - 30 October.

ES8964 Camping El Molino de Cabuerniga

Sopeña de Cabuérniga, Ctra. C625, km. 42, 39510 Cabuérniga

Located in a peaceful valley with magnificent views of the mountains, beside the river Saja and only a short walk from the old and attractive village, this gem of a site is on an open, level, grassy meadow with trees. Wonderful stone buildings and artefacts are a feature of this unique site. There are 114 marked pitches, all with electricity, although long leads may be needed and the site is lit at night. This comfortable site is very good value and ideal for a few nights while you explore the Cabuérniga Valley which forms part of the Reserva Nacional del Saja. The area is great for just resting or indulging in active pursuits with opportunities for mountain biking, climbing, walking, swimming or fishing in the river, horse riding, hunting, paragliding and 4x4 safaris. Sopeña Fiesta is in mid-July each year.

Facilities

A single, modern sanitary block provides showers in curtained cubicles, washbasins with cold water only. Dishwashing (H&C) and laundry sinks outside. Washing machines and ironing. Facilities for disabled campers planned. Small shop for basics. Restaurant/bar (June - Sept). Wonderful playground in rustic setting – supervision recommended. Fishing. Bicycle hire. Stone cottages and apartments for rent. Barbecue. No English is spoken. Off site: Fishing 200 m. Riding 4 km.

At a glance

| Welcome & Ambience | ✓✓✓✓✓ | Location | ✓✓✓✓✓ |
| Quality of Pitches | ✓✓✓✓✓ | Range of Facilities | ✓✓✓✓✓ |

Directions

From N634 at Cabezon de la Sal turn on C625, continue for approx. 10 km. to km. 42 where site is signed before Valle de Cabuerniga. Turn into village (watch out for low eaves/gutters on buildings), bearing right, watching carefully for small site signs through village (the locals always point for you!). automatic barrier at entrance arch.

Charges 2003

Per pitch	€ 6.61
adult	€ 3.31
child	€ 3.01
electricity	€ 2.10

All plus VAT.

Reservations

Contact site. Tel: 942 706 259.
Email: c.m.cabuerniga@campingcabuerniga.com

Open

All year.

Cantabria

ES8970 Camping Las Arenas–Pechon
Ctra. Pechon - Unquera, km. 2, 39594 Pechon

This campsite is in a very quiet, but rather spectacular location bordering the sea and the Tina Mayor estuary, with views to the mountains and access to an excellent beach. Otherwise, enjoy the pleasant kidney shaped pool that also shares the views. Unusually there is yet another beach on the far side of the site, this for the more adventurous as the access path is a little steep. Las Arenas is a very green, 10 hectare site with lots of shade from acacias, oak and poplar trees, and is good value. Taking 337 units, half of the site is divided into marked, grassy pitches (60 sq.m) in various bays or on terraces with stunning sea and mountain views, with electricity available and connected by asphalted roads. There are some quite steep slopes to tackle - the restaurant along with reception is at the top. Children need to be supervised in some areas and infirm campers may find the slopes difficult.

Facilities
Clean, well tiled sanitary facilities are in the older style. Various blocks include showers (no divider), plus dishwashing, laundry sinks and washing machines. Well stocked supermarket Restaurant (open to public). Snack bar. (open when site open). Playground. Fishing. Opportunities for fishing, swimming, diving, windsurfing or cycling from site. Windsurfer and bicycle hire. Torches necessary. English is spoken. Off site: For older teenagers a disco/bar 1 km. Golf 28 km.

At a glance
Welcome & Ambience	✓✓✓✓	Location	✓✓✓✓✓
Quality of Pitches	✓✓✓✓✓	Range of Facilities	✓✓✓✓

Directions
Nearest large city is Santander. Turn off the N634, Santander - Coruna road, just east of Unquera onto the road to Pechon. Site is 4.5 km.

Latest charges
Per adult	€ 3.60
child	€ 3.99
caravan	€ 4.80
tent	€ 3.00 - € 3.60
car	€ 3.60
motorcycle	€ 2.60
motorcaravan	€ 6.00
electricity (5A)	€ 2.15

All plus 7% VAT.

Reservations
Contact site. Tel: 942 717 188. Email: lasarenas@ctv.es

Open
1 June - 30 September.

ES8971 Camping Caravaning Playa de Oyambre
Finca Peña Guerra, 39547 San Vicente de la Barquera

This exceptionally well managed site is ideally positioned to use as a base to visit the spectacular Picos de Europa or one of the many sandy beaches along this northern coastline. In lovely countryside (good walking and cycling country), the site has some views of the fabulous Picos mountains, and is near the Cacarbeno National Park. The owner's son Pablo and his wife Maria are assisted by Francis in providing a personal service and both men speak excellent English. The 200 marked pitches are mostly of a good size (average 80 sq.m. with the largest ones often taken by tightly packed seasonal units). They are arranged on wide terraces with little shade and with electricity in most places. All pitches are flat and most have water and drainage. The site is well lit and a guard patrols at night (high season). The site gets busy with a fairly large Spanish community in season and there can be the usual happy noise of them enjoying themselves at weekends.

Facilities
Good sanitary facilities are in one, well kept block, with cleaners on duty all day and evening. Showers are spacious but have a frustrating mixture of push-button hot and ordinary cold controls. Facilities for babies and disabled visitors. Dishwashing (H&C) and laundry sinks (cold only). Washing machines (tokens from reception). Motorcaravan services. Well stocked supermarket open until 10 pm. with deliveries of fresh fish three days a week (15/6-15/9). Restaurant features fresh local dishes. Bar/TV lounge. Games area with machines. Swimming pools with lifeguard (1/6-15/9). Playground. Basketball. Football. Off site: Fishing 1 km. Superb beaches 1 km. Riding 5 km. San Vicente de la Barquera 5 km.

At a glance
Welcome & Ambience	✓✓✓✓✓	Location	✓✓✓✓
Quality of Pitches	✓✓✓✓✓	Range of Facilities	✓✓✓✓✓

Directions
Site is signed at the junction to Comillas, at km. 265 on the E70, 5 km. east of San Vicente de la Barquera. The entrance is quite steep (take care with caravans). Exercise caution as there is another 'Camping Playa de Oyambre' within 500 m. (on the beach) which is not recommended.

Latest charges
Per pitch	€ 6.95
adult	€ 3.45
child	€ 2.95
electricity (10A)	€ 2.50

All plus VAT.

Reservations
Advised, particularly if you have a large unit. Write to site. Tel: 942 711 461. Email: camping@oyambre.com

Open
Easter/1 April - 30 September.

Cantabria

ES8973 Camping Santillana

Ctra. de Comilias s/n, 39330 Santillana del Mar

This is an attractive site on sloping ground eight kilometres from the beaches of the north coast with full facilities. It has a fine swimming pool complex, a restaurant and self service café which operate all year. pitches mostly for tents are informally arranged on a slope, with other pitches for caravans and motorcaravans on the lower part of the site. With numbered but unmarked pitches, some over-crowding may occur. Pitches alongside the road will experience some road noise as this is a busy arterial route. Many permanent types of accommodation on site and a large separate complex across a small street has many mobile homes. The site is directly off the main road and a fairly steep entry brings you to a reception where English is spoken.

Facilities

Toilet blocks are well placed (onlt one open in low season), fully equipped and with facilities for disabled campers. Washing machines and irons. Supermarket. Souvenir shop. Bar/restaurant (popular with locals at weekends) and self service cafe (all year). Swimming pool complex with separate children's pool. Play area for toddlers and an inventive play complex for older children. Minigolf. Tennis. Bicycle hire. Satellite TV. Drinks machines. Electronic games. Film processing service. Entertainment in high season.

At a glance

| Welcome & Ambience | ✓✓✓✓ | Location | ✓✓✓✓ |
| Quality of Pitches | ✓✓✓✓✓ | Range of Facilities | ✓✓✓✓✓ |

Directions

Nearest large city is Santander. Site is directly off Santanilla - Comillas road (C6316) between the 5 km. and 6 km. markers. Exit the N634 west of Torrelavega. Alternatively, exit A67 at km. 16 and follow signs to Santillana.

Charges 2003

Per person	€ 4.95
child (6-10 yrs)	€ 3.85
caravan or tent	€ 4.95
car	€ 4.80
motorcaravan	€ 6.00
electricity	€ 3.00

No credit cards. Camping Cheques accepted.

Reservations

Advisable in July and August. Tel: 942 818 250. Email: campingsantillan@ceoecant.es

Open

All year.

ES8985 Camping Valderredible

Ctra. Polientes - Ruerrero. s/n, Valderredible, 39220 Polientes

This is a pleasant site owned by the Gutierrez brothers who designed and constructed this site using their past campsite experience. Jose and Jesus are very keen to welcome you to their establishment. All facilities on site are modern and kept spotlessly clean. There are 100 flat pitches with 80 for tourers and 20 for tents. Most have electricity and trees have been planted, although there is little shade at the moment. The pools enjoy river and mountain views, as does the patio to the bar and restaurant. The bustling bar, with TV, is pleasantly decorated with local artefacts and offers a range of tapas in season. There are some lovely walks in this unspoilt area (ask for guidance). The site is about 80 km. south of Santander and is good as a stopover or for longer stays if you wish for a peaceful break. On the first Sat and Sun of August there is a Fiesta here with all night celebrations so the site is full and extremely noisy.

Facilities

The good central sanitary block is fully equipped and comfortable. Washing-up sinks outside but covered Two washing machines (free) and a dryer. No facilities for disabled campers. Small well stocked shop. Bar selling tapas and more formal restaurant, good service and reasonably priced. Swimming pool and children's pool (caps required; June - Sept). Play area (supervision required). Volleyball. Bar billiards. Table football. Torch useful. Off site: Canoeing and fishing in river Ebro 200 m. (March - June). Riding and bicycle hire 15 km. Buses run to local village which has a few bars and some restaurants.

At a glance

| Welcome & Ambience | ✓✓✓✓ | Location | ✓✓✓✓✓ |
| Quality of Pitches | ✓✓✓✓ | Range of Facilities | ✓✓✓✓ |

Directions

Exit from A623 Burgos - Santander road around the village of Quintanilla Escalada onto minor road to Polientes. The site is clearly signed along the 21 km. of road and is just past the village of Ruijas. It is a spectacular drive in from the main road.

Charges 2003

Per adult	€ 3.15
child (3-10 yrs)	€ 2.79
tent	€ 3.25
caravan	€ 3.25
car	€ 3.25
motorcaravan	€ 5.26
electricity	€ 2.17

Plus 7% VAT.

Reservations

Necessary in August. Tel: 942 776 138. Email: valderrecamp@mundivia.es

Open

1 April - 4 November.

Cantabria

ES8995 Camping Los Molinos

Ctra. La Ria S/N, 39180 Noja

Camping Los Molinos is ideally located for touring the local area and as an overnight stop en route when travelling by ferry via Bilbao or Santander. It is close to the village of Noja and near the Playa del Ris beach which has fine sand and clear water. The site is divided into two main areas, both with a large number of permanent units. There are 500 average sized touring pitches, on level ground, but with little shade; all have electricity. There is a large separate area for tents. Each half of the site has its own main building with catering facilities. The right side has the main restaurant/bar, disco, supermarket, while the left has the reception, café/bar, supermarket and the swimming pools. Unusually the site has its own karting complex.

Facilities

The fully equipped modern sanitary building is central and kept very clean. Washing machines, dishwashing (H&C) and laundry sinks under cover. Facilities for disabled campers have access ramps. Supermarket, butcher and fishmonger (1/6-30/9). Main restaurant/bar good decoration and tablecloths with cafe bar providing tapas, pizzas or takeaway food. (1/6-30/9). Swimming pool and children's pool with life guard (15/6-10/9). Playground. Basketball. Tennis. Team games. Medical room. Security at gate. ATM. Torch useful. Off site: Indoor pool 100 m. Beach 300 m. Fishing 300 m. Golf 1 km. Riding and bicycle hire 500 m. Boat launching 7 km. Free bus hourly to the beach and town in high season.

At a glance

Welcome & Ambience	✓✓✓✓	Location	✓✓✓✓
Quality of Pitches	✓✓✓✓	Range of Facilities	✓✓✓✓✓

Directions

From E70/A8 Bilbao - Santander, take exit 185, CA147 to Noja take first right S403. It is 10 km. to Noja. In town look for multiple campsite signs going off to left. Follow signs to Playa del Ris. At beach roundabout turn left and look for a left turn at further large signs. Reception is in the building to the left.

Charges 2003

Per pitch	€ 6.50 - € 9.50
adult	€ 3.25 - € 4.40
child	€ 2.60 - € 3.40
tent	€ 4.50 - € 5.50
car	€ 2.00 - € 2.60
electricity	€ 2.45

No credit cards.

Reservations

Write to site. Tel: 942 630 426.
Email: losmolinos@ceoecant.es

Open

12 February - 15 November.

ES9000 Camping Playa Joyel
Playa de Ris, 39180 Noja

This very attractive, holiday and touring site is some 40 km. from Santander and 70 km. from Bilbao. It is a high quality, comprehensively equipped busy site, by a superb beach; providing 1,000 well shaded, marked and numbered pitches, including 80 large pitches of 100 sq.m. Electricity is available (with new blue Euro-sockets). The swimming pool complex with lifeguard is free to campers and the superb beaches are cleaned daily 15/6-20/9. One of the beach exits leads to the main beach, or if you turn left out of the other you will find a safe, placid estuary with water at rising tide. An unusual feature is the natural park within the site boundary which has a great selection of animals to see. It overlooks a protected area of marsh where European birds spend the winter. A 'no cycling on site' rule operates in July/Aug. There are security patrols at night. This good value, well managed site has a lot to offer for family holidays with much going on in high season when it gets very busy. Used by tour operators (150 pitches).

Cantabria

Facilities
Six excellent, spacious and fully equipped toilet blocks (voted amongst the cleanest in Europe) include baby baths and dishwashing facilities. Large laundry. Motorcaravan services. Gas supplies. Freezer service. Supermarket (all season). General shop. Kiosk. Restaurant (14/4-29/9). Bar, café takeaway and snacks (14/4-28/9). Swimming pools, bathing caps compulsory (15/5-15/9). Entertainment organised with a soundproof pub/disco (July-Aug). Games hall. Gym park. Recreation area and sports field. Tennis. Playground. Riding.Fishing. Natural animal park. Barbecue area. Hairdresser (July/Aug). Pharmacy. ATM and money exchange. Torches necessary in some areas. Medical centre. Dogs are not accepted. Off site: Bicycle hire 500 m. Large complex with multiple facilities including golf and indoor pool (fee) 1 km. Golf 20 km.

Directions
From A8 (E70) toll-free motorway at Beranga (km.185) take the N634 then, almost immediately, take the S403 for Noja. Follow signs to site.

Latest charges
Per adult	€ 3.70 - € 5.50
child (under 10 yrs)	€ 2.50 - € 4.10
pitch	€ 9.90 - € 11.70
electricity (3A)	€ 2.45 - € 2.70

All plus 7% VAT. No credit cards. Camping Cheques accepted.

Reservations
Made for 1 week or more. Early arrival or reservation is essential in high season. Tel: 942 630 081.
Email: campingplayajoyel@yahoo.es

Open
23 March - 29 September.

At a glance
Welcome & Ambience	✓✓✓✓	Location	✓✓✓✓
Quality of Pitches	✓✓✓✓	Range of Facilities	✓✓✓✓

the travel service
TO BOOK THIS SITE
0870 405 4055
Expert Advice & Special Offers

- Only 40 km from Santander (ferry) and 70km from Bilbao (ferry), easily and quickly reached along the magnificent, new, toll-free autovia and the coast roads.
- A 25 ha. holiday site with a large (4 ha) recreation and sports area and a precious, 8 ha natural park with animals in semiliberty.
- Modern, first category installations. Beautifull surroundings with direct access to wide, clean beaches. Surrounded by meadows and woods.
- Service and comfort for the most exacting guests. Properly marked pitches.
- English spoken.
- Open from Easter to 30th September.

Great on-line holiday deals alanrogersdirect.com

Pais Vasco-Euskadi

Located in northern Spain, this is a region steeped in Basque traditions, which is reflected in the architecture, native language, local sports and cuisine.

There are three provinces:
Alava, Gipuzkoa and Bizkaia

The regional capital is Vitoria

The province of Gipuzkoa adjoins France in the east. Its capital, San Sebastian, is a bustling, picturesque seaside town with a strong Basque identity. Overlooking La Concha Bay and enclosed by rolling low hills, this popular resort boasts four good beaches, including the celebrated La Concha Beach. As cider production is one of oldest traditions in Basque country there are also plenty of sidrerías (cider houses) to visit. Heading along the rocky fringe of Costa Vasca towards Bilbao in Bizkaia are more excellent beaches and pretty fishing villages including Orio, Zarautz and Getaria. The biggest attraction in Bilbao is the famous Guggenheim Museum. Opened in 1997 this spectacular building is completely covered with titanium sheets and houses a collection of modern and contemporary art from around the world. The city also boasts a beautiful old quarter with a Gothic cathedral, the Plaza Nueva and a museum. Further inland in Alava is Vitoria, the region's capital. Its medieval streets intermingle with Renaissance Palaces and fine churches and are lined with lively bars and tavernas. In the summer the city plays host to a jazz festival. Elsewhere in the province are various nature reserves.

Cuisine of the region

Basque cuisine is considered to be the finest in Spain. Tapas or *pintxos* is readily available in bars, served with the local white wine *txakolí*. Fish is popular, especially *bacalao* (cod) and seafood is often used to make casseroles and sauces. Lots of milk based desserts. Founded in the 19th century, the tradition of dining clubs or *txokos* are unique to the Basque country

Alubias pochas: white haricot bean stew

Chipirones en su tinta: squid cooked in its ink

Goxua: sponge cake with whipped cream and caramel

Intxaursalsa: milk pudding with cinnamon and walnuts

Marmitako: fish and potato stew

Pantxineta: custard slice

Places of interest

Encartanciones: one of the world's largest cave chambers Torca del Carlista, wildlife sanctuary

Hondarribia: fishing port, beaches, charming walled old town

Laguardia: old walled town with cobbled streets, historic buildings, in wine-growing district of Rioja Alavesa

Oñati: Baroque architecture, old university

Tolosa: impressive old town square, carnival in February

Zarautz: seaside town, famous for production of *txakoli*

Zumaia: beaches, good coastal walks, July fiesta with Basque sports, dancing and bull racing

tip

BASQUE SPORTS FEATURE IN MANY LOCAL FIESTAS. WATCH OUT FOR *AIZKOLARITZA* (LOG-CHOPPING), *HARRI-JASOTZEA* (STONE-LIFTING) AND *SEGALARITZA* (GRASS-CUTTING)!

www.alanrogers.com for latest campsite news

Pais Vasco-Euskadi

ES9035 Camping Portuondo
Ctra. Gernika - Bermeo, 48360 Mundaka

From some of the 119 pitches on site there are stunning views over the ocean and estuary. Among the lovely gardens the pitches are mainly for medium size vans and tents but there are 6 large pitches at the lower levels for caravans and motorhomes. In high season (July/Aug) it is best to ring to book your space. This well cared for, impressive little site could either be a very pleasant site to stay or a good base from which to explore the local area and the friendly owner Inmanol is keen to help you. The site is mostly terraced, with pitches split, one section for your unit the other for your car and there is shade in parts. Most pitches are very slightly sloping and all have electricity (some may need long leads). Above the larger sanitary block the building becomes a lofty picnic area with long benches, open on all sides, but perfect for occupants of tents in periods of rain. There is a stylish, safe swimming pool in the lower area of the site but no facilities for disabled campers. We stress that this site is on a steep incline.

Facilities
Two very good quality, fully equipped, sanitary units can be heated and include mostly British style WCs and a smart baby bathroom. Dishwashing and laundry sinks outside under cover. Washing machines and dryers. Automated shop (all season). Bar and two restaurants, one open to public offering full range of meals and snacks, plus barbecue food (16/1-15/12). Takeaway (15/6-15/9). Swimming pools (15/6-15/9). Table tennis. Sky TV. Barbecue area. Bicycle hire. Caravan storage. Torches necessary. English spoken. Off site: Fishing 100 m. Beaches 500 m. bracing walk. Surfing on Mundaka beach (500 m) is so good they hold international championships there. Boat launching 1 km. Bicycle hire 2 km. Bars and restaurants 2 km. Sailing 5 km.

Directions
From N634 or autopista (S. Sebastian-Bilbao), turn at Amorebieta onto the C6315 road to Gernika - Bermeo. Approach site from Bermeo direction due to oblique, steep (18%) access.

Charges 2003
Per adult	€ 4.10 - € 4.55
child (under 10 yrs)	€ 3.50 - € 4.00
pitch	€ 8.80 - € 9.20
pitch with electricity (6A)	€ 11.85 - € 12.15

All plus 7% VAT. Less 5-10% for longer stays.

Reservations
Write to site. Tel: 946 877 701.
Email: recepcion@campingportuondo.com

Open
All year.

At a glance
Welcome & Ambience	✓✓✓✓	Location	✓✓✓✓
Quality of Pitches	✓✓✓✓	Range of Facilities	✓✓✓✓

ES9038 Camping Orio
20810 Orio

This site has 260 pitches, with many long stay units and privately owned static units, but there should always be adequate space in the 190 pitches allocated for tourers. It is only 100 m. from the beach and there is little shade. The pitches are in rows divided by tarmac roads and hedges, all with electricity (5A). Like most of the north coast sites, it is fairly expensive in high season, with the cheaper pitches furthest from the beach, but the bonus is that they are closer to the sanitary facilities. The beach is in a pretty bay contained by towering hills which overlook the site. The beach is of soft sand (real sand castle stuff) and shelves gently. Fishing is popular off the extremely long jetty or in the local river. This is a decent site for transit stops, west of San Sebastian or a little longer if you wish to enjoy the beach.

Facilities
The modernised main sanitary block is fully equipped and includes baby baths. Two additional smaller, older sanitary blocks are opened in the main season. Large kitchen with additional dishwashing and laundry sinks (cold water) outside under cover. Good facilities for disabled campers. Mini-market and good restaurant/bar attached to the site (open July/Aug). Swimming pools. Playground. Squash and tennis courts. Fishing. Barbecue area. Dogs are not accepted. Torches are necessary. Some English is spoken. Off site: Fishing 100 m. Sailing. Indoor pool. Aviary 100 m. Golf 6 km.

Directions
Turn off N634 road at the Orio junction and follow signs to site. The approach is straightforward.

Latest charges
Per unit incl. 2 persons	€ 12.70 - € 22.55
extra adult	€ 2.30 - € 3.65
child (2-10 yrs)	€ 1.80 - € 3.10

VAT included.

Reservations
Write to site. Tel: 943 834 801.
Email: kampina@terra.es

Open
1 March - 1 November.

At a glance
Welcome & Ambience	✓✓✓✓	Location	✓✓✓✓
Quality of Pitches	✓✓✓	Range of Facilities	✓✓✓

Great on-line holiday deals alanrogersdirect.com

Pais Vasco-Euskadi

ES9039 Gran Camping Zarautz

Monte Talai-Mendi, Ctra. N634 San Sebastian - Bilbao, km. 17, 20800 Zarauz

This friendly site sits alongside vines high in the hills to the east of the Basque town of Zarautz and has commanding views of the excellent beaches and the island of Isarria. Twenty percent of the 500 pitches are permanent which brings Spanish life and colour to the site at weekends. The pitches are of average size, shaded by mature trees, are reasonably level and have electricity. We recommend a call to reserve one of the perimeter pitches which enjoy magnificent views over the bay. Between the site and the sea is a protected public area where flora and fauna flourish. On approaching the site you will pass a Bodega producing the local white wine, Txakoli (pronounced Char-coal-lee). The locals drink it young with shellfish. The town of Zarautz offers a cultural programme in summer and the pedestrian promenade with modern sculptures is a good vantage point to enjoy the beach and surfers.

Facilities

Two sanitary blocks - the more modern is circular and open plan with facilities for disabled campers. Two washing machines. Restaurant/bar with TV. Well stocked shop. Play area. Drinks machines. Recycling bins. English spoken. Off site: Bus/train service 1 km. Two good restaurants very close by. Below site at beach level is a 9 hole golf course. For a special treat visit the ancient siderías (cider houses). These open in January and offer tastings with superb traditional food until the cider runs out. Ask for assistance at reception.

At a glance

| Welcome & Ambience | ✓✓✓✓ | Location | ✓✓✓✓✓ |
| Quality of Pitches | ✓✓✓✓ | Range of Facilities | ✓✓✓ |

Directions

From N634 Donostia - San Sebastian road at 17 km. marker take sign to Zarautz and site is well marked on the roundabout at the eastern side of town.

Charges 2003

Per adult	€ 3.80
child (0-10 yrs)	€ 3.25
caravan or tent	€ 4.50
car	€ 3.80
motorcaravan	€ 8.30
electricity (5A)	€ 3.10

Reservations

Contact site. Tel: 943 831 238.

Open

All year.

ES9045 Camping Angosto

Ctra. Villanane - Angosto no. 2, 01425 Villanañe

This is a smart eco-friendly site with excellent facilities surrounded by wooded hills near the Valderejo National Park. Opened in 2002, the facilities are improving every year remaining smart and clean. A keen young team run things here, and there is an emphasis on adventure sports. The site is occasionally busy with parties of local youngsters enjoying the various activities organised by the management (it can be noisy when this happens). With ample manoeuvring space, the 71 pitches are flat and of average size, 25 having electricity. There is a large area for tents. Young trees have been planted around the site and are beginning to provide shade. An attractive pool has been built with a sliding roof for inclement weather. Attractive walks start just outside the site perimeter. As the site is one hour from Bilbao we see it as a most pleasant stopover or a chance to sample the rustic simplicity of the area and enjoy the facilities and a tranquil setting.

Facilities

Central, fully equipped sanitary block of attractive design with facilities for disabled campers. Dishwashing sinks outside, under cover. Washing machine. Good shop also used by the local villagers. Stylish bar. Attractive and terraced restaurant. Small fenced children's play area close to entrance and grass toddler play area. Mountain bike hire. Fishing. Adventure sports incl. para-ascending organised. Table football. Table tennis. TV. Fishing. Ice machine. Drinks machine. Torches necessary in some areas. Off site: Heated municipal pool 1.4 km. Bus service from pretty local village 1 km.

At a glance

| Welcome & Ambience | ✓✓✓✓ | Location | ✓✓✓✓✓ |
| Quality of Pitches | ✓✓✓✓✓ | Range of Facilities | ✓✓✓✓✓ |

Directions

Nearest town is Miranda de Ebro. From Bilbao and the Longrono autoroute, exit at village of Pobes and take road to Salinas and Espejo (N625). Site is clearly signed. If towing a caravan continue to Miranda de Ebro proceed towards Burgos for one exit (no 4) and take the N1 to the N625 then north to Villanane.

Latest charges

Per adult	€ 3.16
child	€ 2.70
tent	€ 2.85
caravan	€ 3.16
car	€ 2.85
motorcaravan	€ 4.81
electricity	€ 2.70

All plus 7% VAT.

Reservations

Contact site. Tel: 945 353 271.
Email: info@camping-angosto.com

Open

April - September (plus weekends Sept - March).

La Rioja

This small region located in the north eastern part of the country is the most outstanding wine-growing area in Spain. Its production, Rioja wine, figures among the finest wines in the world.

This is a one province region

The capital is Logroño

The capital of the region Logroño did not gain importance till the 11th century, when the rise in popularity of the Pilgrims' Route to Santiago de Compostela attracted people. Indeed the 12th century Codex Calixtinus, the first guide to the route, mentions the city. And throughout the region, every town along the way has a church dedicated to the saint.

Pilgrimages aside, La Rioja is best known for its wine. At the centre of the region's wine production is Haro, a stately town northwest of Logroño, and obviously a good place to stock up on a bottle or two! For those interested in the wine processes the Museum of Wine is worth a visit; admission includes cheese and wine tasting. During the last week of June the town comes alive with festivities. With free outdoor concerts, costumed characters on giant stilts, wine tastings and bargain buys, the climax of these fiestas is the Battle of the Wine, where thousands of people happily gather to be drenched in wine.

Cuisine of the region

Asparagus, beans, peppers, garlic, artichokes and other vegetables and pulses are the basic ingredients of a long list of dishes such as vegetable stew, potatoes a la riojana, lamb cutlets with vine shoots or stuffed peppers. Traditional desserts include pears in wine, almond pastries from Arnedo or marzipan from Soto

Camerano Cheese: cheese made from goat's milk, typical of La Rioja, usually eaten as a dessert with honey.

Fardelejo: pastry cake filled with marzipan

Riojan-style potatoes: prepared with chorizo, peppers, garlic and lamp chops (optional)

Places of interest

Calahorra: main town in Lower Rioja, Cathedral Museum

Ezcaray: in the Sierra de la Demanda mountains, the surrounding area is made up of streams, forests and peaks over 2,000 metres high

Nájera: monastery of Santa María la Real, built in 1032, History and Archaeological Museum

San Millán de la Cogolla: traditional town, Monasteries of Suso and Yuso where the first texts written in Spanish are preserved

Santo Domingo de la Calzada: last great staging post of the Pilgrim's Route in La Rioja, Cathedral of San Salvador

tip

TO THE SOUTH OF THE REGION YOU CAN TOUR THE ROUTE OF THE DINOSAURS, AN ITINERARY WHICH TAKES IN THE TRACKS LEFT BY THESE PREHISTORIC CREATURES.

www.alanrogers.com for latest campsite news

ES9040 Camping de Haro

Avenida Miranda 1, 26200 Haro (La Rioja)

This quiet riverside site is on the outskirts of the village of Haro, which is the commercial centre for the renowned Rioja wines. It is a family run site with excellent pools and good supporting facilities. There is considerable room to manoeuvre at the entrance with modern reception and a welcome from the cheery young owner, Carlos who speaks excellent English. The river Ebro running alongside the site can provide fishing, and there is secure fencing. Approximately 30% of the good sized pitches on level ground are occupied by permanent campers. The area is very popular with Spanish holidaymakers in summer. Electricity connections are provided, although long leads may be required on some pitches. The site gives information on the jewel of a town, and tastings at the Bodegas close by.

Facilities

Two modern sanitary blocks incorporates excellent facilities for disabled campers. Laundry. All facilities were spotlessly clean and well maintained when visited. Mini market offers fresh bread in season. Restaurant, bar and supermarket (all in season only). Large smart adult pool. Three toddler pools. Drinks and ice machine. New children's play area and animation in season. Fishing. Torch useful. Off site: Beautiful old town square with bustling bars, excellent restaurants and wine tastings. Order a 'Banda' in the bars, sold as a cheap house wine and be rewarded with a glass of 'Banda Azul' which is in fact a superb quality Rioja.

At a glance

| Welcome & Ambience | ✓✓✓✓ | Location | ✓✓✓✓✓ |
| Quality of Pitches | ✓✓✓✓✓ | Range of Facilities | ✓✓✓✓ |

Directions

Take E804 road from Bilbao south to Logroño; enter Haro at exit 9 and the site is well signed just west of the river on the western side of town.

Charges 2003

Per adult	€ 2.93 - € 3.45
child	€ 2.31 - € 2.72
tent or caravan	€ 2.93 - € 3.45
car	€ 2.93 - € 3.45
motorcaravan	€ 5.06 - € 5.96
electricity (3A)	€ 2.05
dog	€ 1.42 - € 1.67

Camping Cheques accepted.

Reservations

Write to site. Tel: 941 312 737.
Email: campingdeharo@fer.es

Open

All year except 10 Dec. - 10 Jan.

Navarra

The region of Navarra lies in the north of Spain, on the border with France separated by the Pyreenes. With mountain retreats, beautiful valleys and an array of attractive towns and historic buildings littered throughout the region, it is also popular for those wishing to follow the Pilgrim's Route to Santiago de Compostela.

There is only one province also known as Navarra

The capital is Pamplona

Founded by the Roman general Pompey in 75 BC, the region's capital Pamplona is perhaps best known for the Fiestas de San Fernmín (July), when the *encierro* takes place – a tradition which involves people running through the streets in front of bulls. The city is also boasts its fair share of sights including the old town, with its ancient churches and elegant building. Outside the city is the Sierra de Aralar, a great hiking spot with well-marked paths of all grades. A wander through here will take you past waterfalls and caves and in Excelsis you'll come across Navarra's oldest church, the Sanctuario de San Miguel, a popular pilgrimage destination. In the south, the historic medieval town of Olite is home to an outstanding 15th century castle, with turrets galore, and a Romanesque and Gothic church. To the west is the Urbasa and Andía Nature Reserve. Further north and in the east, the villages and valleys of the Pyrenees provide some of the most beautiful landscapes in the province and offer the perfect place to relax. Of particular note are the Valle de Baztán and the Valle de Salazar. For the more active, the Valle de Roncal is a good place to explore the mountains as is the Pirenaico National Park.

Cuisine of the region

Typical products found in abundance in this area include asparagus grown on the river banks, small red peppers and artichokes from Tudela, pork from Estella, cherries from Ciriza, cheese made in the Roncal Valley and *chorizo* from Pamplona

Ajoarriero: cod cooked with garlic, potato, 'choricero' peppers and tomatoes

Canutillos de Sumbilla: sweet pastry made with aniseed, filled with lemon flavouring

Chorizo: shaped like a candle, stuffed in thick tripe with pork and beef, seasoned with salt, paprika, garlic and sugars. It is eaten raw.

Cordero al chilindrón: lamb stew

Cuajada: made from sheep's milk and natural curd, sweetened by honey or sugar

Pacharán: traditional aniseed liquor

Places of interest

Andía Nature Reserve: forests, ponds, wildlife including the golden eagle, wild boar and wildcat

Camino de Santiago: ancient Pilgrim's route. There are variants but the most popular point of entry into Spain was the pass of Roncesvalles, in the Pyrenees. It then continues south through Navarra via Sangüesa, Puente La Reina and Estella, then west through the provinces of La Rioja and Castilla-León till it reaches Santiago in the Galicia province

Orreaga-Roncesvalles: a town established as a sanctuary and hospital in 1132 and first staging post for pilgrims, musuem with exhibition on Pilgrim's Route.

Sangüesa: small town, 14th century churches, medieval hospital

Ujué: medieval defensive village, Romanesqe church

tip

VISIT THE CAVES AT ZUGARRAMURDI. IN THE MIDDLES AGES THE CAVERN WAS A MAJOR CENTRE FOR WITCHCRAFT AS 'CELEBRATED' IN THE LOCAL WITCHES' FESTIVAL (JULY).

www.alanrogers.com for latest campsite news

ES9042 Camping Etxarri

Paraje Dambolintxulo s/n, 31820 Etxarri-Aranatz

Situated in the Valle de la Burunda the site is a peaceful oasis with superb views of the 1,300 m. high San Donato Mountains. The approach to the constantly improving site is via a road lined by huge 300 year old beech trees, surrounding the tiny site, which nestles behind an enormous pool. Reception is a purpose built chalet with a touring reference library (mostly in Spanish). There are 100 average sized pitches on flat ground, 50 for tourers, with electricity to all and water to 25. The site is well placed for fascinating walks in unspoilt countryside and is close to three recognised nature walks catering for all tastes and abilities. Animation is organised in August for children and there are many other activities available (see below). There is hostel accommodation for young Navarra students as part of their curriculum, and this is also used as standard accommodation especially at the time of the Fiestas de San Fermín (bull-running) in Pamplona. It is essential to make a reservation if you wish to stay for the week of 6-14 July. A visit to Pamplona is recommended, although parking is difficult. Try to the west of the bullring, then wander down to Plaza de Toros (renamed Plaza Hemingway) to savour the atmosphere. A useful tip: it is common to use dual-naming of places and roads, one in Spanish, the other in the Basque language. It can be confusing – ask for advice if in doubt.

Facilities

Single, very modern sanitary block includes sinks and baby bath. Laundry. Gas supplies. Essential supplies available in high season. Bar. Restaurant with traditional fare at reasonable prices (1/6-30/9). Very large swimming pool plus children's pool (ex municipal and open to the public). Archery (small fee). Bicycle hire. Minigolf. Skateboarding. Table tennis. Small football pitch. Volleyball. Play area. Games room. Off site: Good bus services. Local village at 2 km. has bars, restaurants and shops.

At a glance

Welcome & Ambience	✓✓✓✓	Location	✓✓✓✓
Quality of Pitches	✓✓✓✓	Range of Facilities	✓✓✓

Directions

From A8 San Sebastian - Bilbao motorway take exit to Pamplona A15 at the junction at Irurzun (about 17.5 km. northwest of Pamplona) take N240 to Vitoria. At 40 km. marker take road to Etxarri-Aranatz where site is signed.

Charges 2003

Per adult	€ 2.75 - € 3.35
child	€ 2.50 - € 3.00
caravan	€ 3.40 - € 4.10
tent	€ 2.75 - € 3.25
car	€ 2.75 - € 3.35
electricity (6A)	€ 3.10

Reservations

Contact site. Tel: 948 460 537.
Email: info@campingetxarri.com

Open

1 April - 1 October.

Situated amidst a leafy oakwood in the centre of the Sakana Valley.

Its magnificent setting makes it a perfect base for visiting two outstandingly beautiful areas: the mountains of Urbasa and Aralar.

These are lands of shepherds inhabitated since the paleolithic times, and they still boast many prehistoric remains.

Due to varying altitudes, they are accessible to all ages.

**Camping ETXARRI . E-31820 ETXARRI ARANATZ (Navarra) . Tel./fax: (34) 948 46 05 37
info@campingetxarri.com . www.campingetxarri.com**

ES9043 Camping Caravaning Errota el Molino
31150 Mendigorria

This is an extremely large, sprawling site set by an attractive weir near the town of Mendigorria, alongside the river Arga. Regardless of the mini-windmill (molino) at the entrance, it really takes its name from an old disused water-mill close by. Reception is housed in the lower part of a large prefabricated building along with the bar/restaurant which has a cool shaded terrace, there is a large separate more formal dining room and a supermarket and other support facilities. The chirpy owner Anna Beriain will give you a warm welcome. The upper floor provides dormitory accommodation for backpackers. The site is split into separate permanent and touring sections. The touring area is a new development which is divided into sections. There are good-sized flat pitches with electricity and water for tourers, however there is no electricity in the tent area. Many trees have been planted around the site but there is little shade as yet. There is a small tour operator presence and backpackers and campers abound during the festival of San Fermin in July. Tours of the local bodegas (groups of ten) to sample the fantastic Navarra wines can be organised by reception.

Facilities
The single, fully equipped, toilet block is very clean and well maintained, with cold water to washbasins. Services could become busy during San Fermin but then access is allowed to the sanitary facilities on the permanent side. Dishwashing (cold only) and laundry sinks (H&C). Facilities for disabled campers. Washing machine. Large restaurant, pleasant bar. Supermarket (Easter - Sept). Excellent pools for adults and children. Football. Table tennis. Volleyball. Golf. Bicycle hire. Riding. Weekly animation programme (July/Aug) and many sporting activities. Pleasant river walk. Sophisticated dock and boat launching facility, pedaloes and canoes for hire and an ambitious water sport competition programme in season with a safety boat present at all times. Torches useful. Off site: Bus for town 1 km. Tours to Pamplona.

Directions
From N111 Pamplona - Logroño road take exit to Puente la Reina. Take N6030 towards Mendigorria and after approx 6 km. take Larraga turn by the wide river Arga, where site is signed.

Charges 2003
Per person	€ 3.60
child	€ 2.95
pitch incl. car and electricity	€ 10.50

Plus 7% VAT. Discounts outside high season.

Reservations
Made with 25% deposit. Advisable during San Fermin. Tel: 948 340 604. Email: info@campingelmolino.com

Open
All year.

At a glance
Welcome & Ambience	✓✓✓✓	Location	✓✓✓✓
Quality of Pitches	✓✓✓✓	Range of Facilities	✓✓✓✓

Navarra

Aragón

In the north eastern part of Spain, Aragón borders France with the Pyreenes lying between them. It is a region rich in folklore, with rural mountainside villages renowned for their Romanesque architecture, beautiful valleys and awe-inspiring peaks.

Aragón is made up of three provinces: Huesca, Zaragoza and Teruel

The capital of the region is Zaragoza

The region can be separated into three different areas: the central area consisting of the Ebro basin, a vast flat lowland; the northern area where the Pyrenees lie; and the area made up of the Iberian mountain range in the northwest and south-east of the region. The northern-most province of Huesca is located in the foothills of the Pyrenees Mountains, a beautiful area with plenty of picturesque towns and villages to visit. It is also good walking country with numerous trails offering anything from short day-walks in the valleys to long-distance treks in the mountains. Skiing is popular too. Bordering Huesca, the province of Zaragoza is home to the region's capital, also of the same name. Zaragoza is a lively town with plenty of bars and restaurants, plus numerous museums and architectural treasures. Outside the capital you'll find more villages, countryside, and vineyards where the best of the region's wine is produced; the mapped out Ruta del Vino will take you through the area. The third province of Teruel is largely comprised of the Iberian mountain range, with attractive towns, medieval sights and more dramatic scenery to admire.

Cuisine of the region

Specialities include lamb, locally-produced ham and sausages; fruit is also used a lot in desserts.

Chilindrones: sauces of tomato and pepper

Frutas de Aragón: sugar-candied fruits covered in chocolate

Pollo al chilindrón: chicken (or lamb) stew with onions, tomatoes and red peppers

Salmorrejos: cold soups

Suspiros de amante: dessert with cheese and egg

Ternasco: roast lamb

Tortas de alma: made with pumpkin, honey and sugar

Trenza de Almudévar: with nuts and raisins soaked in liqueur

Places of interest

Aljafería Palace: spectacular Moorish monument

Basílica de Nuestra Señora del Pilar: Baroque temple from the 17th and 18th centuries

Benasque: attractive alpine town, gateway to Pyrenees

Casa-Museo de Goya: art museum, including engravings by Goya

Jaca: home of the country's oldest Romanesque cathedral

Monasterio de San Juan de la Peña: 17th century Baroque monastery and 10th century Old monastery in Romanesque style

Parque Nacional de Ordesa y Monte Perdido: alpine national park

FOR FOLK MUSIC LOVERS, THE PYRENEES FOLK FESTIVAL IS HELD IN JACA, LATE JULY AND THE CITY OF ZARAGOZA INTERNATIONAL FOLKLORE EVENT TAKES PLACE IN SEPTEMBER.

www.alanrogers.com for latest campsite news

Aragón

ES9060 Camping Peña Montañesa

Ctra. Ainsa - Francia, km. 2, 22360 Labuerda

A large, riverside site situated quite high up in the Pyrenees, near the Ordesa National Park, Pena Montanesa is easily accessible from Ainsa or from France via the Bielsa Tunnel (steep sections on the French side), and is ideally situated for exploring the beautiful Pyrenées. The site is essentially divided into three sections opening progressively throughout the season and all have shade. The 288 pitches on fairly level grass are of approximately 75 sq.m. and electricity is available on virtually all. This is quite a large site which has grown very quickly and througout it may at times be a little hard pressed, though it is very well run. Grouped near the entrance are the facilities that make the site so attractive. Apart from a fair sized outdoor pool and children's pool (lifeguard 1/3-1/10), there is a glass covered indoor pool (heated in winter) with jacuzzi and sauna (open all year) and an attractive bar/restaurant (with open fire) and terrace with the supermarket and takeaway opposite.There is an entertainment programme for children (21/6-15/9 and Easter weekend) and twice weekly for adults (July/Aug).

Facilities

A newer toilet block, heated when necessary, has free hot showers but cold water to open plan washbasins, facilities for disabled visitors and a small baby bathroom. An older block in the original area has similar provision. Washing machine and dryer. Bar. Restaurant. Takeaway. Supermarket. Outdoor swimming pool and children's pool (March - Oct). Pool complex (all year). Playground. Boules. Table tennis. Bicycle hire. Riding. Rafting. Only gas barbecues are permitted. Torches required in some areas. Off site: Fishing 100m. Skiing in season. Canoeing near.

At a glance

Welcome & Ambience	✓✓✓✓✓	Location	✓✓✓✓✓
Quality of Pitches	✓✓✓✓	Range of Facilities	✓✓✓✓✓

Directions

Site is 2 km. from Ainsa, on the road from Ainsa to France.

Charges 2003

Per person	€ 4.40 - € 5.50
child (1-9 yrs)	€ 3.44 - € 4.30
pitch	€ 12.00 - € 15.00
dog	€ 2.64 - € 3.30
electricity	€ 4.30

All plus 7% VAT.

Reservations

are made for camping with € 100 deposit by visa or giro. Tel: 974 500 032.
Email: info@penamontanesa.com

Open

All year.

ES9062 Camping Boltana

Ctra. N-260, km. 442, 22340 Boltaña

Nestled in the Rio Ara valley, surrounded by the Pyrennes mountains and below a tiny but enchanting, historic, hill top village, is the very pretty, thoughtfully planned Camping Boltana. Generously sized, grassy pitches have good shade from a variety of trees and a stream meanders through the campsite. The landscaping includes ten charming rocky water gardens (though these can dry up in summer months) and a covered pergola doubles as an eating and play area. A stone building houses the site's new reception, social room and supermarket. Opposite is a terrace for enjoying tapas, listening to music, casual eating, animation and games and above this is the charming stone and wood restaurant. Special meals and paellas can be ordered the day before for you to eat in the restaurant or take away. Angel Moreno, the owner of the site, is a charming host and has tried to think of everything to make his guests comfortable.

Facilities

Two modern sanitary blocks include facilities for disabled visitors and laundry facilities. A casual restaurant and bar and a more formal restaurant (April-Oct). Supermarket. Swimming pools and children's pool (15/5-30/9). Playground. Barbecues. Full size soccer pitch. Animation for children, music at weekends in high season. Pentanque. Guided tours organized, plus hiking, canyoning, rafting, climbing, mountain biking and caving. Torches may be necessary in some parts. Local bus service.

At a glance

Welcome & Ambience	✓✓✓✓✓	Location	✓✓✓✓
Quality of Pitches	✓✓✓	Range of Facilities	✓✓✓✓

Directions

South of the Park Nacional de Ordesa, site is about 50 km. from Jaca near Ainsa. From Ainsa travel northwest on N260 toward Boltana (near 443 km marker). 1 km. from Boltana turn south toward Margudged. Camping Boltana is well signed and is approx. 1 km. along this road.

Charges 2003

Per adult	€ 4.60
child (1-10 yrs)	€ 3.70
caravan or tent	€ 5.10
car	€ 5.10
motorcycle	€ 4.10
motorcaravan	€ 9.20
dog	€ 2.35

Camping Cheques accepted.

Reservations

Contact site for details. Tel: 974 502 347.
Email: info@campingboltana.com

Open

All year.

Aragón

ES9064 Camping Gavín
Ctra. N260, km. 503, 22639 Gavín

Camping Gavín is set on a terraced, wooded hillside. At about 900 m, it is surrounded by towering peaks at the portal of the Tena Valley. The National Park of Ordesa, the valleys of Hecho, Broto and Tena and their associated ravines, lakes and rivers all offer a great variety of opportunities for physical activities. The site offers 150 pitches of 80 sq m.in size and with electricity available to all (6/10A). The main site buildings are built of natural stone. There are also eleven superb, balconied apartments for four to six persons. You will find a friendly welcome with English spoken.

Facilities
Excellent shower and toilet facilities in three main buildings with subtle, tasteful décor include facilities for babies and disabled people. Dishwashing and laundry facilities. Bar and snacks. Well stocked supermarket. Swimming pool and children's pool. Tennis. Table tennis. Playground. Barbecues are not permitted at some times of the year. Off site: Windsurfing, rafting, riding, fishing, walking and climbing in the vicinity. Bicycle hire 2 km. Day excursions to the Monastery of San Juan de la Pena or over the border into France possible.

At a glance
Welcome & Ambience	✓✓✓✓	Location	✓✓✓✓
Quality of Pitches	✓✓✓✓	Range of Facilities	✓✓✓✓✓

Directions
Site is off the N260, 2 km. from Biescas at km 503.

Charges 2003
Per person	€ 3.25 - € 4.50
caravan or tent	€ 3.25 - € 4.50
car	€ 3.25 - € 4.50
motorcaravan	€ 5.50 - € 7.80
electricity	€ 3.15 - € 4.50

Camping Cheques accepted.

Reservations
Advisable for Holy week and July/Aug.
Tel: 974 485090. Email: info@campinggavin.com

Open
All year.

ES9070 Centro de Vacaciones Pirineos
Ctra. N240, km. 300, 22791 Santa Cilia de Jaca

This pretty, site which is open most of the year is directly on the pilgrimage route to Santiago. As well as the campsite, with chalets to hire, there is a small hotel. It has a mild climate, being near the River Aragon, not too high and convenient for touring the Pyrenees. The trees provide good shade. There is an attractive irregular shaped swimming pool and children's pool. The restaurant with a varied menu and a good value menu of the day has a large comfortable terrace and a patio for drinks and snacks. There is an open fronted room for barbecuing and all equipment is provided. A major feature here is the huge recreational area with all manner of sports and amusements. It is a friendly site which is useful for transit stops and off-season camping on the large, mostly level wooded area which can accommodate 250 units (no marked pitches), with electric points throughout. There is some road noise along the south side of the site.

Facilities
One heated sanitary block is open all year, providing a quite satisfactory supply, including dishwashing and laundry sinks with hot water. A second, more modern block is open April - September only. Launderette. Restaurant. Bar. Supermarket (15/6-15/9, otherwise essentials kept in bar). Swimming pools (15/6-15/9). Two tennis courts. Table tennis. Playroom with electronic games. Petanque. Bicycle hire. Gas supplies. 5-side-soccer. Torches required in some areas. Off site: Fishing and bathing in river 200 m.

At a glance
Welcome & Ambience	✓✓✓	Location	✓✓✓✓
Quality of Pitches	✓✓✓	Range of Facilities	✓✓✓✓

Directions
Site is 15 km. west of Jaca on N240 at km 300 (65 km. northwest of Huesca).

Charges 2003
Per adult	€ 4.80
child (2-9 yrs)	€ 4.45
caravan or tent	€ 4.80
car	€ 4.50
motorcaravan	€ 8.50
electricity (6A)	€ 3.90

All plus 7% VAT.

Reservations
Made with deposit (€ 60). Tel: 974 377 351.
Email: pirineos@pirinet.com

Open
All year excl. 3 November - 3 December.

Aragón

ES9125 Camping Lago Barasona
Ctra. N -123a, km. 25, 22435 La Puebla de Castro

This site, alongside its associated ten room hotel, is beautifully positioned in terraces by the shores of the Lago de Barasona (a large reservoir), with views of hills and the distant Pyrenees. There are two excellent restaurants here one being in the hotel the other with a pretty terrace with wonderful views. The menu and cooking is outstanding, specialising in the regional cuisine. The very friendly, English speaking owner is keen to please and has applied very high standards throughout the site. The grassy, fairly level pitches are generally around 100 sq.m. with 35 high quality pitches of 110 sq m for larger units. All have electricity, many are well shaded and some have great views of the lake and/or hills. Waterskiing and other watersports are available in July and August. You may swim and fish in the lake which has a shallow area extending for around 20 m. If you prefer, the site also has a round outdoor pool plus the pleasant standard pool in the hotel (these open from as early as April when the weather is often quite warm). The disco is well away from the site by the lakeside. The local administration has put together some excellent tourist and walking route information (in English) and the owner has matched this with his own quality brochure. This is a most pleasant and peaceful site in a lovely area and will suit families who wish for quality and choice in their camping. The views really are beautiful.

Facilities
Two toilet blocks in modern buildings have high standards and hot water throughout including cabins (3 for ladies, 1 for men). Bar/snack bar and two excellent restaurants (all season). Shop (15/5-15/9). Swimming pools (15/5-15/9). Tennis. Table tennis. Mountain bike hire. Canoe, windsurfing motor boat and pedalo hire. Mini-club. Lake swimming, fishing, canoeing, etc. Facilities for volleyball, football and a new play area were under construction. Walking (maps provided). Money exchange. Mini-disco. Off site: Riding 4 km.

At a glance
Welcome & Ambience	✓✓✓✓	Location	✓✓✓✓✓
Quality of Pitches	✓✓✓✓	Range of Facilities	✓✓✓

Directions
Site is on the west bank of the lake, close to km. 25 on the N123A, 4.5 km. south of Graus (approx. 80 km. north of Lleida/Lerida).

Latest charges
Per person	€ 3.50 - € 4.85
child (2-10 yrs)	€ 2.50 - € 3.95
car	€ 3.50 - € 4.85
caravan or tent	€ 3.50 - € 4.85
motorcaravan	€ 5.50 - € 7.85
electricity	€ 3.45

Plus VAT @ 7%. Camping Cheques accepted.

Reservations
Made with 25-50% deposit, but probably not needed outside mid-July - mid-August. Contact site for details. Tel: 974 545 148. Email: info@lagobarasona.com

Open
1 April - 30 September.

ES9100 Camping Casablanca
50012 Zaragoza

Although not a sophisticated site, Casablanca is considered acceptable for overnight or for a short stay to visit the fascinating city of Zaragoza. Although a city site it is surprisingly quiet. On a flat meadow (with little grass), there are 192 pitches with electricity. It can be very hot here in summer but there is some shade and the site has a pleasant medium sized swimming pool with a small area separated for children, although this is only open in July/August.

Facilities
The sanitary block is basic with hot water and could be hard-pressed at busiest times. British style WCs. Shop and restaurant/bar (July/Aug). Swimming pool (July/Aug). Play area. Torches required. Off site: Town shop 200 m.

At a glance
Welcome & Ambience	✓✓✓	Location	✓✓✓✓
Quality of Pitches	✓✓✓	Range of Facilities	✓✓✓

Directions
Site is just outside town to southwest in the Val de Fierro district; access roads lead off N11 Madrid road (km. 316a) or N330 Valencia road and are well signed. The site lays back from the road across apiece of open ground so keep a good lookout.

Latest charges
Per adult	€ 3.79 - € 4.12
child	€ 3.09 - € 3.41
car	€ 3.79 - € 4.12
tent or caravan	€ 3.79 - € 4.12
motorcaravan	€ 5.95 - € 6.62
motorcycle	€ 3.34 - € 3.89
electricity (10A)	€ 3.05

Reservations
Can be made to Campings Betsa, C/Nov. 139, 17600 Figueras (Gerona). Tel: 976 753 870.

Open
1 April - 15 October.

Great on-line holiday deals alanrogersdirect.com

Aragón

ES9105 Camping Lago Park

Ctra. Alhama de Aragon-Nuevalos, 50210 Nuevalos

Lago Park is situated in an attractive area surrounded by mountains. The site has a rather steep access and slopes so is considered unsuitable for disabled campers. It is just outside the attractive ancient village, between lake and mountains, and suitable as a base for exploring this really attractive area. Set on a steep hillside, the 300 pitches (250 for tourers) are on terraces. Only the lower rows of terraces are suitable for large caravans. These pitches, are numbered and marked by trees, most having electrical connections. Facilities on site include a large pool (unheated and chilly with its mountain water), a restaurant/bar and small shop. The restaurant is disappointing with restricted hours, mediocre cooking and is pricey, but there are many good restaurants in town. The site is suitable for transit stops. It is not recommended for extended stays.

Facilities
The single sanitary block has Turkish and British style WCs. washbasins with hot water and controllable hot showers (no dividers). Restaurant/bar (June-Sept). Shop (all season). Swimming pool (late June-Sept). Play area. Gas supplies. Torches needed in some areas. Off site: Fishing 300 m. Riding 2 km.

At a glance
Welcome & Ambience	✓✓✓	Location	✓✓✓✓
Quality of Pitches	✓✓✓	Range of Facilities	✓✓✓

Directions
From Zaragoza (120 km.) take fast A2/N11/E90 road and turn onto C202 road beyond Calatayud to Nuévalos (25 km.). From Madrid exit A2 at Alhama de Aragón (13 km.). Follow signs for Monasterio de Piedra from all directions.

Latest charges
Per person	€ 4.21
child (up to 10 yrs)	€ 4.06
car	€ 4.21
motorcycle	€ 3.16
caravan	€ 4.66
tent	€ 4.51
motorcaravan	€ 8.11
electricity (6A)	€ 3.61

Reservations
Contact site. Tel: 976 849 038.

Open
1 April - 30 September.

ES9095 Camping Ciudad de Albarracin

Junto al Polideportibo, 44100 Albarracin

This neat and clean family site is set on three levels on a hillside behind the town, with a walk of one kilometre to the centre. It is very modern and has high quality facilities including a superb building for barbecuing (all materials provided). There are 130 pitches, all with electricity and separated by trees. Some require cars to be parked separately. The homely bar/restaurant, with terrace and TV, is open all season and has a limited but very pleasant menu. The site is good value, is well run and is a good bet for exploring the area or just enjoying the peace and quiet in this area of natural beauty.

Facilities
The two spotless, modern sanitary buildings provide British style WCs, quite large showers and hot water throughout. Baby bath in the ladies' and a smart area for dishwashing and laundry with washing machines. Bar/restaurant (all season). Essentials from bar. Special room for barbecues with fire and wood provided. Play area. Fronton. Five-a-side soccer. Torches required in some areas. Off site: Municipal swimming pool 100 m. (high season). Town with shops, bars and restaurants 500 m.

At a glance
Welcome & Ambience	✓✓✓✓	Location	✓✓✓✓
Quality of Pitches	✓✓✓	Range of Facilities	✓✓✓

Directions
From Teruel north on the N330 for about 8 km. then west onto A1512 for 37 km. Well signed in town.

Latest charges
Per person	€ 2.40
child (under 14)	€ 1.80
car	€ 2.30
caravan	€ 2.55
tent	€ 2.40
motorcaravan	€ 4.35
electricity	€ 1.80

Plus 7% VAT.

Reservations
Tel: 978 710 197 or 710 107.

Open
1 April - 31 October.

The Regions of Portugal

Portugal

Portugal is a relatively small country occupying the southwest corner of the Iberian peninsula, bordered by Spain in the north and east, with the Atlantic coast in the south and west. In spite of its size, the country offers a tremendous variety in both its way of life and traditions.

Most visitors looking for a beach type holiday head for the busy Algarve, with its long stretches of sheltered sandy beaches, and warm, clear Atlantic waters, great for bathing and watersports. With its monuments and fertile rolling hills, central Portugal adjoins the beautiful Tagus river that winds its way through the capital city of Lisbon, on its way to the Altantic Ocean. Lisbon city itself has deep rooted cultural traditions, coming alive at night with buzzing cafes, restaurants and discos. Moving south east of Lisbon the land becomes rather impoverished, consisting of stretches of vast undulating plains, dominated by cork plantations. Most people head for the walled town of Evora, an area steeped in two thousand years of history. The Portuguese consider the Minho area in the north to be the most beautiful part of their country, with its wooded mountain and wild coastline, a rural and conservative region with picturesque towns.

Population: 10 million

Capital: Lisbon

Climate: The country enjoys a maritime climate with hot summers and mild winters with comparatively low rainfall in the south, heavy rain in the north.

Language: Portuguese, but English is widely spoken in cities, towns and larger resorts. French can be useful.

Currency: The Euro ( ).

Telephone: The country code is 00 351.

Banks: Mon-Fri 08.30-11.45 and 13.00-14.45. Some large city banks operate a currency exchange 18.30-23.00

Shops: Mon-Fri 0900-1300 and 1500-1900. Sat 0900-1300.

Public Holidays: New Year; Carnival (Shrove Tues); Good Fri; Liberty Day 25 Apr; Labour Day; Corpus Christi; National Day 10 June; Saints Days; Assumption 15 Aug; Republic Day 5 Oct; All Saints 1 Nov; Immaculate Conception 8 Dec; Christmas 24-26 Dec.

Tourist Office:

ICEP Portuguese Trade & Tourism Office,
Second Floor, 22/25a Sackville Street, London W1S 3LY

Tel: 09063 640 610   E-mail: iceplondt@aol.com
Fax: 020 7494 1868   Internet: www.portugalinsite.com

Algarve

The Algarve, Portugal's southernmost province, is a true sunseekers paradise, offering all year round sunshine and over 150 miles of beautiful sandy beaches.

The Algarve has one district: Faro

The coast of the Algarve offers mile after mile of golden beaches and small sandy coves with interesting rock formations, interspersed with busy fishing ports. The capital, Faro, boasts excellent beaches, while the thriving fishing port and market centre of Lagos is one of the most popular destinations in the Algarve. Although the earthquake of 1755 caused great damage to Lagos, the streets and squares of the town have retained much of their charm. Within walking distance are some superb beaches, including Praia de Dona Ana, which is considered to be the most picturesque of all, and the smaller coves of Praia do Pinhão and Praia Camilo. Further inland and to the north, the hills mark the edge of a greener and more fertile region, brilliantly coloured by fig-trees, orange-groves and almond-trees that come into blossom in the winter. Here you will also find a series of typical villages that have successfully preserved their ancestral traditions. The walled town of Silves has a Moorish fortress, 13th century cathedral and archaeology musuem. It also has a lively summer beer festival. Nearby, the narrow streets of the old spa town of Monchique wind up a steep hillside, revealing magnificent views of the surrounding countryside.

Cuisine of the region

Fresh fish and seafood are popular; the local speciality is *Ameijoas na Cataplana* (clams steamed in a copper pan). One of the most traditional dishes is *caldeiradas* (stew made with all kinds of different fish) and *sardinha assada* (grilled sardines). Given the abundance of trees in the region, figs and almonds are used a lot in desserts including *bolinhos de amêndoa* (small cakes made from marzipan and almond paste), which are moulded into the shape of fruits and vegetables in all kinds of different sizes.

Places of interest

Albufeira: popular resort, daily market, good nightlife

Cape São Vicente: south westernmost point of Europe

Faro: monuments, churches, museums, Gothic cathedral, good shopping centre

Sagres: 17th century fortress

Tavira: picturesque town, 17th and 18th century architecture

Vilamoura: good sporting faciles including golf courses

THE ALGARVE HAS A WHOLE HOST OF GOLF COURSES, SOME OVERLOOKING THE SEA, WHERE YOU CAN PLAY ALL YEAR ROUND.

www.**alanrogers**.com for latest campsite news

PO8200 Orbitur Camping Valverde

Estrada da Praia da Luz, Valverde, 8600 Lagos

A little over one kilometre from the village of Praia da Luz and its beach and about seven kilometres from Lagos, this large, well run site is certainly worth considering for your stay in the Algarve. It has 600 numbered pitches, of varying size which are enclosed by hedges. All are on flat ground or broad terraces with good shade in most parts from established trees and shrubs. On site is a swimming pool with long slide and a children's pool (under 10's free, adults charged). This is an excellent site with well maintained facilities and good security. It attracts a good number of long-term winter visitors. The site, which is one of the better Orbitur sites, is extremely well managed by Sra. Pinto, who is helpful and friendly.

Facilities

Six large, clean, toilet blocks have some washbasins and sinks with cold water only, and hot showers. Units for disabled people. Laundry. Motorcaravan services. Supermarket, shops, restaurant and bar complex with both self-service and waiter service in season (all April - Oct). Takeaway. Coffee shop. Swimming pool with water slide and children's pool (Jun - Sep). Playground. Tennis court with markings for other sports. General room with TV. Excursions. Medical post. Disco. Pub. Off site: Fishing and bicycle hire 3 km. Golf 10 km. The road to the beach is quite narrow with fast traffic.

At a glance

Welcome & Ambience	✓✓✓✓✓	Location	✓✓✓✓
Quality of Pitches	✓✓✓✓	Range of Facilities	✓✓✓✓

Directions

Fork left on N125 road 3 km. west of Lagos to Praia da Luz and site is under 1 km.

Charges 2003

Per unit incl. 2 persons,
electricity, water € 15.60 - € 29.70
extra adult € 2.50 - € 4.90
child (5-10 yrs) € 1.25 - € 2.45
Off season discounts (up to 70%).

Reservations

Contact Orbitur - Central de Reservas, Rua Diogo do Couto, 1149 - 042 Lisboa. Tel: 811 70 00 or Tel: 811 70 70. Fax: 21/814 80 45. Tel: 282 78 92 11. Email: info@orbitur.pt

Open

All year.

BOOK NOW YOUR PLACE IN THE BEST LAWN OF PORTUGAL! TAKE A HOLIDAY ALL YEAR ROUND!

www.orbitur.pt
Explore PORTUGAL

ORBITUR · INTERCÂMBIO DE TURISMO, SA
INFORMATION AND RESERVATION:
R. Diogo do Couto, 1-8° F · 1149-042 Lisboa · PORTUGAL
Tel. +351.218117000/70 Fax +351.218148045
e-mail: info@orbitur.pt

Algarve

PO8210 Parque de Campismo Albufeira
EN 125 Ferreiras-Albufeira, 8200-555 Albufeira

The spacious entrance to this site will accommodate the largest of units. One of the better sites on the Algarve, with installations and amenities well above the usual standard. The 1,500 pitches are on fairly flat ground with some terracing, trees and shrubs giving reasonable shade in most parts. There are some marked and numbered pitches of 50-80 sq.m. Winter stays are encouraged with many facilities remaining open including a heated pool. An attractively designed complex of traditional Portuguese style buildings on the hill forms the central area of the site, has pleasant views and is surrounded by a variety of flowers, shrubs and well watered lawns, complete with a fountain. The waiter and self-service restaurants, a pizzeria, bars and a sound proofed disco, have views across the three pools.

Facilities
The toilet blocks include hot showers. Washing machines. Waiter and self-service restaurants, and pizzeria. Bars. Sound proof disco. Swimming pools. Playground. ATM. Car hire. Off site: Site bus service to Albufeira (2 km).

At a glance
Welcome & Ambience	✓✓✓✓	Location	✓✓✓
Quality of Pitches	✓✓✓	Range of Facilities	✓✓✓✓

Directions
From N125 coast road or N264 (from Lisbon) at new junctions follow signs to Albufeira. Site is approx. 1 km. from junctions, on left.

Charges 2003
Per adult	€ 4.00 - € 5.70
child (1-9 yrs)	€ 3.10 - € 4.10
pitch	€ 4.00 - € 9.80
electricity	€ 3.20
animal	€ 1.50

Reservations
Made to give individual pitch, no deposit or fee. Tel: 289 58 76 29.
Email: campingalbufeira@mail.telepac.pt

Open
All year.

PO8202 Parque de Campismo de Espiche
Estrada Nacional, 125, Espiche, 8600 Lagos

This site has been taken over by the previous owners of Camping L'Amfora in Spain and has been recommended by our Spanish agent. With their experience and expertise, the new owners are fully refurbishing the site, adding new toilet blocks, a large swimming pool, new bungalows and much more. It will be open all year round and should prove to be one of the best campsites in Portugal. There are 300 pitches, all with electricity and water and trees provide some shade. The sea is two kilometres and the city of Lagos four kilometres with all the attractions of the Algarve within easy reach.

Facilities
Two toilet blocks are supplemented by a further block in high season. Washing machines. Shop. Restaurant/bar. Bicycle hire. Swimming pool. Internet point. Entertainment in high seaosn on the bar terrace. Bungalows to rent. Off site: Praia da Luz village 1 km.

Directions
From Lagos on road N125 towards Sagres, site is 3 km.

Charges 2004
Per adult	€ 2.00 - € 4.50
child	€ 1.00 - € 2.25
pitch	€ 1.75 - € 4.50
car	€ 1.25 - € 3.00
electricity	€ 2.00 - € 2.50
dog	€ 0.50 - € 1.00

Reservations
Contact site. Tel: 0282 789 256.
Email: info@turiscampo.com

Open
1 January - 31 December

PO8230 Camping Olhao

Pinheiros de Marim, 8700 Olhao

This site, taking around 1,000 units and open all year, has mature trees to provide reasonable shade. The pitches are marked, numbered and in rows divided by shrubs with electricity and water to all parts. Permanent and long stay units take 20% of the pitches and the tourist pitches fill up quickly in July and August, so arrive early. Amenities include very pleasant swimming pools and tennis courts, a reasonable restaurant/bar, all very popular with the local Portuguese, and a café/bar with TV and games room. There is some noise nuisance from the nearby railway. The large, sandy beaches in this area are on offshore islands reached by ferry and are, as a result, relatively quiet; some are reserved for naturists. This site can get very busy in peak periods and maintenance can be variable. There was a large, low season British contingent when we visited enjoying the low prices.

Facilities

Eleven sanitary blocks are adequate, clean when seen, and are specifically sited to be a maximum of 50 m. from any pitch. One block has facilities for disabled visitors. Laundry. Supermarket. Kiosk. Restaurant/bar (all year). Café and general room with TV. Playgrounds. Swimming pools (April - Sept) and tenni courts (fees for both). Volleyball. Bicycle hire. Internet. Off site: Bus service 50 m to the nearest ferry at Olhao. Riding 1 km. Fishing 2 km. Golf 20 km.

At a glance

Welcome & Ambience	✓✓✓✓	Location	✓✓✓✓✓
Quality of Pitches	✓✓✓	Range of Facilities	✓✓✓✓

Directions

Just over 1 km. east of Olhão, on EN125, take turn to Pinheiros de Marim. Site is 300 m. on left. Look for white triangular entry arch as the site name is different on the outside wall – a foible of the owner.

Charges 2003

Per adult	€ 1.80 - € 3.45
child (5-12 yrs)	€ 0.95 - € 1.85
car	€ 1.45 - € 2.85
tent	€ 1.35 - € 2.45
caravan	€ 2.35 - € 6.90
motorcaravan	€ 2.35 - € 6.90
electricity	€ 1.20

Less for longer winter stays.

Reservations

Contact site. Tel: 289 70 03 00.
Email: sbsicamping@mail.telepac.pt

Open

All year, as are all facilities.

Great on-line holiday deals *alanrogersdirect*.com

Algarve

PO8220 Orbitur Camping Quarteira
Estrada da Fonte Santa, 8125 Quarteira

This is a large, busy attractive site on undulating ground with some terracing, taking 795 units. On the outskirts of the popular Algarve resort of Quarteira, it is 600 metres from a sandy beach which stretches for one kilometre to the town centre. Many of the unmarked pitches have shade from tall trees and there are a few small individual pitches of 50 sq.m. with electricity and water for reservation. There are 680 electrical connections. Like others along this coast, the site encourages long winter stays. The swimming pools are excellent, featuring pools for adults (with a large flume) and children (fountains), (open in high season incurring an extra charge). There is a large restaurant and supermarket which have a separate entrance for local trade.

Facilities
Five sanitary blocks provide British and Turkish style toilets, individual washbasins with cold water, hot showers plus facilities for disabled visitors. Washing machines. Motorcaravan services. Gas supplies. Supermarket, self-service restaurant (Feb - Nov). Separate takeaway (from late May). Swimming pools (June - Sept). General room with bar and TV. Tennis. Kiosk. Open air disco. Medical room. Off site: Fishing 1 km. Bicycle hire (summer) 1 km. Golf 4 km.

At a glance
Welcome & Ambience	✓✓✓✓✓	Location	✓✓✓✓✓
Quality of Pitches	✓✓✓✓	Range of Facilities	✓✓✓✓

Directions
Turn off N125 south towards Quarteira in Almancil (8 km. west of Faro). Site is 5 km. from the junction.

Charges 2003
Per unit incl. 2 persons, electricity and water	€ 15.60 - € 29.70
child (5-10 yrs)	€ 1.25 - € 2.45
extra adult	€ 2.50 - € 4.90
Off season discounts (up to 70%).	

Reservations
Contact Orbitur - Central de Reservas, Rua Diogo do Couto, 1149 - 042 Lisboa. Tel: 21/811 70 00 or Tel: 811 70 70. Fax: 21/814 80 45. Tel: 289 30 28 26. Email: info@orbitur.pt

Open
All year.

PO8410 Parque de Campismo de Armacao de Pera
8365 Armacao de Pera

A modern site with a wide attractive entrance and a large external parking area, the 1,200 pitch areas are in zones on level grassy sand. They are marked by trees that provide some shade, and are easily accessed from tarmac and gravel roads. Electricity is available for most pitches. The facilities are good. The restaurant, self service café and bar, and well stocked supermarket should cater for most needs, and you can relax around the swimming pools. The disco near to the entrance and café complex is soundproofed which should ensure a peaceful night for non-revellers. The site is within easy reach of Albufeira and Portimão and makes an excellent base for stays in this region.

Facilities
Three modern sanitary blocks provide British and Turkish style WCs, some with bidets, washbasins, showers with hot water on payment, and facilities for disabled campers. A reader reports that maintenance can be variable. Laundry. Supermarket. Restaurant (1/5 - 30/9). Self service café. Three bars (1/5-30/9). Kiosk. Games and TV rooms. Tennis. Well maintained play area with safe, sandy base. Swimming pool and children's pool (May - Sept). ATM. Off site: Fishing, bicycle hire and watersports nearby.

At a glance
Welcome & Ambience	✓✓✓✓✓	Location	✓✓✓✓
Quality of Pitches	✓✓✓✓	Range of Facilities	✓✓✓✓✓

Directions
Site is west of Albufeira. Turn off N125/ IC4 road in Alcantarilha, taking the EN269-1 towards the coast. Site is on left side before Armação de Pêra. There are other sites with similar names in the area, so be sure to find the right one.

Charges 2003
Per adult	€ 2.30 - € 4.90
child (4-10 yrs)	€ 1.40 - € 2.70
car	€ 1.40 - € 2.80
tent	€ 1.80 - € 4.00
caravan or motorcaravan	€ 1.80 - € 5.00
motorcycle	€ 1.30 - € 2.50
electricity (6A)	€ 2.00 - € 3.50
Min. stay 3 nights 1 June - 31 Aug.	

Reservations
Write to site. Tel: 282 31 22 96.

Open
All year.

PO8430 Orbitur Camping Sagres

Cerro das Moitas, 8650 Sagres

Camping de Sagres is a pleasant site at the western tip of the Algarve, not very far from the lighthouse in the relatively unspoilt southwest corner of Portugal. With 960 pitches for tents and 120 for tourers, the pitches are sandy and located amongst pine trees that give good shade. There are some hardstandings for motorhomes and electrical connections throughout. The fairly bland restaurant, bar and café/grill provide a range of reasonably priced meals. This is a reasonable site for those seeking winter sun, or as a base for exploring this 'Land's End' region of Portugal, as it is away from the hustle and bustle of the more crowded resorts. The beaches and the town of Sagres are a short drive.

Facilities
Three spacious toilet blocks are showing some signs of wear but provide hot and cold showers, washbasins with cold water and footbaths. Dishwashing and laundry sinks (cold water) are under cover outside. Washing machines and ironing boards. Motorcaravan services. Supermarket (1/4-1/11). Restaurant/bar and café/grill (all 1/4-30/9). TV room. Bicycle hire. Barbecue area. Playground. Fishing. Medical post. Car wash. Off site: Beach 2 km. Fishing 2 km. Boat launching 8 km. Golf 12 km.

At a glance
Welcome & Ambience	✓✓✓✓	Location	✓✓✓✓
Quality of Pitches	✓✓✓✓✓	Range of Facilities	✓✓✓✓

Directions
Turn off road N268 East to EN268, after approx. 2 km. after turn to Sagres, site (as a camping site only – no name) is signed off to right.

Charges 2003
Per person	€ 2.40 - € 4.30
child (5-10 yrs)	€ 1.20 - € 2.15
car	€ 2.10 - € 3.70
motorcycle	€ 1.50 - € 2.90
tent	€ 2.00 - € 5.70
caravan	€ 2.70 - € 5.90
motorcaravan	€ 3.10 - € 6.30
electricity (5A)	€ 2.25

Off season discounts (up to 70%).

Reservations
Write to site or contact Orbitur - Central de Reservas, Rua Diogo do Couto, 1149 - 042 Lisboa. Tel: 282 62 43 71.

Open
All year.

PO8440 Parque de Campismo Quintos dos Carriços

Praia da Salema, Vila do Bispo, 8650-196 Budens

This is an attractive and peaceful, valley site with a dedicated naturist area. A traditional tiled Portuguese style entrance leads you down a steep incline into this excellent and well maintained site which has a village atmosphere. With continuing improvements, the site has been developed over the years by the Dutch owner. It is spread over two valleys (which are real sun-traps), with the 300 partially terraced pitches marked and divided by trees and shrubs (oleanders and roses). A small stream (dry when seen) meanders through the site. The most remote part, 250 m. from the main site, is dedicated to naturists. Although the site is lit, torches may be required in more remote areas. A very popular site for summer and winter sun-worshippers, within easy driving distance of resorts. The many fine beaches in the region provide ample opportunities for diving, swimming and fishing.

Facilities
Four modern, spacious sanitary blocks, well tiled with quality fittings, are spotlessly clean and include washbasins with cold water and hot showers on payment (€ 0.60). Dishwashing, laundry sinks and washing machine. Excellent facility for disabled people. Gas supplies. Well stocked minimarket (all year). Restaurant (daily 1/3-15/10). Bar (daily in season, once a week only 15/10-1/3). TV room. Bicycles, scooters, mopeds and m/cycles for hire. Internet. Library. Games room. Off site: Nearby tennis, squash, riding golf and excellent walks. Fishing and golf 1 km. Riding 8 km. Bus service operates from the site. Beach 1 km.

At a glance
Welcome & Ambience	✓✓✓✓✓	Location	✓✓✓✓
Quality of Pitches	✓✓✓✓	Range of Facilities	✓✓✓✓

Directions
Turn off RN125 (Lagos-Sagres) road at junction to Salema (17 km. from Lagos); site is signed.

Charges 2003
Per adult	€ 3.80
child	€ 1.90
tent	€ 3.80 - € 4.90
caravan	€ 5.40
car	€ 3.80
motorcycle	€ 2.70
motorcaravan	€ 5.40 - € 6.45
electricity	€ 2.00
dog	€ 1.15

Discounts for long winter stays.

Reservations
Contact site. Tel: 282 69 52 01.
Email: quintacarrico@oninet.pt

Open
All year.

Alentejo

With huge, sparsely populated plains dominated by vast cork plantations, which provide nearly half of the world's cork, Alentejo's main attractions include the historic city of Évora and the coastal resorts with their fine, sandy beaches.

Alentejo is made up of four districts: Beja, Évora, Setúbal and Portalegre

One of the most impressive cities in Portugal, Évora lies on a gently sloping hill rising out of the huge Alentejo plain. A city steeped in history, it was occupied by the Romans and Moors for centuries. With its narrow streets, of Moorish origin, and white-washed houses, it also boasts one of the best-preserved Roman temples in the coutry plus various palaces and monuments, the majority dating from the 14th-16th centuries. One of the more extraodinary sights can be found in the Capela dos Ossos in the church of São Francisco – adorning the walls and pillars of this chamber are the bones of more than 5000 monks.

On the Alentejo coast is the small peaceful town of Santiago do Cacém, which has two of the best beaches in Portugal. The nearby archaelogical site at Miróbriga includes ruins of a hippodrome, several houses (some of which have mural paintings) and a clearly defined acropolis. Further south along the coast is Porto Côvo and the larger, popular resort of Vila Nova de Milfontes, which has a little castle and ancient port.

Cuisine of the region

Alentejo was traditionally an important wheat-growing region (it is frequently referred to as the 'granary of Portugal'). Local specialities include *sopa de cação* (skate soup), made from fish and bread, and *ensopado de borrego* (lamb-stew). Cheeses of the region include *queijo de Serpa* and *queijos de Niza*, made from goats milk. The *queijos de Évora*, made from ewe's milk, is smaller in size with a strong, spicy flavour. *Arroz Doce* (rice pudding topped with cinnamon) is the traditional dessert for festivals and parties and is to be found all over the country.

Places of interest

Arraiolos: ancient town, 17th century castle, famous for its carpets

Beja: provincial town founded by Julius Caesar, 13th century castle

Borba: pretty town, noted for its marble and wine

Elvas: ancient fortress town, 15th century aqueduct

Estremoz: market town, medieval castle

Odemira: quiet, characterful country town

Reguengos de Monsaraz: charming, unspoiled village with whitewashed houses

Vila Viçosa: attractive hillside town, 16th century convent

tip

THE SERRA DE SÃO MAMEDE NATURAL PARK OFFERS GOOD WALKS, WITH EXCELLENT VIEWS AND ALSO HAS AN INFORMATION CENTRE HOLDING TEMPORARY EXHIBITIONS.

PO8170 Parque de Campismo São Miguel

São Miguel, Odeceixe, 7630-592 Odemira

Nestled in green hills near two pretty white villages, four kilometres from the beautiful Praia Odeceixe (beach) is the attractive camping park Sao Miguel. The main building (with its traditional Portuguese architecture) is built around two sides of a large grassy square, it houses reception, restaurant, bars and supermarket. There are 'Lisbon Arcade' style verandas to sit under and enjoy a drink, coffee or meal while enjoying the view across the square to the pool tennis courts and camping which is hidden under a canopy of trees. Unusually the site works on a maximum number of 700 campers, you find your own place (there are no defined pitches) under the tall trees, there are ample electrical points, the land slopes away gently. The wooden chalet style accomodation is in a separate area, but some mobile homes share the two traditional older style but clean sanitary blocks. An outdoor cinema operates in summer showing films for children and adults. The self serve restaurant and bars are excellent, there is a pizzeria by the pool with its own terrace (summer only) and for those who want to self cater the supermarket has a bakery, as well as wide range of goods including cooked chicken, fresh fruit and vegetables.

Facilities

Two older style sanitary buildings with British style WCs and free hot showers. Washing machines, dishwashing and laundry sinks are at the end of the block under cover. Toilets and basins for disabled campers but no shower. Shop (Jun - Sep). Restaurant/bar (March - Oct) Bar, snacks and pizzeria (June - Sept). Playground. Tennis courts (extra charge). Swimming pool (extra charge). No animals are accepted. Torches useful. Off site: Village has a range of shops bars and restaurants. Fishing and sailing 4 km. Riding 20 km. Historic village of Odemira 2 km. Camping is situated inside the Nature Park of Alentejo.

At a glance

| Welcome & Ambience | ✓✓✓✓✓ | Location | ✓✓✓✓ |
| Quality of Pitches | ✓✓✓✓ | Range of Facilities | ✓✓✓✓✓ |

Directions

Between Odemira and Lagos on the N120 just before the village of Odeceixe on the main road well signed.

Latest charges

Per adult	€ 2.60 - € 4.00
child (5-10 yrs)	€ 1.40 - € 2.25
tent	€ 2.60 - € 6.00
caravan	€ 4.00 - € 5.50
car	€ 2.60 - € 3.50
motorcaravan	€ 5.00 - € 8.00
electricity	€ 2.10

Plus 7% VAT.

Reservations

Write to site. Tel: 282 947145.
Email: camping.sao.miguel@mail.telepac.pt

Open

Easter - September.

PO8350 Camping Markádia

Barragem de Odivelas, Apartado 17, 7920-999 Alvito

A tranquil, lakeside site in an unspoilt setting, this will appeal most to those nature lovers who want to 'get away from it all' and to those who enjoy country pursuits such as walking, fishing or riding. The lake is in fact a 1,000 hectare reservoir, and more than 120 species of birds can be found in the area. The open countryside and lake provide excellent views and a very pleasant environment, albeit somewhat remote. The stellar veiws in the very low ambient lighting are wonderful at night. The site is lit but a torch is required. There are 130 casual unmarked pitches on undulating grass and sand with ample electricity connections. The friendly Dutch owner has carefully planned the site so each pitch has its own oak tree to provide shade. The bar/restaurant with a terrace is open daily in season but weekends only during the winter. One can swim in the reservoir and rowing boats, pedaloes wind-surfers are available for hire. You may bring your own boat, although power boats are not allowed on environmental grounds.

Facilities

Four modern, clean and well equipped toilet blocks are built in traditional Portuguese style with hot water throughout. Dishwashing and laundry sinks are open air. Washing machines and ironing boards. Motorcaravan services. Bar and restaurant (1/4-30/9). Shop (all year, bread to order). Lounge. Playground. Fishing. Boat hire. Tennis. Riding. Medical post. Car wash. Dogs are not accepted in July/August. Facilities and amenities may be reduced outside the main season.

At a glance

| Welcome & Ambience | ✓✓✓✓✓ | Location | ✓✓✓✓✓ |
| Quality of Pitches | ✓✓✓✓✓ | Range of Facilities | ✓✓✓✓✓ |

Directions

From A2 between Setabul and the Algarve take exit 10 on IP8 signed Ferreira and Beja. Take road to Torrao and 13 km. later at 1 km. north of Odivelas, turn right towards Barragem and site is 3 km. after crossing head of reservoir following small signs (one small section of poor road).

Charges 2003

Per adult	€ 4.40
child (5-10 yrs)	€ 2.00
tent or caravan	€ 4.40
car or motorcycle	€ 4.40
motorcaravan	€ 8.80
electricity (16A)	€ 2.20

Discounts of 10-20% outside June - Aug, and for longer stays. No credit cards.

Reservations

Contact site for details. Tel: 284 76 31 41.

Open

All year.

Alentejo

PO8160 Parque de Campismo Porto Covo
7520-436 Porto Covo

This is a site in a popular, small seaside resort where a fairly large proportion of the pitches are occupied by Portuguese units. However, it has a reasonable sense of space as you pass the security barrier to reception which is part of an uncluttered and attractively designed 'village square' area with some well established apartments to rent. The pitches are rather small but are hedged, reasonably level, all have electricity, and are shaded. A mini market stocks the essentials and some souvenirs. If you do not want to venture out to the beach then the swimming pools are behind the restaurant and have areas for sunbathing, the children's pool separated from the adults'. Dedicated barbecue areas are close to the pools. A jolly bar and restaurant with terrace cleverly operates across the boundary of the site and it offers a varied Portuguese menu (popular with the locals) at very reasonable prices. A second smaller restaurant operates in the site in low season. The beaches are a short walk and feature steep cliffs and pleasant sandy shores.

Facilities
The toilet blocks are clean with the usual amenities including hot showers, plus cold outside showers, foot baths and ironing facilities. Motorcaravan services. Restaurant/bar. Mini-market in season. Recreation room with games and a TV. Play area. Swimming pools. Tennis. Barbecue areas. Boat trips and fishing trips organised. Off site: The village is a short walk from a range of shops, bars and restaurants in pretty new roads. Bus service to Lisbon from site. Fishing 500 m. Riding 20 km. Golf 25 km.

At a glance
Welcome & Ambience	✓✓✓✓✓	Location	✓✓✓✓
Quality of Pitches	✓✓✓✓	Range of Facilities	✓✓✓✓✓

Directions
From E120-1 Cercal - Sines road (note: the road changes from the E120 at Tanganheira). Take left turn (southwest) to Porto Covo. The signs are misleading hereon so look for a large white water tower with site logo for confirmation of the signs.

Charges 2003
Per adult	€ 3.70 - € 4.80
child	€ 1.85 - € 2.40
tent	€ 3.70 - € 6.00
caravan or motorcaravan	€ 4.50 - € 7.50
car	€ 2.30 - € 3.20
motorcycle	€ 1.70 - € 2.40
electricty	free

All plus 7% VAT. Reductions in low season.

Reservations
Write to site. Tel: 269 90 51 36.

Open
All year.

CAMPSITE INSPECTIONS

Every campsite in this guide has been inspected and selected by one our seasonal campsite inspection teams.

Our teams are required to visit typically between 30 and 50 sites and submit detailed reports on each site visited.

We now have a number of vacancies for campsite Inspectors and would be interested to hear from candidates with a good knowledge of camping and caravanning. A fee is paid for each inspection, as well as travel expenses.

For applications for these posts and further information, please contact:

Rod Wheat
Alan Rogers Guides Ltd, 96 High Street, Tunbridge Wells TN1 1YF
Fax: 01892 51 00 55   Email: contact@alanrogers.com

Lisbon & Vale do Tejo

With its deep-rooted cultural traditions, range of leisure activities, year-round sunshine, sandy beaches, historic towns and villages, Lisbon and Vale do Tejo has something for everyone. It is also the centre of Fado, the traditional haunting folk song of Portugal.

This region divided into four districts: Leiria, Lisbon, Santarém and Setúbal

(Part of Setúbal also features in the Alentejo region)

Standing on the banks of the river Tagus, Lisbon has been the capital of Portugal since 1255. Places of interest in the city include the medieval quarters of Alfama and Mouraria, with their cobbled streets and alleys, colourful buildings, markets and castles, and Belém, with its tower and the 16th century Jerónimos monastery. Lisbon also boasts an assortment of museums. Not far from the capital lies the romantic town of Sintra, which has an array of cottages, manor houses and palaces. Its mountains also form part of the Sintra-Cascais Natural Park.

Along the Atlantic coast ,high sweeping cliffs lead down to white sandy beaches, backed by lagoons. Europe's westernmost point, Cabo da Roca, is found here as are plenty of coastal towns and villages including Peniche, Nazaré and Óbidos, a small medieval walled town with cobbled streets, tiny whitewashed houses and balconies brimming with flowers. Further inland, at Alcobaça, Tomar and Batalha, are ancient monasteries and convents, with castles in Leiria, Tomar and Santarém. Recreational pursuits include water sports, fishing and golf; courses are found throughout the region. In summer there are also open air music festivals.

Cuisine of the region

Fish soups, stews and seafood are popular, including *sardinha assada* (grilled sardines) and *Bifes de Espardarte* (swordfish steaks). Sintra is famed for its cheesecakes, which according to ancient documents were already being made in the 12th century, and were part of the rent payments. Wine-producing regions include Azeitão, Bucelas, Carcavelos and Colares.

Caldeiradas: fish stews

Queijadas: cheese tarts

Pastéis de Belém: custard tarts

Travesseiros: puff pastries stuffed with a sweet eggy mixture

Places of interest

Estoril: casino, golf course and racing track

Fátima: one of the most important centres of pilgrimage in the Catholic world

Leiria: medieval royal castle, 16th century cathedral, Romanesque church

Mafra: 18th century Palace-Convent, the largest Portuguese religious monument

Santarém: castle, archaeology museum, Gothic convent and churches

Sesimbra: picturesque small fishing town, medieval castle, the Lagoa de Albufeira is a favourite spot for windsurfers

Setúbal: natural reserve, beaches, golf courses,

Tomar: 12th century Templars' Castle, Gothic and Renaissance churches, 15th century synagogue

tip

INTERESTED IN LOCAL CRAFTS AND CUISINE? VISIT THE ESTORIL HANDICRAFTS FAIR (JULY-AUG) OR THE NATIONAL GASTRONOMY AND HANDICRAFTS FESTIVAL IN SANTARÉM (OCT-NOV).

Lisbon & Vale do Tejo

PO8150 Orbitur Camping Costa da Caparica

Ava. Alfonso de Albuquerque, Quinta de Ste Antonio, 2825 Costa da Caparica

This is very much a site for 600 permanent caravans but it has relatively easy access to Lisbon (just under 20 km) via the motorway, by bus or even by bus and ferry if you wish. It is situated near a small resort, favoured by the Portuguese themselves, which has all the usual amenities plus a good sandy beach (200 m. from the site) and promenade walks. There is a small area for touring units which includes some larger pitches for motorcaravans. We see this very much as a site to visit Lisbon rather than for prolonged stays. Some activities and shows are organised in season in an outdoor disco/entertainment area.

Facilities
The three toilet blocks have mostly British style toilets, washbasins with cold water and some hot showers – they come under pressure when the site is full. Facilities for disabled visitors. Washing machine. Motorcaravan services. Supermarket. Large bar/restaurant (Feb-Nov). Playground. Doctor calls daily in season. Gas supplies. Off site: Fishing 1 km. Riding 4 km. Golf 5 km.

At a glance
Welcome & Ambience	✓✓✓✓	Location	✓✓✓✓
Quality of Pitches	✓✓✓	Range of Facilities	✓✓✓✓

Directions
Cross the Tagus bridge (toll) on A2 motorway going south from Lisbon, immediately take the turning for Caparica and Trafaria. At 7 km. marker on IC20 turn right (no sign); the site is at the second roundabout.

Charges 2003
Per unit incl. 2 persons, electricity, water	€ 15.20 - € 28.30
extra adult	€ 2.40 - € 4.40
child (5-10 yrs)	€ 1.20 - € 2.20

Off season discounts (up to 70%).

Reservations
Contact Orbitur - Central de Reservas, Rua Diogo do Couto, 1149 - 042 Lisboa. Tel: 21/811 70 00 or Te: 811 70 70. Fax: 21/814 80 45. Tel: 212 90 13 66. Email: info@orbitur.pt

Open
All year.

PO8130 Orbitur Camping Guincho

E.N.247, Lugar da Areia - Guincho, 2750-053 Cascais

Although this is a popular site for permanent Portuguese occupants with 1,295 pitches, it is nevertheless quite attractively laid out among low pine trees and with the A5 autostrada connection to Lisbon (30 km), it provides a useful alternative to sites nearer the city. Located behind sand dunes and a wide, sandy but somewhat windswept beach, the site offers a wide range of facilities. These include a fairly plain bar/restaurant, supermarket (all year), general lounge with pool tables, electronic games, TV room and a good laundry. There is a choice of pitches (small – mainly about 50 sq.m) mostly with electricity, although siting amongst the trees may be tricky, particularly when the site is full. This is viewed as an alternative for visiting Lisbon, not a holiday site.

Facilities
The three sanitary blocks, one refurbished, are in the older style but are clean and tidy. Washbasins with cold water but hot showers. Dishwashing sinks have cold water. Three washing machines, two dryers. Facilities for disabled visitors. Motorcaravan services. Supermarket. Restaurant, bar and terrace (all year). General room with TV. Tennis. Playground. Entertainment in summer. Medical post. Car wash. Gas supplies. Off site: Excursions. Riding 500 m. Beach 800 m. Fishing 1 km. Golf 3 km.

At a glance
Welcome & Ambience	✓✓✓✓	Location	✓✓✓✓
Quality of Pitches	✓✓✓✓	Range of Facilities	✓✓✓✓

Directions
Approach from either direction on N247. Turn inland 6.5 km. west of Cascais at camp sign. Travelling direct from Lisbon, the site is well signed as you leave the A5 autopista.

Charges 2003
Per adult	€ 3.30 - € 5.80
child (2-10 yrs)	€ 1.70 - € 3.30
pitch for caravan or tent with car incl. electricity	€ 11.75 - € 21.10
motorcaravan incl. electricity	€ 10.10 - € 16.80
dog	€ 3.00

Off season discounts (up to 70%).

Reservations
Contact Orbitur - Central de Reservas, Rua Diogo do Couto, 1149 - 042 Lisboa. Tel: 21/811 70 00 or Tel: 811 70 70. Fax: 21/814 80 45. Tel: 214 87 04 50. Email: info@orbitur.pt

Open
All year.

PO8100 Orbitur Camping Sao Pedro de Moel

Rua Volta do Sete, 2430 Sao Pedro de Moel

This quiet and very attractive site is situated under tall pines, on the edge of the rather select small resort of São Pedro de Moel. The attractive, sandy beach is about 500 m. walk downhill from the site (you can take the car, although parking may be difficult in the town) and is sheltered from the wind by low cliffs. The shady site can be crowded in July and August. The 525 pitches are in blocks and unmarked (cars may be parked separately). There are 404 electrical connections (15A), and a few pitches are used for permanent units. Although there are areas of soft sand, there should be no problem in finding a firm place. The large restaurant and bar are modern as is the superb swimming pool, children's pool and flume (there is a lifeguard).

Facilities

Four clean toilet blocks have mainly British style toilets (some with bidets), some washbasins with hot water. Hot showers are mostly in one block. Laundry. Motorcaravan services. Supermarket. Large restaurant and bar with terrace (Apr - Sept). Swimming pools (June - Sept). TV and games room. Playground. Table tennis. Tennis. Medical post. Car wash. Gas supplies. Off site: Bus service 100 m. Beach 500 m. Fishing 1 km.

At a glance

Welcome & Ambience	✓✓✓✓	Location	✓✓✓✓✓
Quality of Pitches	✓✓✓✓✓	Range of Facilities	✓✓✓✓✓

Directions

Site is 9 km. west of Marinha Grande, on the right as you enter São Pedro de Moel.

Charges 2003

Per unit incl. 2 persons, electricity, water	€ 13.70 - € 24.90
extra adult	€ 2.10 - € 4.00
child (5-10 yrs)	€ 1.05 - € 2.00

Off season discounts (up to 70%).

Reservations

Contact Orbitur - Central de Reservas, Rua Diogo do Couto, 1149 -042 Lisboa. Tel: 21/811 70 00 or Tel: 811 70 70. Fax: 21/814 80 45. Tel: 244 59 91 68. Email: info@orbitur.pt

Open

All year.

The Orbitur Chain of Campsites

Orbitur is the largest campsite chain in Portugal. It owns sites all over the country and boasts a central booking agency and e-mail service which may be used to avoid disappointment in peak season. There are 22 campsites in the chain providing good pitches and supporting facilities, along with bungalows and mobile homes to rent.

Reservations for any of the sites should be made through the central office (not with individual sites); write to Orbitur at:

Orbitur – Central de Reservas,
Rua Diogo do Couto, 1149-042 Lisboa
Tel: 21 811 70 00 or 811 70 70. Fax: 21 814 80 45
Email: info@orbitur.pt Internet: http://www.orbitur.pt

Membership of the Orbitur Camping Club, taken either with your booking or at any site (free for pensioners) grants a 10% discount on site charges. Camping charges are reasonable and there is a general reduction of 40% to 70% (depending on length of stay) from October to March inclusive.

Lisbon & Vale do Tejo

PO8110 Orbitur Camping Valado

E.N.8 - 5 Alcobaca - Valado, 2450 Nazaré

This popular site is close to the old, traditional fishing port of Nazaré which has now become something of a holiday resort and popular with coach parties. The large sandy beach in the town (about two kilometres steeply downhill from the site) is sheltered by headlands and provides good swimming. The campsite is on undulating ground under tall pine trees, has 503 pitches and, although some smallish individual pitches with electricity and water can be reserved, the bulk of the site is not marked out and units could be close together especially during July/August. About 375 electrical connections are available. The functional restaurant, bar and supermarket are contained in one white-walled block.

Facilities

The three toilet blocks have British and Turkish style WCs, washbasins (some cold water), and 17 hot showers, all very clean when inspected. Dishwashing and laundry sinks under cover. Laundry. Motorcaravan services. Supermarket. Bar, snack bar and restaurant with terrace (-Feb - Nov). TV/general room. Playground. Tennis. Medical post. Car wash. Gas supplies. Off site: Bus service 20 m. Fishing and bicycle hire 2 km.

At a glance

Welcome & Ambience	✓✓✓✓	Location	✓✓✓✓
Quality of Pitches	✓✓✓✓	Range of Facilities	✓✓✓

Directions

Site is on the Nazaré - Alcobaca N8-5 road, 2 km. east of Nazaré.

Charges 2003

Per unit incl. 2 persons, electricity, water	€ 12.30 - € 22.20
extra adult	€ 1.90 - € 3.40
child (5-10 yrs)	€ 0.95 - € 1.70

Off season discounts (up to 70%).

Reservations

Contact Orbitur - Central de Reservas, Rua Diogo do Couto, 1149 042 Lisboa. Tel: 21/811 70 00 or Tel: 811 70 70. Fax: 21/814 80 45. Tel: 262 56 11 11. Email: info@orbitur.pt

Open

1 February - 30 November.

PO8400 Campismo O Tamanco

Casas Brancas II, 3100-231 Louriçal

O Tamanco is a peaceful countryside site, with a homely almost farm-stead atmosphere. The young Dutch owners, Irene and Hans, are sure to give you a warm welcome at this delightful little site. The swimming pool is very pleasant as is the small bar and a restaurant (with vegetarian menu options). Courses in printing and sculpture are arranged at certain times of the year. There may also be entertainment for the children during the day. The site is very popular with the Dutch, mature couples and winter campers. The 100 good sized pitches are separated by cordons of all manner of fruit trees, ornamental trees and flowering shrubs, on level grassy ground. There is electricity to 72 pitches and five pitches are suitable for large motorhomes. The site is lit and there is nearly always space available. One can fish or swim in a nearby lake and the resort beaches are a short drive. There may be some road noise on pitches at the front of the site.

Facilities

The single toilet block provides very clean and generously sized facilities including washbasins in cabins, with easy access for disabled visitors. As facilities are limited they may be busy in peak periods. Dishwashing and laundry sinks outside, under cover. Hot water throughout. Washing machine. Bar/restaurant. Roofed patio with fireplace. TV room/lounge. Swimming pool. Off site: Lake 2 km. Beach 11 km. Market in nearby Lourical every Sunday.

At a glance

Welcome & Ambience	✓✓✓✓✓	Location	✓✓✓✓✓
Quality of Pitches	✓✓✓✓✓	Range of Facilities	✓✓✓✓

Directions

From N109/IC1 (Leira-Figuera de Foz) road, 25 km. south of Figuera in Matos de Carriço, turn on to N342 road (signed Louriçal 6 km). Site is directly off the behind high hedges 1.5 km. on left.

Latest charges

Per adult	€ 2.75
child (up to 5 yrs)	€ 1.50
tent	€ 2.10 - € 2.70
caravan	€ 3.00
car	€ 2.10
motorcaravan	€ 5.00
electricity (6A)	€ 1.90

Winter discounts up to 40%. No credit cards.

Reservations

Contact site. Tel: 236 95 25 51.
Email: campismo.o.tamanco@mail.telepac.pt

Open

1 February - 31 October.

PO8460 Camping Caravaning Vale Paraiso
Estrada Nacional 242, 2450-138 Nazaré

A pleasant, well managed site, Vale Paraiso is by the main N242 road in eight hectares of undulating pine woods. It provides over 600 shady pitches, many on sandy ground only suitable for tents. For other units there are around 250 individual pitches of varying size on harder ground with electricity. A range of sporting and leisure facilities includes a good outdoor pool with sunbathing areas a play area for children plus a small adventure playground. There is a bar, takeaway and a recently (2002) refurbished, slightly bland restaurant/bar. Several long sandy beaches are within 2-15 km. allowing windsurfing, sailing, surfing or body-boarding. Animation for children and evening entertainment is organised in season. The owners are keen to welcome British visitors and English is spoken.

Facilities
Toilet facilities are good, with hot water for washbasins, showers, laundry and dishwashing sinks. Nearly all WCs are British style. Facilities for disabled people. Baby baths to borrow. Washing machine and dryers. Motorcaravan services. Shop. Self-service and a la carte Electronic games. Restaurant (March - Sept). Café/bar with TV (all year). Takeaway. Tabac. Supermarket (March - Sept). Swimming pool (March - Sept; free for children under 11 yrs). Petanque. Volleyball. Basketball. Football. Badminton. Leisure games. Amusement hall. Bicycle hire. Safety deposit. Gas supplies. Tourist information. Email and fax facilities (read free, send for a fee). Bus service from gate. Off site: Fishing 1.5 km. Boat launching 2.5 km. Riding 5 km. Golf 35 km.

At a glance
Welcome & Ambience	✓✓✓✓	Location	✓✓✓✓
Quality of Pitches	✓✓✓✓✓	Range of Facilities	✓✓✓✓✓

Directions
Site is 2 km. north of Nazaré, on the EN242 Marinha Grande road.

Charges 2003
Per person	€ 2.90 - € 3.80
child (3-10 yrs)	€ 1.40 - € 3.80
caravan	€ 3.50 - € 4.20
motorcaravan	€ 4.20 - € 4.90
tent	€ 2.50 - € 4.70
car	€ 5.60 - € 6.80
motorcycle	€ 1.70 - € 2.00
electricity (4-10A)	€ 2.40

Reservations
Contact site. Tel: 262 56 18 00.
Email: info@valeparaiso.com

Open
All year.

Animation and Nature
Reservations on-line: www.valeparaiso.com

Estrada Nacional 242
2450-138 Nazaré-PORTUGAL
Tel. 351 262 561 800
Fax. 351 262 561 900
info@valeparaiso.com

vale paraíso ***
camping
bungalows
apartments

Great on-line holiday deals alanrogersdirect.com

Lisbon & Vale do Tejo

PO8450 Parque de Campismo Colina do Sol

2465 Sao Martinho do Porto

Colina do Sol is a well appointed site with its own swimming pool and near to the beach. Only one kilometre from the small town of Sao Martinho do Porto, it has around 350 pitches marked by fruit and ornamental trees on grassy terraces. Electricity is available to all, although some may need long leads. The attractive entrance with its beds of bright flowers, is wide enough for even the largest of outfits, and the surfaced roads are very pleasant for manoeuvring. There is a warm welcome and good English is spoken. A well stocked supermarket and a restaurant, cafeteria, and a bar with a delightful paved terrace beside the large clean swimming pools, one for children. The beach is at the rear of the site, with access via a gate which is locked at night (10 pm-8 am). This is a convenient base for exploring the Costa de Prata. Market in Sao Martinho do Porto is on Sunday.

Facilities
Two large, clean and modern toilet blocks provide British style WCs (some with bidets), washbasins - some with hot water. Dishwashing and laundry sinks are outside but covered. Ironing facilities. Motorcaravan services. Supermarket, restaurant/café with bar. Off site: Shop, restaurant and bar within 200 m.

At a glance
Welcome & Ambience	✓✓✓✓	Location	✓✓✓✓
Quality of Pitches	✓✓✓✓	Range of Facilities	✓✓✓✓

Directions
Turn from EN 242 (Caldas-Nazaré) road northeast of San Martinho do Porto. Site is clearly signed.

Latest charges
Per adult	€ 2.87
child (4-10 yrs)	€ 1.37
small tent	€ 2.47
large tent	€ 2.92
caravan	€ 3.29 - € 3.57
car	€ 2.37
motorcycle	€ 1.60
motorcaravan	€ 4.39
electricity (6/10A)	€ 1.60

Less 25-50% in low seasons.

Reservations
Contact site. Tel: 262 98 97 64.

Open
All year except 15 Dec. -15 Jan.

PO8480 Orbitur Camping Foz do Arelho

EN360 - km. 3, Foz do Arelho, 2500 Caldas da Rainha

This is a large and roomy ex-municipal site, new to the Orbitur chain and improvements are still taking place. It is two kilometres from the beach and has a new central complex with a most impressive swimming pool and separated children's pool with lifeguard. The large two storey, brick-faced building contains all the site's leisure facilities but has no ramped access and there are no sanitary facilities anywhere on site for disabled campers. The building is somewhat sterile and the furniture is bland but there are pleasant views over the pool from the restaurant and terrace. The pitches are generally sandy with some hardstandings, vary in size and are unmarked on two main levels with wide tarmac roads. There is a little shade and some permanent Portugese units occupied in high season and weekends at other times. All touring pitches have electricity (5/15A). This is a site with work in progress and it will improve to the usual Orbitur standards but if you have special needs we recommend a telephone call first.

Facilities
Four identical modern sanitary buildings (solar heating) with seatless British and Turkish style WCs and free showers. Washing machine in one, dishwashing and laundry sinks have cold water only. No facilities for disabled campers. No chemical disposal point. Supermarket. Children's club. Games room. Tabletennis. Small new amphitheatre. Electronic games. Bar/snacks and restaurant. (April - Sept). Playground - supervision needed. Bus service. Doctor's room. Torches useful. Off site: Bus 500 m. Seaside town has a range of shops, bars and restaurants 2 km. Fishing 2 km. Watersports 3 km. Riding 15 km. Golf 35 km.

At a glance
Welcome & Ambience	✓✓✓	Location	✓✓✓✓
Quality of Pitches	✓✓✓	Range of Facilities	✓✓✓✓

Directions
Site is north of Lisbon west of Caldos. From A8 Take N360 to Foz de Arehlo. Site is well signed.

Charges 2003
Per adult	€ 5.00
child (4-12 yrs)	€ 3.00
pitch (70-75 sq.m)	€ 12.00 - € 29.00

Reservations
Contact Orbitur - Central de Reservas, Rua Diogo do Couto, 1149-042 Lisboa. Tel: 21/811 70 00 or Tel: 811 70 70. Fax: 21/814 80 45. Tel: 262 978683. Email: info@orbitur.pt

Open
All year.

Beiras is the traditional name for a strip of land flanked by Portugal's two main rivers – the Douro and the Tagus. This region is made up of two contrasting areas: white sandy beaches, fishing villages and pine forests lie along the coast, while inland the mountains dominate the landscape.

Beiras has five districts: Aveiro, Coimbla, Castelo Branco, Guarda and Viseu

Beiras & Centre

One of Europe's oldest university towns, Coimbra was Portugal's capital from 1143 to 1255. The university, founded in 1290, has kept its academic traditions, as seen in the black-capped students, in the soulful tones of the *fado de Coimbra* (traditional song sung to the sound of guitars by the students) and in the Queima das Fitas (Burning of the Ribbons), a boisterous celebration of graduating students. Coimbra also boasts a Romanesque cathedral and south of the town lies Conímbriga, with the most important Roman remains in Portugal. Surrounded by the original walls, the archaeological site features an early Christian burial ground, a set of hot springs and a museum. Further north lies Aveiro. Famous for its lagoon, the town is crisscrossed by canals where colourfully painted moliceiro boats sail. To the east lies the Serra de Estrela, the highest mountain range in the country. It is home to the textile town of Covilha, various attractive villages including Gouveia, Manteigas and Seia, plus the mountain resort of Guarda. Skiing is popular. Along the coast, the pretty seaside resorts of São Martinho do Porto, Nazaré and Figueira da Foz offer fine sandy beaches, good seafood restaurants and water sports facilities.

Cuisine of the region

Roast pork, lamb stew, seafood and fresh fish are popular, including *truta* (trout) from the mountains of Serra da Estrela. The famous ewe's milk cheese Queijo da Serra, is also a produced in the mountains, and can be bought at Cheese Fairs held in villages and towns throughout the region during February and March. Regional desserts include hard and sweet biscuits, pancakes and sponge cake (*ovos-moles*, *pão-de-ló*).

Chanfana: lamb stewed in red wine

Leitão assado da Bairrada: roast pork

Places of interest

Belmonte: hilltop town, castle, Romanesque-Gothic church

Bussaco: national park founded by monks in the 6th century

Castelo Branco: 13th century castle, medieval quarter, 16th-18th century churches

Curia and *Luso*: spa towns

Monsanto: historic village, 12th-century castle, 18th-century manor-houses

Viseu: remains of Gothic walls, cathedral

 **tip**

BUY THE LOCALLY PRODUCED HANDICRAFTS: EMBROIDERED SILK BEDSPREADS FROM CASTELO BRANCO, CERAMICS FROM COIMBRA, AND GLASS AND CRYSTAL FROM ALCOBAÇA.

www.alanrogers.com for latest campsite news

PO8040 Parque de Campismo da Vagueira

Gafanha da Vagueira, Gafanha da Boa Hora, 3840-254 Vagos

This is a large site set 1.5 km. from the beach and 500 m. from the river 'Ria da Gosta Nova'. Shaded under tall pine trees and with comprehensive facilities and reasonable prices. The 800 pitches are unmarked, on sand and pine needles with a large amount of permanent Portuguese units which are here in high season and weekends at other times. Groups are taken in high season. All touring pitches have electricity. The modern buildings have clean lines and are in sympathy with the surroundings, the restaurant/bar/café complex has a disco area outside where music is played at weekends. This complex extends into a large rectangle holding the extremely large supermarket and facilities listed below. The whole site is securely fenced and is kept remarkabley clean. The rules of peace between 2300- 0700 are firmly applied. This is a good family site if you do not need a pool and have transport to get you to the beach. The seaside town here is a mixture of buildings and services which seem to be unsure of which future direction to take, but the beach is excellent.

Facilities
Seven modern sanitary buildings with British and Turkish style WCs and free showers. Washing machines, dishwashing and laundry sinks have cold water only. At the end of each block there are barbeque facilities. Outdoor disco. Facilities for disabled campers (unlocked). Very large supermarket. Children's club. Games room. Electronic games. Bar/snacks and separate restaurant with sound menus and local wines (Jun - Sept). Playground. Bus service. Doctor's room. Internet room. Tennis (charge). Torches useful. Off site: Seaside town has a range of shops bars and restaurants. River fishing 500 m. Bus 500 m. Golf 1 km. Riding 1 km. Water sports at beach 1.5 km.

At a glance
Welcome & Ambience	✓✓✓✓✓	Location	✓✓✓✓
Quality of Pitches	✓✓✓✓	Range of Facilities	✓✓✓✓✓

Directions
Site is south of Aveiro. Take N109 south from Aveiro towards Mira. At Vagos take the N333 right turn towards Vagueira. Site is well signed at this turn and is just off the roundabout you arrive at on the beach road.

Charges 2003
Per person	€ 3.29
child	€ 1.65
pitch and car	€ 5.47 - € 7.41
electricity (6A)	€ 2.47

Reservations
Write to site. Tel: 234 797526.

Open
All year.

PO8050 Orbitur Camping Sao Jacinto

E.N.327, km. 20, Sao Jacinto, 3800 Aveiro

This small site is in the Sao Jacinto nature reserve, on a peninsula between the Atlantic and the Barrinha, with views to the mountains beyond. The area is a weekend resort for locals and can be crowded in high season – it may therefore be difficult to find space in July/Aug, particularly for larger units. Swimming and fishing are both possible in the adjacent Ria, or the sea, 20 minutes walk from a guarded back gate. There is a private jetty for boats and the manager will organise hire of the decorative 'Moliceiros' boats used in days gone by to harvest seaweed for the land. This is not a large site, taking 169 units on unmarked pitches, but in most places trees provide natural limits and shade. A deep bore-hole supplies the site with drinking water.

Facilities
Two toilet blocks, very clean when inspected, contain the usual facilities. Dishwashing and laundry sinks. Washing machine and ironing board in a separate part of the sanitary block. Motorcaravan services. Shop. Restaurant/bar (all May - Sept). Playground. Table tennis. Tourist information. Off site: Bus service 20 m. Fishing 200 m. Bicycle hire 10 km.

At a glance
Welcome & Ambience	✓✓✓✓✓	Location	✓✓✓✓✓
Quality of Pitches	✓✓✓✓	Range of Facilities	✓✓✓✓

Directions
Turn off N109 at Estarreja to n109 - 5 to cross bride over Ria da Gosta Nova and on to Torreira and São Jacinto. Or from Porto go south N1/09 turn for Ovar on the N 327 which leads to Sao Jacinto.

Charges 2003
per unit incl. 2 persons, electricity, water	€ 12.30 - € 22.20
extra adult	€ 1.90 - € 3.40
child (5-10 yrs)	€ 0.95 - € 1.70

Off season discounts (up to 70%).

Reservations
Contact Orbitur - Central de Reservas, Rua Diogo do Couto, 1-8o, 1100 Lisboa. Tel: 21/811 70 00 or Tel: 811 70 70. Fax: 21/814 80 45. Tel: 234 83 82 84. Email: info@orbitur.pt

Open
February - November.

PO8070 Orbitur Camping Mira

Estrada Florestal no. 1 - km. 2, 3070 Mira

A small seaside site set in pinewoods, Orbitur Camping Mira is situated to the south of Aveiro and Vagos, in a quieter and less crowded area. It fronts onto a lake at the head of the Ria de Mira, which eventually runs into the Aveiro Ria. A back gate leads directly to the sea and a wide quiet beach 300 m. away, a road runs alongside the site where the restaurant complex is situated resulting in some road noise. The site has around 225 pitches on sand, which are not marked but with trees creating natural divisions. Electricity and water points are plentiful. The site provides an inexpensive restaurant, snack bar, lounge bar and TV lounge. A medium sized supermarket is well stocked, with plenty of fresh produce. The Mira Ria is fascinating, with the brightly painted, decorative 'Moliceiros' (traditional fishing boats).

Facilities
The modern toilet blocks are clean, with 14 free hot showers and washing machines. Motorcaravan services. Shop, restaurant and bar (Feb - Nov). Snack bar. TV room. Smart playground. Gas supplies. Off site: Bus service 150 m. Bicycle hire 200 m. Fishing 500 m. Golf 1 km. Indoor pool, lake swimming and riding at Mira 7 km.

At a glance
Welcome & Ambience	✓✓✓✓	Location	✓✓✓✓✓
Quality of Pitches	✓✓✓✓	Range of Facilities	✓✓✓✓

Directions
Turn off N109 at Mira, about 27 km. south of Aveiro towards Praia de Mira. After about 5 km. (watch for speed bumps close to site!) a small sign shows a left turn which leads direct to the site. If you miss it, the site is signed from the beach resort. Make sure you ask for the Orbitur site if stuck - there are others here which are not as pleasant!

Charges 2003
Per person	€ 2.10 - € 3.70
child (5-10 yrs)	€ 1.05 - € 1.85
tent	€ 1.60 - € 5.10
motorcycle	€ 1.25 - € 2.50
motorcaravan	€ 2.50 - € 5.95
caravan	€ 2.10 - € 5.60
electricity (5/15A)	€ 2.25

Off season discounts (up to 70%).

Reservations
Contact Orbitur - Central de Reservas, Rua Diogo do Couto, 1-8o, 1100 Lisboa. Tel: 21/811 70 00 or Tel: 811 70 70. Fax: 21/814 80 45. Tel: 231 47 12 34. Email: info@orbitur.pt

Open
1 March - 30 November.

PO8090 Orbitur Camping Figueira da Foz

E.N. 109 - km. 4 Gala, 3080 Figueira da Foz

This site of around 450 pitches is on sandy terrain under a canopy of pine trees and well cared for. Some pitches near the road may be rather noisy. One can drive or walk the 300 m. from the back of the site to a private beach; you should swim with caution when it is windy – the warden will advise. The site fills in July and August and units may be very close together, but there should be plenty of room at other times.

Facilities
The three toilet blocks have British and Turkish style toilets, individual basins (some with hot water) and free hot showers. Motorcaravan services. Laundry. Supermarket and restaurant/bar with terrace (all May - Sept). Lounge. Playground. Tennis. TV. Doctor visits in season. Car wash area. Gas supplies. Off site: Beach 300 m. Fishing 1 km. Bicycle hire and riding 3 km.

At a glance
Welcome & Ambience	✓✓✓✓✓	Location	✓✓✓✓✓
Quality of Pitches	✓✓✓✓	Range of Facilities	✓✓✓✓✓

Directions
Site is 4 km. south of Figueira da Foz beyond the two rivers; turn off N109 1 km. from bridge on southern edge of Gala, look for Orbitur sign on roundabout it is then 600 m. to site.

Charges 2003
Per person	€ 2.10 - € 3.70
child (5-10 yrs)	€ 1.05 - € 1.85
car	€ 1.80 - € 3.40
motorcycle	€ 1.25 - € 2.50
tent	€ 1.60 - € 5.10
caravan	€ 2.10 - € 5.80
motorcaravan	€ 2.50 - € 5.95
electricity (5/15A)	€ 2.25

Off season discounts (up to 70%).

Reservations
Contact Orbitur - Central de Reservas, Rua Diogo do Couto, 1-8oF, 1149-042 Lisboa. Tel: 233 43 14 92. Email: info@orbitur.pt

Open
All year.

PO8330 Camping Municipal Arganil

E.N. 17 - km. 5 Sarzedo, 3300 Arganil

This quiet, inland site is attractively located in the hamlet of Sarzedo, some two kilometres from the town of Arganil. A spacious and well planned site, it is high quality for a municipal and prices are very reasonable! Delightfully situated among pine trees above the River Alva where one can swim, fish, canoe and windsurf. The 150 pitches, most with electricity, are of a reasonable size, mainly on flat sandy grass terraces shaded by tall trees. The site is kept beautifully clean and neat and access roads are tarmac. A small but excellent restaurant serves local food and has an unusual attached bar with terrace.

Facilities

Sanitary facilities are clean and well maintained, with Turkish and British style WCs, controllable hot showers, washbasins in semi-private partitioned cabins and a hairdressing area with electric sockets. Ramped entrances make it suitable for disabled visitors. Washing machines. Bar, restaurant and snacks (all year). Shop (July - Sept). TV room. Tennis. Car wash. Off site: Bus service 50 m. Fishing 100 m. River beach 100 m. Watersports 200 m. Swimming pool in nearby Arganil. Golf 25 km.

At a glance

Welcome & Ambience	✓✓✓✓	Location	✓✓✓✓
Quality of Pitches	✓✓✓✓✓	Range of Facilities	✓✓✓✓

Directions

From EN17/N2 Coimbra - Sarzedo at 324.4 km marker exit to Sarzedo site is signed. Ignore first campsite sign to Avelar as there is a much better access some 500 m. further up the road on the right also signed.

Charges 2003

Per person	€ 1.50 - € 1.70
child (5-10 yrs)	€ 1.00 - € 1.20
car	€ 1.50 - € 2.00
motorcycle	€ 1.20 - € 1.70
tent	€ 1.40 - € 2.80
caravan	€ 2.00 - € 5.00
motorcaravan	€ 2.20 - € 5.00
electricity (5/15A)	€ 1.90 - € 2.20
Plus 7% VAT.	

Reservations

Contact site. Tel: 235 20 57 06. Email: campingcma@hotmail.com

Open

All year.

PO8360 Parque Campismo de Municipal

Barragem de Idhana-a-Nova, 6060 Idanha-a-Nova

With its high level of sophistication, this attractive and well laid out site is unlike most municipal sites. It is located in quiet, unspoilt countryside close to a reservoir, near the small town of Idanha-a-Nova. The site has around 500 spacious unmarked pitches on wide grassy terraces and there is a little shade from young trees. Electricity is provided. Amenities on the site include tennis courts with stadium-style spectator seating and a medium sized swimming pool with child's pool, together with several playgrounds. A good supermarket, restaurant, bar and terrace complex is located centrally on site, open in high season.

Facilities

Four large toilet blocks, built in the traditional Portuguese style, provide quality installations with some washbasins in private cabins, hot showers with dividers, foot baths and facilities for disabled visitors. Dishwashing and laundry sinks (cold water). Laundry. Supermarket (1/7-30/9). Cafe, bar and restaurant (1/7-30/9). Swimming pool. Tennis courts. TV room. Vending machines. Medical post. Car wash. Canoe hire.

At a glance

Welcome & Ambience	✓✓✓	Location	✓✓✓
Quality of Pitches	✓✓✓✓	Range of Facilities	✓✓✓✓

Directions

Using the N240, turn off at Ladoeiro onto the N354 (32 km. east of Castelo Branco) and follow signs to Barragem and site. Do not approach via the town of Idanha-a-Nova.

Latest charges

Per adult	€ 1.25
child (4-10 yrs)	€ 0.62
tent	€ 0.62 - € 1.87
caravan	€ 2.24
car	€ 1.25
motorcycle	€ 0.62
motorcaravan	€ 2.49
electricity (16A)	€ 0.60

Reservations

Write to site. Tel: 277 20 27 93.

Open

All year.

Porto & North

Originally inhabited by Celtics, Romans and Moors, the North is a region steeped in history. Renowned for its beautiful countryside, the River Douro winds its way past mountains, valleys, vineyards and cliffs until it reaches the sandy beaches of the Atlantic coast near the city of Porto.

The region is comprised of five districts: Braga, Bragança, Porto, Viana do Castelo and Vila Real

Situated in the north western corner of Portugal, the Costa Verde boasts lush green pine forests and unspoilt sandy beaches, dotted with picturesque seaside villages, including Caminha and Vila Nova de Cerveira. It is also renowned for its wine, being the home of Port and Vinho Verdo. Located on the banks for the River Douro, the attractive city of Porto is the centre of the Port wine trade – free tastings are offered at the wine cellars in Vila Nova de Gaia – and terraced vineyards can be found across the Douro Valley.

The region is also a perfect place for walking, mountain trekking, canoeing or simply relaxing in the spa towns of Carvalhelhos, Chaves and Pedras Salgadas. Vidago has a magnificent park with swimming pools and a golf course, while the mountains of Peneda, Soajo and Gerês form the Peneda Geres National Park, an area covering 170,000 acres, with an abundance of wildlife. Vila Nova de Foz is the centre for visits to the Côa Archaeological Park, which houses one of the world's largest collections of outdoor Palaeolithic rock art, dating back 22,000 years.

Cuisine of the region

Typical dishes include *bacalhau* (dried and salted cod), *rabanadas*, *papos-de-anjo* and *barrigas-de-freiras* (sweetmeats). Porto has its own tripe dish *Tripas à moda do Porto*.

The Minho region is renowned for its *Vinhos Verdes*, whose vines are grown on trellises (being suspended high in the air on special frames). In the Douro region, the vines are grown on terraces, giving the impression of huge natural staircases leading down to the banks of the river. Both red and white wines are produced here including the famous *Vinho do Porto* (Port Wine).

Caldo verde: thick soup made with green cabbage, potatoes and spicy sausage

Feijoada à transmontana: bean stew

Places of interest

Barcelos: medieval walled town with dungeon, ceramics museum, archaeology museum

Bragança: medieval castle and walls, 16th century cathedral, railway museum with 19th century locomotives and carriages.

Chaves: Roman bridge, 14th century castle with Archaeology and Epigraphy Museum.

Guimarães: medieval castle and walls, palace

Lamego: medieval castle, 12th century fortress

Ponte de Lima: beautiful small town, Roman bridge, medieval towers, manor houses

Viana do Castelo: town famous for its handicrafts and colourful regional costumes

Vila do Conde: ancient medieval shipyard, famous for its manufactured lace

TAKE A BOAT TRIP ALONG THE RIVER DOURO AND ADMIRE THE BEAUTIFUL TERRACED VINEYARDS WHERE THE GRAPES ARE GROWN FROM WHICH PORT WINE IS MADE.

www.alanrogers.com for latest campsite news

PO8010 Orbitur Camping Caminha

E.N.13 - km. 90, Mata do Camarido, 4910 Caminha

A pleasant site in northern Portugal close to the Spanish border; this site is just 200 m. from the beach with an attractive and peaceful setting in woods alongside the river estuary that marks the border with Spain. With a pleasant, open feel about it, fishing is possible in the estuary and bathing, either there or from the rather open, sandy beach. The site is shaded by tall pines with other small trees planted to mark the large sandy pitches. The main site road is surfaced but elsewhere take care not to get trapped in soft sand accessing some pitches. Pitching and parking can be haphazard. Water points, electrical supply and lighting are good.

Facilities
The clean, well maintained toilet block has British style toilets, washbasins (cold water) and hot showers, plus beach showers, extra dishwashing and laundry sinks (cold water). Laundry with ironing boards. Motorcaravan services. Small restaurant, snacks and supermarket (all April - Sept). Off site: Beach 100m. Bus service 800 m. Fishing 1 km. Riding 5 km. Golf 40 km.

At a glance
Welcome & Ambience	✓✓✓✓✓	Location	✓✓✓✓
Quality of Pitches	✓✓✓✓✓	Range of Facilities	✓✓✓✓

Directions
Turn off main coast road (N13-E50) just after camping sign at end of embankment, approx. 1 mile south of ferry.

Charges 2003
Per person	€ 2.10 - € 3.50
child (5-10 yrs)	€ 1.05 - € 1.85
tent	€ 1.60 - € 5.10
caravan	€ 2.10 - € 5.30
car	€ 1.90 - € 3.40
m/cycle	€ 1.25 - € 2.50
motorcaravan	€ 2.50 - € 5.95
electricity	€ 2.25 - € 2.90

Off season discounts (up to 70%).

Reservations
Contact Orbitur - Central de Reservas, Rua Diogo do Couto, 1149 - 042 Lisboa. Tel: 21/811 70 00 or Tel: 811 70 70. Fax: 21/814 80 45. Email as site address. Tel: 258 92 12 95. Email: info@orbitur.pt

Open
16 January - 30 November.

PO8020 Orbitur Camping Viana do Castelo

Rua Diogo Alvares, Cabadelo, 4900-161 Darque

This site in northern Portugal is worth considering as it has the advantage of direct access, through a gate in the fence (locked at night) to a large and excellent soft sand beach (400 metres), which is popular for windsurfing. There are 225 pitches on undulating sand, most with good shade. There are some flat good sized pitches for caravans and electricity in all parts. As usual with Orbitur sites, pitches are not marked and it could be crowded in July/August. A pleasant restaurant terrace overlooks the swimming pool and site. A ferry crosses the river to the town centre.

Facilities
Clean, well kept toilet facilities are in two blocks. Both blocks have washbasins with cold water and hot showers. Good facilities for disabled campers. Laundry. Motorcaravan services. Supermarket. Small restaurant with terrace and bar (all May -Sep). Reading room with TV, video and fireplace. Playground. Tennis. Medical post. Gas supplies. Off site: Fishing 1 km. Riding 2 km.

At a glance
Welcome & Ambience	✓✓✓✓✓	Location	✓✓✓✓✓
Quality of Pitches	✓✓✓✓	Range of Facilities	✓✓✓✓

Directions
On N13 coast road driving north to south drive through Viana do Castelo and over estuary bridge, turn immediately right off N13 towards Cabedelo and the sea. Site is the third camp signed, the other two are not recommended.

Charges 2003
Per unit incl. 2 persons, electricity and water	€ 13.70 - € 24.90
extra adult	€ 2.10 - € 4.00
child (5-10 yrs)	€ 1.05 - € 2.00

Off season discounts (up to 70%).

Reservations
Contact Orbitur - Central de Reservas, Rua Diogo do Couto, 1149 - 042 Lisboa. Tel: 21/811 70 00 or Tel: 811 70 70. Fax: 21/814 80 45. Email as site address. Tel: 258 32 21 67. Email: info@orbitur.pt

Open
16 January - 30 November.

PO8380 Parque Natural de Vilar de Mouros

4910 Vilar de Mouros

Located some 15 minutes walk above the village of Vilar de Mouros and very close to the Spanish border, this small site is ideal for those looking for an uncomplicated traditional campsite giving really good prices. Along with several permanent units, the 45 marked pitches for touring units, all with electricity, are on slightly sloping, grassy terraces, with a separate unmarked area for tents, all set amongst trees and vines on a hillside. Not many are suitable for larger units. This friendly site has a good range of other amenities which include a tennis court, one large and one small unusual small stone swimming pools. There is a small but good café/bar (open 8 am-11 pm), takeaway, a simple self-service restaurant with shady terrace, and a mini-market. Occasional Saturday evening organised gastronomic and folklore trips are popular.

Facilities
The two toilet blocks, very much in the quainter, older Portuguese style, provide British style WCs (some with bidets), washbasins (cold water), and hot showers. Dishwashing and laundry sinks (cold water) are under cover. Washing machine and dryer in a separate building. Mini-market (high season). Café/bar. Self-service restaurant. Swimming pool. Tennis court. TV room. Washing machine. Children's pool and playground. Medical post. Bicycle hire. Local folklore entertainment trips. Little English spoken. Dogs are not accepted. Off site: Fishing 4 km. River Minho 4 km. Riding 5 km. Golf 20 km.

Directions
Site is signed from the N13, just north of Seixas, turn towards Vilar de Mouros. Site is on right just before village.

Charges 2003
Per adult	€ 2.10 - € 3.50
child	€ 1.02 - € 1.70
pitch	€ 2.04 - € 4.40
car	€ 1.80 - € 3.00
m/cycle	€ 1.50 - € 2.50
electricity (2/9A)	€ 2.30

Reservations
Contact site. Tel: 258 72 74 72.

Open
All year.

At a glance
Welcome & Ambience	✓✓✓✓	Location	✓✓✓✓
Quality of Pitches	✓✓✓✓	Range of Facilities	✓✓✓✓

PO8030 Orbitur Camping Rio Alto

E.N.13 - km. 13 Rio Alto-Estela, 4490 Póvoa de Varzim

This site makes an excellent base for visiting Porto (by car) which is some 35 km. south of Estela. It has around 700 pitches on sandy terrain and is next to what is virtually a private beach (access via a novel double tunnel under the dunes). The beach shelves steeply at some tidal stages. The 18 hole golf course is adjacent and huge nets along one side of the site protect campers from any stray balls. There are some hardstandings for caravans and motorcaravans and electrical connections to most pitches. The area for tents is furthest from the beach and windswept, stunted pines give some shade. There are special arrangements for car parking away from camping areas in peak season. There is a quality restaurant, snack bar and a large swimming pool plus children's pool across the road from reception. The beach tunnel is open 9 am-7 pm. and the beach has a lifeguard from 15 June - 15 September.

Facilities
Four well equipped toilet blocks have hot water. Dishwashing and laundry sinks under cover. Washing machines and ironing facilities. Facilities for disabled campers. Restaurant. Bar and snack bar (1/1 -30/11), mini-market (15 May - 15 Sept). Swimming pool (1/6-30/9). Tennis. Children's playground. Games room. Surfing. TV. Medical post. Car wash. Gas supplies. Evening entertainment twice weekly in season. Off site: Fishing 800 m. Golf 1 km. Bicycle hire 13 km. Riding 19 km.

Directions
Site is reached via a cobbled road leading directly off the EN13 coast road towards the sea (just north of Estela), 12 km. north of Póvoa de Varzim. Travel 2.6 km. along the narrow cobbled road and look to the right for an Orbitur sign (well back from the road). Take this for 0.8 km. to site (beware speed bumps). You will be travelling through intensive greenhouse farming for the last 2km but keep going its worth it!

Charges 2003
Per person	€ 2.10 - € 4.30
child (5-10 yrs)	€ 1.05 - € 2.15
tent	€ 2.10 - € 6.20
caravan	€ 3.10 - € 7.10
motorcaravan	€ 3.80 - € 7.50
car	€ 2.00 - € 4.20
m/cycle	€ 1.55 - € 2.90
electricity (5/15A)	€ 2.25

Off season discounts (up to 70%).

Reservations
Contact Orbitur - Central de Reservas, Rua Diogo do Couto, 1149 - 042 Lisboa. Tel: 21/811 70 00 or Tel: 811 70 70. Fax: 21/814 80 45. Email as site address. Tel: 252 61 56 99. Email: info@orbitur.pt

Open
All year.

At a glance
Welcome & Ambience	✓✓✓✓✓	Location	✓✓✓✓✓
Quality of Pitches	✓✓✓✓	Range of Facilities	✓✓✓✓✓

PO8370 Parque de Campismo de Cerdeira
4840 Campo do Gerês

Placed in the National Park of Peneda Gerês, amidst spectacular mountain scenery, this excellent site offers modern facilities in a truly natural area. The well fenced, professional and peaceful site has some 600 good sized unmarked, mostly level, grassy pitches in a shady woodland setting. Electricity is available for most pitches, though some long leads may be required. A very large timber complex, tastefully designed with the use of noble materials, granite and wood provides a superb restaurant with a comprehensive menu (including breakfast). There are unlimited opportunities in the area for fishing, riding, canoeing, mountain biking and climbing.

Facilities
Three very clean sanitary blocks provide mixed style WCs, controllable showers and hot water. Dishwashing and laundry sinks under cover. Laundry. Gas supplies. Mini-market. Restaurant/bar (15/4- 30/9, plus weekends and holidays). Playground. Bicycle hire. TV room. Medical post. Good tennis courts. Mini Golf. Car wash. Barbeque area. Torches useful. English spoken. Dogs are not accepted in July/August. Off site: Fishing 800 m. Riding 800 m.

At a glance
Welcome & Ambience	✓✓✓✓	Location	✓✓✓✓✓
Quality of Pitches	✓✓✓✓	Range of Facilities	✓✓✓✓✓

Directions
From north, N103 (Braga-Chaves road), turn left at N205 (7.5 km north of Braga). Follow N205 to Caldelas Terras de Bouro and Covide where the campsite is clearly marked to 'Campo do Geres'. An alternate route from the N103 looks easier on the map but is in fact more difficult.

Charges 2003
Per adult	€ 3.00 - € 4.00
child (5-11 yrs)	€ 1.80 - € 2.50
tent	€ 3.00 - € 4.50
caravan	€ 4.00 - € 5.00
car	€ 2.80 - € 3.50
motorcycle	€ 1.80 - € 2.50
motorcaravan	€ 4.50 - € 5.50
electricity (5/10A)	€ 2.00 - € 3.00

Reservations
Contact site. Tel: 253 35 1005.
Email: parque.cerdeira@portugalmail.pt

Open
All year.

Driving in Europe

If you are planning to take your caravan, tent, trailer tent or motorcaravan to the continent you will need to be familiar with the rules, regulations and customs that pertain to driving abroad.

A recent survey looked at why many Britons would not entertain a holiday abroad and why many foreigners would not contemplate coming here. According to the findings, the biggest single put-off was driving on the 'wrong' side of the road. However, statistics clearly show that you are less at risk of being involved in accidents – and that includes minor shunts – when driving in another country. The theory is that motorists of that country recognise that the nationality plate on your vehicle means that you might be slightly hesitant and give you that extra few inches which makes the difference between a minor ding and a trouble free journey. Of course it could also be that when driving in another country we take things a bit easier, so we are less at risk of being involved in an accident.

With European harmonisation eliminating most of the differences between driving in your home country and another, there has never been a better time to consider driving abroad. Where there are differences, they are in the detail.

For example all European countries require you to carry your driving documents whenever you are behind the wheel; there's no three day's grace to get to your local police station. Amongst the documents you are required to carry is your vehicle registration document, the V5 (what used to be called the log book). If yours is a hire or company vehicle you may have difficulties getting your hands on the V5. However the police will accept a photocopy of the V5 provided it is accompanied by a brief letter – signed by the vehicle owner – saying you have their permission to take the vehicle abroad.

European harmonisation also means that most common road signs are the same in all countries. Where mainland Europe differs from the UK is in the use of direction signs. If you are following signs through a town and arrive at a junction without signage – don't panic. The logic is that if all major routes are straight on, you don't need another sign to tell you the obvious.

As to language difficulties, you will find that most continental road signs are similar in style to those in the UK, although what is written on them will be in the language of the country concerned (for example Barcelona is spelt Barcelone in French), so it's worthwhile mugging up some of the more important and/or more usual ones. See articles on individual countries – the main signs have been translated for you.

When it comes to traffic regulations around school entrances, the Europeans are also ahead of us. In mainland Europe the law, or common practice, is that you should not pass a parked school bus unless it is absolutely safe to do so. If you can pass, you must keep your speed to a walking pace. It is the same when you drive past a school when the children are outside. The law, or best practice, says you should reduce your speed to a crawl.

We would never dream of suggesting that you would ever break the speed limit, but if you are tempted it is worth remembering that European police seem to have as many speed cameras as British police. The difference between speeding in the UK and mainland Europe is in the way fines can be levied. If you are caught in a manned speed trap you may be expected to pay an on-the-spot fine, so it's no good arguing that you haven't got enough money to pay the fine. Most manned speed traps will take cash, traveller's cheques, debit and credit cards.

Driving in Europe

Checklist

Before you set off for a holiday abroad it's worth making yourself a checklist of things to do, and what to pack – we've been travelling abroad several times a year for more than thirty years and we still don't rely on our memory for this, so it's best to consult a checklist; here's the one we use:

- ☐ Passports
- ☐ Tickets
- ☐ Motor Insurance Certificate, including Green Card or Continental Cover clause
- ☐ V5 Registration Document and/or (if not your own vehicle) the owners authority
- ☐ Breakdown Insurance Certificate
- ☐ Driving Licence (The new PHOTO style licence is now MANDATORY in most European countries)
- ☐ Form E1-11 (to extend NHS Insurance to European destinations)
- ☐ Foreign Currency (EUROS, and Swiss Francs if appropriate) and/or Travellers Cheques
- ☐ Credit Card(s)
- ☐ Campsite Guide(s) and Tourist Guide(s)
- ☐ Maps/Road Atlas
- ☐ GB Stickers on car and caravan/trailer
- ☐ Beam deflectors to ensure that your headlights dip towards the right hand side
- ☐ Red Warning Triangle
- ☐ Spare vehicle/caravan driving light bulbs
- ☐ Torch
- ☐ First-Aid Kit, including mosquito repellent
- ☐ Fire extinguisher
- ☐ Basic tool kit (e.g screwdriver, pliers, etc)
- ☐ Continental mains connector/adaptor, and a long cable – for continental sites
- ☐ Polarity tester
- ☐ Spare fuses for car and caravan
- ☐ Spare fan/alternator belt

Finally bear in mind it's well worth having your car and caravan serviced before you go, and do check that your outfit is properly 'trimmed' before you set off.

Be sensible at all times and do not leave valuables in your vehicle or leave anything visible which could tempt a petty thief. Take care if waved down by anyone; in the past tactics like this have been used to get you to leave your car so an accomplice can have a field day rummaging through your belongings.

Driving in France

The most likely thing to catch out the unwary first time motorist in France is their *Prioite a Droite* rule whereby you are required to give way to traffic entering from the right, even when they are joining a main road from a minor one. In recent years this rule has been abandoned on the approach to most main roads where there are now *Passage Protégé* signs (a yellow diamond, indicating you have priority) or by a sign saying *Vous n'avez pas Priorite* (ie. it's NOT your right of way).

French drivers have a reputation for driving fast, but recently the laws have been tightened up, the fines for speeding increased, and generally they probably don't drive any faster than we do in Britain, although the maximum speed limit on Autoroutes (motorways) in dry weather is 130 kph which is about 83 mph (110 kph in the wet, about 68 mph). Unlike Britain there are no lower limits for towing caravans.

Within towns, there are no speed limit signs as such, but usually the 'town sign' as you enter a town or village has a red reflective border around it and these signs serve as a 50 kph (30 mph) speed limit sign. It is actually a clever idea as it saves cluttering up the environment with loads of separate speed limit signs – the end of the speed-limited area is indicated by a similar sign on leaving the town or village, but this time the sign has a diagonal black line across it.

With regards to drinking and driving – don't! The limit is actually LOWER in France than it is in the UK (50 mg of alcohol per 100 ml of blood, as opposed to 80 mg in the UK).

The most important essential equipment which must be carried at all times is a warning triangle and a spare set of light bulbs. The minimum driving age in France is 18 years, and children under 10 years of age must occupy a rearward facing child seat, with a belt. Driver and passengers are all required to wear seat belts, and motor-cyclists are required to wear crash hats, and to ride with their headlights on at all times.

The following are particularly common road signs:

Allumez vos phares	switch on headlights
Peage	Toll booth ahead
Ralentissez	slow down
Rappel	continue to hold your speed down
Attention travaux	road works ahead
Deviation	diversion
Cedez le Passage	Give Way
Toutes Directions	means 'all directions' so keep following this route
Autres Directions	means all directions EXCEPT for places individually signed
Sens Interdit	no entry
Risque de Verglas	risk of black ice
Serrez a droite/gauche	keep to the right/left
Sortie	exit (from Autoroute)

Driving in Spain & Portugal

Spain

Driving in Spain presents few problems, but there is one piece of advice in particular which we would highlight, namely the need to have a Bail Bond (obtainable via your motor insurers) to avoid the risk of your car being impounded following an accident. It is also necessary to carry two warning triangles in Spain, as well as a spare set of bulbs.

Seat belts for all passengers are compulsory, and children under 12 years of age are not allowed to sit in the front unless using a proper child seat/harness; motorcyclists must wear crash hats. The maximum speed limits are roughly similar to those in the UK: 120 kph, or 75 mph on motorways, known as Autopistas, and 90 kph on main roads – there is a lower limit of 80 kph when towing.

The following are some of the more important road signs:

Ceda el Paso	Give Way
Despacio	Slow Down
Peligro	Danger!
Prioridad	Right of way
Peaje	Toll Booth
Prohibicion	Prohibited
Salida	Exit (from Autopista)

Portugal

Unfortunately Portugal has a very poor road safety record, particularly around the Algarve coastal area. Quite why this should be so is not entirely clear, but it may well have something to do with the fact that road surfaces vary from excellent to dreadful, sometimes with little or no warning! It is not uncommon to be driving along a well surfaced smooth tarmac road one moment only to be confronted with a stretch of cobbled road the next – somewhat unnerving to say the least, so concentration and care are the order of the day. Be prepared to give way to traffic on your right, even if it looks as if you have the right of way.

Speed limits are 120 kph (75 mph) on motorways (Auto-Estradas) and 90 kph on other main roads, but there are lower limits for towing (100 kph and 70 kph respectively).

Essential equipment consists of a warning triangle and spare set of light bulbs. Seat belts all round are mandatory, and children under 12 years of age are not allowed in the front seats unless wearing a child restraint; motorcyclists are required to wear crash hats and keep their headlights on at all times.

Driving Routes to Spain

Driving through Europe to Spain and Portugal

If you're planning to go on holiday to Spain or Portugal you can of course avoid the need to drive across Europe by taking one of the direct services from the UK to northern Spain operated by Brittany Ferries (Plymouth-Santander) or P&O (Portsmouth-Bilbao).

Route via the tunnel or short-sea ferry crossing

If you decide to cross the channel either via the tunnel or via one of the short-sea ferry crossings from Kent the most obvious route is to drive south through France as far as the city of Orange.

This route involves either driving round Paris on the crowded 'Peripherique' (the inner ring road) or via the slightly less crowded outer ring road the Franciliene. The alternative to these busy routes around Paris is to use the A26 and head for Reims, thus avoiding Paris completely.

From Reims continue on the A26 southbound to Troyes where you join the A5 to Langres.

At Langres join the A31 which by-passes Dijon to join up with the A7 near Beaune (the 'Autoroute du Soleil', the busiest autoroute in France during the summer) where you continue heading south past Lyon to Orange.

We suggest the following campsites for overnight stops; full details can be found in the Alan Rogers guide to France or on www.alanrogers.com.

A1 (south)
FR80030M   Camping du Port de Plaisance at Peronne

A26 (south)
FR02000   Camping-Caravaning du Vivier aux Carpes at Seraucourt-le-Grand
FR02060M   Camping Municipal at Guignicourt

A26/A4 (south)
FR51020M   Camping Municipal at Chalons-sur-Marne

A5 (south east)
FR52030   Camping Lac de la Liez at Langres

A6 (south towards Mediterranean)
FR89030M   Camping Les Coullemieres at Vermenton
FR21020M   Municipal Les Cents Vignes at Beaune
FR21030M   Municipal Savigny-les-Beaune, near Beaune
FR21060   Camping Les Bouleaux at Vignoles
FR71070   Castel Chateau de l'Eperviere at Gigny-sur-Saone
FR71010M   Camping Municipal at Macon

A7 (south towards Mediterranean)
FR26020   Castel Camping du Senaud at Albon
FR26030   Sunelia Le Grand Lierne at Chabeuil
FR26110   Les 4 Saisons Camping at Grane
FR26120   Gervanne Camping at Mirabel-et-Blacons

At Orange you'll need to take the A9 (signposted to Montpelier and Barcelone) which will take you right through to the Spanish border at Le Perthus, south of Perpignan.

Driving Routes to Spain

Suggested campsites for overnight stops

A9 (south towards Spain)
FR11080   Camping La Nautique at Narbonne
FR66180   Mas Llinas Camping at La Boulou

Once over the border the road number changes to the E15 which runs south past all the Costa Brava resorts to Barcelona. From Barcelona you have a choice depending on your ultimate destination – for Tarragona and the Costa Daurada, for Valencia and the Costa Blanca, or for the Costa del Sol and Gibraltar simply continue on the E15. At Malaga you have the choice of continuing west on the E15 towards Gibraltar, Cadiz and Seville, or of heading north on the A92/ N331 to Granada, and on to Madrid via the E5. If you are headed for Portugal, the E15 becomes the E5 at Algeciras (west of Gibraltar) heading north-west towards Cadiz and Seville. At Seville the E1 autoroute heads west through Huelva to the Portuguese border, Faro and the Algarve, whereas the E803/N433 running northwards from Seville by-passes the Algarve and heads directly for Lisbon.

Western Channel crossing via Normandy or Brittany

For those readers choosing a Western Channel crossing to Normandy or Brittany, there are a couple of alternative routes to Spain which from our own experience we've found to be a lot less busy. For Barcelona, Valencia and the Costa Blanca we would choose to travel down the west coast of France on the N137/ A83 south from Rennes to Niort where the Autoroute southwards becomes the A10 through to Bordeaux.

Suggested campsites for overnight stops:

N137 Rennes/Nantes road
FR44140M   Camping Municipal Henri Dubourg at Nozay

A10
FR17200   Camping-Caravaning Au Fil de l'Eau at Saintes
FR40140   Camping-Caravaning Lou P'tit Poun at St Martin-de-Seynanx

At Bordeaux there is a further choice – for San Sebastian, the Costa Verde, Madrid, the Costa del Sol or the Algarve we would pick up the A63 and the N10 via Biarritz to the Spanish border at Hendaye and continue to San Sebastian (where you have a further choice of heading southwest towards Madrid, the Costa del Sol or the Algarve, or continuing west towards Bilbao and Santander).

For those making for Barcelona, the Costa Brava, the Costa Daurada or even the Costa Blanca at Bordeaux we would take the A62 in a south-easterly direction to Toulouse, from where you have the choice of continuing on the autoroutes (A61 and A9) via Perpignan or of taking the new A66 Autoroute (signposted Andorre) and the N20 via Andorra more or less direct to Barcelona; quite a bit shorter, and cheaper in terms of autoroute tolls, but significantly slower if you're driving a fast car.

Suggested campsites for overnight stops:

A62 (soth east)
FR47100M   Camping Municipal at Tonneins

A66/N20 (south towards Andorre and Spain)
FR09060   Camping Le Pre Lombarde at Tarascon-sur-Ariege
FR09060   Camping du Lac at Foix

Driving Routes to Spain

As this route crosses directly over the Pyrenees, rather than skirting around them, it can also be quite challenging during the winter, especially as the weather can be extremely changeable: clear and sunny one moment, heavy snowfalls the next. It is worth bearing in mind that many passes across the Pyrenees and in the mountain ranges of Spain and Portugal, which are difficult to negotiate at the best of times (particularly with a caravan in tow), become impassable or completely closed during the winter. The following table gives an indication of the situation regarding the better known passes in SW France, Spain and Portugal:

Area	Name	From-to Road number	Height (metres) Gradient %	Comments
SW France	Aubisque	Argeles-Gazost/Eaux-Bonnes	1700 (10%)	Closed Oct-Jun Unsuitable for caravans
Andorra	Envalira	L'Hospitalet/Andorra N2	2400 (12.5%)	Sometimes closed Nov-Apr
Spain	Escudo	Santander/Burgos	1010 (14%)	Difficult in winter
Spain	Guadarrama	Guadarrama/St.Rafael	1510 (14%)	Usually open
Spain	Alto do Canizo	Verin/ Puebla de Sanabria	1100 (5.5%)	Usually open
France/Spain	Roncevalles	St.Jean-Pied-de-Port/ (Ibaneta) Pamplona C135	1060 (10%)	Usually open
Spain	Navacerrada	Madrid/Segovia	1880 (17%)	Slow but scenic
Spain	Picos de Europa	Unquera/ Riano	1600 (12%)	Sometimes closed Unsuitable for caravans
France/Spain	Pourtalet	Eaux-Chaudes/ Biescas	1800 (10%)	Usually open
France	Puymorens	Toulouse/Bourg-Madame	1920 (10%)	Closed Nov-May Unsuitable for caravans
France	Quillane	Quillan/Mont-Louis	1714 (8.5%)	Often closed Nov-Apr
Spain	Somosierra	Madrid/Burgos	1450 (10%)	Often closed Nov-Mar
France/Spain	Somport	Huesca/Pau N330/N134	1630 (10%)	Often closed Mar-Dec
Spain	Tosas	Puigcerda/Barcelona N152	1800 (10%)	Usually open
France	Tourmalet	Luz St Sauveur/ Ste Marie Campan	2115 (12.5%)	Often closed Oct-Jun Unsuitable for caravans

Save over 50% on your holiday

- 400 sites – all just £9.95 per night
- Maximum flexibility - go as you please
- Fantastic Ferry Deals

After 5 years Camping Cheque is still the fastest growing programme of its type. For choice, value and unbeatable Ferry Deals there is simply no alternative. Last year 120,000 people used nearly 1 million Camping Cheques and enjoyed half-price holidays around Europe. Make sure you don't miss out this year.

Huge off peak savings

400 quality campsites in 18 European countries, including the UK, all at just £9.95 per night for pitch + 2 adults, including electricity. That's a saving of up to 55% off normal site tariffs. And with special free night deals (14 nights for 11 Cheques, 60 nights for 30 Cheques etc) the price can reduce to under a fiver a night!

ferry savings
Ask about our famous special offers

 Caravans/trailers Go **FREE**
 Motorhomes Priced As Cars

Conditions apply – ask for details

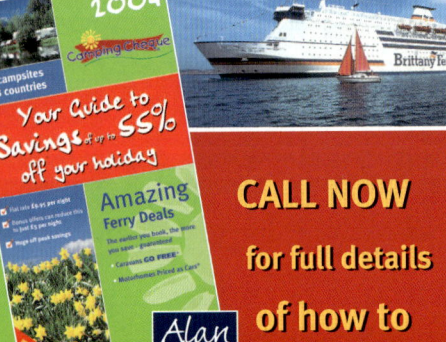

CALL NOW
for full details
of how to
save 50%

For full information visit the all-new website
www.campingcheque.co.uk

Buy Cheques, check ferry availability,
book everything on-line AND SAVE!

0870 405 4057

SAVE UP TO 66%

YOU'VE CHOSEN THE RIGHT CAMPSITE NOW CHOOSE THE RIGHT MAGAZINE...

SAVE 10%
12 issues £32

SAVE 38%
12 issues £21.99

'SAVE 66%' Subscribe to **MMM** & Add 12 issues of **Which motorcaravan** for only £11.99

SAVE 21%
12 issues £28

SAVE 24%
1 Year (10 issues) £22.50

SAVE 11%
1 Year (6 issues) £14.99

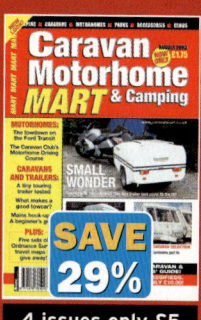

SAVE 29%
4 issues only £5

Call our **HOTLINE** on **01778 391180**
quoting ref: alanrogers04
Email: **subscriptions@warnersgroup.co.uk**
Visit our **website** at **www.warnersgroup.co.uk**
Also available from all good newsagents

Two of the best

Caravan

Your monthly guide to buying and maintaining your tourer, with details of all the UK's current models. It's also packed with touring tips and readers' own site reports

Motor Caravan MAGAZINE

Your practical route to motorhome freedom – which means in-depth tests, touring ideas and valuable practical advice. We want YOU to get the best from your motorhome!

Subscribe and save 25%
Just call our special hotline number below

+44 (0)845 676 7778

Lines are open seven days a week, 9am – 9pm. Closing date 15 November 2004
Quote code **Caravan 28V** or **Motor Caravan 28U** when calling

25% discount is by six-monthly direct debit only. All other payment options will receive a 15% discount

Saga Caravan and Motorhome Insurance

Wide-ranging cover at low prices

Saga is one of the main providers of caravan and motorhome insurance in the UK for people aged 50 and over. If you are looking for high levels of cover at low prices, it could pay to call us.

Saga Caravan and Motorhome Insurance includes:

- All year round cover throughout Europe, at no extra cost

- 'New for old' caravan or motorhome replacement - if your caravan is less than five years old or your motorhome is less than two years old and with a mileage of under 12,000, and it is either stolen or damaged beyond repair, providing you were its first owner

- Substantial cover for your personal belongings and camping equipment

- No Claim Discount available, subject to your past claims experience.

SAGA

For a personal quotation or instant cover call free on

0800 096 4087

stating reference GP8321

Lines are open 8.30am-7pm weekdays and 9am-1pm Saturday.
Telephone calls may be monitored or recorded for staff training purposes.

For more information or to e-mail us, visit www.saga.co.uk

Saga Services would like to send you information about other Saga products and services and may pass on your details to other Saga companies for this purpose.

TRY AN ISSUE FOR 1p

No risk, no commitment

Practical Caravan is written by enthusiasts for enthusiasts. Each issue is packed with superb photography, great holiday locations, model and park reviews, technical advice, reader tips and stories, and much more. So, try the first issue for 1p.

It beats paying £3.15 for an issue in the shops! And if for some reason you don't enjoy your issue, simply write to us within the first month and no further payment will be taken! But we are sure you'll love it - and you don't have to do anything - your subscription will automatically continue at the low rate of £8.50 every 3 issues - saving you 10% off the shop price!

PLUS
- **GET EVERY ISSUE DELIVERED TO YOUR DOOR**
- **NEVER MISS AN ISSUE**
- **PAY IN HANDY INSTALMENTS**

call our hotline number now

CALL 08456 777 812

PLEASE HAVE YOUR BANK DETAILS READY AND QUOTE ARFW3

the travel service

Save Time, Save Money

THE LOW COST PITCH AND FERRY RESERVATION SERVICE FOR READERS OF THE ALAN ROGERS GUIDES

INSPECTED CAMPSITES & SELECTED

We'll book your preferred campsite(s)
Choose from 150 of the finest inspected and selected sites across Europe (look for the Alan Rogers logo alongside the site descriptions in all Guides). We can even book site-owned mobile homes and chalets (ask for our other brochure).

Ask about our incredible Ferry Deals:
- ✓ **Caravans GO FREE**
- ✓ **Motorhomes Priced as Cars**

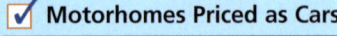

We'll organise your low cost Channel crossing - call us for a quote or visit **www.alanrogersdirect.com**

We'll provide comprehensive information
Leave it to the experts and enjoy peace of mind. Our own unique Travel Pack, complete with map and guide book will prove invaluable.

Don't leave it to chance, leave it to us

For your FREE colour brochure
0870 405 4055

alanrogersdirect.com
book on-line and save

Insurance

In theory European law means that a vehicle insured for use in the UK is still insured in any other European country. But some insurers know that doesn't really mean what you think it means. Somewhere in the fine print on page 37 of your policy you could find that if you take your vehicle abroad your insurance coverage is reduced to third party only. So two weeks before you venture abroad contact your vehicle insurer and find out if you need additional coverage.

Most vehicle breakdown insurance schemes claim to offer pan-European cover. But again it is worth asking just how good that cover is. If you car expires beside the road in a cloud of steam you don't want to have to try explaining the problem to a telephone receptionist who is fluent in every language – except yours.

The travel insurers Alan Rogers work with (see advert on page 188) operate language-specific call centres. If anything goes wrong you'll speak to somebody totally fluent in your language. What all insurers will insist on is that your vehicle must be in good condition before you set off on holiday. A full service a few weeks before your departure date will take care of that.

There is probably no subject which causes campers, caravanners and motorcaravanners venturing abroad more worries than insurance, so notwithstanding the notes above, if you're in any doubt about insurance it may be worthwhile you giving the subject some further thought, and the following will hopefully help to clarify things:

The problem with insurance is that there is often an 'overlap', so that sometimes one aspect is apparently covered on two insurance policies. To avoid confusion let's cut through the hype and take a clear look at the different types of insurance.

If you are planning on camping, caravanning or motorcaravanning abroad, this is what you will need.

Road traffic insurance

As previously stated, your ordinary car or motorcaravan road insurance will cover you anywhere in the EU. *However* many policies only provide minimum cover. So if you have an accident your insurance may only cover the cost of damage to the other person's property.

To maintain the same level of cover abroad as you enjoy at home you need to tell your vehicle insurer. Some will automatically cover you abroad with no extra cost and no extra paperwork. Some will say you need a Green Card (which is neither green or on card) but won't charge for it. Some will charge extra for the green card. Ideally you should contact your vehicle insurer 3-4 weeks before you set off, and confirm your conversation with them in writing.

A good insurance company will provide a European recognised accident report form. On this you mark details of damage to yours and the other party's property and draw a little diagram showing where the vehicles were in relation to each other. You give a copy of your form to the other motorist; he gives you a copy of his. It prevents all the shouting which often accompanies accidents in this country.

Holiday insurance

This is a multi-part insurance. One part covers your vehicles. If they breakdown or are involved in an accident they can be repaired or returned to this country. The best will even arrange to bring your vehicle home if the driver is unable to proceed.

Many new vehicles come with a free breakdown and recovery insurance which extends into Europe. Some professional motoring journalists have reported that the actual service this provides can be patchy and may not cover the recovery of a caravan or trailer. Our advice is to buy the motoring section of your holiday insurance.

The second section of holiday insurance covers people. It will include the cost of doctor, ambulance and hospital treatment if needed. If needed the better companies will even pay for English language speaking doctors and nurses and will bring a sick or injured holidaymaker home by air ambulance.

The third part of a good holiday insurance policy covers things. If someone breaks in to your motorhome and steals your passports and money, one phone call to the insurance company will have everything sorted out. If you manage to drive over your camera, it's covered.

An important part of the insurance that is often ignored is the cancellation section. Few things are as heartbreaking as having to cancel a holiday because a member of the family falls ill. Cancellation insurance can't take away the disappointment, but it makes sure you don't suffer financially as well.

There are a number of good insurance policies available including those provided for their members by the two major clubs and those offered by the leading camping holiday agents already mentioned in this guide.

Which ever insurance you choose we would advise not picking any of the policies sold by the High Street travel trade. Whilst they may be good, they don't cover the specific needs of campers, caravanners and motorcaravanners. And ideally you should arrange your holiday insurance at least four weeks before you set off.

Form E111

By arrangement between the British Government and rest of the European Community Governments, British holidaymakers can enjoy the same health care as that Government offers its own citizens. The form which shows you are entitled to take advantage of this arrangement is called E111.

E111 doesn't replace holiday insurance, but is in addition to. The form is available from all main UK Post Offices. Fill out one for every member of your family. Get it stamped by the counter staff and take it on holiday with you.

In theory one Form E111 lasts you for ever. But we've had reports that in some rural areas in Europe they may not understand that, so our advice is to get a new E111 every year. It is free.

And that is all you need to know about insurance. You know what they say about insurance, don't you? You'll only need it if you haven't got it.

www.insure4europe.com

Taking your own tent, caravan or motorhome abroad?
Looking for the best cover at the best rates?

Our prices considerably undercut most high street prices and the 'in-house insurance' of many tour operators whilst offering equivalent (or higher) levels of cover.

Our annual multi-trip policies offer superb value, covering you not only for your european camping holiday but also subsequent trips abroad for the next 12 months.

Total Peace of Mind

To give you total peace of mind during your holiday our insurance policies have been specifically tailored to cover most potential eventualities on a self-drive camping holiday. Each is organised through Voyager Insurance Services Ltd who specialize in travel insurance for Europe and for camping in particular. All policies are underwritten by UK Underwriting Ltd, on behalf of a consortium of insurance companies that are members of the Association of British Insurers and the Financial Ombudsman services.

24 Hour Assistance

Our personal insurance provides access to the services of Inter Group Assistant Services (IGAS), one of the UK's largest assistance companies. European vehicle assistance cover is provided by Green Flag who provide assistance to over 3 million people each year. With a Europe-wide network of over 7,500 garages and agents you know you're in very safe hands.

Both IGAS and Green Flag are very used to looking after the needs of campsite-based holidaymakers and are very familiar with the location of most European campsites, with contacts at garages, doctors and hospitals nearby.

Save with an Annual policy

If you are likely to make more than one trip to Europe over the next 12 months then our annual multi-trip policies could save you a fortune. Personal cover for a couple starts at just £95 and the whole family can be covered for just £115. Cover for up to 17 days wintersports participation is included.

Low Cost Annual multi-trip insurance

Premier Annual Europe self-drive
including 17 days wintersports
£95.00 per couple

Premier Annual Europe self-drive
including 17 days wintersports
£115.00 per family

Low Cost Combined Personal and Vehicle Assistance Insurance

Premier Family Package
10 days cover for vehicle, 2 adults plus dependent children under 16.
£75.00*

Premier Couples Package
10 days cover for vehicle and 2 adults
£61.00*

* Motorhomes, cars towing trailers and caravans, all vehicles over 4 years old and holidays longer than 10 days attract supplements – ask us for details. See leaflet for full terms and conditions.

One call and you're covered – ask us for a leaflet or no-obligation quote.

Policies despatched within 24 hours

0870 405 4059

insure4europe.com is a trading name of Alan Rogers Guides Ltd. 96 High Street, Tunbridge Wells, Kent TN1 1YF

Open all year

The following campsites are understood to accept caravanners and campers all year round, although the list also includes some sites that are open for at least ten months. These are marked with a star (*) – please refer to the site's individual entry for details. It is always wise to phone them to check as the facilities available, for example, may be reduced.

SPAIN

Cataluña-Catalunya
ES8063	El Llac*
ES8072	Les Medes*
ES8102	Mas Patoxas
ES8130	Calonge
ES9144	Stel
ES9121	Vall d'Ager
ES9123	El Solsones
ES8235	Bon Repos
ES8240	Bona Vista Kim
ES8390	Vilanova Park
ES8392	El Garrofer*
ES9140	Pedraforca
ES8395	Arc de Bara
ES8502	Montblanc Park
ES8506	Serra de Prades
ES8535	Cala d'Oques
ES8536	Ametlla

Comunidad Valenciana
ES8558	Vinaros
ES8570	Torre La Sal 2
ES8580	Bonterra
ES8612	Euro Camping (Oliva)
ES8615	Kiko
ES8625	Kiko
ES8675	Vall de Laguar
ES8680	Armanello
ES8681	Villasol
ES8682	Villamar
ES8683	Benisol
ES8685	El Raco
ES8686	Excalibur Medieval
ES8687	Cap Blanch
ES8689	Playa del Torres
ES8741	Florantilles
ES8742	La Marina
ES8743	Marjal
ES8754	Javea
ES8755	Moraira

Murcia
ES8745	La Fuente
ES8748	Los Madriles
ES8752N	El Portus
ES8753	La Manga

Andalucia
ES8749	Sopalmo
ES8751	Cuevas Mar
ES8760	Mar Azul
ES8765	La Garrofa
ES9270	Suspiro-Moro
ES9275	Los Avellanos
ES9280	Sierra Nevada
ES9285	Las Lomas
ES9290	El Balcon
ES8711	Nerja*
ES8782	Laguna Playa
ES8783N	Almanat
ES8790	La Laguna
ES8800	Marbella Playa
ES8802	Cabopino
ES8803	La Buganvilla
ES8809	El Sur
ES8812	Chullera 2
ES8850	Paloma
ES8855	Tarifa
ES8865	Playa Las Dunas
ES8889	Los Alcornocales
ES8871	Giralda
ES9081	Villsom
ES9082	Sevilla
ES9078	Los Villares
ES9080	El Brillante
ES9084	La Campiña*
ES9085	Carlos III
ES9089	Despenaperros

Extremadura
ES9087	Merida
ES9027	Monfrague
ES9028	Villueracas

Castilla La-Mancha
ES9088	Fuencaliente
ES9094	Aguzadera
ES9090	El Greco

Madrid
ES9091	Soto-Castillo
ES9092	Coto Cisneros
ES9200	El Escorial
ES9210	Pico-Miel

Castilla y Leon
ES9025	Regio
ES9022	El Folgoso
ES9044	Monumento
ES9250	Costajan
ES9253	Picon del Conde

Galicia
ES9024	As Cancelas

Asturias
ES8940	Los Cantiles
ES8965	Picos-Europa

Cantabria
ES8964	Molino
ES8973	Santillana

Pais Vasco-Euskadi
ES9035	Portuondo
ES9039	Gran Zarautz

La Rioja
ES9040	Haro*

Navarra
ES9043	Errota el Molino

Aragón
ES9060	Peña Montañesa
ES9062	Boltana
ES9064	Gavin
ES9070	Pirineos*

PORTUGAL

Algarve
PO8200	Valverde
PO8210	Albufeira
PO8220	Quarteira
PO8230	Olhao
PO8410	Armacao-Pera
PO8430	Sagres
PO8440	Quintos

Alentejo
PO8160	Porto Covo
PO8350	Markádia

Lisbon & Vale do Tejo
PO8100	S Pedro-Moel
PO8110	Valado
PO8130	Guincho
PO8140	Monsanto
PO8150	Caparica
PO8450	Colina-Sol*
PO8460	Vale Paraiso
PO8480	Foz do Arelho

Beiras & Centre
PO8040	Vagueira
PO8050	Sao Jacinto*
PO8090	Figueira da Foz
PO8330	Arganil
PO8360	Idhana

Porto & North
PO8010	Caminha*
PO8020	Viana-Castelo*
PO8030	Rio Alto
PO8370	Cerdeira
PO8380	Vilar de Mouros

Dogs

Since the introduction in 2000 of the Passports for Pets scheme many British campers and caravanners have been encouraged to take their pets with them on holiday. However, not only are the Pet Travel conditions understandably strict, the procedure is quite lengthy and complicated - you can check the current situation via the Passports for Pets website:

http://freespace.virgin.net/passports.forpets

If you are planning to take your dog we do advise you to phone the site first to check – there my be limits on numbers and breeds or times of the year when they are excluded. For the benefit of those who want to take their dogs to Spain and Portugal we list here those that have indicated to us that they NEVER accept dogs.

Never – these sites do not accept dogs at any time:

SPAIN					
Cataluña-Catalunya		**Castilla y Leon**		**PORTUGAL**	
ES8090	Cypsela	ES9251	Rio Lobos	**Alentejo**	
ES8101	Playa Brava	**Cantabria**		PO8170	São Miguel
ES8103	El Maset	ES9000	Playa Joyel	**North**	
ES9143	Pirineus	**Pais Vasco-Euskadi**		PO8380	Vilar de Mouros
ES9123	El Solsones	ES9038	Orio		
ES8420	Stel (Roda)				
ES8481	Cambrils				
ES8530	Playa Montroig				
ES8537N	Templo del Sol				
ES8540	Torre del Sol				
Comunidad Valenciana					
ES8560	Playa Tropicana				
ES8681	Villasol				
ES8682	Villamar				
ES8741	Florantilles				
Murcia					
ES8748	Los Madriles				
Andalucia					
ES8751	Cuevas Mar				

Maybe – accepted at any time but with certain restrictions:

SPAIN			PORTUGAL		
Cataluña-Catalunya			**Alentejo**		
ES8060	Ballena Alegre 2	Special Area	PO8350	Markádia	not July-Aug
ES8072	Les Medes	not July-Aug	**North**		
ES8075	Estartit	not 20/6-20/8	PO8370	Cerdeira	not July-Aug
ES8080	Delfin Verde	not 12/7-15/8			
ES8160	Cala Gogo	not 1/7 - 26/8			
ES8533	Els Prat	not 1/7-31/8			
Andalucia					
ES8803	La Buganvilla	not July-Aug			

Fishing

We are pleased to include details of sites which provide facilities for fishing on site. However, it is always best to contact sites directly to check that they provide for your individual requirements.

SPAIN

Cataluña-Catalunya
ES8010	Castell Mar
ES8015	La Laguna
ES8030	Nautic Almata
ES8035	Amfora
ES8040	Las Dunas
ES8050	Aquarius
ES8060	Ballena Alegre 2
ES8063	El Llac
ES8074	Paradis
ES8080	Delfin Verde
ES8101	Playa Brava
ES8135	Eurocamping
ES8140	Treumal
ES8160	Cala Gogo
ES8200	Cala Llevadó
ES8230	El Pinar
ES8232	Bella Terra
ES9143	Pirineus
ES9142	Solana del Segre
ES8235	Bon Repos
ES8310	Ballena Alegre
ES8312	Tres Estrellas
ES8410	Playa Bara
ES8420	Stel (Roda)
ES8483	Tamarit
ES8486	Torre de la Mora
ES8520	Marius
ES8530	Playa Montroig
ES8533	Els Prat
ES8535	Cala d'Oques
ES8536	Ametlla
ES8537N	Templo del Sol
ES8540	Torre del Sol

Comunidad Valenciana
ES8560	Playa Tropicana
ES8570	Torre La Sal 2
ES8612	Euro Camping
ES8615	Kiko
ES8687	Cap Blanch
ES8689	Playa del Torres
ES8743	Marjal

Murcia
ES8752N	El Portus
ES8753	La Manga

Andalucia
ES8760	Mar Azul
ES8765	La Garrofa
ES8782	Laguna Playa
ES8783N	Almanat
ES8855	Tarifa

Castilla La-Mancha
ES9090	El Greco
ES9091	Soto-Castillo
ES9092	Coto Cisneros

Asturias
ES8945	Lagos-Somiedo
ES8950	Costa Verde
ES8960	La Paz
ES8965	Picos-Europa

Cantabria
ES8962	La Isla
ES8970	Arenas-Pechon
ES9000	Playa Joyel

Pais Vasco-Euskadi
ES9045	Angosto
ES9035	Portuondo

La Rioja
ES9040	Haro

Navarra
ES9043	Errota el Molino

Aragón
ES9060	Peña Montañesa
ES9125	Lago Barasona

PORTUGAL

Alentejo
PO8350	Markádia

North
PO8030	Rio Alto

Horse Riding

We understand that the following sites have horse riding stables on site. However, we do recommned that you contact the campsite to check that they meet your requirements.

SPAIN

Cataluña-Catalunya
ES8015	La Laguna
ES8030	Nautic Almata
ES8506	Serra de Prades

Comunidad Valenciana
ES8625	Kiko

Andalucia
ES8751	Cuevas Mar
ES8760	Mar Azul
ES9290	El Balcon

Extremadura
ES9027	Monfrague

Asturias
ES8945	Lagos-Somiedo

Cantabria
ES8962	La Isla
ES9000	Playa Joyel

Navarra
ES9043	Errota el Molino

Aragón
ES9060	Peña Montañesa

PORTUGAL

Alentejo
PO8350	Markádia

Portugal – Map 1

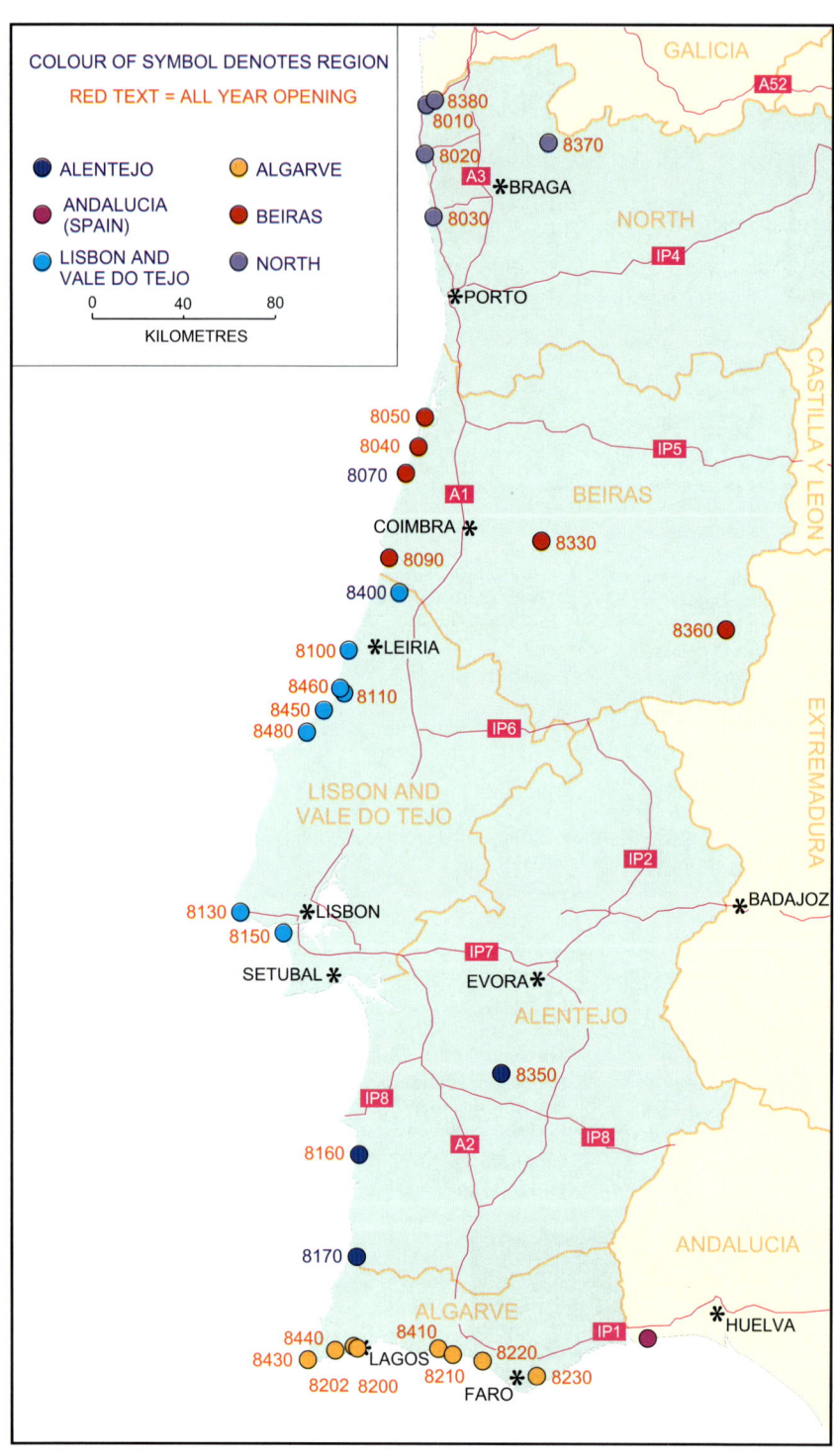

Andalucia & Murcia – Map 2

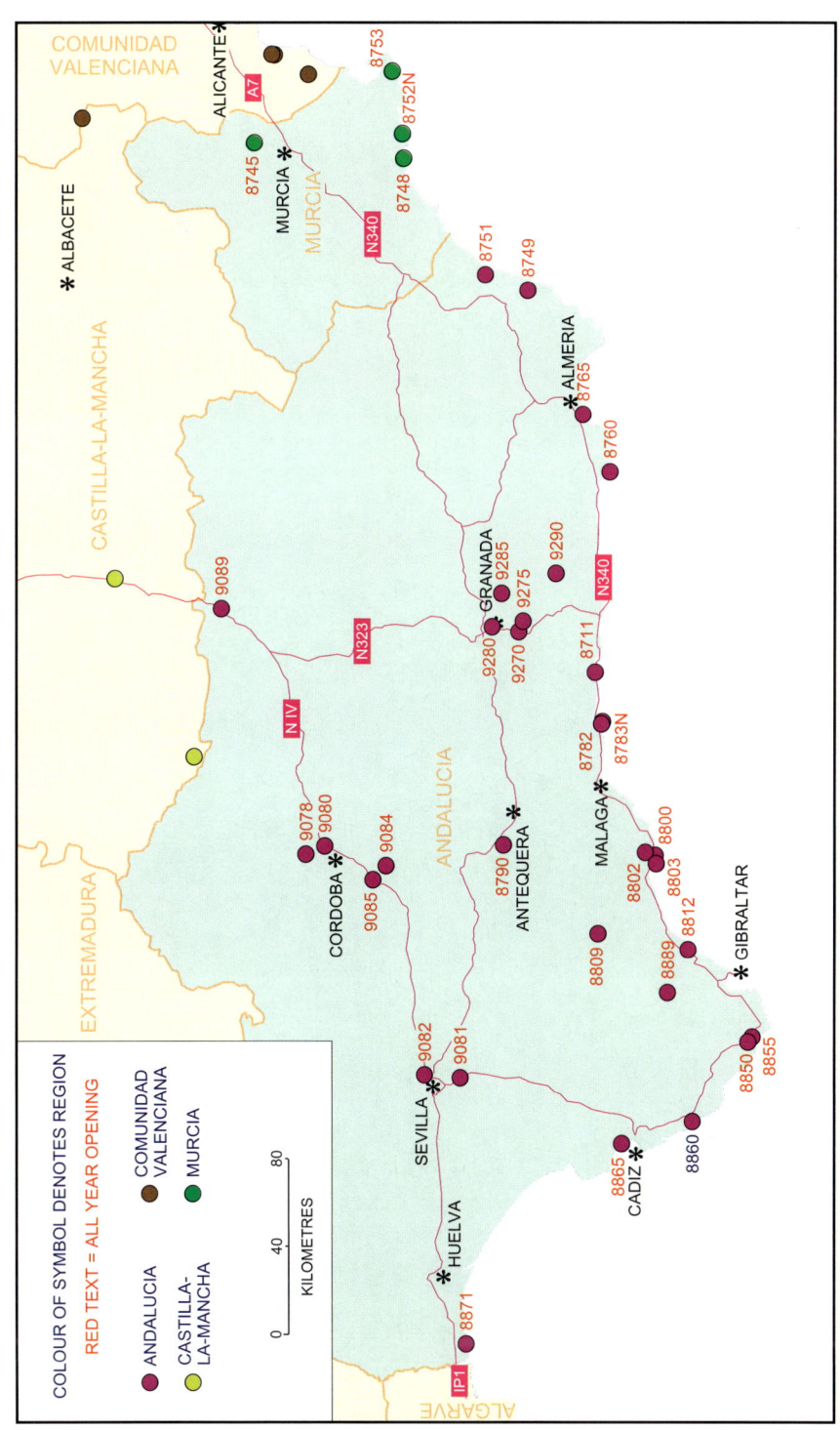

Extremadura, Castilla La-Mancha, Madrid & Comunidad Valenciana – Map 3

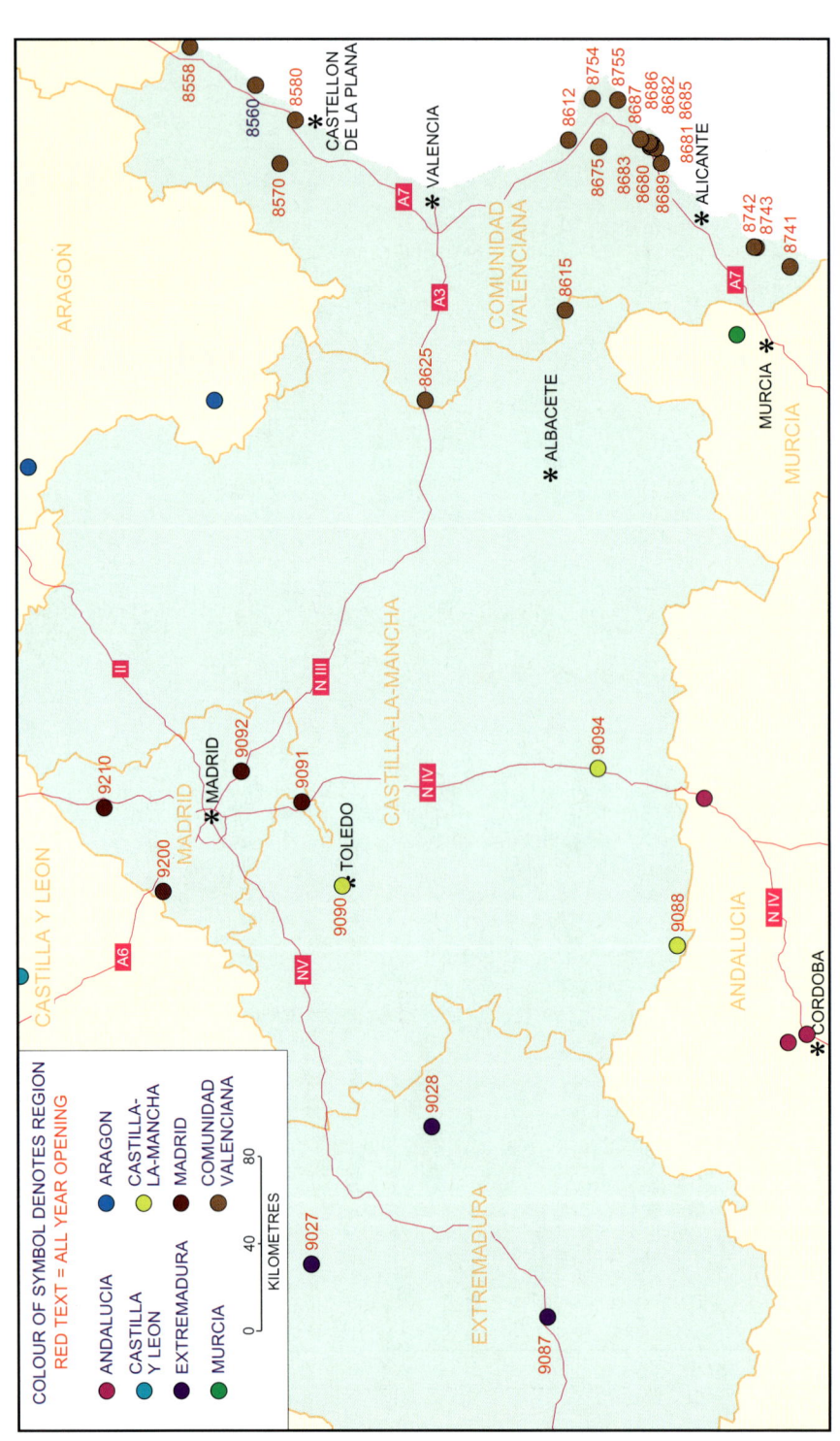

Galicia, Asturias, Cantabria, Pais Vasco-Euskadi, Castilla y León & La Rioja – Map 4

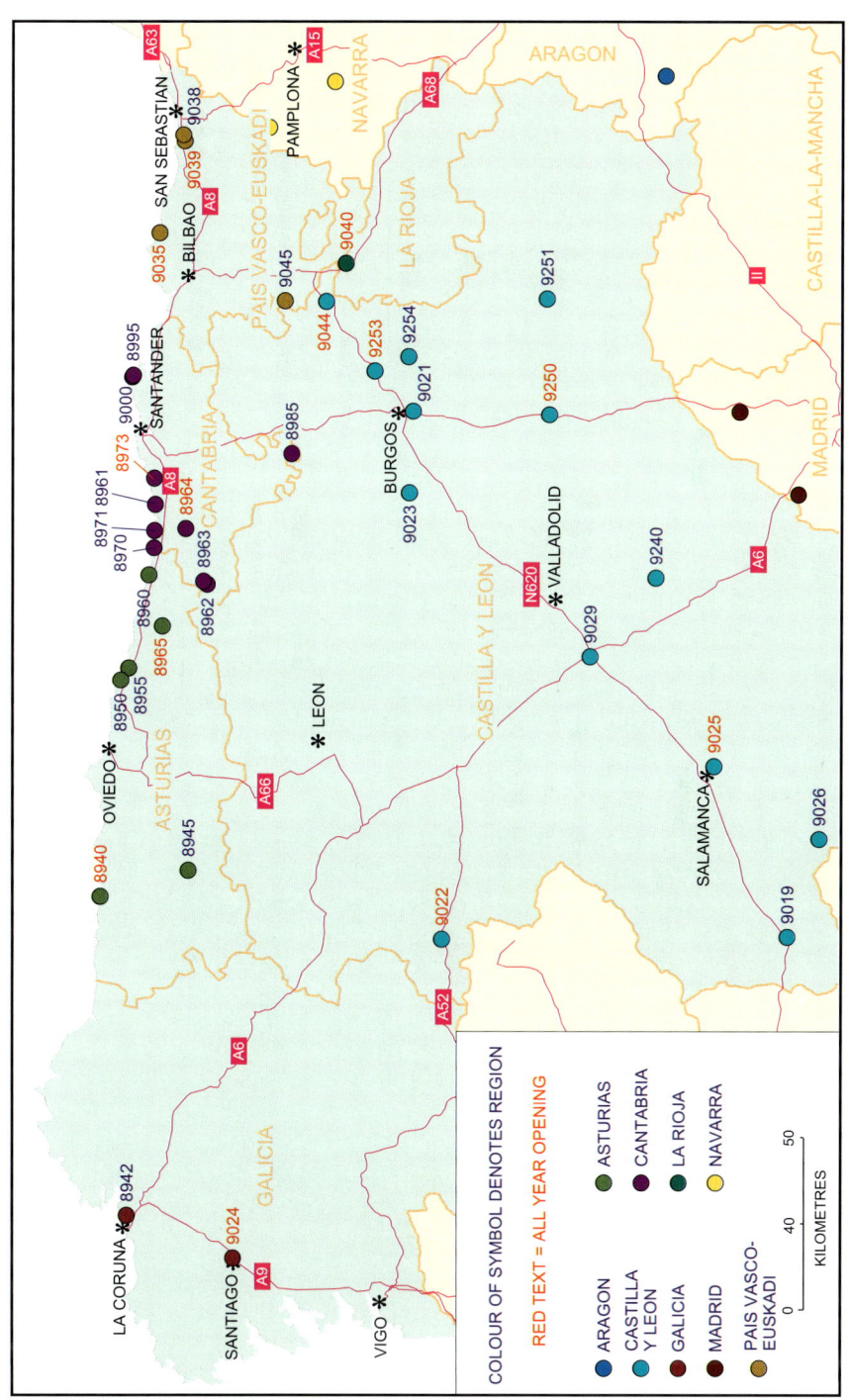

Navarra, Aragón & Catalunya – Map 5

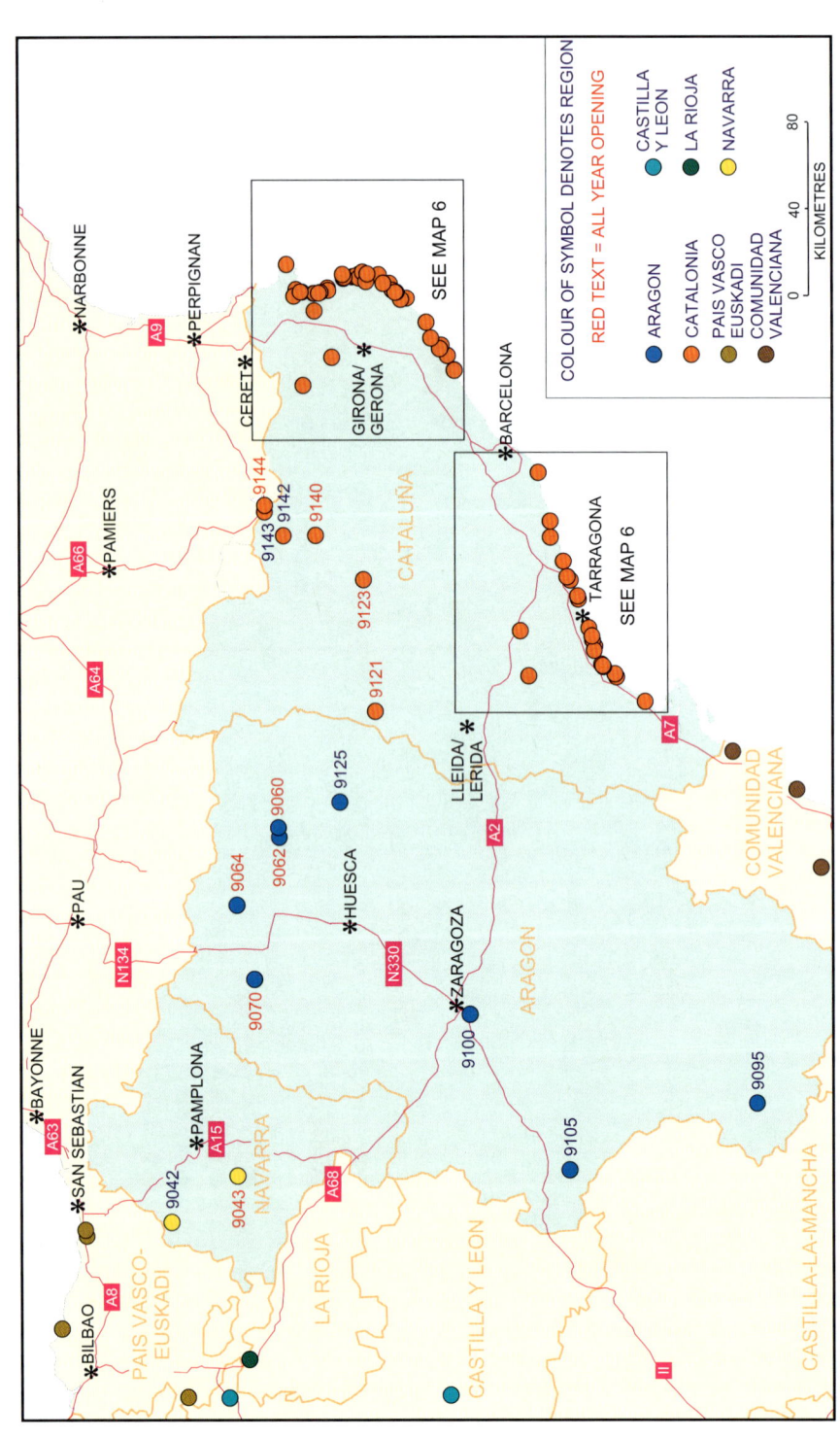

North East Catalunya – Map 6a

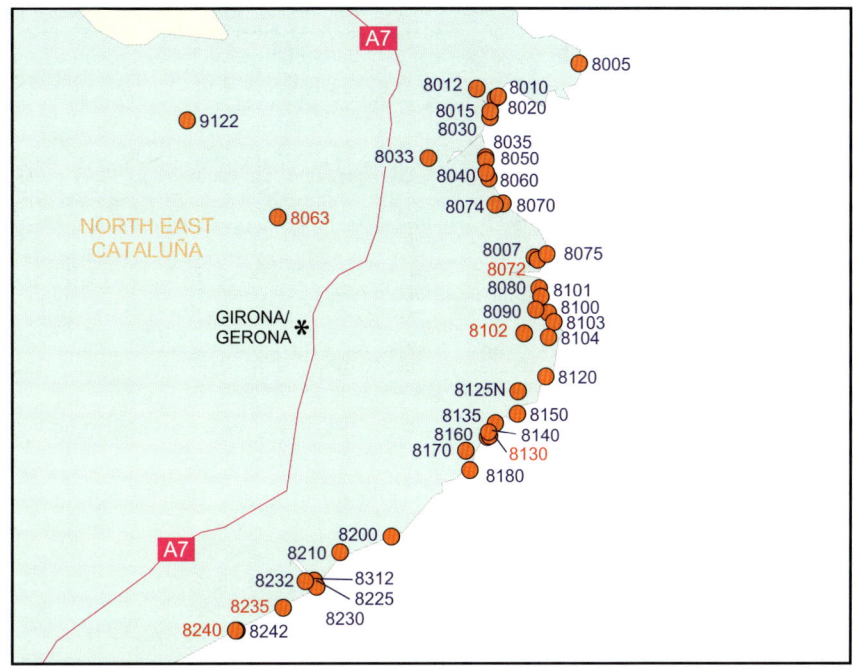

South West Catalunya – Map 6b

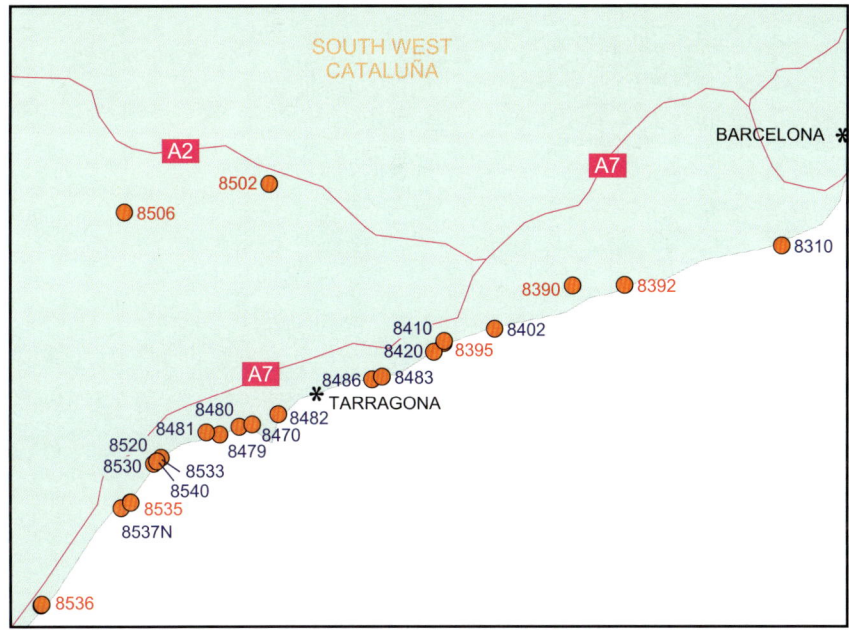

Reports by Readers

We always welcome reports from readers concerning sites which they have visited. Generally reports provide us with invaluable feedback on sites already included in the Guide or, in the case of those not featured in our Guide, they provide information which we can follow up with a view to adding them in future editions. However, if you have a complaint about a site, this should be addressed to the campsite owner, preferably in person before you leave.

Please make your comments either on this form or on plain paper. It would be appreciated if you would indicate the approximate dates when you visited the site and, in the case of potential new sites, provide the correct name and address and, if possible, include a campsite brochure. Send your reports to:

Alan Rogers Guide, Manor Garden, Burton Bradstock, Bridport DT6 4QA

Name of Campsite and Ref. No. (or address for new recommendations):

....

....

Dates of visit: ....

Comments:

Reader's Name and Address: ....

....

....

....

Town and Village Index

Ager	47	Granada	89	Platja de Pals	34, 40
Albarracin	146	Guadalupe	105	Polientes	131
Albufeira	152	Guardamar del Segura	81	Porto Covo	158
Alcossebre	70	Güejar-Sierra	90	Potes	129
Alfaz del Pi	76	Guils de Cerdanya	44	Póvoa de Varzim	171
Almayate	93	Haro	138	Puigcerdá	44
Almeria	88	Hospitalet de L'Infant	66	Quarteira	154
Almerimar	88	Hospitalet del Infante	67	Ribera de Cabanes	71
Altea	77	Idanha-a-Nova	168	Roda de Bara	54, 55
Alvito	158	Isla Cristina	98	Ronda	95
Ameyugo	116	Isla Plana	83	Ruiloba	128
Aranda de Duero	117	Jávea	80	Sabinillas-Manilva	96
Aranjuez	110	Jimena de la Frontera	98	Sagres	155
Arganda del Rey	110	La Cabrera	111	Saldés	49
Arganil	168	La Carlota	101	Salou	56, 58, 60
Armacao de Pera	154	La Manga del Mar Menor	84	San Miguel de Salinas	78
Aveiro	166	La Marina	79	San Pere Pescador	29
Avin-Onis	126	La Pineda	61	San Vicente de la Barquera	130
Banos de Fortuna	83	La Puebla de Castro	145	Sant Antoni de Calonge	45
Banyoles	45	Labuerda	143	Sant Feliu de Guíxols	43
Begur	36	Lagos	151, 152	Sant Pere Pescador	26-28
Bellver de Cerdanya	47	L'Ametlla de Mar	66	Santa Cilia de Jaca	144
Benicasim	71	L'Escala	30, 32	Santa Cruz	122
Benidorm	74-77	L'Estartit	32, 33	Santa Elena	102
Blanes	41, 42	Lisboa		Santa Marta de Tormes	114
Boltaña	143	Llafranc	38	Santa Susana	52
Budens	155	Lloret de Mar	46	Santaella	102
Burgos	115	Louriçal	162	Santiago	121
Cabuérniga	129	Luarca	124	Santillana del Mar	131
Calafell	55	Malpartida de Plasencia	104	Sao Martinho do Porto	164
Caldas da Rainha	164	Marbella	93, 94	Sao Pedro de Moel	161
Calella de la Costa	48	Maro	91	Sevilla	99
Calonge	38, 39	Mendigorria	141	Sitges	50
Cambrils	60	Mérida	104	Solsona	46
Caminha	170	Miami-Playa	63, 64	Somiedo	124
Campell	74	Mira	167	Tarifa	95, 96
Campo do Gerês	172	Miranda del Castañar	113	Tarragona	58, 63
Caravia Alta	125	Mojacar	87	Toledo	108
Cartagena	84	Monasterio de Rodilla	117	Tordesillas	119
Cascais	160	Montagut	43	Torre del Mar	92
Castelló d'Empúries	23, 24, 26	Montblanc	53	Torroella de Montgrí	30
Castrojeriz	116	Mont-Roig Del Camp	64	Tossa de Mar	42
Ciudad Rodrigo	113	Montroig	62	Turieno-Potes	128
Coca	119	Moraira-Teulada	81	Ucero	118
Colunga	125	Mundaka	135	Vagos	166
Conil de la Frontera	97	Nazaré	162, 163	Valdepeñas	107
Cordoba	100, 101	Noja	132, 133	Vidiago-Llanes	126
Costa da Caparica	160	Nuevalos	146	Vigo de Sanabria	115
Darque	170	Odemira	157	Viladecans 49	
Dilar	90	Olhao	153	Vilanova de Prades	53
El Escorial	111	Oliva	72, 73	Vilanova i la Geltru	51
El Puerto de Santa Maria	97	Orio	135	Vilar de Mouros	171
Empúria-Brava	22	Palamos	37	Villajoyosa	78
Etxarri-Aranatz	140	Palomares	87	Villanañe	136
Figueira da Foz	167	Pals	35	Villargordo del Cabriel	72
Fuencaliente	107	Pechon	130	Villasur de Herreros	118
Fuente de Piedra	92	Pitres	91	Vinaros	70
Gavá	52	Platja d'Aro	40	Zaragoza	145
Gavín	144	Platja de Pals	34	Zarauz	136

Campsite Index by Number

SPAIN

ES8010	Camping Castell Mar	24
ES8012	Camping Mas Nou	23
ES8015	Camping-Caravaning La Laguna	26
ES8020	Camping Internacional de Amberes	22
ES8030	Camping Nautic Almata	24
ES8033	Camping Las Palmeras	26
ES8035	Camping L'Amfora	27
ES8040	Camping Las Dunas	28
ES8050	Camping Aquarius	28
ES8060	Camping La Ballena Alegre 2	29
ES8063	Camping El Llac	45
ES8070	Camping L'Escala	30
ES8072	Camping Les Medes	33
ES8074	Camping Paradis	32
ES8075	Camping Estartit	32
ES8080	Camping El Delfin Verde	30
ES8090	Camping Cypsela	34
ES8100	Camping Inter-Pals	40
ES8101	Camping Playa Brava	34
ES8102	Camping Mas Patoxas	35
ES8103	Camping El Maset	36
ES8104	Camping Begur	36
ES8120	Kim's Camping	38
ES8125N	Camping Relax-Nat	37
ES8130	Camping Int. de Calonge	39
ES8135	Eurocamping	45
ES8140	Camping Treumal	38
ES8150	Camping Int. de Palamos	37
ES8160	Camping Cala Gogo	39
ES8170	Camping Valldaro	40
ES8180	Camping Sant Pol	43
ES8200	Camping Cala Llevadó	42
ES8210	Camping Tucan	46
ES8225	Camping La Masia	41
ES8230	Beach Camp El Pinar	42
ES8232	Camping Bella Terra	41
ES8235	Camping Bon Repos	52
ES8240	Camping Botànic Bona Vista Kim	48
ES8242	Camping Roca Grossa	48
ES8310	Camping La Ballena Alegre	49
ES8312	Camping Tres Estrellas	52
ES8390	Camping Vilanova Park	51
ES8392	Camping El Garrofer	50
ES8395	Camping Arc de Bara	54
ES8402	Camping Vendrell Platja	55
ES8410	Camping Playa Bara	54
ES8420	Camping Stel	55
ES8470	Camping La Siesta	60
ES8479	Camping Playa Cambrils-Don Camilo	60
ES8480	Camping and Bungalows Sanguli	56
ES8481	Camping Cambrils Park	58
ES8482	Camping La Pineda de Salou	61
ES8483	Camping Tamarit Park	58
ES8486	Camping Torre de la Mora	63
ES8502	Camping Caravaning Montblanc Park	53
ES8506	Camping Serra de Prades	53
ES8520	Camping Marius	63
ES8530	Playa Montroig	62
ES8533	Camping Els Prats	64
ES8535	Camping-Pension Cala d'Oques	67
ES8536	Camping-Caravanning Ametlla	66
ES8537N	Camping Naturista El Templo del Sol	66
ES8540	Yelloh! Village La Torre del Sol	64
ES8558	Camping Vinaros	70
ES8560	Camping Playa Tropicana	70
ES8570	Camping Torre La Sal 2	71
ES8580	Camping Bonterra	71
ES8612	Euro Camping	72
ES8615	Kiko Park	73
ES8625	Kiko Park Rural	72
ES8675	Camping Vall de Laguar	74
ES8680	Camping Armanello	74
ES8681	Camping Villasol	75
ES8682	Camping Villamar	75
ES8683	Camping Benisol	76
ES8685	Camping Caravaning El Raco	77
ES8686	Excalibur Medieval Camping	76
ES8687	Camping Cap Blanch	77
ES8689	Camping Playa del Torres	78
ES8711	Nerja Camping	91
ES8741	Camping Florantilles	78
ES8742	Camping Internacional La Marina	79
ES8743	Complejo Ecoturistico Marjal	81
ES8745	Camping La Fuente	83
ES8748	Camping Los Madriles	83
ES8749	Camping Sopalmo	87
ES8751	Camping Cuevas Mar	87
ES8752N	Camping Naturista El Portus	84
ES8753	Caravaning La Manga	84
ES8754	Camping Jávea	80
ES8755	Camping-Caravanning Moraira	81
ES8760	Camping Mar Azul	88
ES8765	Camping La Garrofa	88
ES8782	Camping-Caravaning Laguna Playa	92
ES8783N	Camping Naturista Almanat	93
ES8790	Camping La Laguna	92
ES8800	Camping Marbella Playa	93
ES8802	Camping Cabopino	94
ES8803	Camping La Buganvilla	94
ES8809	Camping El Sur	95
ES8812	Camping Chullera 2	96
ES8850	Camping Paloma	95
ES8855	Camping Tarifa	96
ES8860	Camping Fuente del Gallo	97
ES8865	Camping Playa Las Dunas	97
ES8871	Camping Giralda	98
ES8889	Camping Los Alcornocales	98
ES8940	Camping Los Cantiles	124
ES8942	Camping Los Manzanos	122
ES8945	Camping Lagos de Somiedo	124
ES8950	Camping Costa Verde	125
ES8955	Camping Arenal de Moris	125
ES8960	Camping La Paz	126
ES8961	Camping El Helguero	128
ES8962	Camping La Isla	128
ES8963	Camping La Viorna	129
ES8964	Camping El Molino de Cabuerniga	129
ES8965	Camping Picos de Europa	126
ES8970	Camping Las Arenas-Pechon	130

Code	Name	Page
ES8971	Camping Playa de Oyambre	130
ES8973	Camping Santillana	131
ES8985	Camping Valderredible	131
ES8995	Camping Los Molinos	132
ES9000	Camping Playa Joyel	133
ES9019	Camping La Pesquera	113
ES9021	Camping Municipal Fuentes Blancas	115
ES9022	Camping El Folgoso	115
ES9023	Camping Camino de Santiago	116
ES9024	Camping As Cancelas	121
ES9025	Camping Regio	114
ES9026	Camping El Burro Blanco	113
ES9027	Parque Natural de Monfrague	104
ES9028	Camping Las Villueracas	105
ES9029	Camping El Astral	119
ES9035	Camping Portuondo	135
ES9038	Camping Orio	135
ES9039	Gran Camping Zarautz	136
ES9040	Camping de Haro	138
ES9042	Camping Etxarri	140
ES9043	Camping Errota el Molino	141
ES9044	Camping Monumento al Pastor	116
ES9045	Camping Angosto	136
ES9060	Camping Peña Montañesa	143
ES9062	Camping Boltana	143
ES9064	Camping Gavín	144
ES9070	Centro de Vacaciones Pirineos	144
ES9078	Camping Los Villares	100
ES9080	Camping Municipal El Brillante	101
ES9081	Camping Villsom	99
ES9082	Camping Sevilla	99
ES9084	Camping La Campiña	102
ES9085	Camping Carlos III	101
ES9087	Camping Merida	104
ES9088	Camping de Fuencaliente	107
ES9089	Camping Despenaperros	102
ES9090	Camping El Greco	108
ES9091	Camping Soto del Castillo	110
ES9092	Camping Lagos Coto Cisneros	110
ES9094	Camping La Aguzadera	107
ES9095	Camping Ciudad de Albarracin	146
ES9100	Camping Casablanca	145
ES9105	Camping Lago Park	146
ES9121	Camping de la Vall d'Ager	47
ES9122	Camping Montagut	43
ES9123	Camping El Solsones	46
ES9125	Camping Lago Barasona	145
ES9140	Camping Repos del Pedraforca	49
ES9142	Camping Solana del Segre	47
ES9143	Camping Pirineus	44
ES9144	Camping Stel	44
ES9200	Caravanning El Escorial	111
ES9210	Camping Pico de la Miel	111
ES9240	Camping El Cantosal	119
ES9250	Camping Costajan	117
ES9251	Camping Cañon del Rio Lobos	118
ES9253	Camping Picon del Conde	117
ES9254	Camping Puerta de la Demanda	118
ES9270	Camping Suspiro del Moro	89
ES9275	Los Avellanos de Sierra Nevada	90
ES9280	Camping Sierra Nevada	89
ES9285	Camping Las Lomas	90
ES9290	Camping El Balcon de Pitres	91

PORTUGAL

Code	Name	Page
PO8010	Orbitur Camping Caminha	170
PO8020	Orbitur Camping Viana do Castelo	170
PO8030	Orbitur Camping Rio Alto	171
PO8040	Parque de Campismo da Vagueira	166
PO8050	Orbitur Camping Sao Jacinto	166
PO8070	Orbitur Camping Mira	167
PO8090	Orbitur Camping Figueira da Foz	167
PO8100	Orbitur Camping Sao Pedro de Moel	161
PO8110	Orbitur Camping Valado	162
PO8130	Orbitur Camping Guincho	160
PO8150	Orbitur Camping Costa da Caparica	160
PO8160	Parque de Campismo Porto Covo	158
PO8170	Parque de Campismo São Miguel	157
PO8200	Orbitur Camping Valverde	151
PO8202	Parque de Campismo de Espiche	152
PO8210	Parque de Campismo Albufeira	152
PO8220	Orbitur Camping Quarteira	154
PO8230	Camping Olhao	153
PO8330	Camping Municipal Arganil	168
PO8350	Camping Markádia	158
PO8360	Parque Campismo de Municipal	168
PO8370	Parque de Campismo de Cerdeira	172
PO8380	Parque Natural de Vilar de Mouros	171
PO8400	Campismo O Tamanco	162
PO8410	Parque de Campismo de Armacao	154
PO8430	Orbitur Camping Sagres	155
PO8440	Parque de Campismo Quintos	155
PO8450	Parque de Campismo Colina do Sol	164
PO8460	Camping-Caravaning Vale Paraiso	163
PO8480	Orbitur Camping Foz do Arelho	164

Campsite Index by Region

SPAIN

Cataluña-Catalunya

ES8020	Camping Internacional de Amberes	22
ES8012	Camping Mas Nou	23
ES8010	Camping Castell Mar	24
ES8030	Camping Nautic Almata	24
ES8015	Camping-Caravaning La Laguna	26
ES8033	Camping Las Palmeras	26
ES8035	Camping L'Amfora	27
ES8040	Camping Las Dunas	28
ES8050	Camping Aquarius	28
ES8060	Camping La Ballena Alegre 2	29
ES8070	Camping L'Escala	30
ES8080	Camping El Delfin Verde	30
ES8074	Camping Paradis	32
ES8075	Camping Estartit	32
ES8072	Camping Les Medes	33
ES8090	Camping Cypsela	34
ES8101	Camping Playa Brava	34
ES8102	Camping Mas Patoxas	35
ES8103	Camping El Maset	36
ES8104	Camping Begur	36
ES8125N	Camping Relax-Nat	37
ES8150	Camping Int. de Palamos	37
ES8120	Kim's Camping	38
ES8140	Camping Treumal	38
ES8130	Camping Int. de Calonge	39
ES8160	Camping Cala Gogo	39
ES8100	Camping Inter-Pals	40
ES8170	Camping Valldaro	40
ES8225	Camping La Masia	41
ES8232	Camping Bella Terra	41
ES8200	Camping Cala Llevadó	42
ES8230	Beach Camp El Pinar	42
ES8180	Camping Sant Pol	43
ES9122	Camping Montagut	43
ES9143	Camping Pirineus	44
ES9144	Camping Stel (Puigcerdá)	44
ES8063	Camping El Llac	45
ES8135	Eurocamping	45
ES8210	Camping Tucan	46
ES9123	Camping El Solsones	46
ES9121	Camping de la Vall d'Ager	47
ES9142	Camping Solana del Segre	47
ES8240	Camping Botànic Bona Vista Kim	48
ES8242	Camping Roca Grossa	48
ES8310	Camping La Ballena Alegre	49
ES9140	Camping Repos del Pedraforca	49
ES8392	Camping El Garrofer	50
ES8390	Camping Vilanova Park	51
ES8235	Camping Bon Repos	52
ES8312	Camping Tres Estrellas	52
ES8502	Camping-Caravaning Montblanc Park	53
ES8506	Camping Serra de Prades	53
ES8395	Camping Arc de Bara	54
ES8410	Camping Playa Bara	54
ES8402	Camping Vendrell Platja	55
ES8420	Camping Stel (Roda de Bará)	55
ES8480	Camping and Bungalows Sanguli	56
ES8481	Camping Cambrils Park	58
ES8483	Camping Tamarit Park	58
ES8470	Camping La Siesta	60
ES8479	Camping Playa Cambrils - Don Camilo	60
ES8482	Camping La Pineda de Salou	61
ES8530	Playa Montroig Camping Park	62
ES8486	Camping Torre de la Mora	63
ES8520	Camping Marius	63
ES8533	Camping Els Prats	64
ES8540	Yelloh! Village La Torre del Sol	64
ES8536	Camping Ametlla Village Platja	66
ES8537N	Camping Naturista El Templo del Sol	66
ES8535	Camping-Pension Cala d'Oques	67

Comunidad Valenciana

ES8558	Camping Vinaros	70
ES8560	Camping Playa Tropicana	70
ES8570	Camping Torre La Sal 2	71
ES8580	Camping Bonterra	71
ES8612	Euro Camping	72
ES8625	Kiko Park Rural	72
ES8615	Kiko Park	73
ES8675	Camping Vall de Laguar	74
ES8680	Camping Armanello	74
ES8681	Camping Villasol	75
ES8682	Camping Villamar	75
ES8683	Camping Benisol	76
ES8686	Excalibur Medieval Camping	76
ES8685	Camping Caravaning El Raco	77
ES8687	Camping Cap Blanch	77
ES8689	Camping Playa del Torres	78

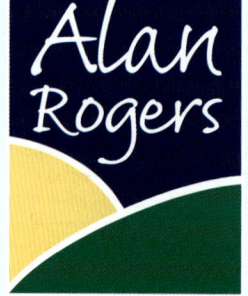

Code	Name	Page
ES8741	Camping Florantilles	78
ES8742	Camping Internacional La Marina	79
ES8754	Camping Jávea	80
ES8743	Complejo Ecoturistico Marjal	81
ES8755	Camping-Caravanning Moraira	81

Murcia

Code	Name	Page
ES8745	Camping La Fuente	83
ES8748	Camping Los Madriles	83
ES8752N	Camping Naturista El Portus	84
ES8753	Caravaning La Manga	84

Andalucia

Code	Name	Page
ES8749	Camping Sopalmo	87
ES8751	Camping Cuevas Mar	87
ES8760	Camping Mar Azul	88
ES8765	Camping La Garrofa	88
ES9270	Camping Suspiro del Moro	89
ES9280	Camping Sierra Nevada	89
ES9275	Los Avellanos de Sierra Nevada	90
ES9285	Camping Las Lomas	90
ES9290	Camping El Balcon de Pitres	91
ES8711	Nerja Camping	91
ES8782	Camping-Caravaning Laguna Playa	92
ES8790	Camping La Laguna	92
ES8783N	Camping Naturista Almanat	93
ES8800	Camping Marbella Playa	93
ES8802	Camping Cabopino	94
ES8803	Camping La Buganvilla	94
ES8809	Camping El Sur	95
ES8850	Camping Paloma	95
ES8812	Camping Chullera 2	96
ES8855	Camping Tarifa	96
ES8860	Camping Fuente del Gallo	97
ES8865	Camping Playa Las Dunas	97
ES8889	Camping Los Alcornocales	98
ES8871	Camping Giralda	98
ES9081	Camping Villsom	99
ES9082	Camping Sevilla	99
ES9078	Camping Los Villares	100
ES9080	Camping Municipal El Brillante	101
ES9085	Camping Carlos III	101
ES9084	Camping La Campiña	102
ES9089	Camping Despenaperros	102

Extremadura

Code	Name	Page
ES9087	Camping Merida	104
ES9027	Parque Natural de Monfrague	104
ES9028	Camping Las Villueracas	105

Castilla La-Mancha

Code	Name	Page
ES9088	Camping de Fuencaliente	107
ES9094	Camping La Aguzadera	107
ES9090	Camping El Greco	108

Madrid

Code	Name	Page
ES9091	Camping Soto del Castillo	110
ES9092	Camping Lagos Coto Cisneros	110
ES9200	Caravanning El Escorial	111
ES9210	Camping Pico de la Miel	111

Castilla y León

Code	Name	Page
ES9019	Camping La Pesquera	113
ES9026	Camping El Burro Blanco	113
ES9025	Camping Regio	114
ES9022	Camping El Folgoso	115
ES9021	Camping Fuentes Blancas	115
ES9023	Camping Camino de Santiago	116
ES9044	Camping Monumento al Pastor	116
ES9250	Camping Costajan	117
ES9253	Camping Picon del Conde	117
ES9254	Camping Puerta de la Demanda	118
ES9251	Camping Cañon del Rio Lobos	118
ES9240	Camping El Cantosal	119
ES9029	Camping El Astral	119

Galicia

Code	Name	Page
ES9024	Camping As Cancelas	121
ES8942	Camping Los Manzanos	122

Asturias

Code	Name	Page
ES8940	Camping Los Cantiles	124
ES8945	Camping Lagos de Somiedo	124
ES8950	Camping Costa Verde	125
ES8955	Camping-Caravaning Arenal de Moris	125
ES8960	Camping La Paz	126
ES8965	Camping Picos de Europa	126

Cantabria

Code	Name	Page
ES8961	Camping El Helguero	128
ES8962	Camping La Isla	128
ES8963	Camping La Viorna	129
ES8964	Camping El Molino de Cabuerniga	129
ES8970	Camping Las Arenas-Pechon	130
ES8971	Camping Playa de Oyambre	130
ES8973	Camping Santillana	131
ES8985	Camping Valderredible	131
ES8995	Camping Los Molinos (Noja)	132
ES9000	Camping Playa Joyel	133

Pais Vasco-Euskadi

Code	Name	Page
ES9035	Camping Portuondo	135
ES9038	Camping Orio	135
ES9045	Camping Angosto	136
ES9039	Gran Camping Zarautz	136

La Rioja

Code	Name	Page
ES9040	Camping de Haro	138

Navarra

Code	Name	Page
ES9042	Camping Etxarri	140
ES9043	Camping Errota el Molino	141

Campsite Index by Region

Aragón

ES9060	Camping Peña Montañesa	143
ES9062	Camping Boltana	143
ES9064	Camping Gavín	144
ES9070	Centro de Vacaciones Pirineos	144
ES9125	Camping Lago Barasona	145
ES9100	Camping Casablanca	145
ES9105	Camping Lago Park	146
ES9095	Camping Ciudad de Albarracin	146

PORTUGAL

Algarve

PO8200	Orbitur Camping Valverde	151
PO8202	Parque de Campismo de Espiche	152
PO8210	Parque de Campismo Albufeira	152
PO8230	Camping Olhao	153
PO8220	Orbitur Camping Quarteira	154
PO8410	Parque de Campismo de Armacao	154
PO8430	Orbitur Camping Sagres	155
PO8440	Parque de Campismo Quintos	155

Alentejo

PO8170	Parque de Campismo São Miguel	157
PO8160	Parque de Campismo Porto Covo	158
PO8350	Camping Markádia	158

Lisbon & Vale do Tejo

PO8130	Orbitur Camping Guincho	160
PO8150	Orbitur Camping Costa da Caparica	160
PO8100	Orbitur Camping Sao Pedro de Moel	161
PO8110	Orbitur Camping Valado	162
PO8400	Campismo O Tamanco	162
PO8460	Camping-Caravaning Vale Paraiso	163
PO8450	Parque de Campismo Colina do Sol	164
PO8480	Orbitur Camping Foz do Arelho	164

Beiras & Centre

PO8040	Parque de Campismo da Vagueira	166
PO8050	Orbitur Camping Sao Jacinto	166
PO8070	Orbitur Camping Mira	167
PO8090	Orbitur Camping Figueira da Foz	167
PO8330	Camping Municipal Arganil	168
PO8360	Parque Campismo de Municipal	168

North

PO8010	Orbitur Camping Caminha	170
PO8020	Orbitur Camping Viana do Castelo	170
PO8030	Orbitur Camping Rio Alto	171
PO8380	Parque Natural de Vilar de Mouros	171
PO8370	Parque de Campismo de Cerdeira	172

Widely regarded as the 'Bible' by site owners and readers alike, there is no better guide when it comes to forming an independent view of a campsite's quality. When you need to be confident in your choice of campsite, you need the Alan Rogers Guide.

- Sites only included on merit
- Sites cannot pay to be included
- Independently inspected, rigorously assessed
- Impartial reviews
- 36 years of expertise

THIS FORM WILL save you money

TO QUALIFY FOR SOME MONEY SAVING OFFERS, AND USEFUL INFORMATION, SIMPLY RETURN THE COUPON.
NO STAMP REQUIRED.

Register me for savings - today

Ferry savings
Please keep me posted with the latest ferry savings, special offers and up to date news

Discounts on Alan Rogers Guides
Please offer me discounts on future editions of the Alan Rogers' Guides plus other camping and caravanning publications

www.**alanrogers**.com

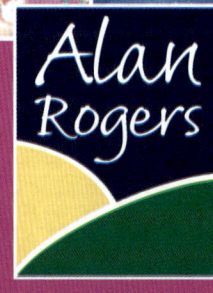

Register me for: (Please tick)
❏ Ferry Savings   ❏ Discounts on Alan Rogers guides

Mr/Mrs/Ms _____ Initial _____ Surname _____
Address _____
_____ Postcode _____
Telephone _____ Email _____

Brickbats and Bouquets
Tell us what you think of the Alan Rogers Guides
_____
_____

Priority Subscription 2005
Want a brand new copy of the 2005 Alan Rogers Guides hot off the press? If so we'll rush you a priority copy - and guarantee you'll pay no more than this year's prices. Of course postage and packaging will be completely free.

❏ BRITAIN & IRELAND   ❏ FRANCE   ❏ EUROPE
❏ SPAIN & PORTUGAL   ❏ ITALY   ❏ MOBILE HOMES & CHALETS

Credit card number ☐☐☐☐ ☐☐☐☐ ☐☐☐☐ ☐☐☐☐
Expiry date ___/___   Issue no. (switch) _____

No funds will be taken before 1st January 2005, or publication, whichever is soonest. Alternatively enclose a cheque (post-dated to 1st January 2005).

Return in an envelope to address overleaf - **NO STAMP REQUIRED!**

THIS FORM WILL save you money

POST THE COUPON TODAY! - NO STAMP REQUIRED!

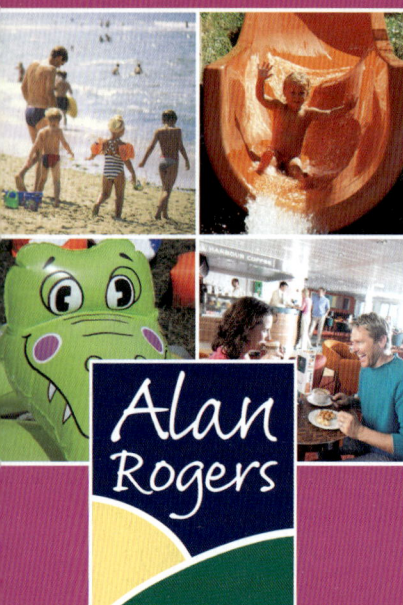

www.**alanrogers**.com

POP IN AN ENVELOPE AND RETURN TO:

Alan Rogers Guides
FREEPOST SEA 8263
96 High Street
Tunbridge Wells
Kent TN1 1RB

NO STAMP REQUIRED!